COGNITIVE PROCESSES AND EMOTIONAL DISORDERS

THE GUILFORD CLINICAL PSYCHOLOGY AND PSYCHOTHERAPY SERIES

MICHAEL J. MAHONEY, EDITOR

PAIN AND BEHAVIORAL MEDICINE:
A COGNITIVE–BEHAVIORAL PERSPECTIVE
Dennis C. Turk, Donald Meichenbaum, and Myles Genest

COGNITIVE PROCESSES AND EMOTIONAL DISORDERS:
A STRUCTURAL APPROACH TO PSYCHOTHERAPY
V. F. Guidano and G. Liotti

AGORAPHOBIA: NATURE AND TREATMENT
Andrew M. Mathews, Michael G. Gelder, and Derek W. Johnston

COGNITIVE ASSESSMENT
Thomas V. Merluzzi, Carol R. Glass, and Myles Genest, Editors

COGNITIVE THERAPY OF DEPRESSION
Aaron T. Beck, A. John Rush, Brian F. Shaw, and Gary Emery

IN PREPARATION

RELAPSE PREVENTION
G. Alan Marlatt and Judith Gordon

INSOMNIA
Richard Bootzin and Thomas Borkovec

ATTRIBUTIONAL PROCESSES IN CLINICAL PSYCHOLOGY
Lyn Abramson, Editor

COGNITIVE PROCESSES AND EMOTIONAL DISORDERS

A STRUCTURAL APPROACH TO PSYCHOTHERAPY

V. F. GUIDANO AND G. LIOTTI

Psychiatric Clinic of the University of Rome

Foreword by Michael J. Mahoney

THE GUILFORD PRESS

New York   London

To John Bowlby

© 1983 The Guilford Press
A Division of Guilford Publications, Inc.
200 Park Avenue South, New York, N.Y. 10003

Printed in the United States of America

LIBRARY OF CONGRESS CATALOGING IN PUBLICATION DATA

Guidano, V. F.
  Cognitive processes and emotional disorders.

  (The Guilford clinical psychology and psychotherapy series)
  Bibliography: p.
  Includes indexes.
    1. Cognitive therapy. 2. Cognition. 3. Psychology, Pathological. 4. Cognitive styles.
I. Liotti, G. II. Title. III. Series. [DNLM: 1. Affective disorders—Therapy. 2. Cognition.
3. Self concept. 4. Anxiety disorders—Therapy. 5. Psychotherapy. WM 420 G945s]
RC489.C63G84   616.89'14   81-13188
ISBN 0-89862-006-6

ACKNOWLEDGMENTS

This book is the result of more than 10 years of clinical research and practice with people suffering from emotional disorders. For the clinical observations that made this work possible we are indebted to colleagues cooperating with us both in the Psychiatric Clinic of the University of Rome and in the Rome Center of Behavioral Psychotherapy.

We also thank our colleagues who have read the manuscript and offered valuable suggestions for its improvement: Mario Reda, Antonio Caridi, Cesare De Silvestri, Daniela Amoni Guidano, and Sandra De Biase.

We are grateful to Priscilla De Angelis and Flavia Nati of the translation center Il Melograno in Rome, and to Mrs. Carol Hendrickson for helping us in the difficult task of translating the manuscript into English.

The editorial staff of The Guilford Press gave invaluable aid in the final composition of the manuscript, as well as in the preparation of the indexes. To the whole staff our warmest thanks are due.

It is impossible to mention the names of all the colleagues to whom we are indebted for stimulating ideas and useful criticisms. Had we not discussed with them so many points and read their works, this book would probably never have been written.

One to whom we are especially grateful is Michael J. Mahoney. From many points of view it is thanks to his encouragment and advice that our ideas on the possibility of an integrative paradigm for psychotherapy have taken the form expressed in these pages.

FOREWORD

In February of 1980 I was invited to speak at the University of Rome. My talk, which was focused on transformational processes in psychotherapy, drew heavily on the parallels between Thomas Kuhn's analysis of scientific revolutions and the more personal revolution processes that seem to be exhibited by many psychotherapy clients. Much to my surprise and delight, after my talk I learned that a small group of researchers in Rome had been working on some similar ideas that borrowed from and extended the work of Imre Lakatos. Where Kuhn had offered a sociological analysis of the structure of scientific revolutions, Lakatos had directed his attention to the psychological structure of belief changes. But the Rome group had gone well beyond Lakatos's model and had developed—over several years of theoretical refinements and clinical explorations—a much more comprehensive view of the processes involved in personal knowing and significant personal change. This book represents the first presentation of their work in English.

With the help of their co-workers and clients, Vittorio Guidano and Gianni Liotti have developed a provocative and heuristic model of personal knowledge organization and its change. Besides extending Lakatos's important work in epistemology, they have integrated some of the most significant features of evolutionary theory and the writings of John Bowlby on affectional bonding and the development of individual styles of adaptation. In what must be regarded as an impressively broad and ecumenical treatise, they have managed to integrate the works of such traditionally disparate writers as Piaget, Bandura, Beck, Bruch, and Weimer. The reader is thus offered innovative integration of behavior therapy, social learning theory, evolutionary epistemology, cognitive psychology, theories of emotional and cognitive development, psychodynamic formulations, cognitive therapy, and a number of other themes from our highly specialized science of human behavior. The project is truly Herculean in scope and the authors manage to carry it off with a level of scholarship that is exemplary. Moreover, they combine their unique and high-powered theoretical offerings with impressive clinical translations. The first third of the book is devoted to theoretical issues and the second discusses the implications of these issues for our conceptualization and practice of psychotherapy. The final section is devoted to an insightful rendition of the preceding material as it is illustrated in and relevant to the everyday pursuits of the mental health practitioner. Their analysis of common cognitive organizations in depression, eating disorders, obsessive–compulsive patterns, and phobias reflects a rare blend of theoretical sophistication and practical engagement.

Needless to say, I think this book is exciting and I am honored to have been able to participate in some small way in its presentation to the professional community. It is, in my opinion, one of the most creative and stimulating volumes to have appeared in recent years, and it is written in a warm and personable spirit of sensitive scientific humility. As the authors themselves note, it may not be the final word in our quest for an adequate understanding of human adaptation processes. It is, however, a valuable step in that direction.

Michael J. Mahoney

PREFACE

The structural approach to psychotherapy outlined in this book originated about 10 years ago from the perception of a discrepancy between the promising results of a psychotherapeutic practice making wide use of behavior therapy techniques and the limited explicative power of the learning principles forming the theoretical foundation of those techniques.

One has but to pick and choose to find examples of such a discrepancy. For instance, in most cases it was rather difficult to describe, according to learning principles, the intricate context of interpersonal relationships and of subjectively relevant past experiences in which the abnormal behavior to be modified through "behavioristic" techniques had emerged. It was also hard to take into account, within the framework of behavioristic learning theories, the wide employment of imagination, which is so characteristic of many classical behavior therapy interventions. And it was almost impossible to consider, in terms of learning principles, many of the phenomena implied in the therapeutic relationship whose relevance to the final outcome was rather obvious, such as the explanations offered by the therapist in response to the patient's questions concerning the meaning of his or her disturbances and the nature of the therapeutic maneuvers.

For a while, the introduction, within our therapeutics, of the principles and methods of cognitive therapy seemed effective in reducing the perceived discrepancy between theory, techniques, and ongoing clinical observations. However, it was not long before this unpleasant dissonance increased again. The description, analysis, and modification of isolated beliefs, specimens of internal dialogue, fragments of daydreams, and more or less specific deficits or distortions of thought left unsolved the problems posed by a very fundamental and rather obvious clinical observation, that is, the impression of a certain uniformity of an individual's knowledge across different cognitive domains. In other words, not only did the central role of an individual's acquired knowledge of self and the world in regulating the perception of environmental events and his or her consequent behavior appear more and more evident in our reformed clinical practice—as well as being supported by data offered by basic disciplines such as experimental cognitivistic psychology, neuropsychology, and epistemology —but the development, maintenance, and change of individual knowledge during its temporal becoming also appeared uniform (although not necessarily strictly coherent) across different cognitive domains. An individual obviously knows himself or herself, and is known by others as the same individual even while, in different moments, he or she is expressing different or even contradictory beliefs, opinions, emotions, and behaviors.

To reduce incongruity, a proper theoretical foundation for a clinical practice in which centrality and uniformity of individual knowledge so clearly appear has to take into account problems such as the following: How should the patterns of regularity underlying cognitive development be described? What kind of relationship can exist between abnormal patterns of self-knowledge development and emotional disorders emerging in adult life? How is it possible to explain the progressive growth of individual knowledge during the whole life so that the basic impression of its uniformity is taken into account? In which way could the outburst of an emotional "illness" or the "personal revolution" (Mahoney, 1980) that sometimes occurs as a result of psychotherapy be matched with the mechanisms underlying the uniform growth of self-knowledge?

In face of such problems, our need for a theoretical revision seemed to have reached a limit. It seemed impossible to go on progressively widening the range of applicability of the behavioristic and functionalistic paradigm from which we had started. On the other hand, we had no reason for giving up the original motives of our refusal of the psychoanalytic approach to psychotherapy, that is, the poor connection with basic experimental psychology, the length of treatment and its doubtful efficacy, and the rather confused structure of the psychoanalytic theory (Rapaport, 1960). These perplexities induced us to go further into the epistemological foundations of the psychotherapeutic theories, and we were quite surprised to discover that there was a common epistemological principle underlying both the approaches that, for opposite reasons, we refused. Both psychoanalysis and behavior therapy seemed to accept the epistemological assumption known as associationism (cf. Liotti & Reda, 1981). This principle, implying a "passive" idea of knowledge development and convincingly criticized by Popper (cf. Popper & Eccles, 1977), seemed to represent the limit met by our effort of theoretical revision. We had to review *epistemologically*—that is, to change, rather than to widen— our scientific paradigm (Kuhn, 1962).

Since our daily activity is psychotherapy, the planned epistemological revision could not be disconnected, either in logic or in practice, from our clinical practice. Therefore the conception of emotional disorders we were treating and the conceptualization itself of the behavioristic and cognitivistic techniques whose efficacy we had already experienced would be influenced by the epistemological revision we were starting. This book is an account of the results of our search for, and of some specific applications of, a nonassociationistic, nonreductionistic epistemology of psychotherapy in view of both the model of human behavior deriving from it and the general implications for psychotherapy.

Part One of this book is concerned with the basic epistemological tenets to which we have chosen to adhere and with the model of individual knowledge organization that emerges when such an epistemological position is matched with the information on cognitive structures and processes that are likely to be offered to a cognitively oriented psychotherapist during his or her daily practice. The intention to maintain the habit of connecting, as much as possible, our clinical activity with experimental psychology methods and results—a habit we acquired at the beginning of our practice as behavior therapists—was a leitmotif throughout the comparison between basic epistemology and the data of clinical observation. For this reason, the chapters in the first part of the book refer to experimental psychology and to ethology as often as our knowledge of the subject allowed.

In Chapter 1 we describe the fundamental aspects of epistemology that we chose. In short, this epistemology can be characterized as evolutionary, constructivistic, and structuralistic. Its main aspect can be related to critical rationalism as it was outlined in the works of Sir Karl Popper. The model of human behavior and human cognition transpiring from this epistemological position is marked by the concept of the organism's being *active* in response to the environment: "Organisms are problem-solvers and active explorers of their world" (Popper & Eccles, 1977, p. 138). The main aspect of mental functioning is no longer the forming and breaking up of associative ties, but rather the active processing of expectations, hypotheses, and theories. Much of our knowledge reflects our species-specific modes of cognition and is therefore not limited to inductive generalization of outside information. Under such a perspective, knowledge appears as a progressive *construction*, and the consideration of its developmental aspects becomes particularly relevant to understanding both its structure and the dynamics of its growth, maintenance, and change. The second half of Chapter 1 is consequently devoted to an outline of some developmental aspects of human knowledge. Bowlby's attachment theory and Piaget's conceptions concerning cognitive growth are the main interlocking themes around which our account of knowledge development revolves.

In the remaining chapters of Part One, we make wide use of quotations from Popper's work in order to make as clear and explicit as possible how our epistemological position guides and directs the treatment of various aspects of cognitive development, organization, and functioning that seem more relevant to clinical practice.

Chapter 2 is devoted to the development of self-knowledge. From the point of view previously outlined, it becomes possible to define the central role of knowledge, avoiding, at the same time, any "mentalistic" assumption. The famous argument of the "homunculus," through which the cognitivistic approach was counterargued by behavioristic scholars, appears compatible with a passive "sensory" model of the mind (which implies a *regressio ad infinitum* in the search of an active regulatory "inner" principle), but not with an active "motor" model (cf. Weimer, 1977). The "agent" is not the "homunculus," but the self. The self is conceived of as the central aspect of knowledge organization, an aspect that is itself developed (cf. Popper's concept of "learning to be a self," Popper & Eccles, 1977). Although there are at present various clinical and theoretical approaches to the problem of the self (cf., e.g., Arieti, 1967; Bandura, 1978; Raimy, 1975), we preferred to limit ourselves mainly to a description of the developmental conditions and processes involved in defining self-knowledge (Chapter 2) and to a sketch of a model of cognitive organization in which self-knowledge has a central role (Chapter 3).

Chapter 3 is the most "structuralistic" chapter of this book. As A. R. Luria points out,

> Separate events and objects do not constitute the aim of science. As such, they may only represent objects to be distinguished or described. The aim of science is to discover *relations* among objects or events. . . . The inclusion of an object or event in a system of relations is a basic principle of scientific knowledge, in that it reflects the essence of its existence.*

Chapter 3 presents a descriptive model of a "system of relations" in which one may include otherwise separate "objects" and "events" such as theories or beliefs concerning self-identity, images and emotional schemata emerging from personal memories, attitude toward reality, procedures of problem solving, and so forth. In accordance with the general epistemology upon which our clinical research is founded, this model is drawn from the work of Lakatos, a disciple of Popper, on the structure of scientific theories. Once we have duly considered the differences between an epistemological and a psychological model, the formalization supplied by Lakatos of the structure and procedure of a scientific theory seems to be especially suited to describing the organization of individual knowledge and to adhere surprisingly well to the therapist's need to take into account, in a neat, overall way, all of the information supplied by a person about his or her cognitive structure.

Chapter 4 is concerned with the maintenance and change of cognitive structures. When, at the end of development, the construction of individual knowledge has reached the consistency and stability implicit in the model of organization proposed in Chapter 3, the regulation of its subsequent maintenance and growth is mainly connected to the principle of congruity. The reader might well be reminded of the usage by Pribram (1971) of such concepts as consonance–dissonance, congruity–incongruity, match–mismatch, and

---

*This passage has been retranslated into English from an Italian translation of an unpublished Russian manuscript entitled "Protiv Redukcionizma V Psychologii" ["Against Reductionism in Psychology"], dated Moscow, 1975.

novelty–habituation in his account of the neuropsychological organization. Indeed, in our model, ongoing cognition appears mainly as the result of a continuous interaction between the incoming information and the subject's preexisting knowledge, with the search for congruity being the main regulator of such a matching process.

Chapter 5 ends the first, theoretical part of the book with a sketchy account of some conditions in which the structure of personal knowledge is so rigid and loaded with paradoxes that the matching process with novel incoming information is very likely to result in specific cognitive disfunctions and emotional disturbances. Abnormal patterns of attachment during developmental periods are postulated, on clinical and theoretical grounds (to be supported with practical examples and a review of pertinent literature in the third part of the book), to be the *primum movens* of the paradoxes in cognitive organization that will lead to full-fledged clinical syndromes in adult life, given the proper stressors.

Part Two describes the general implications for psychotherapy of the theoretical framework previously outlined. From this theoretical framework, the analogy between man and scientist (Kelly, 1955), by now widely used, emerges as a particularly useful metaphorical image of human behavior. Consequently, a heuristically meaningful way of conceptualizing the whole process of a cognitively oriented psychotherapy may center around this metaphor. The hallmark of a psychotherapist adhering to this approach is, perhaps, his or her consistent effort to adhere to the scientific method, both in the way of gathering data and planning a therapeutic strategy and in the implicit and explicit attempt to teach the "patient"* how to use the same method in dealing with everyday problems. Although obviously the therapeutic relationship, assessment procedures, and therapeutic maneuvers are nothing more than different aspects of the same unitary process (i.e., they are overlapping and simultaneously occurring operations in which the patient and the therapist are equally active), in practice it is necessary to describe them separately.

---

*As Mahoney (1980, p. 171) remarks, it is misleading to call people who have problems "clients" and people who have solutions "therapists." Since it seems impossible to ignore such terms as "clinical," "disorder," "therapist," "treatment," and so forth in a book about "therapy" and "emotional disorders," we have chosen to be consistent and to call our clients "patients." Of course this does not imply that we accept as valid the "diesase model" of abnormal behavior as it is usually understood.

In Chapter 6 the therapeutic relationship is presented as the confrontation between two "scientists" (the patient and the therapist) holding different causal theories about the meaning of the patient's symptoms. However, this confrontation is not meant to be a cold and impersonal one: Bowlby's attachment theory is here, again, a useful tool in understanding the emotional implications of the searching, exploratory activity in which both the patient and the therapist are engaged (Bowlby, 1977b).

Chapter 7 considers the assessment procedures, the crucial step of which is the critical identification and evaluation of the patient's *implicit* causal theories (cf. Nisbett & Wilson, 1977). Two general kinds of considerations are necessary in order to understand how it is possible to make explicit such tacit, implicit theories: First, the therapist's explicit causal theories concerning the patient's problematic behavior must be different from the patient's own theories. Second, the reconstruction of the patient's developmental history becomes a fundamental step in the assessment procedures, since only this reconstruction can confirm the hypotheses expressed by the therapist about the role of causal theories underlying the patient's cognitive organization.

Chapter 8 is about the process of cognitive psychotherapy, in which two basic aspects are considered as most relevant. First, the therapeutic interventions are conceived of and organized according to the general dynamic and structure of scientific inquiry: A descriptive and experimental phase (behavioral and cognitive assessment; behavioral techniques and "superficial" cognitive interventions) is followed by a phase of epistemological critique and revision (reconstruction of the whole cognitive organization and confutation or logical challenge of basic assumptions). Second, the whole therapeutic procedure is strategically oriented. The timing of each therapeutic maneuver and the passage from the first (descriptive–experimental) to the second (epistemological–critical) phase are regulated by the need to consider the patient's ability to integrate new information into his or her preexisting cognitive structure and by the aim of progressively obtaining a deep and persisting cognitive change.

Part Three contains a description of some specific clinical applications of this structural approach to emotional disorders. Four main clinical syndromes are considered: depression (Chapter 9), agoraphobia and related multiple phobias (Chapter 10), obsessive–

compulsive patterns (Chapter 11), and eating disorders (Chapter 12). The outline of a specific knowledge organization underlying the emotional disturbances and problematic behavioral patterns typical of each syndrome constitutes the core of each chapter. The patterned procedure of clinical assessment required in order to recognize this specific knowledge organization (behavioral, cognitive, and developmental analysis) precedes this core, and the outline of a corresponding therapeutic strategy follows it.

The aim that we have pursued in thus shaping the description of the clinical applications of this structural approach to psychotherapy is threefold. We wish to show as clearly as possible how the implications of our theoretical foundations are reflected in everyday clinical practice (i.e., how the model of human individual knowledge organization presented in Part One is recognizable in real people). We also aim to make clear that the central aspect of the psychotherapeutic process is the identification of the patient's specific cognitive organization, since this very knowledge guides the "strategic" planning of the whole therapy, while the single "tactics" that a therapist may choose to utilize (i.e., *in vivo* desensitization vs. imaginal desensitization, coping imagery vs. flooding, etc.) seem largely optional and a matter of personal predilection. Finally, we mean to exemplify how a structural approach to psychotherapy may be useful in reevaluating nosographic concepts and their applicability to everyday psychotherapeutic practice. Whereas a static, objectifying conceptualization of the invariant patterns of abnormal behavior seems largely unreliable and of little practical utility, a structural and dynamic look at what underlies those invariant patterns (i.e., a cognitive organization and its predictable lines of transformation) may constitute a rather powerful tool in the hands of an experienced psychotherapist. For a more detailed account of these problems, refer to Appendix A.

The whole of Part Three presents many clinical vignettes. The purpose of these short descriptions is to exemplify the various steps of the assessment needed to identify all of the cognitive and developmental data that the therapist can frequently expect to find when dealing with the clinical syndromes described herein. For these reasons, only relatively limited attention is paid to the clinical examples of specific therapeutic interventions.

Appendix B gives the composition of the sample of patients

from which the present clinical study derives. Although these patients appear there as figures within a diagnostic framework, in our minds they are courageous living beings to whom we owe considerable intellectual stimulation and a sense of deep personal gratitude.

V. F. Guidano
G. Liotti

CONTENTS

PART ONE

THEORETICAL
FOUNDATIONS

1

HUMAN KNOWLEDGE: SOME EPISTEMOLOGICAL AND PSYCHOLOGICAL NOTES

GENERAL REMARKS

AN EVOLUTIONARY VIEW OF THE RELATIONSHIP BETWEEN COGNITION AND REALITY

It is almost a truism of modern biology that human beings are the product of a long evolutionary history which began millions of years ago from simple unicellular organisms or virus-like ancestors and their still simpler progenitors. During the course of this evolutionary process, the human species, as all other species, has adapted adequately to the environment through a continuous confrontation with reality, regulated by the natural selection paradigm.

We believe that evolution, and, in particular, the adaptation process that characterizes it, can be considered on the same level as knowledge processes. Every progressive adaptation can be seen as a further acquisition of information about that reality and therefore ultimately as a real acquisition of knowledge. Thus the progressive and enormous increase in adaptive adequacy that has paralleled the increase in neural complexity throughout the course of evolution has been gradually recorded (through the onset of more and more organized perceptual and mnemonic patterns) in stored templates, modeling the useful (or meaningful) regularities of the environment. Finally, having attained a unique level of development of the brain and with the onset of language, humans' adaptation to reality is

3

enhanced by sophisticated mechanisms of perceiving and knowing that allow for the construction of representational models of reality through which an exploration of and control on the environment, unprecedented on the zoological scale, becomes possible.

Therefore, from an evolutionary point of view, knowing has evolved along with other aspects of life. It is our opinion that the adoption of an "evolutionary epistemology" viewpoint (cf. Campbell, 1974) can be useful in at least two respects.

First, it allows the concept of knowledge to be emancipated from the exclusiveness of the philosophical field since it provides a biological frame of reference where knowledge can become an object of study, which is compatible with the methodology used in experimental disciplines. Second, this point of view allows us to define in a different way the controversial problem of "realism," that is, of the philosophical position positing the theory of the independent existence of reality, apart from the subject who perceives it, as well as the theory that the perceptual knowledge possessed by an individual has a perfect correspondence to that reality. In particular, the position that fostered the empiricist tradition with its belief that reality not only exists independently from the knowing subject, but that this reality can be known by the subject through sensorial impressions free from prejudice (so-called naive realism), becomes absolutely untenable. Indeed, according to the evolutionary viewpoint, our very perceiving and knowing apparatus is a product of the adaptation that the human species has undergone and therefore is in itself an element of the real world (cf. Lorenz, 1973). Thus human knowledge is strictly connected to information-processing patterns of an evolutionary origin in the sense that the frames of coordinates that regulate our perceiving and knowing are functions of the neurosensorial organization produced in the course of phylogenetic adaptation.

On the other hand, although the human brain is astonishingly complex, it does not and cannot have access to the totality of data regarding the outside world. Therefore there is no doubt that our perceiving apparatus underinforms us: For example, it does not inform us of the existence of infrared light and of many other dimensions of reality for which we have not developed receptor organs. Nevertheless, the information that our brain supplies us with is likely to be quite reliable and to have a real correspondence to the outside world (even though it is obviously reduced and somehow "distorted" in comparison to the potentially available totality of data); otherwise we would not be here.

Thus our perceiving apparatus is not able to provide us with an exact reproduction of external reality, but rather gives us an image of the world that is a somewhat simplified version of reality, construed on the basis of "utilitarian" criteria. In other words, under the pressure of specific selective processes, those perceptual and cognitive patterns have been developed which are functionally adapted to processing information concerning the specific aspects of reality that are of particular importance for the conservation of the species.

Within the limits of an evolutionary viewpoint, the only tenable position on the problem of the intercurrent relationship between the real world and its representation seems to be the so-called critical or hypothetical realism, according to which effective possibilities of knowing reality *as such* do not exist: Each knowledge unit, far from being a copy of the real world, should always be considered a product of the interaction between the knowing subject and the known object, both equally real (Lorenz, 1973). In this way, our knowledge can take the form of an uninterrupted series of constructions with which we tend to draw gradually closer to reality, discovering its properties through a continuous succession of approximations.

Notwithstanding the belief of the impossibility of reaching a final and definite certainty about external reality, critical realism is radically distinct from solipsism and idealism (positions that deny the autonomy of external reality): Reality exists independently from us, and it is the "limit," so to speak, toward which we tend, without ever reaching it.

A SKETCH OF AN ACTIVE MODEL OF THE MIND

The empiricist tradition, which is still influential in modern psychology, has strongly contributed to the formation of models of learning and development based on the theory that the sense organs are the sources of knowledge. This position has been incisively defined by Popper (1972) as "the bucket theory of the mind," to indicate that the mind is considered to be a kind of originally empty or almost empty container where the "material" procured through the senses is accumulated and is finally assimilated.

In its original version, this theory assumed that at birth the organism was a tabula rasa where sensorial messages were progressively impressed. This statement remains substantially unchanged, even in the more recent formulations based on the information-processing approach, which admits that the mind is not really completely empty, but can, at birth, be provided with a sort of computer program. These two versions share the belief that knowledge can be obtained immediately through the direct registration of sensorial data and that the mind is a passive receptor of environmental stimuli. In this viewpoint, the process that regulates and coordinates learning is identified essentially with the association mechanism: On the basis of the acquisition of contingency relationships between chronologically close environmental stimuli (classical conditioning) or between actions and consequent environmental changes (operant conditioning), the organism becomes capable of associating sensations and actions with one another; expectations and beliefs are considered as by-products of these associations.

Today various epistemological criticisms make the bucket theory of the mind untenable, invalidating, above all, its two basic assumptions: (1) the sensorial origin of knowledge and (2) the organism's passivity. The first assumption holds that knowledge can be obtained in a direct and immediate way through the sense organs. This viewpoint can be countered with the following arguments:

a. From an evolutionary point of view, every organism, including the human being, possesses inborn dispositions which, even before any experience, predispose it to attend selectively to the occurrence of determined events. Among these dispositions, the most important ones undoubtedly regard the "need for regularity": The human organism not only is provided with a perceiving apparatus endowed with the ability to select the outside world's regularities, but also has an inborn tendency to search for regularly recurring environmental patterns. As Popper (1963) remarks, this inborn need for regularity corresponds in many respects to the law of causality invoked by Kant. Actually, it constitutes an a priori datum preceding every sensorial experience, appearing as a sort of inborn bias upon which the possibilities of sensorial experience are founded. As Popper says:

> The theory of inborn *ideas* is absurd, I think; but every organism has inborn *reactions* or responses; and among them, responses adapted to impending events. These responses we may describe as "expectations" without implying that these "expectations" are conscious. The newborn baby "expects," in this sense, to be fed (and, one could even argue, to be protected and loved). In view of the close relation between expectation and knowledge we may even speak in quite a reasonable

sense of "inborn knowledge." This "knowledge" is not, however, valid a priori; an inborn expectation, no matter how strong and specific, may be mistaken. (The new-born child may be abandoned, and starve.)

Thus we are born with expectations; with "knowledge" which, although not *valid a priori*, is *psychologically* or *genetically* a priori, i.e., prior to an observational experience. One of the most important of these expectations is the expectation of finding a regularity. It is connected with an inborn propensity to look out for regularities, or with a *need* to *find* regularities, as we may see from the pleasure of the child who satisfies this need.

This "instinctive" expectation of finding regularities, which is psychologically *a priori*, corresponds very closely to the "Law of Causality" which Kant believed to be part of our mental outfit and to be *a priori* valid. One might thus be inclined to say that Kant failed to distinguish between psychologically *a priori* ways of thinking or responding and *a priori* valid beliefs. But I do not think that his mistake was as crude as that. For the expectation of finding regularities is not only psychologically *a priori*, but also logically *a priori*: it is logically a priori to all observational experience, for it is prior to any recognition of similarities, as we have seen; and all observation involves the recognition of similarities (or dissimilarities). (1963, pp. 47–48)

Thus the assumption that knowledge is derived directly from sensorial impressions fails in its own statement. Indeed, in the viewpoint presented, pure sensorial impressions do not exist. Given that expectation theories are genetically incorporated in every sense organ, every sensation is already an abstraction, a construction of the organism.

b. If every sensation is already a construction, the mind is a system capable of producing not only its own output, but also, to a large extent, the input it receives. As an alternative to the sensorial theories, Weimer (1977) has proposed a motor theory of the mind that can explain the undoubtedly more important generative nature of human knowledge processes. As he says:

The mind is intrinsically a motor system and the sensory order by which we are acquainted with external objects as well as ourselves, the higher mental processes which construct our common sense and scientific knowledge, indeed everything mental, is a product of what are, correctly interpreted, constructive motor skills. (1977, p. 272)

The point of view that emerges from this conceptual framework is that of a mind that is no longer a passive container of sensations that form a copy of reality ("naive realism"), but rather a system that constructs its own model of reality, a model comprehending the very basic sensations underlying the construction of itself ("critical or hypothetical realism").

As far as the second assumption of sensorial theories is concerned—that is, the organism's passivity—the previous considerations have already implied that the organism constantly carries out an active role. Nevertheless, the theme of activity can still be developed and made explicit through further considerations.

If pure sensorial impressions do not exist, then it can be logically deduced that no type of passive experience exists. Even in a simple sensation, there is the activity of extracting and detecting regularities with which the sense organs function. On the other hand, from the viewpoint of the "motor" theories of the mind, the organism's activity represents the indispensable basis to any learning and acquisition of knowledge of reality. Indeed, every theory of the mind implicitly presupposes a model of interaction between organism and environment within which the processes that mediate the interaction itself are defined. If in a "sensory" theory the organism–environment interaction has perception as the fundamental mediator, then in a motor theory the organism's activity itself becomes that mediator. However, this does not completely deny the importance of senses or perception: The organism's activity is constantly expressed at a motor level (environmental exploration), a sensorial level (extracting and detecting regularities), and a cognitive level (making and matching hypotheses). In this sense, as Piaget (1970) asserts, to know an object essentially means to act upon it.

According to this view, learning by experience depends on a process of making and matching expectations and hypotheses by an active trial-and-error procedure. Therefore learning is essentially cognitive and depends on a process of concept formation whose important characteristic is the constructive and generative activity of the mind, rather than the simple assimilation of sensorial data. As Popper points out:

> I think that the old story that the senses are primary in learning is wrong (especially in learning something new, i.e., in discovering). I believe that, in learning hypotheses have a primary role; that making comes before matching. The senses have two roles: first, they challenge us to *make* our hypotheses; second, they help us to *match* our hypotheses—by assisting in the process of refutation, or selection. (Popper & Eccles, 1977, p. 429)

The generative and constructive nature of learning processes must be appreciated to understand how the personal models of reality correspond more to real constructions than to simple copies of the world itself. Even though they can have a variable degree of correspondence with the real world, these models of reality have a preponderant role in directing the interaction of the individual with the world. Indeed, such models determine the pattern with which the individual can see and conceive of the world, thus contributing substantially to the form that experience assumes. Popper (1974) expresses this concept with his usual clarity:

> Our theories are our inventions; but they may be merely ill-reasoned guesses, bold conjectures, hypotheses. *Out of these we create a world: not the real world, but our own nets in which we try to catch the real world.* (p. 46; italics added)

TACIT AND EXPLICIT ASPECTS OF KNOWLEDGE

Since Polanyi's (1966, 1968) studies, two aspects of knowledge can be distinguished: tacit knowledge, about which we cannot speak, and explicit knowledge, about which we can. Although there is much evidence that tacit knowledge is connected to almost all aspects of mental processing (cf. Franks, 1974; Turvey, 1974; Weimer, 1973, 1974, 1977), we do not yet possess an adequate conceptual framework that is able to provide us with a satisfactory model of the relationship between tacit and explicit knowledge.

In this section we will attempt to catch a glimpse of this relationship, considering how the distinction between the two types of knowledge originates. First, we will deal with the evolutionary viewpoint and then will see how tacit and explicit knowledge are developed and articulated in a single individual's ontogeny.

The Evolutionary Perspective

From an evolutionary viewpoint, the problem of distinguishing two kinds of knowledge only comes up in the human species, and it is presumably connected to the onset of language and the hemispheric specialization.

The studies carried out by Sperry and his associates (cf. Sperry, 1974) on patients whose corpus callosum was sectioned in the treatment of intractable neurological diseases (the so-called split-brain patients) have furnished extremely interesting data on the functional organization of the human brain. Among these, the discovery of the uniqueness and exclusiveness of the left hemisphere with respect to conscious experience is particularly noteworthy; that is, although the right hemisphere was still able to carry out skilled and purposive movements, especially in the area of spatial and pictorial tests, it became completely incapable of furnishing any conscious experience of its activity. Therefore, with a good approximation, one could come to the conclusion that the right hemisphere's activity in normal persons reaches consciousness only by transmission to the left hemisphere through the corpus callosum. Thus the capability of conscious experience seems to be the exclusive prerogative of the left hemisphere, which contains the linguistic areas.

This hemispheric specialization is unique to human beings; in fact, the homologous cortical areas of primates do not show any evidence of functional asymmetry (see Eccles, in Popper & Eccles, 1977, especially Chapters E5 and E6). It is also probable that such hemispheric specialization has been produced during human evolution in response to the unique demands and the specific pressures imposed by the onset of the unprecedented evolutionary possibility represented by language.

Unlike the sharp and immediate messages that animals give and receive, language offered the human species the possibility of a disengagement from the context through which the potentialities of exploration and control of the environment changed significantly. According to Bronowski and Bellugi (1970), the properties of language that have permitted the attainment of such a disengagement from the immediacy of environmental stimuli can be schematized in the following points:

- Delay between stimulus and utterance of the message that the stimulus provoked
- Separation of the emotional or affective component from the specific content transmitted by the message
- The prolongation of reference, that is, the possibility of using specific messages backward and forward in time

- Internalization of language, which thus became not only an instrument of social communication, but also an instrument of reflection and exploration that the individual could use in elaborating various hypothetical messages before choosing the one he or she believed suitable.

Furthermore, these points are all part of what is surely the most important property offered to the human mind by language: being able to reify experience, structuring it in elements, which, as concepts, have stability and consistency and can therefore be manipulated on the same level as real objects. With this capacity for reifying experience, the human species not only reaches an unprecedented level of disengagement from the context, but also acquires new possibilities for controlling and influencing its own environment, as a result of an ever-increasing level of comprehension of outside reality. Thus the possibilities that have been created by the onset of language can justify how the left hemisphere, more verbal and logical than the right, has progressively become the center of conscious control and experience.

However, this does not mean that the forms of prelogical "thought" produced during the long evolutionary process have become extinct or even atrophied. As Teuber (1974) cogently argues, the concept of a unilateral dominance of the left hemisphere over the right should be abandoned and substituted by one of a complementary specialization. Furthermore, it is possible that from the beginning the functional complementarity of a left hemisphere specialized in analytical and logical tasks and a right hemisphere specialized in synthetic and holistic tasks has notably increased the possibilities of adaptive adequacy. Therefore what has probably been produced is a new functional integration, where the control of this complementary specialization was assumed from the emerging higher cortical functions. In other words, it is as if a kind of "choice of the species" occurred in which the control over environmental exploration was assigned to the logical–conceptual capabilities that appeared and to the new possibilities that they offered. On the other hand, since the forms of prelogical knowledge—which cannot be verbalized and therefore are essentially tacit—have appeared much earlier in the course of evolution, one could think they were more deeply rooted in the phylogenetic structure. In this way, they could have functioned as a continuous reference point through which it became possible to focus conscious control on extremely specialized, but for this reason inevitably partial, "higher" cortical functions.

The Ontological Perspective

Turning to the level of individual development, it is possible to find some formal analogies with what has been explained on a phylogenetic level. Indeed, since embryology was established as an autonomous discipline, it has stressed how ontogeny formally recapitulates phylogeny. If we observe the course of individual development from this viewpoint, we can point out the following formal analogies in sequence.

1. Tacit knowledge is undoubtedly the type of knowledge that appears first in the course of development. In fact, given the relative slowness of cognitive growth, early infancy is essentially characterized by the presence of a direct and immediate knowledge to which the capabilities of verbalization, reflection, and awareness are absolutely secondary.

2. The progressive elaboration of explicit knowledge is much more gradual; this graduality stems from the person's slowness in mastering language and in internalizing it until he or she is able to make use of the concepts themselves, independently from the situations in which they originated. However, also in individual development, the gradual establishment of an explicit knowledge parallels a progressive disengagement from the context by the child. In particular, the slow structuring of logical–conceptual capabilities is accompanied by a progressive detachment of the child's thought from the situational "here and now" of the environment as well as from the immediacy of his or her experiences of self. Thus, for example, while during childhood, the children's self-concepts are still strictly connected to the specific familial context, with adolescence and the onset of logical–deductive thought, they become progressively more competent to structure their personal identities as stable and independent from the social–familial context (see Chapter 2).

3. The conscious control of the entire cognitive organization is assumed by the explicit knowledge of self and the world that the individual has progressively organized. However, also in this case, the tacit knowledge elaborated during the course of development supplies a continuous frame of coordinates through which the control of conscious experience can be focused on the higher cognitive functions. In particular, the deep rules of tacit knowledge, which supply individuals (in a direct and immediate way) with the invariant aspects of their perception of self and the world, allow them to direct their conscious attention and rational thoughts toward specific and definite objectives. Finally, it should be stressed that, even if in a functional complementary relationship, the tacit and explicit aspects correspond to distinct forms of knowledge, each one characterized by its own functional patterns. For this reason, making tacit knowledge explicit never corresponds to a simple linear translation from a nonverbal code to a verbal one; on the contrary, it corresponds to a real, new construction in the sphere of explicit knowledge (see Chapter 3).

THE CENTRAL ROLE OF SELF-KNOWLEDGE[1]

In the first of a series of dialogues between Popper and Eccles, which constitutes the third part of their book *The Self and Its Brain* (1977), Eccles states:

> I am always thinking of myself as central in the first place to my perceptions, my imaginations, my environment. Everything comes to *me* in the first place. Then from all that is inborn in my brain and all that is built in my brain by experiences, I proceed to interpret so that I can act most appropriately in the various situations, and of course assimilate the new knowledge into all the experiental remembrances that I have already accumulated. And so I have the belief that *I am central to my own experiences and interpretations. I escape from solipsism by utilizing these experiences in order to understand other persons and the world around me*. . . . I readily give to each experiencing self the same prerogative of being *primary* to its whole tremendous incoming load of information that is pouring in by its

sense organs and that has to be interpreted in the light of memory.
(p. 426; italics added)

Popper's reply is in substantial agreement, with an important
specification:

> *After* I am established, so to speak, as a self-conscious person, things
> look as these phrases suggest; but the word "primary" carries with it
> the mistaken suggestion that ego is, in time, or logically, the first thing.
> But in time, or logically, I am, first of all, an organism not fully
> conscious of myself—when I am a small baby. . . . What is "primary"
> is the inborn disposition to sense, and the inborn disposition to
> interpret what arrives through the senses. Thus, if you say that I am
> central to my experience, then I accept that, but *only after I am
> constituted as a person or a self; which in itself is the result of learning.*
> (pp. 426–427; italics added).

Thus a rather precise profile of the organization of human
knowledge is being drawn up. At birth, the organism is provided with
a biological identity, but not as yet a personal, psychological one.
Furthermore, it is endowed with precise inborn dispositions to sense
and interpret what arrives through the senses and to actively process
tacit knowledge about the world and its own body, with its rhythms
and feelings.

The development of language and the growing capability of
internalizing it allow for the progressive construction of an explicit
knowledge on the basis of the reference point furnished by tacit
knowledge. Disengagement from the context, and the consciousness
allowed by this development, permit the gradual establishment of a
stable and ordered knowledge or reality. In this reality-construction
process, the "learning to be a self" (Popper & Eccles, 1977) represents
the element that orders and integrates both the already acquired
knowledge and the "tremendous incoming load of information that is
pouring in by the senses" (p. 426).

Thus gradually the human organism actively learns to recognize
itself. It progressively unifies the knowledge it is acquiring about
itself into a personal identity: It identifies with itself and puts itself at
the center of reality, that is, at the center of all its knowledge. In light
of this central role in the organization of knowledge, the developmental aspects of self-knowledge and personal identity deserve special
attention.

DEVELOPMENTAL ASPECTS OF
HUMAN KNOWLEDGE

The progressive integration and organization of knowledge that takes place during the various phases of development is not a process that unfolds itself in a passive individual. Rather, it appears as the active work of an agent, who learns to know himself or herself through this very process and thereupon gradually constructs a unique personal identity. From this perspective, the construction of self-knowledge that progressively emerges during the course of development is the integrating element of the entire process: Through the gradual organization of self-knowledge, the organismic processes inherent in development and the environmental conditions that shape and regulate the individual's learning assume idiosyncratic forms and definite relationships.

Indeed, a satisfying description of development should be unitary and should illustrate the progressive integration of species-specific innate dispositions, developing self-knowledge, cognitive growth, and emotional experiences while taking into account the family and the environmental influences that regulate the entire process.

A CONCEPTUAL FRAMEWORK FOR THE INTEGRATION OF MATURATIONAL PROCESSES AND ENVIRONMENTAL INFLUENCES

Although an infant at birth has a complex repertoire of inborn dispositions, he or she is not yet a self. Rather, through slow and gradual development, the infant has to become a self. Self-recognition, and, later, the acquisition of self-knowledge, cannot come about simply through direct self-observation: As Popper suggests (Popper & Eccles, 1977), this can be achieved only by progressively and actively developing concepts and theories about self. In other words, self-knowledge develops through action. This assumption implies that the organism's interaction with the surrounding environment precedes knowledge development and represents a prerequisite to it.

Therefore an infant learns to know by exploring and actively interacting with his own environment. People are undoubtedly the most important objects in this environment. Through their interest in the child, and through the child's knowledge of his own body, which he gradually acquires, he can learn that he is a person.

In support of the theory that human beings acquire self-knowledge through ongoing interactions with other people (see, e.g., Cooley, 1902; Mead, 1934), many data indicate that a child who grows up in isolation does not achieve a full consciousness of self (Curtiss, Fromkin, Krashen, Rigler, & Rigler, 1974). Studies on primates have also produced some interesting related findings: Chimpanzees raised in human families can perceive themselves as similar to human beings (Hayes & Nissen, 1971). This phenomenon, known as the "looking-glass effect," is so defined by Popper: "Just as we learn to see ourselves in a mirror, so the child becomes conscious of himself by seeing his reflection in the mirror of other people's consciousness of himself" (Popper & Eccles, 1977, p. 110).

Although we consider the looking-glass effect absolutely fundamental to the acquisition of self-knowledge, we do not agree with the original, excessively environmentalist formulation that the construction of "self" is exclusively a social acquisition. According to this viewpoint, self-knowledge is the outcome of social roles and of the knowledge of ourselves that the social environment imposes upon us; in other words, we are what society makes us believe we are. As Hamlyn (1977) has cogently argued, in this formulation of *content* of knowledge is confused with the *conditions* necessary for its development. If interaction with others is an indispensable condition for the acquisition of self-knowledge, the organism's own activity in selecting the content of this knowledge cannot be disregarded. The organism is not a passive container progressively filled up by the definitions that society and others furnish; rather, through those definitions, it actively selects and constructs rules and concepts about itself and others. Also, the peculiarities of developmental processes should be considered within the organism's activity. By influencing the organism's sensitivity and information-processing abilities, maturational changes actively intervene on the conditions of learning (social interactions) and on the organization of knowledge's content.

Attachment theory, the organization of emotional experiences, and cognitive growth are the main areas of concern in an integrative approach to maturational processes, environmental influences, and knowledge organization.

ATTACHMENT THEORY

The "medium" through which developmental processes (cognitive and emotional) advance is the relationships with those people who make up the child's early environment. On the basis of the possibilities offered by the gradual cognitive and emotional growth, this medium supplies a great deal of the material that the child will progressively process into self-knowledge and knowledge of the world.

From this perspective, and in accordance with Ainsworth, Blehar, Waters, and Wall (1978), we consider attachment theory (Bowlby, 1958, 1969, 1973, 1980) as a kind of explanatory theory, which essentially furnishes a guide for understanding and organizing observational and experimental data already available to us. This theory could be a new integrative paradigm of human development, giving us an inclusive and organized vision of all factors that intervene in the evolution of self-knowledge.

Attachment

"Attachment behavior" was formerly defined as the class of behavioral systems aimed at maintaining closeness and contact with other people, particularly the "caregiver," who generally is the mother.

Harlow's famous experimental studies on primates (1958) have proved the early psychodynamic theories on the nature of attachment to be false. According to these theories, feeding, which acts by reducing the hunger drive, is the mediator of attachment. In contrast to the hypothesis that an acquired "dependency need," is secondary to the primary hunger drive, Harlow unequivocally demonstrated that the fundamental mediator of attachment behavior is contact with the caregiver.

Attachment behavior—which can be described in other animal species besides the intensely studied primates—undoubtedly possesses strong phylogenetic determinants. These provide infants with a complex repertoire of action schemes and coding systems that enable them to intervene actively with their caregivers from the very first phases of life (Brazelton, Koslowski, & Main, 1974). On the other hand, a wide variety of environmental situations (illnesses, mother's relative absence, stressful events such as strangers' continuous presence or exposure to unfamiliar situations, etc.) can modify attachment.

A host of observations favor the idea that the inborn programming of attachment behavior is continuously shaped and modified through experience (see Bowlby, 1969); in other words, the individual differences in experience will lead to different "patterns" of attachment behavior. Therefore, even though the general conditions that activate and mold attachment behavior are by now widely described in the literature, we should remember that the principle coordinating the organization of the behavior becomes, early in life, highly specific to the individual as well as characteristic of the particular developmental stage.

Although, during the first phases of life, attachment is expressed essentially by simple contact-seeking patterns of behavior, later on it becomes progressively more articulated and complex, thanks to the emerging cognitive and emotional development. Particularly when internalization has acquired some stability, infants are able to form representational models of their attachment figures, of themselves, and of the surrounding environment. As infants learn more about themselves and their world, these representational models become more articulated and complex too.

Through the consolidation of complex internal representations, infants not only are able to tolerate increasingly longer periods away from their mothers without having anxious reactions, but also can incorporate their expectations regarding their mothers' accessibility and availability into their representational models. They also understand how accessibility and availability can be modified by various circumstances. It is obvious how the very development of these representational models carries the core of future stable cognitive structures concerning the main attributes of the self and outside reality.

At this point it may be useful to distinguish explicitly between attachment behavior and attachment (e.g., Ainsworth et al., 1978). Attachment behavior includes the behavior systems and strategies used for maintaining contact with the attachment figure; attachment is the representational model of the attachment relationship plus the affective bond that the infant establishes with his or her attachment figure. This representational model and affective bond tend to persist and become progressively more independent from contingent situations. Whereas early attachment behavior can be intermittent and elicited by specific situations, attachment is much more constant and stable and is less influenced by environmental situations. For example, if the infant is intent upon exploring his environment and does not openly demonstrate attachment behavior, this does not mean that he is not attached to his mother at that moment or that he is less attached to her than he was when explicit attachment behavior was observed.

Thus "attachment" might be defined as a cognitive structure that is constructed during the course of development, starting from inborn dispositions shaped by experiential data and directing the child's search for physical proximity and affective contact. The distinctive individual quality of attachment behavior patterns exhibited in response to various environmental situations is also a function of this cognitive structure. Moreover, these behavior patterns show a hierarchical organization; that is, the behaviors included in them are more or less interchangeable and can be integrated in various ways into the plans and strategies for adapting to the demands of different environmental situations. Needless to say, attachment acquires a qualitatively distinctive meaning in the human species, where the period of development and family care is by far the most prolonged on the zoological scale.

In concluding this discussion of attachment, we want to emphasize the growing awareness among researchers that the mother's importance has been overestimated and that the father's role has been erroneously considered to be of secondary or little value. This overemphasis on the mother's role most likely stems from the influence of early psychodynamic models and on the immediate and obvious observation that mothers usually spend more time with the infant than fathers do. At least in Western culture, this holds true. However, more than 15 years ago, caution was voiced against the conclusion that the mother is inevitably the main attachment figure. Schaffer and Emerson (1964) have pointed out that quality is a more critical variable in "emotional bonds" than quantity, thereupon introducing the notion of "intense attachment." This can be formed with individuals who are available for relatively limited periods of time, but who react quite intensely with the infant. Thus, if an attentive and available father is associated with a relatively unstimulating mother, he will most likely be first in the hierarchy of attachment objects in spite of the mother's greater temporal availability. Studies carried out in recent years on the father's role in development (cf. Lamb, 1976; Lynn, 1974) have emphasized his role in development from infancy to adolescence. The importance of his role is further documented by the effects that his absence may have on cognitive and emotional development (Biller, 1974).

Detachment[2]

Immediately after early infancy (from about 1 to 2 years of age), with the progressive acquisition of walking and the beginning of language development, children can proceed more quickly toward the exploration of their surroundings. Their specific search for physical closeness, which was almost exclusive up until this period, becomes less intense. The growing infants, because of the stability of their internal representations, become increasingly able to tolerate brief separations. By now they are able to leave the mother more often on their own initiative; each time, they go farther away from her for longer periods. In other words, the detachment process has begun.

Human beings are subject to an unusually long period of parental attachment. This condition would be counteradaptive if it inhibited exploratory behavior. In other words, the advantages of being provided with a secure source of parental care (protection, guidance, etc.) for a long period would be canceled if attachment interfered with the gathering of new information through the autonomous exploration of the environment. Given the evolutionary importance of exploratory behavior, it is rather strange that the detachment process has been studied much less intensively than attachment behavior. Rheingold and Eckerman (1971) argued in favor of the evolutionary meaning of detachment. They observed that detachment from parental figures is a distinctive process whose length and complexity are positively correlated with the higher level of the zoological scale. In accordance with these evolutionary remarks, we believe that the process of detachment deserves a detailed description.

Even if detachment and exploration begin on the infant's initiative, the caregiver's presence is fundamental at least at the beginning. Rheingold (1969) has demonstrated that the mother's absence has an inhibitory effect on exploratory behavior in an unfamiliar environment. The mother's presence (or absence) proved to be a crucial variable that allowed for (or inhibited) exploration of novel environments. Apparently, *just being aware of her presence* gives the infant enough confidence to approach an unfamiliar environment; that is, in her presence the novelty is attractive, whereas without her it becomes a source of fear. Moreover, we should consider that the mother is not at all a passive spectator; she can intervene in the process by either encouraging or discouraging the child's exploration. Presumably, the caregiver's response to the infant's separation initiative will influence how and to what extent the infant moves away. It could be expected that, in order to explore the novelties of the surrounding environment with confidence, the infant not only must have a familiar point of reference to turn back to, but also must conceive of the "secure base" as a steadily accessible and available one. Thus autonomous exploration seems to be correlated with the caregiver's response and with the degree of trust that the infant has in that person.

It must be stressed that the onset of exploratory detachment does not in any way indicate the end of attachment, nor does detachment represent the opposite pole to attachment. On the contrary, attachment and detachment should be considered as "interplay classes of behaviors which develop side by side and *coexist* throughout the life of an individual" (Rheingold & Eckerman, 1970, p. 79; italics added).

Because of the long period of development and parental care typical of the human species, detachment in the human being is gradual and requires much time. The environmental exploration that begins with the onset of walking is only the obligatory initial phase. Subsequent phases will occur when the child enters school, when there is more and more frequent contact with peers, and in social situations involving the child's absence from the family (camping vacations, sports activities, etc.). Finally, a more defined differentiation takes place during adolescence: Stimulated by cognitive development and sexual maturation, the youth not only will be able to form his or her own opinions of reality, which at times will differ from those of the family, but also will be able to establish affective relationships that can be experienced as being of the same importance as the parental relationships. Therefore it is during adolescence that the long process of detachment can begin to be more completely organized on the cognitive and affective levels (cf. Bloom, 1980).

Certainly, in such a long and gradual process, many factors can interfere with the developing cognitive structures related to detachment. For instance, if the caregiver negatively interferes with the child's autonomous exploration, the child could easily develop the belief that the outside world is full of danger and that it is unsafe to detach himself or herself from "protective" figures. Moreover, the length of the detachment process makes detachment gradually less dependent on the caregiver's immediate response and more dependent on the presence of other variables, such as the possible existence of significant models at school or among peers and the quality of the family's "social network," which, in turn, determines the quantity, quality, and variability of cultural stimulations. For instance, even under the influence of parents who repress the detachment process, children who are furnished with a culturally stimulating environment might obtain enough information with which to construct alternative self-images and rules in order to detach themselves from the family and directly face the outside world.

As already stated, detachment does not represent the opposite pole to attachment; rather, it influences the quality and the development of the attachment itself. It is a plausible hypothesis that the progressive development of language and conceptual abilities allows children to communicate to other people who are significant to them the experiences that they have had during their own exploration. In this way, regular development of detachment might allow the relational structures of attachment to develop further, so that attachment will include not only modalities of physical and affective contact, but also patterns for communicating one's own opinions and emotional meanings. Finally, it can be hypothesized that the patterns of contact seeking and communication that are developed in this way become the basic elements used in constructing the attachments of adult life.

THE DEVELOPMENT OF EMOTIONAL EXPERIENCE

There is considerable evidence to indicate that a repertoire of facial and motor responses exists from the earliest phases of life; these responses are accompanied by feelings that precede learning experiences and that therefore are largely dependent upon the organism's genetic development. Brazelton *et al.* (1974) have demonstrated how an infant is equipped with a whole series of "motor responses" (cycling, visual following, etc.) that seem to be employed exclusively in interacting with other people. Observations of infants who were born blind and deaf (Eibl-Eibesfeldt, 1970) have revealed mimicry and expressive patterns equal to those of normal infants, thus suggesting that they are genetically determined rather than learned through observation. In comparison to the expressive behavior of normal infants, that of deaf and blind babies becomes much less differentiated and more stereotyped as time passes. However, neither the onset nor the pattern of the expressive responses is influenced by previous learning.

These data indicate that, from the earliest phases of development, a child possesses both the primary quality of feelings and the ability to manifest them through expressive motor mechanisms. Moreover, it is evident that emotional communication is closely connected from the beginning to these expressive motor mechanisms, particularly facial expression. Many observations (Eibl-Eibesfeldt, 1972) indicate that an inborn disposition to react selectively to the human face exists and that the first reciprocal communicative systems between infants and caregivers (prior to language) are largely based on expressive motor patterns. In other words, the face supplies a rich and continuous reciprocal feedback that modulates the emotional communication between the infant and his or her caregivers.

On the other hand, although the infant is provided with inborn expressive patterns associated with basic feelings, it is not likely that these can be experienced as "true" emotions at least until the differentiation between self and not-self is accomplished. According to Lewis and Brooks-Gunn (1979), the self–not-self differentiation begins with the construction of enduring experiences, that is, with the Piagetian phase of object permanence and the initial development of internalization (around the end of the first year). At this point, the infant has the possibility of proceeding toward "recognition of self" and therefore of localizing his or her feelings within the self: Only now can basic feelings become "emotional experiences." In other words, without a rudimentary form of representational knowledge, which implies an elementary principle of self-knowledge (i.e., self-recognition), an emotion cannot be subjectively experienced. If the first stage of emotional development coincides with the transition from basic feelings to emotional experiences, this development proceeds during all of infancy, childhood, and adolescence through a progressive differentiation of emotions. Starting as these quite intense, undifferentiated, and not very controllable basic feelings, the emotions undergo a continuous blending, becoming more subtle and articulated and abounding in specific meanings, and are progressively more subject to cognitive control. As a result of this differentiation during the course of development, the range of emotional experiences is greatly increased. This allows the organism to respond to the different and multiform environmental situations with a variety of emotional tones.

Obviously, cognitive development that advances in parallel with emotional development has an important role in the process of emotional differentiation. However, in accordance with Leventhal (1979), we do not consider the "cognitive-arousal" theory of emotions (Schachter & Singer, 1962) completely adequate in explaining emotional development and the organization of emotional experience. As a matter of fact, if the cognitive label totally determines emotions, then cognitive development would necessarily have to *precede* emotional development. This is rendered doubtful by some very elementary observations. For instance, infants have a range of specific emotional reactions that allows their families to regard them as particular persons, with their own "temperaments," much before the onset of language. Furthermore, if emotional differentiation were determined solely through the labeling ability offered by cognitive development, emotions would not have either a specific role in early communication or a relative autonomy (see, e.g., Mahoney, 1980). As Leventhal points out, the argument that emotions are mere epiphenomena of cognitions can be turned around: Situations that are potentially "cognitively" different may be construed as cognitively similar on the basis of the fact that they generate similar feelings. At the present state of knowledge, we can assume that "feelings"— which are far from being epiphenomena of thinking or simple "arousals"—are partially autonomous and concrete experiences with a specific information content, codified mainly in an analogical way.

When internalization has acquired a certain stability, infants are able to hold a constant representation not only of the information that comes from the outside world, but also of that which comes from their internal states. Indeed, a significant share of early stimulation comes from the infant's own body (self-perception), since for him or her, this very body is an object to know. Consequently, in every moment infants come to grips with two distinct, but *simultaneous*, perceptives inputs: Each perception of the outside world corresponds to a self-perception feeling which gives them information on their own status. Since cognitive development progresses more slowly than emotional development, it is likely that self-perception is the earliest condition that allows for a sense of subjective continuity in time.

We are not affirming here that cognitive development is second-ary to, or a derivative of, emotional development; such an affirmation would closely imitate the psychodynamic position. Instead, we mean that, at least until cognitive development reaches a certain level (specifically, the period described by Piaget as the one of concrete operations and then of formal operations; see Flavell, 1963), cognitive and emotional development proceed *together*, reciprocally influencing and determining each other. Feelings and emotions are concrete experiences bringing with them information and meanings "from within" (self-perception) that notably contribute to cognitive develop-ment, whereas cognitive growth influences emotional differentiation. As Elkind (1970) points out, during infancy (in contrast with later childhood and adulthood) the intellectual and affective functions are to a large extent reciprocally undifferentiated. This is why anything that affects affective equilibrium at this age (e.g., problematic emo-tional attachment or stressful events) will deeply influence cognitive functioning and vice versa. A healthy adult is usually able to keep the single sources of emotional suffering separate from cognitive function-ing in different areas.

Emotional experience shows, in each individual, the features of an *organized* experience rather than a fragmentary and episodic one. Emotions certainly differ, and the same emotional experience could appear each time with different shades of meaning. However, a continuous sense of personal singleness pervades each instance of emotional experience and furnishes the individual's perceptive and cognitive experiences with a kind of self-recognizable affective color-ing. Self-perception and perception of the world are simultaneous, as we have already pointed out; perception of the world would be more objective and impersonal if it were not accompanied by self-perception. Which factors preside over this organization of emotional experi-ences? Various data indicate how specific aspects of memory and imagination could intervene in this process.

Leventhal (1979) stresses the importance of an "emotional memory mechanism" during emotional processing. This mechanism would be a relatively concrete memory of an analogical type, made up mainly of images that include "key perceptual features of emotion-eliciting situations," representations of expressive patterns and of the motor and visceral reactions that accompany those situations. Aside from how they should be conceptualized, these "emotional schemata" seem to consist of concrete representations of specific experiences, which can be retrieved through imaginative procedures: They make up real "feeling memories." Among the functions that Leventhal attributes to emotional schemata, the following should be stressed:

1. They furnish a more or less automatic and unconscious reaction repertoire in response to affectively meaningful stimuli.
2. They selectively focus attention on specific details in the perceptual field, influencing the entire "coding" of the current situation.
3. They strongly contribute to the emotional differentiation in the course of development. The progressive elaboration of "schemata" consists of connecting preexisting emotional reactions to new situations, modifying emotions that are already present, and producing new blends of environmental stimuli on the one hand and motor patterns and neurovegetative and instrumental reactions on the other.
4. They contribute through the imaginative procedures to the mnemonic mechanism of retrieval.
5. Finally, they contribute to the structuring of emotional experience, giving the feature of personal singleness to it. On the basis of strictly personal meanings, events that could not have been correlated otherwise are united and connected. In other words, this "collative" characteristic of the emotional bundle is fundamental in shaping the structural aspects of the self-tacit knowledge.

We want to emphasize here that, as representations of emotional experiences and thus being present throughout the entire course of life, emotional schemata are undoubtedly already active while language development is still in its early phases. In keeping with this hypothesis, if the majority of people are asked to go back as far as they can in their life memories, what they invariably recollect are images linked to specific and intense "feelings." In particular, it is likely that, because of the still scarce cognitive differentiation, the emotional schemata structured during infancy acquire a peculiar functional stability which makes them "prototypic emotions." As such, they mediate those idiosyncratic emotional responses to particular stimuli that are considered expressions of the person's "character." During later childhood and adolescence, the individual becomes capable (thanks to cognitive maturation and growth) of paying attention to the cognitive aspects of his or her own emotions and thereupon progressively elaborates beliefs and theories on his or her own emotional experience and on that of others. Instances of beliefs that are inferred by concrete emotional experience concern how one comes to react to certain situations with specific emotions, as well as the nature of emotional experiences, the causes that determine them, and the effects produced once they have been aroused. Because of the logical–deductive capability of adolescent thought, true theories about internal states are elaborated from these first beliefs and will become part of the personal identity structure in adulthood.

COGNITIVE GROWTH

In this section we want to emphasize those aspects of cognitive development that, from our clinical viewpoint, seem to particularly affect the development and organization of self-knowledge.

Thanks to Piaget's work in this field, much more is known about cognitive development than about emotional development (cf. Flavell, 1963). Stemming from the construction of enduring experience (the so-called phase of object permanence), the first distinction between self and not-self is accomplished. When internalization begins to be somewhat stable, infants actively proceed to extract "sets" of regularities from their surrounding heterogeneous and multiform environment; from these "sets" they begin to elaborate more or less complex rules for categorizing the experience that they gradually acquire. Through a dynamic and reciprocal relationship with their environment, they infer increasingly complex rules for coordinating their actions, emotions, and thoughts.

The progressive disengagement of the person's thought from the situational "here and now," as well as from the immediacy of his or her experiences of self, is perhaps the most outstanding feature of the slowly unfolding cognitive abilities. Gradually, during the course of development, the child becomes aware of himself or herself, comes to accept the norms of logical coherence, and masters the abstract concepts of language. When the individual reaches adolescence, the internalization of language is usually such that it allows for abstract thought and for a beginning satisfactory disengagement: Concepts may be dealt with as such, apart from the environmental situations to which they apply.

Needless to say, this slow disengagement from the context of experience significantly influences learning during infancy and childhood. In the remainder of this section, we inspect the functional aspects of this progressive disengagement through three essential periods: (1) infancy and preschool years (from about 2½ to 5 years of age—preschool children), (2) childhood (which roughly corresponds to the primary school period), and (3) adolescence (from about 11 or 12 to 15 or 16 years of age). These phases only partly correspond to those described by developmental psychologists; the reason for this discrepancy is that we have adopted a simplification necessitated by the practical requirements of clinical practice. (We have to reconstruct our patients' developmental histories through direct clinical interviewing, and therefore we need reference points—such as school years—that are easy for the average patient to recollect.)[3]

Infancy and Preschool Years

Infants are considerably self-centered regarding their own representations; that is, "decentering" (see, e.g., Beck, 1976; Bedrosian & Beck, 1980) is almost impossible. It is as if they assumed that all other people see things as they do. It is absolutely impossible for them to understand that others might have different points of view. They do not feel any need for justifying their reasoning to others or to themselves, since they find it extremely difficult to deal with the results of their thought processes as "objects" for new thinking. The distinctive feature of this age is that, even though the children can respond to and solve problems posed verbally, they are almost incapable of verbalizing the solutions they find (Elkind, 1970). Little by little as they approach the sixth year, the number of overt trial errors for finding solutions decreases; it seems that, with their increasing abilities of internalizing and using language, they can rely more and more upon mental manipulations.

In this period the imaginal mode of thought representation plays an essential role in reasoning and problem solving. The use of internalized language (inner dialogue) as a mediator in problem solving is quite elementary and most likely is useful mainly in prolonging imaginal processes rather than in substituting for them. In other words, thinking during infancy tends to operate mainly through relatively static and concrete images of reality. Contrary to what occurs in subsequent phases, during which formal mental operations become possible, thoughts are very close to sequences of explicit actions. At this age children limit themselves to mentally rescanning the real, concrete sequences as they would if they were involved in an explicit action. One of the most functionally interesting aspects of this concreteness is that which Piaget calls "infantile realism": Things are what they seem to be in the immediate self-centered perception, without any possible alternatives, and the incorporeal phenomena (dreams, emotions, thoughts, duties, etc.) are materialized in almost tangible entities.

Childhood

During the primary school years, the ability to decenter begins to develop. In comparison to the subjective centralization of infancy, where all the infant's attention is focused on sensorial, emotional, and imaginative immediacy, the primary-school-age child's attention is shifted toward the formal properties of objects and on the coordination of the actions that he or she carries out on them. Thus actions can be progressively internalized and become mental operations (*concrete* operations), gradually assuming the characteristics of reversibility. For instance, the child is now able to reconstruct the probable initial conditions of a given situation before it was modified by an ongoing action. Thereupon internalized actions are progressively organized in a coordinated system of actions, conditions for actions, and consequences, in a close relationship to each other. A typical feature of this childhood period in comparison to infancy is that the inner representation of reality assumes a definite organization, endowed with stability, order, and coherence.

Notwithstanding the importance of this initial decentering, children's thinking is still quite bound to the context of immediate experience. They act as if their principal and exclusive task is to arrange and organize data of present experiences. This close dependence on the phenomenal world, besides often compelling them to deal with the qualitative properties of effects or events one at a time, also limits their ability in problem solving. In fact, they are not yet able to use the hypothesis-testing approach, but rather must proceed by trial and error (even if less so than during infancy), based mainly on available concrete data. Furthermore, when the solution to a problem has been found, they cannot easily generalize it to other analogous problems; this makes them relatively incapable of understanding general rules and of drawing general conclusions from their own trials.

In spite of this limitation, childhood marks an extremely important step in the progressive disengagement of thinking from the immediacy of experience. In the period of concrete operations, children gradually begin to extend their thought from what is actual to what is possible. By the end of childhood, this extension has reached such a degree that it makes up the premises for the adolescent "formal operations" revolution.

Adolescence

With the onset of formal logical–deductive operations in adolescence, thoughts not only gradually break away from the phenomenal context, but become, as such, objects of further reasoning.

Perhaps the most important property of logical–deductive thinking concerns the relationship between what is real and what is possible; that is, reality comes to be conceived of as a particular subset within the totality of events and things, a subset, furthermore, that not only can be experienced, but also is *deducible* by means of hypotheses and causal theories. This distinction between what is real and what is possible sets in motion a radical change in the relationship with reality. Unlike the child, the adolescent not only is interested in arranging and organizing the data present in immediate experience, but also can use these data for elaborating hypotheses and explanatory theories. From these theories, he or she can now imagine "what could happen," thereupon reversing the logical roles between "real" and "possible." Consequently, thought processes are now dominated by hypothetical–deductive types of strategies. The hypothesis-testing approach is used mainly in problem solving: Through hypothetical reasoning, the implicit consequences of a hypothesis can be inferred, and it is possible to discard subjectively unsuitable hypotheses *before* testing them out in reality. Finally, we should emphasize that in adolescence the contents of thought are largely propositional. The entities that the adolescent manipulates in his or her reasoning are no longer the raw data of childhood, but rather formulations and theories which include reality data as particular cases.

The subordination of the real world to the possible world, while orienting attention toward problems that go beyond the field of immediate experience, also modifies the concept of time, particularly of the future. The future is no longer something vague and indefinite as it was in childhood; it appears to be a set of definable and pursuable possibilities that one can use in planning his or her own life.

Metaphors that compare the individual to the scientist are often used in cognitive psychology; we say that, as the scientist's behavior is constantly directed by the theories that he follows, so an individual's behavior is directed by the concepts that he has constructed regarding self and the world. Staying within the metaphor, we could say that an individual's scientific career officially begins with adolescence, after a long, gradual period of preparation.

NOTES

1. William James (1892) distinguished the "empirical self" from the "conscious self." The former can be the object of one's own scrutiny; the latter does the scrutinizing. The conscious self experiences, but can never, paradoxically, be experienced in itself. We can experience the world that impinges upon us, and we can experience the memories and the thoughts derived from our interaction with that world, but we can only infer the "ego" that makes those conscious experiences. In this book, when speaking of self, self-knowledge, personal identity, attitude toward oneself, and so forth, we are speaking of James's "empirical self."

2. Bowlby (1969, 1973, 1980) uses the term "detachment" with reference to the *pathological* condition in which attachment behavior has become deactivated. In Bowlby's terminology, the processes that we are describing under the label of "detachment" (following mainly Rheingold and Eckerman's use of the term; see Reingold & Eckerman, 1970, p. 79) would be subsumed under the term "development of self-reliance." Although Bowlby's use of the term "detachment" is certainly very appropriate from the point of view of the clinical applications of attachment theory, we have preferred (given the present state of knowledge on these matters) to stay in the vague, giving to this term a meaning that may cover also positive and healthy aspects of a child's behavior.

3. When an adult patient recollects stressful events from his or her childhood, it is important to place them in a proper time perspective. A stressful event occurring when the patient was in primary school impinges upon a different cognitive–maturational background than if the same event occured, say, during adolescence, and its effect on the ongoing organization of knowledge will be correspondingly different. In other words, it is useful to relate stressful events, maturational phases (with correspondingly varying degrees of possible disengagement), and roughly defined (since it is usually impossible to recollect exact dates) periods of development.

2

THE DEVELOPMENT OF
SELF-KNOWLEDGE

How do we obtain self-knowledge? Not by self-observation, I
suggest, but by becoming selves, and by developing theories
about ourselves.—Popper and Eccles (1977)

In the preceding chapter, mainly using Eccles's and Popper's words,
we stated that the "self" is somehow central in the organization of
knowledge and that it is a "learned" construct. In this chapter, we deal
with some major aspects of the development of self-knowledge,
taking it for granted that the "looking-glass effect" (Cooley, 1902;
Mead, 1934) is valid. The reader may feel that assumptions and
hypotheses are more the subject of this chapter than experimental
data; admittedly, we have only been careful in our discussion not to
contradict the already-existing experimental data and the more obviously observable facts concerning human development. Considering
the clinical purpose of this book, we hope the reader will forgive our
frequent reference to metaphors that we have made in order to avoid
lengthy and boring discussions.

Turning our attention once again to the "looking-glass effect,"
we would like to stress that this principle not only concerns the
relationship with other people, even if its importance is much more
evident at this level, but also reflects the basic modalities that seem to
preside over the whole organization of knowledge. Metaphorically
speaking, external reality is like a mirror through which we recognize
our own image; later on we elaborate this image into our personal
identity, while becoming more or less aware of it. On the other hand,
the mirror of reality is not complete at the beginning, but is reconstructed from fragments that we gradually extract from our experience
and thereafter put together, as in a mosaic. The fragments from

which the construction begins are almost entirely given, coinciding with aspects of parents' personalities, the quality of parents' affective relationship, and the family's social–cultural characteristics. The reason for this is that, at least during infancy, reality almost coincides spatially with the family environment. Subsequently and gradually, other fragments (extracted from scholastic experiences, other early social interactions, sentimental life, etc.) can be progressively added to the construction. Obviously, the form that the construction has achieved at any particular time will determine the type and quality of the next fragment to look for among the available ones and will influence the way in which this fragment is inserted in the already-existing mosaic.

In other words, from the first phases of development, every human being actively abstracts some regularities for differentiating and integrating two stimulus flows that are distinct, but always simultaneous: perception of the outside world and self-perception. Thus any information about the outside world always and inevitably corresponds to information about self. In this way the elaboration of knowledge appears to be a *unitary* process that occurs through the dynamic interplay of two polarities, the self and the world, which can be metaphorically equated to the two sides of a coin: A subject's self-knowledge is always correlated with his or her concept of reality. Not only do the two polarities of knowledge appear as parts of the same organization, but the dynamic aspect of knowledge growth and integration conveys the impression of a single, uninterrupted construction. Environmental and body changes are experienced while passing from one developmental phase to another, and the knowledge organization reached in each phase is not cancelled by the subsequent discoveries and acquisitions. Rather, as Piaget's work clearly shows, each phase of knowledge organization becomes the starting point for the evolution of the next phase and is finally absorbed or integrated into it (cf. Flavell, 1963).

During early infancy (from birth to 2 years of age), the basic prerequisites for the further development of knowledge are established. The first of these prerequisites is the construction of enduring experience, that is, recognition that objects and people still exist when they are perceptually absent. The construction of enduring experience implies the discovery of "self-permanence": when infants are in some way conscious that the existence of other objects is not contingent on their own presence, they become capable of demarcating self and not-self. Permanence of objects and self-permanence then develop side by side (around 8 to 9 months of age; cf. Lewis & Brooks-Gunn, 1979).

Self-permanence implies a form of rudimentary self-recognition, which enables infants to reciprocate more and more actively in the ongoing relationship with their parents. Another basic prerequisite for the further development of knowledge is very likely drawn from the quality of this relationship: a kind of "feeling tone" about the social world, similar to Erikson's (1963) concept of "basic trust." Roughly, this basic feeling tone corresponds to emotional schemata, which convey the information that the social world is more or less reliable or the expectation of how satisfactorily one's needs will be met. The principal factor that determines the quality of this feeling tone is, of course, the quality of the caregivers' response to the infant. Particularly during the early period of life, infants will acquire a feeling that the world and the people in it are reliable the more his parents offer an atmosphere of unconditional acceptance beyond the necessary care and protection. The critical period for acquiring this feeling tone seems to be about the first 2 years of life (Elkind, 1970). By the end of this period, with the possession of the two basic prerequisites mentioned and the ability to walk autonomously and to master a rudimentary language, infants may proceed in acquiring new knowledge and organizing it in a more and more complex structure. The further development of knowledge is regulated mainly by the information on self and the world that infants obtain through their emotional bonds with significant others and by the characteristics that the phases of cognitive growth impress upon the learning process. We shall follow in our discussion of the further development of self-knowledge the same steps used in describing cognitive growth in the preceding chapter.

INFANCY AND PRESCHOOL YEARS

As infants acquire a stable inner representation of self and family members, they become better able to elaborate plans and strategies not only for seeking physical closeness, but also for actively seeking modification of their caregivers' behavior. It is likely that an infants' relational strategies at least partially determine the quality of his or her attachment figure's response: Through reciprocal reinforcement (or confirmation), the parent–child relationship gradually acquires a distinctive form. Within this reciprocal relationship, new information becomes available to the infant, and his or her representational model of self and people correspondingly becomes more articulated. Former "predictions" regarding how to get physical contact are gradually enlarged, and predictions concerning reciprocal relational and emotional availability are added to the model. As Lewis and Brooks-Gunn (1979, p. 230) put it, "Any knowledge gained about the other also must be gained about the self." That is, if others, as a mirror, supply infants with an image of themselves, this does not remain a mere sensorial datum, but rather orients and coordinates self-perception until they are able to perceive themselves consistently with it.

THE INFLUENCE OF EMOTIONAL ATTACHMENT

As we said in Chapter 1, attachment theory may be regarded as an integrative paradigm of development. The influence of the emotional bond with caregivers on the developing self-knowledge can be exemplified in various ways in light of this theory.

A good reciprocal emotional attachment with their caregivers enables infants to perceive themselves as capable of attaining affection, availability, and protection in the people that surround them, while the earlier positive "feeling tone" about the social environment is formalized into a primitive idea that people are reliable. In circumstances where the quality of the emotional relationship with parents is seriously distorted, it is likely that infants come to perceive themselves as incapable of attaining affection, availability, and protection from others. They can, therefore, draw an unlovable self-image connected to an impression of unreliability in the people that surround them.

Obviously, the situations responsible for the development of images connoted by unlovableness and unreliability are manifold. Parents can be detached from their infants (e.g., an undesired pregnancy), they can be discontinuous and fluctuating in their devotion to their infants (e.g., as a result of marital problems or social problems connected to work), or they can be affected by neurotic or psychotic disturbances that can limit, to some extent, their abilities regarding emotional responses. Another example of "pathogenic" attachment can occur when parents' attempts to obtain control over the child's behavior consist of threatening desertion or withdrawal of love; if, later on, such threats are effectively followed by clear-cut periods of separation (hospitalization of one of the parents as a result of illness, conjugal separations between parents, work necessities, etc.), these can be perceived by the child as directed toward him and provoked in some way by him. (As Rutter, 1972, points out, it is not so much the separation itself that has an influence on the child, as the quality of the relationship that precedes, accompanies, and follows it.)

These experiences effectively make infants fear losing one of their caregivers and can produce a kind of "anxious attachment" (Bowlby, 1969, 1973), characterized by the infant's repetitive, stereo-typed, and incessant search for contact and protection. In a circular way, this kind of behavior on the child's part can even further stabilize the established relationship model, since threats of desertion or withdrawal of love end up becoming more and more effective instruments of control.

The emotional quality of attachment also has an influence on the course of detachment processes, as we have already noted. This influence may become manifest precisely when the infant begins to walk and talk. Parents seem to be decisive in this process, not only in their implicit and explicit responses to the infant's detachment initia-tives, but also because they represent a "safe home base" when the infant ventures out to explore his or her environment. Thus infants with an anxious attachment will surely be inhibited in their environ-mental exploration even if their parents encourage detachment, since a great deal of their attention will be permanently devoted to main-taining physical closeness to their caregivers, toward whom they are nurturing a sense of impending loss. Also, the uncertainty about their parents being an available and safe "base" to be counted on every time they are frightened by something while exploring will sub-stantially limit the frequency and the extent of exploratory excursions.

PARENTAL INTERFERENCE IN THE DETACHMENT PROCESS

Possible parental interference in the detachment process can con-tribute to the development in infants of primitive beliefs regarding the unreliability of the environment and the overestimated potential dangers of its novelties, together with a limited "self-reliance," that is, beliefs regarding the inadequacy of their own abilities to cope with the environment. Obviously, this kind of developing self-knowledge seriously hampers the infant's ability to tolerate ever-increasing periods of separation; the "immature" behavior of contact seeking will tend to persist up until the school years.

Nursery school during infancy and the beginning of school later on represent key situations in which an outside observer can reconstruct both the infant's degree of autonomy (pointed out by his ability in dealing with brief separations) and the quality of the parental responses that have intervened in the process. Blurton-Jones and Leach (1972) studied the behavior of a group of children aged 2 to 4 years who were attending nursery school for the first time, correlating it to their mothers' behavior at the moment of separation and at the moment of rejoining (when they came back to pick the children up). They observed that the relationship pattern of children who protested more at the moment of separation ("criers") was centered mainly on the search for physical contact with their mothers ("clinging relationship"), whereas the relationship pattern of those who willingly accepted the separation ("noncriers") was oriented more toward attention and approval seeking ("talking and smiling relationship"). The significant variable seemed to be the "smiling response" that existed between mother and child, as if smiling, being a sign of the mother's readiness to respond positively to the child's needs, could function as an effective substitute for physical closeness. As a counter-check, mothers of criers, although more inclined toward physical contact with their children, showed a significantly lower frequency of smiling responses in their repertoire of expressive behaviors.

Another instance of how caregivers' attitudes toward separation may influence children's exploratory behavior is offered by "excessive maternage." Besides pouring out an excessive quantity of attention on the baby, the "overprotective" mother more or less unwittingly represses the detachment and exploration initiatives, striving to keep the child constantly near to her. In this type of situation, infants can form a self-image that contains contradictory elements: On the one hand, the mother's attention and care can give them a positive sense of self-acceptability and self-lovableness, whereas on the other hand, the interference in detachment simultaneously limits their sense of self-reliance with regard to their autonomous exploratory abilities. The attempt to reach a satisfying integration of these contrasting aspects of their own images can represent one of the guiding threads that subsequently regulates the range of models to imitate as well as the domains of experience considered as significant during childhood and adolescence.

INFANTILE REALISM

We must remember that the level of cognitive development determines how the infant processes the available information. In infancy, the achieved cognitive level is the period of egocentrism and infantile realism characterized by an absolute predominance of imaginal schemata. Since internal language is hardly used, it is impossible to decentralize these images, which for the infant correspond to absolute reality. In other words, these imaginal schemata, which are endowed with intense emotional coloring (emotional schemata) because they are derived from prior concrete experiences whose content is formed mainly of feelings, convey essentially tacit and analogical information on the self and others. The consequences of this tacit and strongly emotionally tinged information (which it is impossible for the infant to verbalize because he or she has not yet mastered subtleties of the language) are noticeable. Since verbalization most likely makes it possible to give temporal and historical dimensions to available data, emotional (tacit) schemata are mainly "presentified"; that is, without the possibility of being inserted in a temporal frame, these schemata come to correspond as such to reality and therefore have a particularly stable nature. In this way, they become a kind of primordial nucleus of knowledge, which is held to be "true" and is preserved as such because it is not "thinkable" or criticizable. As Berger and Luckmann (1966) have argued, this "protorealism" probably performs an important adaptive function in ontogeny. The stability upon which our feeling of singleness is founded and which we continually notice in perceiving our personal identity very likely depends on it.

Infantile realism makes the emotional bonds between parents and infants idiosyncratic. Infants do not internalize the world of people who are meaningful to them as one of many possible worlds, but as *the* world, the only one that exists and the only conceivable one. The infant's early relationship with his or her parents is indeed absolutely unique. On the one hand, infants have a compulsory need for contact, affection, and protection—their very survival depends on it. On the other hand, for many years they will not be able to depict an alternative relationship to the one that historical contingencies have imposed upon them (Berger & Luckmann, 1966). Within an emotional bond without alternatives, parents are the only possible mediators of the world; thus they have an extremely important role in determining what information on self and the world will be considered significant and how it will be processed.

In a recent paper, Bowlby (1979) called attention to some interesting consequences of this peculiar situation. For instance, when parents determine the exclusion of important environmental data, the children are compelled to refuse their own senses' testimony and to accept the parents' point of view. Rather often, it seems, children who will develop emotional disturbances observe scenes that their parents would prefer that they did not see (e.g., suicides or attempted suicides, family dramas connected to unfaithfulness, etc.). Many data uphold the hypothesis that children, when they are subjected to parental pressures or are merely aware of parents' desires to avoid discussing certain topics, usually conform to their parents' wishes, excluding from further processing what they have already registered. The consequence of this exclusion is an apparent unawareness of what has happened: It is as if they had never observed these scenes nor drawn certain impressions or emotions from them. Excluding already-formed schemata from subsequent processing makes it impossible to verbalize them later on, that is, to transform them into objects of thought. Nevertheless, even if they are scarcely recognizable, these schemata will function as kind of "criterion images," yielding a central theme for the progressing organization of emotional states. More specifically, it is very likely that, whenever these emotional schemata are excluded from the thinking process, they will influence the emotional differentiation, contributing to the exclusion of definite feelings from the emotional repertoire and to the engraining of a feeling of unreliability toward one's own sensorial and intellectual abilities (and/or to the development of a basic mistrust of other people's intentions).

Besides these rather dramatic (and fortunately rare) situations, many subtler ones are frequently discovered in the course of individual or family psychotherapy: situations in which data concerning the private world of thoughts and emotions are excluded from further processing because of parents' influence. Even though these situations are widespread—they are almost the rule in families with distorted communicative styles—they are more difficult to recognize than the former, rarer ones. Whenever the child's personal experience differs from the parents' explanation of the feelings they suppose the child is having, thoughts and emotions that have already been produced are excluded, and the parents' redefinition of them is likely to be further processed.

A common example is children's sadness about a temporary separation from a friend of their own age; the parent denies the child's sadness and redefines it as happiness over the fact that the friend is returning home to his or her parents. The typical scheme is: "It's not true that you feel emotion x. Instead, you feel emotion y." These situations can have considerable repercussions on emotional differentiation. On the one hand, they can contribute to the exclusion of a whole range of emotional experience from the self-image so that it will be consistent with the image that the parents seem to accept more favorably; on the other hand, they create a feeling of unreliability concerning one's ability to recognize and define properly one's own internal states. Should this kind of parental redefinition occur repeatedly, the child can reach the "psychotic" point of needing the approval of a significant person in order to be certain that he or she is experiencing a given emotion and not another one.

THE REGULATING FUNCTION OF EARLY EXPERIENCE

In concluding this schematic exposition of the influences on the infant's developing self-knowledge, it might be useful to turn our attention briefly toward the hypothesis that early experiences can have serious and long-lasting effects on the course of development—and therefore on the individual's life (cf., e.g., Rutter, 1972, 1979). Although we believe that such a hypothesis is supported by many clinical and some statistical observations, we also think that it should not be interpreted in a deterministic way. The psychoanalytical tenant that the first 5 or 6 years of life determine the individual's personality and life is, in our opinion, false. It seems safer at the present state of scientific knowledge to assume that early experiences work as "criterion images," which essentially *regulate*, but do not totally determine, the subsequent making and matching processes through which the individual actively constructs knowledge of the self and the world.

From this viewpoint, the consequences of early learning and early experiences that become evident in adult life are not simply a repetition or a manifestation—through the distorting influence of defensive mechanisms—of accumulated and repressed childhood "schemata." Instead, these consequences might be better conceived of as the result of the knowledge organization that has been progressively structured *beginning* with those experiences.

Thus we might say that infancy is characterized by the formation of a relatively stable nucleus of knowledge, which is largely tacit or implicit. This nucleus has a regulating function in the elaboration and construction of subsequent experiences long before the child is able to remember and reflect upon it. In one of his fascinating books, Castaneda (1972) summarizes as follows Don Juan's opinion on how adults influence the child's attainment of knowledge:

> He pointed out that everyone who comes into contact with a child is a teacher who incessantly describes the world to him, until the moment when the child is capable of perceiving the world as it is described. According to Don Juan, we have no memory of that portentous moment, simply because none of us could possibly have had any point of reference to compare it to anything else. (pp. 8–9)

CHILDHOOD

Childhood represents an important turning point in the individual's development: He or she can establish more direct and immediate relationships with the social environment through school and, thanks to maturational processes and cognitive growth, is now endowed with wider information-processing abilities. Infancy's impulsive behavior, which is notably egocentric and accompanied by a sense of immediate certainty, is gradually substituted by a more reflective behavior. The child is now able to proceed toward the construction of new coordinates for relating different impressions and behaviors to each other; that is, he or she becomes better able to discover rules and formulate beliefs about the self and the outside world. The more clinically relevant steps in and influences on the development of self-knowledge that takes place in this life phase could be described under three headings: identification, the role of parents, and the emergence of self-conception.

IMITATION AND IDENTIFICATION

Relationships between the child and other people—the obligatory channel for the child's acquisition of knowledge—are notably influenced by the cognitive growth that coincides with childhood. In the infant's relationships with others, imitation is the almost exclusive way of learning, whereas during childhood identification gradually takes place due to the process of cognitive development.

The relevance of learning by imitation for the human knowledge processes (modeling; cf. Bandura, 1969) might be attributed to the fact that it implies little effort. Through modeling, as compared to operant learning, fewer trials and errors and less expenditure of energy are required in order to acquire, for example, problem-solving strategies. If imitation is, so to speak, the behavioral side of modeling, identification is its cognitive aspect, that is, an aspect that becomes possible when cognitive development has reached a level that permits the acquisition of rules and beliefs through the mere observation of significant models' behavior and verbalized opinions.[1] The definition of the term "identification" is quite debatable, and many clinicians unsympathetic toward the psychoanalytical approach prefer not to use it at all. Nevertheless, it is a rather common observation in clinical practice that individuals tend to resemble the people with whom they have relationships; children and adolescents, in particular, frequently exhibit behavioral and cognitive styles that can easily be detected as being similar to those of their parents.[2]

Cognitive modeling, or identification, thus seems important to understanding many clinical phenomena, and it deserves some brief remarks.

To begin, identification does not simply entail direct and passive counterfeiting of other people's knowledge. On the contrary, the individual actively selects aspects of the model's attitudes to imitate and reconstructs these data on the basis of the cognitive structures he or she already possesses. Therefore the individual's definitely constructive selective attention and retention processes are decisive in cognitive modeling (cf. Rosenthal & Bandura, 1978).

The presence of an emotional involvement also seems to be important in cognitive modeling, although it is not exactly clear how it fosters this process. To a certain extent, the tendency to assume a model's viewpoints and behaviors does not depend upon their outcome, and at times it occurs in spite of the outcome. Variables such as admiration, faith in the model's abilities, and empathy (typical hall-marks of an affectional relationship) might intervene in fostering identification with a model who is obviously socially unsuccessful. A feeling of solidarity stemming from the intention of sharing the "exploration" of the same world with the model might add to the emotional influences on cognitive modeling.

Another relevant feature of cognitive modeling is that children do not seem to identify with only one model; rather, they select a whole range of distinct models (parents, brothers and sisters, children of the same age, teachers, etc.), arranging them according to a hier-archical criterion based mainly on the meaningfulness of their re-lationships with these models. The main variables that operate in selecting a range of possible models might be the following two:

1. The quality of the nucleus of knowledge formed during infancy. This nucleus directs the perception of self and of others' characteristics and thus *influences* the choice of pos-sible models, which would have to fall within the range of these preformed attributions.
2. The availability of alternative models (to family ones) in the social network in which the child lives.

If the number of candidates for modeling is small (reduced social interactions outside the family, hampered social exploration due to parental intolerance to detachment, etc.), it is likely that the child will choose the parent with whom he or she has the more *intense* emotional relationship as a principal model, *apart from the negative or positive quality of the involvement*. In other words, even in a "negative" relationship with a parent (frequent quarrels, reciprocal opposition, etc.), emotional involvement can be intense enough to cause modeling effects. This impression, which is easily drawn from clinical observations of patients who show both a very negative relationship with one of their parents and a clear-cut "identification" with that same parent, might be matched with the well-known fact that many children actively manipulate the level of emotional stimula-tion in the relationship with their parents, preferring to be beaten or punished rather than ignored. In other words, children who have selected a detached parent as a model (because of the lack of alterna-tive models and the effect of the preformed nucleus of self-knowledge) might strive to gain at least his or her "punitive" attention, and the "bad" relationship that is hitherto established does not adversely influence the modeling process at all. The implications of such a modeling situation for understanding certain kinds of adult "neurotic" behavior and cognition (e.g., "ambivalence" toward self and other significant people, provocative opposition behavior that appears as soon as a positive relationship is established, etc.) are perhaps obvious to the reader.

Finally, we should point out that identification is carried out largely through a process of implicit learning (see Bandura & Huston, 1961, for a description of identification as a form of incidental or latent learning). According to Bandura and Huston, a very meaningful part of cognitive modeling concerns behaviors and attitudes that are insignificant and implicit regarding the concrete observed situation. In comparison with the focal awareness of the moment, learning through modeling can be described as "latent." A simple example might clarify this aspect and also explain the differences between imitation and identification.

A son helps his father tidy up the flower beds in the yard on a weekend. While the son *explicitly* imitates the father's behavior, he can also tacitly copy (identification) the father's emotional attitude (pleasure or dislike) toward this work. As far as the practical result of this learning situation is concerned, the father's emotional attitude is not only implicit, but also incidental. The boy's attention is focused on the actions that his father has carried out; he has to learn them if he wants to be helpful. The tacit copying of the father's emotional attitude toward that particular job (which, by the way, may correspond to his beliefs on his role in the home, on how the family is getting along, etc.) may, however, have a much longer story. The boy's perception of the father's "insignificant" behavior can produce emotional schemata that will function as "criterion images" in mediating the development of equivalent attitudes, and these attitudes in turn will manifest themselves when the boy is once again faced by requests to work in the home. Furthermore, these emotional attitudes could influence the construction of the boy's own beliefs on what role he, as a male, must assume in the home. It goes without saying that, in this oversimplified example, we have taken for granted that the emotional relationship between father and son is good enough to ensure a prompt identification, that there are no other competing models for the child at least as far as "working in the home" is concerned, and that there are no adverse influences on identification (e.g., the mother's negative appraisals of the father's emotional attitudes).

Our discussion has implied that behavioral, emotional, and purely cognitive variables coexist in identification. Most likely because of the growing logical–deductive abilities, cognitive variables acquire a greater importance as the child draws nearer to adolescence.

THE ROLE OF PARENTS

Identification with the parent of the same sex (or with an alternative model) during childhood is, although not absolutely essential, certainly important to the child in developing a self-conception as a man or woman and in elaborating the attributes of masculinity and femininity.

Although a child is for himself or herself an object to know, knowledge about one's sex (as any other aspects of self-knowledge) cannot be obtained only by observing one's own body. Besides the results of self-observation, probable sex-bound inborn dispositions that predispose the child to certain behaviors, and other people's verbal definitions of his or her gender role, the child, at least during this phase, tends to choose a homologous model from which to draw a set of regularities helpful in defining "gender identity" (Money & Ehrhardt, 1972). This does not mean that the parent of the opposite sex is ignored or is not helpful in the definition of gender identity. On the contrary, this parent, besides providing emotional and instrumental support to the child, becomes the comparison element through which the child (and later on, the adolescent) may perceive and recognize the specificity of the relationship with the homologous parents. In other words, while the child approaches adolescent sexual maturation, the parent of the opposite sex can acquire the important role of "testing bench," where the adolescent weights the acceptability and lovableness of his or her own gender identity. Needless to say, the effectiveness of sexual identification is influenced by how clearly the homologous model presents his or her gender role. When a parent's masculine or feminine characteristics are ambiguous and alternative models are lacking, the child can easily develop a confusing gender identity.

Besides being useful for the proper development of gender identity, the process of identification with the homologous parent seems to have a considerable role in determining how the child evaluates himself or herself. Dickstein and Posner (1978) have demonstrated on a group of males and females aged 8 to 11 years how self-esteem is positively correlated with the closeness of the parent–child relationship; males' self-esteem is closely associated with the relationship with the father, whereas girls' self-esteem is closely associated with the relationship with the mother.

The distinction of roles between parents is quite specific in Western culture. Social, economic, and cultural factors, although changing somewhat today, add to the biological factors (pregnancy, breast-feeding, etc.) that make the mother–infant relationship a closer one than the father–infant relationship. This fact, however, far from depriving the father–child relationship of significance, allows for wider qualitative variations, which may reflect themselves in manifold relevant influences on the development of the child's self-knowledge. Lewis and Weinraub (1976) have suggested that the father's role could be examined in this respect under three major headings:

1. How the father is described when he is absent. For instance, comments on the father's successfulness or unsuccessfulness in his job, or on his attitude toward the various ups and downs in life, give the child information on what characterizes masculinity, on how he or she should behave as an adult, on what dangers he or she needs to look out for, and so forth.
2. The quality of the mother–father relationship. The emotional support that the father offers to the mother is an important observation upon which the child may form expectations and beliefs on the nature of affective relationships. In particular, the male child will form rules regarding the masculine role in an affective relationship (subsequently following them or rebelling against them according to the quality of his relationship with his father), whereas the female child will form rules on what she can expect from a man in an affective relationship, establishing thereupon a first "draft" of her future approach–avoidance strategies toward males.
3. The father's observable interaction with the family's social network. This interaction will allow the child to draw a whole series of rules on how to act in social relationships and how to face the outside world.

As childhood advances (and more so during adolescent phases), youngsters can have two attachment figures, the mother and the father, both of whom have authority over them and can have different opinions of and expectations for them. According to Lewis and Weinraub (1976), this divergence can act as a stimulus in the differentiation of personal identity, since it can increase discrimination ability and thus self-analytical skills. Furthermore, attempts at integrating this divergence can lead to a rather well-defined and stable commitment to oneself in postadolescence. However, if the divergence is so great that integration attempts fail, the construction of personal identity (and therefore self-esteem) may be adversely influenced.

One of Jules Feiffer's cartoons illustrates this point very well. In the cartoon, a man confides in a friend, saying something like this: "I took everything from my father: the way he walks, his style of behavior, the way he talks, his mentality." "And what about your mother?" interrupts the friend. "From her I learned to despise my father," he answers.

THE EMERGENCE OF SELF-CONCEPTION

During childhood, a structured self-conception gradually emerges. Children become able to describe the elements that characterize their masculinity or femininity, the distinguishing traits and habits of their "personality," and the values and duties they must comply with.

However, on a purely cognitive level, the conceptual definitions of self that children are able to formulate are still closely bound to the concrete situations that suggest them and to episodic definitions offered by relatives, other children, teachers, and so forth. On the emotional level, both self-esteem and the control of feelings and emotions are still directly bound to ongoing affective relationships. In other words, although the child can describe himself as a person, his personal identity is barely outlined, and he succeeds more or less in defining it mainly through ongoing identification (e.g., "I am like Daddy.") and through environmental clues (e.g., "I am a good boy. I haven't broken the vase. John is wicked, he has broken it.").

The gap described here is characteristic of childhood. In the progressive organization of knowledge, children elaborate rules, beliefs, and opinions about themselves and the people that surround them; however, as we have seen in Chapter 1, the cognitive structuring of these rules cannot go beyond the specific context in which they originated. Studies on metacognitive development (Flavell, 1977) clearly support the hypothesis that children (unlike adolescents and adults) do not monitor their memory and communication or their perceptions and appraisals.

> The young child converts messages into cognitive representations and vice versa, but both messages and representations are largely invisible to him. They do not themselves become objects of cognitive scrutiny and evaluation, and their continual generation and reception by the young child are not consciously monitored by him. (Flavell, 1978, p. 234)

Thus the primitive structures of personal identity are continually reelaborated on a strictly "intuitive" and "prelogical" level and become manifest outside the original context only through games, fantasies, fairy tales, or stories with heroes or heroines in which children identify themselves. It is through these activities that an attentive observer can reconstruct the developing concepts of self and the world that the child is unable to systematize.[3]

The cognitive development achieved up to this point does not allow the child to make that "intellectual" discovery of self that will characterize adolescence. However, the logical–conceptual structuring that is typical of adolescence will begin to take form from this "prelogical" reelaboration of the "intuitive" and fantastic content of childhood self-conception and conceptions of the world.

ADOLESCENCE

With adolescence, the individual progresses toward a noteworthy personal rearrangement. An entire set of deep transformations is concentrated in this period: Physical and emotional changes connected to sexual maturation cut across the intellectual changes connected to the onset of abstract thought. Driven by the changes and by other people's demands for a more adult behavior, the adolescent strives to behave according to "adult" values, goals, and ideals.

After a slow, gradual development, the adolescent seems well-endowed with the necessary abilities for an autonomous relationship with outside reality and for a formal organization of self-knowledge. Nevertheless, although the cognitive repertoire seems almost complete, its full use is usually delayed until early adulthood. Perhaps because of social influences that delay economic autonomy, but more likely because of the repercussions of the very novel transformations that have taken place, adolescents seem much more prone to analyzing and observing the new cognitive and somatic endowments than to finding a practical use for them.

This is the so-called phase of adolescent egocentrism. Unlike children in the infant egocentric phase, who are absolutely unable to assume other people's viewpoints, adolescents excel in the ability. They are perfectly able to grasp and theorize about other people's opinions and to compare them with their own. Yet, it is as if all this theorization is an end in itself, aimed at nourishing a new self-concept that includes the proud awareness of the ability to use theoretical elaboration and plans, which can even change the phenomenal appearance of reality. Theorizations, political opinions, and/or social fashions are typically extreme and rarely influenced by reality testing. Indeed, sometimes it seems as if reality should bend to the adolescent's will. This contraposition between one's theories and existing reality usually disappears little by little in adulthood, when one's own opinions may (more or less!) be progressively considered not as unavoidably antagonistic to reality, but, rather, as capable of interpreting it and eventually capable of adapting to it or to a well-planned effort to modify it.

Three major aspects of how adolescent transformations influence the deveopment of self-knowledge are considered in this section: the formalization of self-conception, cognitive modeling, and autonomy from the family.

FORMALIZATION OF SELF-CONCEPTION

The possibility of considering one's own thoughts and emotions as objects of thinking, and the consequent ability to elaborate true causal theories about them, allow for the progressive emergence of self-awareness. Indeed, one of the typical features of adolescents is their strong tendency toward self-analysis and personality diagnosis. This introspective activity has important effects on the conceptual formalization of self.

Montemayor and Eisen (1977) have longitudinally studied the development of self-conception, following a group of children from childhood to adolescence. They have found that the self-construct, which is concrete and relatively undifferentiated during childhood, gradually becomes more articulated as the final phases of adolescence draw near, until it becomes characterized by a high level of abstraction, is well differentiated from the context, and appears hierarchically organized. In other words, whereas children describe themselves in an extremely concrete manner related mainly to the family environment, adolescents describe themselves in terms of personal beliefs and attitudes. For instance, a child, when talking about sports, might say "I like soccer" and describe concretely how he plays, whereas an adolescent would say "I have athletic tendencies" and would illustrate his beliefs on the utility of physical fitness.

The adolescent emphasis on more abstract and qualitative aspects of self proves that a formal, organized definition of personal identity is emerging. However, in this phase of development, the conceptual world of beliefs and hypotheses on self and reality upon which the definition of personal identity is founded usually is full of contradictions and still lacking a coherent integration. During the search for coherent integration, the various schemata, theories, and beliefs that were gathered during infancy and childhood are continually rehearsed and matched with the novelties stemming from sexual maturation, cognitive growth, and environmental changes. Through this rehearsal and matching, self-identity and self-esteem acquire the quality of a stable cognitive–emotive structure. By the end of adolescence, this structure is almost completely independent of the relational context from which its elements origniated. The resulting autonomous and stable personal identity will now direct the youth's behavior in novel environments, showing a remarkable resistance to change.

COGNITIVE MODELING

The new cognitive abilities emerging in adolescence make cognitive modeling somehow different from what it was in the preceding developmental phases.

During childhood, identification is strongly influenced by the emotional aspects of the model–observer relationship and is largely bound to the specific context of current observations. During adolescence, the emotional component may be substantially reduced, and cognitive modeling mainly concerns the model's global attitudes toward life and personal beliefs, which may be influential even when the model is not physically present (e.g., through readings or memory rehearsal). An extreme clinical example might demonstrate how a powerful and long-lasting modeling effect becomes possible in adolescence through an active extraction of the model's beliefs, which are implicit in his or her attitudes and behavior, and might also explain the basic reason for this effect, that is, the adolescent search for a satisfactory adult identity.

Several years ago we had the opportunity to observe a young physician suffering from phobic reactions to almost everything regarding hospitals (wards, operating rooms, etc.). Since he stated that he had never had a particular enthusiasm for medicine, we were surprised (as was he) that he had decided to become a physician, and we began a clinical inquiry about the reason for his professional choice.

His family was rather isolated until the beginning of his youth because they lived in a tendentiously hostile foreign country, and his father was intolerant toward any social relationship that his son might have. The father was the absolute ruler of the home. He was a quick-tempered man, violent and unpredictable; he undervalued his son, treating him as if he were inept or mediocre. Moreover, he acted this way with everyone; he could find faults or shortcomings in anybody and almost always succeeded in imposing his opinions on others.

The only person he did not have this attitude toward was the family physician. The father became courteous and available when the practitioner came to visit. The adolescent boy, according to the psychotherapeutic reconstruction of his developmental history (see Chapter 7), noticed this change in his father's attitude and from this observation seemingly inferred that his father believed the medical profession to be a particularly honorable one. The boy "modeled" on this father's belief and concluded that, if he also became a physician, maybe his father would finally acknowledge his value. Because of the family's isolation, the father was the only available model for the boy. This modeling effect was almost completely implicit, and the young man was not even aware of it when he went to enroll at the university. Since he had refused to enroll in the department that his father had chosen for him and had imposed his own choice—

medicine—he was astonished that, unlike what usually happened, his father not only did not get angry, but seemed to respect and value his son's choice. He was not aware of what had happened even when he asked for psychotherapy as a result of his phobias. (The only plausible reason he held at that time for his professional choice was that of wanting to rebel against his father).

Reconstructing the story, we were able to establish that the deference and respect that the father demonstrated toward the doctor were very likely mainly due to his hypochondriacal worries. In fact, the patient was able to recollect that his father was frequently anxious about his own health and sometimes unable to control or conceal this anxiety. Only the doctor's visit cheered him up and restored his self-confidence for a while. Should the son have attributed the father's deference toward the medical professional to hypochondriacal beliefs instead of to a supposed conviction on the intrinsic honorableness of the medical profession, the cognitive modeling effect would have been rather different. It is therefore evident that the boy did not directly and passively acquire his father's knowledge. Instead, he selected one of his father's beliefs, which assumed a specific meaning only after it was related to the beliefs on self and personal value that the boy already possessed.

From the adolescent period on, it is likely that many "knowledge units"—or "memes," to use a term proposed by Dawkins (1976) for the gene-analogous "replicators" involved in the transmission of acquired knowledge—are acquired, as in our patient's case, through implicit or latent learning. Most likely, these "memes" can be tacitly learned even within an identification process with a model whose relationship with the learner is emotionally "neutral," because of the capability of disengagement from the context that the adolescent has now reached. Tacitly acquired knowledge units may function as reference criteria in the making and matching processes in which the subsequent construction of knowledge is carried on. In other words, cognitive modeling in adolescence and youth can give way to the tacit elaboration of cognitive structures that one will become aware of only later on, when these have become operative instruments in dealing with reality. As Robert Musil puts it in his masterpiece *The Man without Qualities*, adolescents and youth frequently consider the teaching of adult morality ridiculous or boring, only to discover suddenly, later on in life, that they have nevertheless acquired it and are behaving according to it.

THE ADOLESCENT'S SEARCH FOR AUTONOMY

Pubertal maturation and cognitive growth enable the adolescent to detach from the family and begin an autonomous search for affective and sexual partners.

In clinical practice the recollection of adolescent history is frequently useful for catching a glimpse of the patient's style in making and breaking affectional bonds; this life phase is the first in which the inner representations concerning emotional bonds may be clearly reflected in overt behaviors, and therefore the observable behavioral patterns concerning attachment and detachment appear in a more simplified and recognizable form than in adulthood. The influence of "pathogenic" relationships with parents—according to their different roles (see the section on the role of parents in childhood, p. 45)—may now become manifest.

Hetherington (1972), studying the affectional and mating behavior of a group of adolescent girls whose fathers were absent, observed clear-cut distortion and difficulty in their interaction with male peers and adult men. Daughters of divorcees were prone to search actively for many contacts with men, but once they succeeded in establishing these contacts, they tended to behave aggressively toward their partners. Widow's daughters appeared excessively timid and withdrawn, preferring the company of women and avoiding social situations in which meeting men was likely.

Biller (1974) observed that male teenagers with dominant, overprotective mothers and a relatively absent father figure easily took the initiative with girl friends and were usually successful in establishing flirting relationships, but tended to withdraw promptly whenever the flirt seemed to change into a more enduring relationship requiring a stronger emotional commitment. Their style of affective and sexual behavior somewhat resembled the Don Juan stereotype.

Hetherington's and Biller's data are in keeping with many of our clinical observations. To them we might add that these kinds of relational styles usually hamper the adolescent's and youth's detachment from the original family. It is rather evident, and usually confirmed by clinical experience, that the impossibility of a full emotional commitment to new affective partners seriously hinders autonomy from parents.

Without the pretense of offering a complete picture of the obstacles to autonomy that may become manifest during adolescence, we shall briefly outline some patterns that are frequently encountered in clinical practice.

1. Precarious identification with the homologous parent (because of his or her absence or of a very disturbed relationship and lack of alternative models). Although this situation does not inevitably influence heterosexual adjustment (see the already-quoted data of Biller), the capability of adapting to conjugal life and to stable affective relationships seems adversely affected by it. For instance, a male can have difficulties in structuring roles such as husband and father, while masculinity, for him, tends to coincide essentially with heterosexuality (i.e., with sexual performance paralleled by superficial love affairs). Similarly, in the female, while there can be a fairly good repertoire of social techniques bound to heterosexuality, the correspondent roles of wife and mother can be precarious.

2. Lack of the parent of the opposite sex (because of premature death, early divorce between parents, etc.). In these cases social skills related to courtship or to heterosexual relationships may appear rather rudimentary or inadequate. Perhaps more frequently, subjects who have undergone this kind of experience seem to consider themselves prone to being deserted in future affectional bonds or otherwise destined to loneliness. It is possible to hypothesize that this kind of self-knowledge stems from both modeling with the remaining homologous parent and the lack of a "testing bench" (see p. 45) for ascertaining one's lovableness in heterosexual relationships. These individuals usually appear to be rather passive and withdrawn in their affective relationships or otherwise prone to various kinds of provoking, aggressive behavior toward the partner, which, indeed, makes it very likely for desertion to occur (cf. the already-quoted data of Hetherington).

3. Conflicting relationship with the parent of the opposite sex. A rebuffing parent of the opposite sex (i.e., an unaffectionate, critical, judging one) makes the development of overall negative beliefs about the opposite sex very likely, particularly so if the conjugal relationship between parents is disturbed. As a consequence, the affective or sexual life of subjects who have had this kind of experience is usually problematic and tinged with many aggressive displays.

4. Overcontrolling parent of the opposite sex. An individual whose parent of the opposite sex is perhaps affectionate enough, but tends to control the behavior of everybody in the family can expect (usually in a tacit way) that such a situation will most likely be repeated in his or her own affective relationships. As a consequence, the individual is apt to break off even pleasant relationships as soon as they become more involving and demanding and to search almost compulsively for noncontrolling partners, sometimes with paradoxical results (e.g., see Chapter 10, p. 224).

The preceding outline of the cognitive, emotional, and behavioral development in adolscence is far from being complete or even sufficiently accurate. Its purpose is to pinpoint some relevant features for the psychotherapist's work and to lay the groundwork for the discussion of the structural organization of knowledge, the topic of the next chapter.

NOTES

1. One might observe that cognitive modeling is also important in another respect: Without a child's "identifying" with significant models, many data concerning the self-conception would remain in an extremely fragmentary state, whereas identification would yield a sort of template within which these data could find a first raw organization or structure.

2. Sometimes on closer inquiry astonishing similarities appear where a superficial observation seemed to indicate a strong discrepancy—or even a neat opposition —between parents' and sons' (or daughters) attitudes. For instance, a hippy son of a conservative father stated that he was merely living according to his father's verbal complaints concerning the harshness of working in contemporary society: "When I was a child, my father always repeated that it was an enormous sacrifice to go to work every morning in this city with noisy traffic and awful air. Why, then, does he wonder that I'm refusing to work and trying to live in a pleasant countryside?" Another instance is that of a very promiscuous daughter of a strictly religious mother. It turned out that the mother had wanted to become a nun before marriage, but had renounced this desire because of her strong "sexual temptations," always being very "excited" by sexual topics in the newspaper, even if in order to condemn them. Still another instance is that of a politically leftist son of a rightist father. They both were fascinated by "revolution," the only difference being the predilection for the Trotskyist or Hitlerian way of planning violent transformations of society.

3. Since identification with heroes or heroines from fairy tales is the first occasion in life in which the constructs of personal identity begin to take a definite form, it is useful in clinical practice to ask adult patients what kind of fairy tales they preferred in childhood (see Berne, 1972).

3

A DESCRIPTIVE MODEL OF KNOWLEDGE ORGANIZATION

> Only if we can imagine ourselves as acting bodies, and bodies
> somehow inspired by mind, that is to say, by our selves, only then,
> by way of all this reflexiveness—by way of what could be called
> liaison reflexiveness—can we really speak of a self.—Popper and
> Eccles (1977)

THE FORMALIZATION OF SELF-KNOWLEDGE

PRELIMINARY REMARKS

The knowledge acquired by a person during the course of development can be further structured with the full development of logical–
deductive abilities during the period from adolescence to adulthood
(from about 15 to about 20 years of age).

Epistemology, the discipline that traditionally deals with the
constitution and evolution of scientific theories, can furnish formal
analogies that are useful in describing the cognitive transition from
adolescence to adulthood. According to Popper (1974), two phases
can be schematically distinguished during the elaboration of scientific
theories that we use for exploring and arranging our surrounding
world: a dogmatic or prescientific phase, generally followed by a
critical or scientific phase. Through trial and error, mythical and
dogmatic theories are developed in the prescientific phase, which are
the end result of the inborn human disposition to seek and discover
patterns of regularities (e.g., settled routines, settled expectations).
Moreover, these theories are indispensable for the exploration of this
unknown and multiform world, since they furnish the frame of
coordinates necessary for classifying and arranging the discoveries
that are gradually being made. Only later, with the increase in experiences and cognitive resources, is it possible to recognize the
explanatory limits and errors that characterize mythical theories.

These can then progressively approach a critical appraisal and a logical–conceptual structuring that respond to the norms of coherence and experimental verification.

In our opinion it is important to stress that, in both the formation of an individual's systematic knowledge and the formation of scientific theories, the critical or scientific phase is necessarily preceded by a dogmatic or acritical phase. Using this analogy, we could say that the elaboration of knowledge that takes place during the course of a person's development has many of the characteristics of the dogmatic or prescientific phase, or, to use Kuhn's terminology (1962), it is essentially preparadigmatic. Only later, thanks to the emergence of conceptual and abstract thinking, a process of conceptual reelaboration ensues that allows for a logical restructuring of preacquired knowledge, so that a knowledge organization endowed with an internal coherence that makes it similar to a "scientific paradigm" is finally established.

In the phases of knowledge acquisition and structuring, it is also possible to find formal analogies with the evolutionary process that takes place at a biological level. One of the characteristic aspects of biological evolution is that the information is first stored in the genomes and then progressively decoded during ontogeny in close relationship to environmental pressures. Bearing in mind that we are comparing two obviously distinct levels of observation, it is possible to discern, in the development of individual knowledge, patterns that are similar to the ones of biological ontogeny. Thus, during the long period of human development and parental care, knowledge is constructed and stored; only later, when new conceptual instruments emerge at an adult age, can stored knowledge be decoded and further amplified. In other words, analogously to what happens on the biological level, the evolution of knowledge is a unitary process: The previously acquired self-knowledge represents the essential basis for further decoding and amplification. Indeed, we could say that, even though the knowledge acquired during development does not totally determine the subsequent phases, it somehow defines the boundaries within which the subsequent articulation and elaboration of cognitive structures—in response to ongoing environmental pressures—will take place. It should be specified that these boundaries are essentially determined by the fact that acquired self-knowledge is the inevitable initial condition for the subsequent construction and that they are not usually so narrow as to limit in only one specific way the following development.

Thus, for example, if a feeling of unreliability and distrust toward others has been engrained within the structures of early knowledge, this does not mean that one is inevitably going to develop social anxiety at best or paranoia at worst. Both results could come to pass, but only as possible by-products of how the individual actually came to deal with other people in the organization and programming of his or her life. In this way the problem represents only a given starting condition; the way in which the problem will be progressively formulated and the solutions that will be worked out each time will contribute to developing a cognitive organization that will depend only partly upon the initial condition.

THE DEFINITION OF PERSONAL IDENTITY

The ability to transform one's own cognitive and emotional processes into objects of thought is the condition that, beginning with adolescence, allows an individual to start decoding and conceptualizing his or her previously acquired knowledge. Before adolescence, the self-knowledge previously developed, although appearing in games, fantasies, and interpersonal behavior as a complex structure abounding in rules, attributions, and meanings, is largely immediate and tacit. That is, it is more or less directly experienced by the individual through the invariant aspects of mental processing with which his or her way of perceiving and knowing has been structured and is, in a way, a constitutive part of his or her person.

With the emergence of self-analytical skills resulting from abstract thought, individuals can finally begin to explain and arrange into theories and beliefs a large part of what was previously known to them in a tacit and direct form. These theories and beliefs, arranged in more or less coherent sets, will thereafter be used mainly by individuals to think about themselves and about the attitudes and activities that are unique to them. It should be specified that these theories correspond to those aspects of self-knowledge which have been made explicit, which the persons have become aware of, and with which they define their personal identity at a conscious level. In other words, the formalization of personal identity does not correspond in any way to a simple conceptual "translation" of previously acquired self-knowledge, but rather to a further construction. If self-knowledge is a constitutive part of the individual, a kind of tacit, general view of oneself that can account for the individual's specific pattern of experiencing himself or herself and the world, then, as Hamlyn puts it, "a central fact about self-knowledge is that there is no *thing* to be known" (1977, p. 196).

The relationship with self-knowledge can be only of an indirect type; that is, individuals use mainly inferential procedures in order to construct those characteristics that they consider to be their distinctive features. In particular, this construction is constantly mediated by a kind of decision or commitment to oneself resulting, on the one hand, from the specific way in which self-knowledge affects the individual and, on the other hand, from the relationship that, consequently, the individual is able to establish with himself or herself. Identity elaborated in this way implies, on the one hand, an attitude toward oneself, and on the other hand (according to the perspective of the looking-glass effect), an attitude toward reality that includes what the individual believes he is for others and what others are for him.

Therefore, in parallel to the formalization of personal identity, a life program—which is more or less consistent with the aspects of self that the individual is inferring and conceptualizing—begins to take form (Piaget, 1972).

However, it is perhaps useful to incidentally note that Western culture makes this process even more critical and pressing than other contemporary cultures or, possibly, previous eras. In fact, many sociologists (e.g., Luckmann, 1979) have pointed out a characteristic gap, in evolved societies, between primary socialization (connected to the period of development and the acquisition of a constitutive self-knowledge) and secondary socialization (bound to a more direct interaction with social reality and the acquisition of more specialized and conceptual knowledge). Besides other possible considerations, it is obvious that a gap of this type corresponds to a sort of environmental pressure, which, emphasizing the need for a clear-cut self-definition, urges a rather precise and enduring commitment to oneself in order to cope efficiently with the complexity of the surrounding reality.

At this point, we briefly define how, in our opinion, the concept of personal identity should be understood.

The gradual and unitary process that begins with the biological individuation of the self at birth and proceeds during the course of development toward psychological individuation (recognition of the self, self-conceptualization during childhood, etc.) reaches the stage of conceptual and abstract formalization represented by personal identity. Therefore the subjective and temporal continuity on which personal identity is based is inseparable from the person, since it makes up the immediately available reference point and horizon of expectations enabling the person to perceive and evaluate himself or herself with respect to the surrounding world. This conscious personal identity is a basic human experience; to lose it means to lose reality.

Nevertheless, personal identity should not be considered a separate conceptual structure, but rather the result of the continuous relationship existing between tacit self-knowledge—which determines and regulates the initial patterns of perception, feeling, and reality categorization—and the conscious conception that individuals have of themselves and with which they attempt to explain and interpret what they are experiencing. It is a dynamic relationship, subject to temporal becoming. Personal identity is not defined once and for all, but rather accepts continuous feedback from ongoing self-perception and self-evaluation, which, in turn, affect and are affected by the individual's interaction with his or her world.

Finally, the relationship between tacit and explicit self-knowledge is rather complex and does not simply coincide with one's becoming conscious of one's own actions, emotions, and thoughts or with "repressing" and "removing" conscious experiences into the tacit knowledge realm. The belief regarding the "primacy" of explicit self-knowledge (which is in keeping with the tempting optimism toward the power of reason so typical of many cognitive approaches to clinical problems) would place disproportionate emphasis on rationality with respect to the reality of human beings, which is, after all, basically biological. Furthermore, this viewpoint would more or less explicitly identify with awareness the polarity in which the relationship between tacit and explicit knowledge should have its logical conclusion. Instead, in our opinion this relationship is based on a continuous interplay between the individual's intentionality, regulated by conscious knowledge about oneself, and the aspects of his or her imaginative and emotional life, which are mainly regulated by tacit self-knowledge.

This interplay cannot be reduced to either one or the other polarity, both of which coexist during the whole life of each individual. The tacit aspects of self-knowledge are concrete experiences to the individual and seemingly form the basis for continuous development of explicatory, causal theories aimed at integrating these experiences into the realm of explicit, "intentional" knowledge. In other words, explicit self-knowledge does not coincide with total self-knowledge. To use a metaphorical image, tacit self-knowledge is like one plate of a scale, with which the other plate—explicit self-knowledge (or conscious formalized personal identity)—should be in dynamic balance.[1]

THE ORGANIZATION OF COGNITIVE STRUCTURES

I looked on human knowledge as consisting of our theories, our hypotheses, our conjectures; as the *product* of our intellectual activities. There is of course another way of looking at "knowledge": we can regard "knowledge" as a subjective "state of mind", as a subjective state of an organism. But I chose to treat it at *a system of statements*—theories submitted to discussion. "Knowledge" in this sense is *objective*.
—Popper (1974; italics added)

PRELIMINARY REMARKS

As individuals proceed in their conceptual formalization, their knowledge gradually assumes the features of an articulate organization, similar in its complexity to a true "scientific theory."

Usually the organization of cognitive structures is referred to as the "beliefs system" (cf., e.g., Ellis, 1962; Meichenbaum, 1977), a term used to indicate the set of more or less coordinated abstract principles, specific beliefs, and problem-solving procedures that the individual has gradually developed. It is generally assumed that, within such a "coordination," transformation rules exist, which, although they are not explicitly defined, make it possible to pass from abstract principles of a general nature to more concrete and specific beliefs within the system. These "concrete" and well-defined beliefs, in turn, regulate the individual's behavior with respect to a changing environment.

We believe that it would be useful to formalize the concept of "beliefs system" in such a way as to include in it the following considerations:

- All the elements (abstract principles, specific beliefs, problem-solving procedures) that make up the system are organized such that there is a stable and defined structural relationship among the elements. This relationship enables the transformations within the system to come about according to coherent and definite criteria; that is, the transition from general beliefs to more specific ones is always activated in the same way—a way that is plausible to the individual who holds the beliefs.

• The structural relations defining the organization should justify the recurrent regular patterns with which it is carried out and activated in the surrounding environment.

However, we must consider that psychologists are still seeking a precise definition of cognitivism on both a theoretical (e.g., Weimer, 1977) and a therapeutic (e.g., Mahoney, 1980) level. In the present search for a paradigm, the use of conceptual tools developed within more consolidated disciplines operating in close areas of research— such as epistemology—is perhaps justified.

As a matter of fact, during recent years we have witnessed the progressive intensification of exchanges between epistemology and cognitive psychology; this is because practitioners in both disciplines have directed their research toward the formulation of a model to describe the way in which the human being elaborates and organizes self and world knowledge. Epistemology, having the evolution of science as its object of study, has furnished a useful conceptual system for the investigation of organization patterns of human knowledge. Furthermore, epistemologists themselves appear to be increasingly interested in the study of the single individual's knowledge (cf. Popper & Eccles, 1977).

On the other hand, in the field of psychology, Piaget (1970) first dealt with the problem of psychogenesis in children by following a purely epistemological method. At present, epistemology is becoming increasingly influential in cognitive psychology as well as in the field of development. Consider, for instance, how many cognitive psychologists, following the example of Kelly's (1955) pioneering work, share the view that the human being is similar to a scientist, that is, equipped with a complex theory on self and the world that is used to actively direct and control his or her own behavior in interaction with the surrounding environment (see, e.g., Mahoney, 1976; Tweney, Doherty, & Mynatt, 1981).

LAKATOS'S "RESEARCH PROGRAMS"

In view of the preceding considerations, we believe that the structural analysis proposed by Lakatos (1974)—which considers a scientific theory to be organized as a "research program"—is a useful model for the study of the organization and functioning of a single individual's knowledge. Overlooking the epistemological debate still in progress, which goes far beyond the aims of our treatise (for further and detailed information, see the works of Feyerabend, 1975, or Laudan, 1977), the main reasons that we have selected Lakatos's program as a model are essentially as follows.

- It considers a scientific theory as an *organized* and *open structure*, capable of furnishing both a heuristic description of the world and a program of research to follow.
- The emphasis of rationality is relatively reduced, while "metaphysical" or "dogmatic" aspects of the theory's structure are stressed. In particular, it is emphasized how scientists, frequently being unaware of their own metaphysical assumptions, can seek confirmations rather than falsifications, so that the poor results of an experiment or anomalous observation do not, according to them, challenge the validity of the theory they hold as true.

Schematically, the structure of Lakatos's research program may be described as follows: Every program is centered around a "metaphysical hard-core," which contains the basic assumptions that, because of a methodological choice, must not be disproved since they make up the general hypotheses on which the future development of the entire program is based. The metaphysical hard-core is formulated through a slow and gradual process of trial and error preceding the structuring of the research program.

Once the metaphysical hard-core has been formed, an extremely rigid "negative heuristic" originates from it; its task is to preserve the nucleus without confutation, through the selective exclusion of incompatible research findings and areas of scientific concern.

Finally, a "positive heuristic" originates from the nucleus; it is more flexible and articulated than the negative heuristic. Its tasks are to define the fields of investigation toward which research should be directed and to protect the nucleus from further confutations that could arise during the course of research. For this purpose, the positive heuristic gives rise to a series of auxiliary hypotheses, which, in consecutive order, create the following structures:

1. "Protective belt." The auxiliary hypotheses forming the protective belt place themselves around the nucleus, exposing themselves to eventual confutations and anomalies and therefore safeguarding the nucleus' integrity. In this way eventual incongruities between the research program that is carried out and observational data can be attributed not so much to the nucleus' assumptions as to its protective belt, which then can be broadened or rearranged.
2. "Research plans." The auxiliary hypotheses that make up research plans are complex and articulate structures, modeling the fields of investigation with which the research program is concerned. This allows the scientist to turn his or her attention solely toward the reciprocal articulation of these structures, without having to take the anomalies and experimental counterchecks into consideration one at a time (which would be a hard test of their plausibility).

Thus the research program is made up of a series of assumptions and hypotheses (metaphysical hard-core, protective belt, and research plans) arranged in a relationship that coordinates the possible patterns of its development in reality. The development of the program entails a progressive articulation of the basic assumption of the nucleus, realized by means of the continuous modification of the protective belt in relation to experimental data, which in turn come forth during the course of the research plans.

It should be emphasized that the protective belt is the "testing bench" of the entire research program, and the experimental outcomes produced by research plans can influence the nucleus only *through* its protective belt.

In particular, when a research program is carried out, it can have two general outcomes.

1. Research plans will have a good experimental outcome, yielding data that corroborate the assumptions of the nucleus. Depending on the degree of corroboration obtained, a re-

structuring of the protective belt will take place, and thus it will be able to accept other implications from the nucleus; once reorganized in this way, it can begin to elaborate further, more sophisticated research plans and therefore will be better able to explain already-known phenomena and to predict new ones with an overall increase in assimilated experience ("progressive shift").

2. Research plans will not have a good experimental outcome and will not obtain data that corroborate the nuclear assumptions. Nevertheless, the nucleus will be safeguarded from confutation, thanks to a "thickening" of the protective belt that will proliferate "defensive theories," thereupon "overcontrolling" the research program. In other words, the program is not suspended because of confutations, but instead tends to organize itself mainly in a defensive strategy, only refraining—at least in part—from attempting to articulate and develop the assumptions of the nucleus. The entire research program will then become rather static and redundant; it will not be able to predict new facts, and there will be an overall reduction of experience assimilation ("regressive shift").

THE ORGANIZATION OF PERSONAL COGNITIVE STRUCTURES

Before describing the structural organization of individual knowledge in light of Lakatos's model, we must point out that we will use this model only as a kind of metaphorical guide. As a matter of fact, the different levels of application—the course of scientific theories in epistemology and the organization of a single individual's theories in psychology—compel us to seriously consider the discrepancies between the model and the object of our study. So, whereas in epistemology we deal with a process that has an impersonal subject (science), in psychology we deal with a process that has a definite existential subject. For this reason, clinical psychologists face a greater dynamism and variability of phenomena, which will inevitably make their research program considerably different from those studied by an epistemologist.

With this caution in mind, we now consider the structures that make up the organization of individual knowledge that is analogous to an articulate theory capable of directing the unfolding of a research program (i.e., a life program). The functional aspects of this structural organization are dealt with in the final section of the chapter.

Structural Aspects

Metaphysical Hard-Core. The organization of human knowledge is characterized by the presence of a deep, relatively indisputable metaphysical hard-core. This deep structure is identified essentially in the tacit self-knowledge that has been progressively elaborated during the course of development and that, as we have already mentioned, is for individuals a kind of implicit general view of themselves, which is given to them directly by the invariant aspects of their mental processing.

Self-knowledge is irrefutable, more because of a methodological *necessity* (determined by the absolute lack of real alternatives) than because of a methodological *choice* (as in the case of the scientific metaphysical hard-core). Indeed, the construction of self-knowledge during the course of development essentially follows a "situational logic" type of procedure (cf. Popper, 1974). As infants, we cannot perceive the life that characterizes us and our world *as such*, but only through the limited reference scheme of our particular situation (family features, nature and course of attachment and detachment processes, quality of the wider social network in which development takes place, quality and quantity of identification models, etc.). In this way, whereas the elaboration of self-knowledge, with the gradualness and limits imposed on it by the slow pace of cognitive development, is logically *part of the situation itself*, the patterns of regularities and the implications drawn from the situation are progressively generalized, until they form a kind of general model capable of directly explaining the reality to the individual.

Even when this model is further structured and developed—thanks to the onset of logical–conceptual thought—its course is always of a situational logic type, although at a more sophisticated level. Thus, whereas during the early course of development it was the concrete situation to which the model belonged that formed the limited reference scheme, in the phase of conceptual elaboration of knowledge the previously formed self-knowledge becomes the limited reference scheme. The formalization of personal identity and the gradual construction of a life program necessarily proceed from this limited repertoire. The deep structure's irrefutability is therefore a real methodological necessity. For us as individuals, our own tacit self-knowledge is a constitutive part of ourselves, with no real alternatives. In the event that we imagine ourselves as another, this fantasy itself would not leave the unvarying aspects of self-perception out of consideration; that is, it could be led back to the limited reference scheme of our own self-knowledge, making us wish to be another person. In other words, we do not have alternatives to ourselves and can do nothing else but assume ourselves to be an indisputable fact.

The self-knowledge that forms the nucleus of the individual's research program includes a set of deep general rules which determine the invariant aspects of the person's mental processing, through which he or she tacitly and directly obtains the frames of coordinates that sustain recognition of self and the surrounding world. These rules regulate the patterns of both perception and selective attention, extracting only specific patterns of regularity and actively excluding all others. Furthermore, these rather general rules—endowed with a remarkable heuristic power—act as a continuous reference criterion in the making and matching processes through which further theories, beliefs, and expectations are elaborated and become part of the other structures of the program.

These rules are also likely to influence the development of a sort of "theory of time"[2] (intended as the organization of temporal routines that characterize the subjective passing of time). The "internal logic" of this theory consists of regulating the progressive unfolding of the implications derived from the deep structures in the objective reality of temporal becoming. This regulating function operates by

- Coordinating the rhythms of attention and perception through internal representation.
- Coordinating the ongoing modulation of information provided by memory's unifying and constructive activity.
- Coordinating deductive thought in regulating the succession of hypotheses or solutions to problems (depending on the "logic of becoming" which belongs to it).

Finally, the deep structures of self-knowledge, through feeling tones and feeling memories (emotional schemata) processed during the course of development, direct and coordinate most of the individual's emotional and imaginative life. In accordance with Hamlyn (1977), we believe that a complete theory of self-knowledge (which we are far from possessing at present) should include a conceptual model of the "regulators" that preside over the development and organization of emotional experiences.

Protective Belt. The protective belt corresponds to the structures that define and maintain personal identity. As we stated in the first part of this chapter, personal identity is the expression of a dynamic relationship. It is inevitable that, as individuals, we assume our own ways of being and of experiencing the world as a given and indisputable reality; therefore necessarily we will have to structure an attitude toward ourselves allowing us to hold a plausible definition of ourselves, that is, a definition that is not incompatible with—but that, on the contrary, safeguards—those aspects of self-knowledge that we recognize as "self." In other words, the attitude toward oneself, expressed by personal identity, directs the definition of one's own "being," a definition that the individual considers as tenable in the face of the events and varying situations that characterize his or her interaction with the environment.

Personal identity is a rather complex structure. For the sake of a concise description, we may—a bit simplistically—consider it to have two main components, which we shall call "self-identity" and "self-esteem."

Self-identity includes the overall pattern of traits and attitudes that an individual considers "personal" and distinctive and that are immediately available in the conscious representation that the individual has of himself or herself. This representation is the codified and therefore synthesized way of thinking about and evaluating oneself in a given moment. Namely, it is the "ready-for-use" self-image that does not have to be reelaborated each time.

Such an image can also be defined as the outcome of the overall structural relationships that exist between the various domains of beliefs constituting an individual's knowledge. Every human being possesses a wide number of beliefs concerning various domains. For example, there will be beliefs concerning attachment (the meaning that is generally given to affective and interpersonal relationships), duties (what duties one must set for oneself in life, how one should face up to them, etc.), values (what personal values one must aim for, what objectives one must set for one's life, etc.), attribution of causality (e.g., the sense of fatalism or personal responsibility with which one explains various life events), and so forth. From the way in which we compose an overall outline of the various domains, we extract an image of the reality that surrounds us and, at the same time, an image of ourselves moving about in that reality.

For example, suppose that an individual's beliefs about attachment exclude the attribution of a profound meaning to affective experiences in his life program. Also suppose that this person has a rather high concept of personal value ("I cannot stand to be a low- or middle-value man") and a strong sense of duty ("To be worthy of respect, one must never, in any circumstance, deviate from his duties") connected to an attributive style centered on personal responsibility ("Luck and chance do not exist; what one achieves in life is the result of commitment and sacrifice"). This individual will most likely have an image of himself as a person who gives order and meaning to his life through his sense of responsibility and almost missionary-like dedication to his work. Similarly, in his affective relationships, his self-image will not be that of a husband or father who is happy for the affection he gives and receives, but rather that of a person who "sacrifices" himself so that his family does not lack anything, expecting to receive in exchange respect and consideration. Needless to say, a structural relationship combining this man's beliefs in an overall picture (a picture that corresponds to the man's self-image) may be not so clearly defined as to be readily (or directly) available in his sphere of awareness. Nevertheless, he can succeed in deducing the overall picture with relative ease whenever he is provided with adequate data (e.g., in an interpersonal relationship or during psychotherapy), but he will not be able to do so with the principles of self-knowledge from which the attitude toward himself has stemmed.

Self-esteem is the second main component of personal identity. In trying to adhere, in behavior and experienced emotions, to a specific self-image, every human being becomes prone to self-evaluation. The degree of congruence between beliefs concerning one's "value" and ongoing estimates of one's own behavior and emotions corresponds to the degree of self-acceptability and self-esteem. In short, we might say that self-esteem implies the "theory of emotions" to which we adhere in the relationship that we establish with ourselves. This theory defines what range of emotions we can recognize as part of ourselves, how such emotions are labeled and controlled, and in what circumstances and manners it is possible to express them.

As mentioned earlier, it is utterly arbitrary to distinguish the theory of emotions from self-identity, since both are inseparable parts of personal identity. The distinction is drawn here only to call attention to the way one considers one's own emotions, since the acknowledgment of these idiosyncratic "theories" assumes importance at a clinical level. In fact, it often occurs that individuals cannot recognize certain feelings as their own emotions because the emotional range congruent with their self-image is rather limited. The clinical relevance of this phenomenon is noteworthy.

For instance, the man in the previous example whose self-image was centered on a general sense of duty and personal responsibility would not be able to recognize as his own a "despicable" feeling of anger or resentment toward his wife. The more intense the feeling, the more he will try to decode it through "external causal theories," for example, through the concept of illness. Therefore, in anger-evoking situations, he will talk about "dizziness" or "a faint feeling." Repeated episodes of improperly labeled anger can make him believe he is affected by a "strange illness" which doctors cannot diagnose. Self-image as "ill" is acceptable, whereas self-image as "angry" is not. In this way, by maintaining the self-image he thinks he must adhere to, he can succeed in preserving an acceptable level of self-esteem, while preventing himself from becoming aware of his own resentment toward his wife. The psychodynamic concept of "repressed" emotions is radically changed in the cognitive perspective. The cognitive coding (theory of emotion) through which the individual labels internal states—and therefore attributes to them the meaning of emotional experience or, instead, of an externally caused strange phenomenon—takes the place of the "forces" hypothetically responsible for "defense mechanisms."

Research Plans. Personal identity, besides being the expression of one's attitude toward oneself, correspondingly directs one's attitude toward reality. In other words, the structures that enable the entire research program to be carried out in the surrounding reality are elaborated under the direct control of the cognitive structures of personal identity and within the limits of coherence that they imply. The elaboration of research plans essentially consists of the production of *models that simulate and anticipate reality*, whose coherence and representational stability are constantly controlled by at least two kinds of rules: rules that coordinate the assimilation of experience (defining which domains of experience are to be held as significant, as well as the patterns of integration of these experiences within preformed cognitive structures) and rules that coordinate problem-solving procedures (defining both the nature of significant problems and the strategy for dealing with them).

Structural Scheme. What we have said up until now can be summarized by the scheme presented in Figure 3-1. This scheme shows how knowledge organization as a research program is hierarchically ordered in its structure. The ongoing flow of reality's representational models can influence self-knowledge only through the personal identity structure. At the same time, the assumptions or implications of self-knowledge find their way into the representational models of reality only by passing through the structures of personal identity. Therefore personal identity represents a kind of "testing bench" of the entire organization, and the research program's advancement actually implies its continuous remodeling.

As stated previously, personal identity is not defined once and for all, but is continuously remodeled according to the advancement of one's own life program until it reaches a more or less stable organization. This remodeling must follow a specific procedural and temporal pattern, so that the basic sense of subjective temporal continuity (upon which the very perception of self and the world is founded) is preserved while personal identity is modified. In this way personal identity appears as the main control structure of the entire organization. Usually, the control function exercised by personal identity tends to increase progressively with the passing of time: During the juvenile and intermediate phases of life, even consistent remodeling of one's own identity is possible, whereas in adulthood the possibility of significant change in identity generally decreases progressively.

It should be noted that in our model the control function exercised by personal identity is explicated through the same structural relationships that are implied in the requests for continual remodeling. On that account, in every given moment, this structure can be considered the result of a dynamic equilibrium between the requests for change that it receives and the urges for maintenance that it sends out. The main aspects of this balance might be described as shown in Table 3-1.

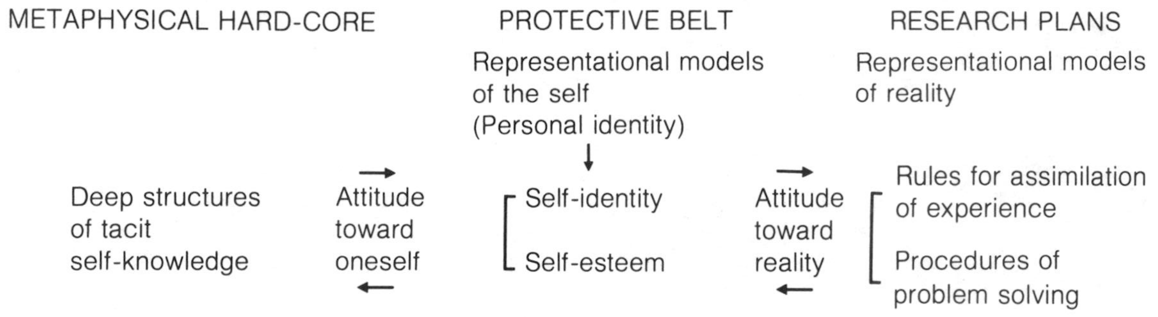

METAPHYSICAL HARD-CORE

Deep structures
of tacit
self-knowledge

Attitude
toward
oneself

PROTECTIVE BELT

Representational models
of the self
(Personal identity)

Self-identity

Self-esteem

Attitude
toward
reality

RESEARCH PLANS

Representational models
of reality

Rules for assimilation
of experience

Procedures of
problem solving

Figure 3-1. Knowledge organization as a research program.

Table 3-1. Elements of the Control Function of Personal Identity

Attitude toward oneself		Attitude toward reality	
Change trends	*Maintenance trends*	*Change trends*	*Maintenance trends*
New material (images, fantasies, emotionally charged information) tends to emerge continuously from tacit self-knowledge. Whenever logical-deductive processes and a proper scanning of other available information on self are set into motion, the individual elaborates further self-description in order to explain the new phenomena, and personal identity change takes place.	Selective attention tends to operate in the individual's self-monitoring, so that only information that is congruous with the preformed structures of personal identity is abstracted from the emotional schemata and stored images of self-knowledge.	Expectancies derived from reality's representational models may be disconfirmed by ongoing events. When a discrepancy between expectations and the outcome of actions is matched by a contemporaneous flow of information from tacit self-knowledge, a change in the internal representation of reality (mediated by a concomitant change in self-description: "I was wrong in believing so and so") becomes possible.	Representation of reality tends to be held constant when faced by contradictory experience. Through selective attention and selective abstraction (focusing on a detail taken out of context, ignoring other features of the situation, and conceptualizing the whole experience on the basis of this detail), expectations partly *form* the objects of experience. Expectations usually differ from simple predictions because of personal, emotional adherence to one's internal representation of reality. If an expected event does not occur, there is usually a tendency to speak of an "illusion" or a "disappointment" rather than simply and impersonally acknowledging that "prediction *x*" did not come true.

A fuller account of the items in this table is given in the next chapter. We now turn to some remarks on the functional aspects of our model.

Functional Aspects

The structures that make up knowledge organization interact with reality through the inner representation that they can determine. The *content* of knowledge (deep rules, beliefs, etc.) is continuously processed by means of structural representations containing both assertions on the situations and events that characterize outside reality and procedures to follow in the represented situations. In the inner representation, the phenomena of the outside world are arranged in models that simulate and anticipate reality. The events and situations that characterize an individual's interaction with the environment are recognized and evaluated through these simulatory–anticipatory models. Inner representation is endowed with flexibility—which allows for adaptation to outside reality's variability—and with internal stability and congruence. It is through these properties that we can perceive the world with those features of regularity and coherence that appear to be indispensable in considering the things that surround us as "real." Indeed, as Polanyi (1968) asserts, "It is the coherence of a thing that makes us attribute reality to it" (p. 28). Passing over the well-known and ancient philosophical controversies on the correspondence between "reality" and its representations (see discussion on this in Chapter 1, pp. 3–5), we want to stress once again that inner models contribute to determining the form of the reality we experience.

In clinical practice, some functional characteristics of knowledge's inner representation deserve particular attention:

1. In comparison with the more abstract structural organization of knowledge, the inner representation depicts the world in a more partial and limited manner. Not all the knowledge contained in the structural organization is represented in the stream of consciousness with all its details and at every moment. Instead, knowledge is represented each time in an episodic way, in accordance with an individual's needs and the events that he or she encounters.

2. Inner representation is in a reciprocal relationship with both the perception of ongoing events and the information derived from past experiences provided by memory. Memory should be considered as an active, ongoing modulation of information rather than a simple retrieval of stored data (Weimer, 1977). The deeper structures of knowledge organization (emotional schemata, personal identity constructs, etc.) influence the inner representation according to the research program's unfolding either through selective attention (and therefore by orienting perception toward specific patterns of environmental regularities) or by directing the modulation of information supplied by memory. In this way, even with the continuous remodeling produced by perceptual and mnemonic feedback, the course of the inner representation satisfies, in every moment and with minimal incongruities, the knowledge contained in the whole organization.

3. It is important to take into account that there are two main interrelated modalities through which deep structures are processed, that is, the analogical and the analytical codes.

Analogical Code. The analogical code mainly processes "images." Images (whether visual, auditory, kinesthetic, etc.) are not to be understood as "pictures" of the world, that is, as "sensorial copies" of stored past events or expected future events elicited by specific external or internal stimuli. Rather, they should be regarded as structural phenomena containing information in the form of assertions (i.e., relationships among the elements that make up the represented situation) and of procedures (i.e., patterns with which the relationships among a situation's elements can be interpreted or dealt with).

From this perspective, which is very similar to that which asserts the constructional and propositional nature of images (cf. Kieras, 1978; Pylyshyn, 1973), an image is not "something" that is simply stored. On the contrary, that which is stored is the corresponding information, and on the basis of this information, the image is reconstructed each time. In this way every reconstruction of the image contains not only the specific information that characterizes it, but also other collateral information derived from the relationships that the representation's specific informative content has in the meantime assumed with the individual's knowledge organization. In other words, imagining is an active mode of information processing, which makes the elaboration of each image a *unique construction*. For example, when we repeatedly imagine a past situation, we do not always represent it in the same way, as if it were a slide; rather, each time it will contain our ongoing interpretations of that same situation, with either additional details or significant omissions.

Another characteristic of imaginal processes is their emotional coloring. This most likely depends on the fact that imagination is the principal mediator in the retrieval process of the "schematic memory" (see Leventhal, 1979, on emotional schemata) in which various experiences are codified, especially through the storage of feelings that make them similar or different. Events that have been coded as being similar because they have the same emotional component recur as similar events in inner representation (with subsequent generalization) resulting mainly from the repeated emotional experience accompanying their reproduction in the imaginal mode. Rather than a simple accompaniment of emotions to imagination, a reciprocal relationship seems to exist between images and emotions; for instance, an unexpected emotion may be followed by a series of images that contribute to characterizing and specifying its nature and meaning.

Also typical of imaginal processes—and especially of daydreams —is their extremely variable course, which at times gives the impression of an arbitrary mental phenomenon, with no meaning whatsoever. Images often run quickly, at other times they seem to stop, and at still other times they tend to "reverberate" and to continue in the direction of singling out specific situations, even when there is no "evident" scope. Furthermore, the patterns that combine images are not based on logical consequentiality, and for this reason they can rove indifferently in various sectors. Moreover, given the affective coloring that accompanies them, images always have such a strong individual characterization that, even though they become automatized as a kind of "mental attitude," they are so always within a personal conventionalism, which the individual himself or herself may find difficult to communicate. In other words, because of its analogical coding and accompanying emotions, the information content of imagination is mainly tacitly and directly noticed by the individual, who would have difficulty in explicating it for himself or herself and for others according to the analytical, sequential, and descriptive terms of language.

Precisely because of these features, the imaginal stream can be considered as one of the more characteristic ways in which an individual's tacit self-knowledge is manifested. In particular, it represents one of the main patterns with which the deep structures of self-knowledge can feed new "material" to the research program's organization, so that it can be elaborated and become part of the individual's explicit knowledge. This material sometimes represents an important demand for change in personal identity, since the imaginal stream tends to circumvent the individual's attempts to maintain specific beliefs on self and reality through selective exclusion of incompatible stored or actual information. Although problems of this kind are frequently observed in clinical practice, they are not easily subject to adequate experimental controls and therefore at present are difficult to formalize at a theoretical level. A clinical anecdote is perhaps still the best way to describe these problems.

Some years ago we observed an interesting phenomenon in a patient who had come to us for treatment. The specific problems for which the patient had sought therapy have no particular bearing on this discussion and may be omitted. While gathering the history, a particular recurrent nightmare became evident which had persecuted the patient since he was 14 years old, and he could explain it to himself only as a bizarre idiosyncrasy. The nightmare depicted a man's face, which, according to the patient, stared at him threateningly and advanced toward him with the intention of killing him. For many years the patient experienced this nightmare frequently (at times, almost every month), so that he had become capable of recognizing it during his sleep and succeeded in waking up before the imagined scene went any further.

Puzzled by the patient's insistence on talking about this phenomenon during the sessions, we asked him to describe as precisely as possible the features of the face that appeared to him, for the purpose of constructing a kind of "identity kit." As could be expected, the patient did not recognize any face he knew in the "identity kit" that had been drawn up. Because we were suspicious about the absolute confidence with which he denied that it could be anyone he knew we asked him to bring, in subsequent sessions, photographs of his relatives, especially his immediate family, since the nightmare had begun when he was 14 years old.

When he brought us these photographs, we were impressed by the resemblance between the "identity kit" and his father's photograph. Although the patient was also struck by the incredible resemblance, he denied that the face that appeared to him during the nightmare could be his father's. He had an almost "heavenly" image of his recently deceased father. His mother had died when he was a baby, and therefore he was left with his father; he looked upon his father as a kind of "saint" who had sacrificed everything in order to dedicate himself exclusively to taking care of his son. On the other hand, it was true that as a child he was almost always with his grandmother, since his father was usually out, generally arriving home late at night. But all of this was always part of the sacrifice and "saintliness" of the father who took on extra jobs so that his son was not in need of anything.

We had no other alternative but to proceed with the investigation, and since the father's elderly sister was living nearby at that time, we decided to interview her. A very interesting story came forth. Briefly, some years after his wife's death, the patient's father had had a romantic affair with a woman in show business, which had gone on for years. She always traveled and was firm in saying that their relationship could continue only if he changed his life so that he could travel with her. The father was willing to make this change, and therefore the only obstacle to this union was represented by his son. (The latter was kept completely in the dark about the relationship; the father justified his absence by saying that he worked overtime for his son's benefit.) The father's sister revealed how, in various desperate moments of his romantic relationship, the father had confided his intention of getting rid of his son by leaving him in a boarding school and then running away with his mistress. This never came to pass, since the woman finally left him for good, tired of the precarious situation.

Our patient was astonished by the story he had heard, but he could not deny it since his aunt offered incontrovertible proof. Naturally, the myth about his father as a saintly and virtuous man crumbled. The most interesting thing was that only then did he have a sudden recollection; that is, one night when he was about 14 years old, passing by his father's room he had seen an unusual expression on his father's face through the open door—without speaking, his father had "glared at him." It immediately occurred to him that the glaring face that had persecuted him for years in his dreams was the same he had seen that night and had completely forgotten "for some unknown reason." His aunt's story revealed that the most dramatic moments of the father's relationship with his mistress had occurred precisely when the patient was 14 years old.

Analytical Code. The analytical code mainly processes lexical units. The processing of these units appears in inner representation in various patterns, one of the most relevant for clinical purposes being the so-called inner dialogue (see, e.g., Meichenbaum, 1977).[3]

Characteristically, verbal thought is aimed at the elaboration of explicit and descriptive knowledge through the production of concepts, which, in comparison to images, are much more stable and enduring entities. Furthermore, once concepts have been elaborated, they are easily detachable from the situational context in which they originated and can be treated as knowledge units in themselves (e.g., like entities, objects) regardless of their origin or actual application.

In inner representations verbal thought can assume extremely different forms, ranging from structured and intentional reasoning to more or less automatic and "stenographic" internal dialogue. Even in the variability of its forms, verbal thought still flows more constantly and regularly than imagination, therefore giving greater stability to the entire internal representation. Furthermore, bound to words by nature, it flows *in sequence* according to formally coherent derivation and combination rules. In this way verbal thought is an instrument of order and coherence for the entire inner representation, since compared to the "eccentricity" of images, it succeeds in defining with fair precision both the general and the particular aspects of a problem, inferring the proper logical and chronological connections.

The processes of verbal thought are extremely important, not only because they allow for the conceptual formalization of knowledge, but also because they are an essential part of the problem-solving procedures that are so important in the research program's practical development. According to Popper (1972), the activity of understanding is essentially that which takes place each time one proceeds toward problem solving. From this perspective, knowing progress is equal to problem solving; that is, the organization of knowledge itself is developed and modified over time through an uninterrupted process of problem solving. A digression on problem solving therefore deserves to be made at this point.

For many years following Newel and Simon's work (1972), it was believed that the formulation and solution of any problem could be traced back to a single set of thought techniques—the so-called General Problem Solver. Whereas the solution procedure was considered to be unique and of a logical–formal type, the formulation of the problem could vary according to the different representations of reality that the individual might have. Models derived from the General Problem Solver theory—which propose a view of reasoning as exclusively propositional and logical—bear little resemblance to everyday thinking. In our opinion they appear to be artifical and limited instruments, which are largely extraneous to the real world's complexity.

Various theoretical considerations and empirical data exist in support of the thesis that problem solving cannot be reduced to a single basic logical type. For instance, Bara (1980a), in a critical review of this topic, reaches the conclusion that a *single* representation of knowledge exists in human beings and that within it there are *different logical types of thought*. In this way the entire area of human problem solving may be considered as a differentiated and articulated set of problem-solving procedures, rather than as a single procedure applicable to all problems.

According to Bara (1980a), the logical types of thought may be classified within six main categories: formal, mundane, physical, interactive, personal, and self problem solving.

1. Formal problem solving coincides with a set of logical–formal and mathematical procedures. Corresponding to the classical area of studies on problem solving, it is intensely studied and overlaps with the paradigm of the General Problem Solver. Nevertheless, it contains procedures (e.g., solutions to logical problems and mathematical equations) that have little importance in everyday life and consequently a low applicability to concrete clinical problems.

2. Mundane problem solving coincides with a set of procedures based on the "common sense" that comes from everyday experience. An "intuitive" exploitation of knowledge or "emotional" decisions that arbitrarily make a problem's premise acceptable or refutable are implied in this class of problem-solving procedures.

Since logical–formal procedures are neglected in mundane problem solving, many "logical passages" may be omitted in arriving at the solution. Although the inferences and solutions drawn through this method may objectively appear incorrect and hurried, subjectively they are usually plausible, so much so that the subject may make vital decisions based on them. The positive side of "alogical" procedures' exploiting "good sense" and emotional drives is, of course, that they allow for rapid and energy-saving conclusions. Far from being "childish" or dangerous, mundane problem solving may be extremely useful for life's everyday purposes.

3. Physical problem solving entails a set of procedures necessary for dealing with problems related to physical reality. It enables us to deal adequately with the outside world, allowing us, for instance, to solve problems of spatial or temporal orientation. Furthermore, it allows us to reason about the intercorrelations that concern concrete things around us or physical events that we face—for example, we can foresee the possible consequences of an impending storm on a picnic and plan the day accordingly.

4. Interactive problem solving coincides with the set of procedures regarding social rules and is therefore useful in understanding interactions between two or more people. This type of problem solving is quite similar to the personal and self problem solving and we can treat them as overlapping sets.

In interactive problem solving, the distinctive element is that the individual is only a spectator; upon becoming an active participant in the interaction, he or she will mainly use personal problem solving. Social rules shared by the group to which the person belongs and the education he or she received from the family are generally the two main sources of interactive problem-solving procedures. In fact, from these, a youth can progressively draw abstract rules of social behavior, which can be used to explain what he or she can expect from people.

5. Personal problem solving entails a set of procedures used in social interaction when the individual is one of the actors. In this case the problem-solving techniques, even though they are derived from social rules and family learning, become extremely personalized. In fact, apart from the general observation that it is one thing to know how one should behave and another to know how one actually behaves, it is obvious that, whenever somebody is directly involved in a relationship, procedures derived from the individual's personal experience must be added to the more impersonal ones of interactive problem solving. One's experience in affective relationships, which is such a relevant part of knowledge organization, is used so continuously by each of us during our lives that one can definitely affirm that all behavior implies a certain degree of personal problem solving.

6. Self problem solving coincides with the set of procedures with which we represent ourselves in everyday life. Through these procedures, one's own image is held constant, on a purely descriptive (self-description) and an evaluative (self-evaluation) level, in the face

of the various problematic situations that may be encountered in everyday life. Needless to say, self problem solving does not furnish us with a representation of ourselves as we are in "reality," but rather of how we believe we are. In other words, these procedures express our attitude toward ourselves more than the self-knowledge that characterizes us. It follows that one cannot pretend that introspection is like a "window" open on internal affective processes, but rather on a biased model of them. As was true for personal problem solving, we may confidently believe that all behavior implies a certain degree of self problem solving (see Chapter 4).

NOTES

1. Every human being, while living in a social and public world, is always characterized by an inner, private, and immediate world, defining in terms of personal uniqueness his or her interaction with the outside world. Socrates, employing the Delphic saying "Know thyself," used to exhort his disciples to act according to a system of life choices based on their inner world, on their feelings and their perceived capabilities and limitations, rather than merely according to rules coming from the outside world.

Let us consider how this old advice can be applied to the ideas we have expressed so far. We are not completely given to ourselves, nor is our life something static; on the contrary, we and our lives are constantly changing. Consequently, our knowledge of self and the world is a continuous construction. In this sense the continuous remodeling of our explicit self-knowledge implies a continuous remodeling of the commitment to ourselves so far constructed. The cues used to make up this constant activity should come not only from data belonging to the realm of explicit knowledge, but also from our tacit knowledge (i.e., our emotional and imaginative life).

From this perspective, the balance between explicit and tacit self-knowledge can be considered achieved if "knowing thyself" corresponds, with only slight incongruities, to "being oneself," if, that is, the person is actively and constantly matching the explicit self-image and the planning of his or her life with the immediate and direct self-knowledge that characterizes him or her. Of course, this perspective is to be looked upon more as an ideal goal to pursue in the course of life than as the purpose to be reached within a psychotherapeutic situation.

Finally, we can perhaps find in this perspective a connection with the well-known Oriental philosophic notion according to which our image of ourselves and of reality is a sort of "fiction" (i.e., a construction) necessary to our functioning, but not corresponding to our whole selves or to a "true" comprehension of reality. Obviously it is quite impossible to go further into such a subject in a scientific book. In fact, science itself belongs by its very nature to the realm of explicit knowledge.

However, also in this sense, the need to seek a balance with anything tacit or implicit can be deduced from the warnings on the limits of science coming from various sources. Among others, see, for example, Bateson's (1979) statement that "science never proves anything" (his Chapter 2) and Wilson's (1978) idea that, as knowledge grows, science must become more and more a stimulus to imagination (his Chapter 9).

2. The psychological study of time is in a revival phase, perhaps thanks to the effects of the Einsteinian revolution that has taken place in physics and that is beginning to extend itself to other fields of human knowledge. At present, the scientific investigation of the experience of time is in its initial stages. We refer the interested reader to the International Society for the Study of Time (ISST) proceedings (Fraser, Haber, & Mueller, 1972; Fraser & Lawrence, 1975; and especially Fraser, Lawrence, & Park, 1978). In cognitive science, data that have emerged from these studies on time have been mainly used by researchers on artificial intelligence and behavior simulation, for the elaboration of models of human cognition. Promising implications of these models for clinical work may be found in Bara's recent paper (1980b).

3. The nomenclature concerning thought modes of representation is rather varied. The "verbal" (lexical) mode of thought representation (Horowitz, 1972) is sometimes identified with "inner monologue" (see, e.g., Mahoney & Mahoney, 1976) or "inner dialogue." The latter term is used in this book, since, phenomenally, verbal thoughts frequently appear in consciousness as a sort of dialogue between different persons. For instance, one can silently appeal to oneself when in trouble with thoughts such as "Let's go, a little more effort" or "Don't be silly, don't give up just now" besides obviously silently saying "I must not give up just now when I'm close to the solution." A phenomenological analysis of verbal thoughts that appeal to oneself with different pronouns ("I", "you", etc.) may be found in Berne's works (e.g., 1961, 1972).

4

MAINTENANCE AND CHANGE OF COGNITIVE STRUCTURES

THE CENTRAL ROLE OF ATTITUDE TOWARD ONESELF AND PERSONAL IDENTITY

The self is not a "pure ego"; that is, a mere subject. Rather, it is incredibly rich. Like a pilot, it observes and takes action at the same time. It is acting and suffering, recalling the past and planning and programming the future; expecting and disposing. It contains, in quick succession, or all at once, wishes, plans, hopes, decisions to act, and a vivid consciousness of being an acting self, a centre of action.—Popper and Eccles (1977)

In Chapter 3 we said that the epistemological model of Lakatos's research program should be understood as a kind of metaphorical guide rather than a one-to-one corresponding model of individual knowledge organization, because shifting from the epistemological to the psychological level, we deal with a process that has a defined existential subject. Indeed, every human being is a unique person, agent of his or her emotional states and thought processes and source of his or her own decisions and actions. In other words, the control over intentions, thoughts, behavior strategies, and so forth lies within the person, and this is an important difference from the more impersonal process of scientific growth.

Mischel and Mischel (1977) came to the following conclusions in their overview of studies concerning self-control: The lack of coherent correlations between trait characterizations (which attempt to specify what people are like in terms of some reasonably small number of dimensions) and people's behavior is evident; the idiosyncratic organization of each individual may be best understood by considering the human being as an active, self-aware problem solver capable of changing himself or herself; "the person or self, then, *is* the behaving organism" (p. 51; see also Royce, 1973).

From our theoretical perspective, the idiosyncratic organization that lies in each of us and that regulates in a specific way our controlling abilities can be understood on the basis of the attitude that each of us assumes toward ourselves. To a large extent, although deep structures correspond to our constitutive, unavoidable way of being (all that we are made of), we formalize our existence in a definite way through the structures of personal identity (all that we make of ourselves). This formalization takes place through a dynamic relationship between the elements of the deep structures (e.g., invariant rules, emotional schemata) and the emergent cognitive abilities (e.g., verbal labeling, distancing). This dynamic relationship, through which we each make ourselves out of what we are made of, unfolds by a continuous process of inner reconstructions. We have called this dynamic relationship "the attitude toward oneself." Personal identity is the emergent conceptualized polarity of this relationship. The idiosyncratic way of controlling the progressive organization of the acquired knowledge of reality is a function of personal identity. Personal identity becomes the point of reference and continuous confrontation with which we are able to monitor and evaluate ourselves in relation to the reality that surrounds us. Furthermore, due to this continuous confrontation, we can proceed to an adequate selection of the available environmental information almost automatically—so quickly, that it occurs beyond our awareness.

The quality and quantity of social stimulation available to us at every moment by far exceed our ability to process and pay attention to all of it. Therefore we are necessarily selective in what we register of the situations featuring our interaction with the world. This selectivity is regulated by the continuous confrontation with the structured self-image, which determines, moment by moment, which of the impinging information is to be held as relevant. Moreover, the continuous confrontation with the perceived personal identity is also decisive in setting the selective limits for the information that comes from ourselves. Only a fraction of potentially available information is processed, whether in the verbal or the imaginal mode of thought representation. Much in the same selective way, inner states (potential emotional experiences) are continuously codified on the basis of the emotional range that we recognize as our own and that is in keeping with the structured self-image. Finally, the same reasoning holds true for memory, toward which we establish an extremely active relationship. Thus, from the modulation of information continuously proposed by the memory, only that information which is considered to be in keeping with the structured self-image is retained and incorporated in it. In the ongoing matching with our perceived personal identity, we have practically unlimited access to past or currently available information about ourselves that we intend to look for, and it is we ourselves who set the limits. (For experimental data on this topic, see Bower & Gilligan, 1979; Markus, 1977; Mischel, Ebbesen, & Zeiss, 1976; Rogers, Kuiper, & Kirker, 1977; Rogers, Rogers, & Kuiper, 1979.)

Thus the attitude toward oneself is more and more characterized as a defined relationship,[1] capable of providing us with a stable and structured self-image, which in turn allows for a continuous and coherent self-perception and self-evaluation in the face of temporal becoming and mutable reality. For this reason the maintenance of our own perceived personal identity becomes almost as important to us as life itself; without it, we would be incapable of proper functioning.

In particular, personal identity exercises its regulatory function in the forward movement of time, making our plans and actions consistent with the quality of the attitude toward ourselves that we have been able to structure. Therefore we could say that the attitude toward oneself is responsible for and coordinates one's corresponding attitude toward reality. That is, our way of seeing reality—and ourselves in reality—essentially depends upon how we see and conceive of ourselves. For example, if we have structured a self-image of a weak and fragile person, we will consequently have a vision of reality as protective on the one hand and as potentially dangerous or hostile on the other. Furthermore, in this reality we will see ourselves move with care and caution, discarding a priori entire domains of experience that are regarded as beyond our possibilities. Therefore, precisely through the corresponding attitude toward reality that it is able to determine, personal identity regulates and coordinates the maintenance and change patterns of our knowledge during our temporal becoming.

MAINTENANCE AND CHANGE OF COGNITIVE ORGANIZATION

The growth of knowledge proceeds from old problems to new problems. . . . The activity of understanding is, essentially, the same as that of all problem solving.
—Popper (1972)

We will now briefly describe the principal ways in which personal identity, through the corresponding attitude toward reality, regulates both the patterns of its own maintenance and the possibilities and patterns of change. Our concluding remarks attempt to outline some aspects inherent in knowledge organization's temporal becoming.

MAINTENANCE

The attitude toward reality is essentially articulated in representational models of reality, which depict the world in congruence with the structured self-image.

The complementarity between self-image and image of reality can certainly be considered one of the fundamental facts on which the maintenance of personal identity rests. The selection of data from outside reality that are coherent with self-image obviously confirms—in an automatic and circular way—the perceived personal identity. For instance, if a man believes that he is not acceptable to people, he will likely be more inclined than others to grasp even minimal signs of criticism or indifference toward himself in various social situations, thereupon confirming his "theory."

Another way to maintain the stability of the structures of personal identity stems from the human ability to formulate problems and actively look for a solution to them. The problem-solving procedures are an instrument through which we can actively manipulate experiential data, obtaining confirmation on our own way of seeing ourselves and the world. On this matter, it is advisable to keep in mind that problems hardly ever exist as such. The problematic nature of a situation is defined more by the "reading code" derived from the individual's organization of knowledge than by the objective difficulty. Consequently, the most suitable hypothesis for solving a problem is not so much that which guarantees the "objectively" better solution, but that which can better state and solve the individual's way of seeing the difficulty. For instance, taking again the preceding example of a man who expects to be rejected, he may try to solve his social problems by assuming an utterly false attitude of brilliantness, only to obtain—at best—a forced compliance to his clumsy jokes, followed by the very factual rejection that he was striving to avoid. Furthermore, as mentioned in the preceding chapter, in reality, problem solving based on logic is only *one* of the possible procedures and certainly not the more frequently used in life's everyday situations. Consequently, patterns of problem solving based on emotional drives or "good common sense" may become ways for many individuals to make effective decisions on life that are not only plausible according to them, but also to the people around them who share the same common sense and its connected "emotional logic." Obviously, this further confirms to the individual the plausibility of the solution taken, in spite of its possible "objective" illogicalness.

Furthermore, in spite of the norms of logic, human beings seem more prone to believing and confirming their own concept of the world than to doubting and disconfirming it when faced with problems of great concern. This tendency toward confirmation may become particularly evident, for instance, as an incapacity for eliminating a trial solution even when it has been proved completely useless. In his work on the failure to eliminate hypotheses, Wason (1977) states that "even intelligent individuals adhere to their own hypotheses with remarkable tenacity when they can produce confirming evidence for them" (p. 313), and it is well known how easy it may be to produce "confirming evidence." Thus, when the trial solution is maintained in spite of the results obtained, it depends directly on the fact that the way the problem is defined and stated is coherent with the subject's representation of reality. In this way the problem's insolubility itself can become a confirmation of the patient's expectations.[2]

On this matter, it may be useful to consider a suitably schematized example (which is more a demonstrative vignette than a real-life occurrence). Let us consider a young woman who has developed a self-image as "intrinsically unlovable." It is highly probable that this image determines an extremely specific attitude toward reality: She may represent men as being not very interested in her and consequently can expect every eventual romantic relationship to come to an end quickly, because her partner will soon recognize her defects and leave her. Once an affective relationship is established, her attitude toward reality makes her define the problem as follows: "What can I do to keep this man from leaving me?" An "adequate" solution—given such a definition of the problem—might well consist of implementing a whole series of behaviors that have the scope of "keeping him at all costs." It is likely that these behaviors in themselves (e.g., incessant demand for affective reassurances, scenes of jealousy, attempts to control the partner's life, etc.) will effectively cause the partner to become tired of the situation and decide to leave her in order to dedicate his attention to a less oppressive and boring woman. However, the young woman will not consider this event as the logical consequence of her own behavior. On the contrary, it will be used as a further confirmation of her own belief that she is intrinsically unlovable and that she is not capable of "keeping her lovers." Therefore in future situations she will tend to intensify her controlling "solution," thus producing further desertions.

Since every time she is abandoned she processes the data derived from the experience on the basis of her self-image (so that it is reconfirmed and made more stable each time), little by little her own "unlovableness" becomes something certain and "proved." It becomes understandable how this belief will orient her toward specific choices in life (regarding work, social engagements, etc.), putting romantic commitments on a secondary level. Progressively, these choices will build a definite "life program," which she will consider as the only one possible for her. In such a situation, the eventual proposal of a new romantic relationship will make the elicitation of the previously described repetitious behavior even easier, with the result of "favoring" the immediate occurrence of the awaited event (desertion by the man). In other words, it is as if the woman "programmed" her own behavior so as to confirm, in the least time possible, the expectation that, at the beginning of her affective experiences, was feared, but that has now become a certainty considered necessary for maintaining and carrying out her own life program.

This vignette is meant to exemplify how, as time passes, the necessity of confirming one's own life choices may be increasingly expressed in the carrying out of behaviors that produce foreseen consequences, functional to the choices made. In this way the occurrence of undesirable, but "certain," events and, in any case, of events that do not challenge the choices made will be "preferable" to the occurrence of desirable events (such as the possibility of a sentimental relationship's continuing) that would imply a change in the life program.

In synthesis, we could say that the tendency toward maintaining one's own conception of self and the world is not manifested only by the production of stereotyped problem formulations and repetitious problem "solutions." Idiosyncratic problem-solving strategies also make it possible to actively manipulate environmental situations until reaching the production of events in consonance with the structured self-image. In this way, through the individual's own stereotyped and repetitious procedures, he or she can "model" the outside environment until reaching the construction of an "environmental niche" that is adequate for his or her personal identity and life program. One of the more singular expressions of human beings as active problem solvers is manifested precisely by their ability to adapt to the mutable surrounding reality while maintaining their own concept of self and the world.

CHANGE

Through the maintenance of the cognitive structures of personal identity, individuals largely "invent" their own experiences, actively operating on their environment through the production of events that are more or less in keeping with their concept of self and the world.

In this sense it is once again possible to grasp the formal analogy between the functioning of individuals and that of scientists. In their attempt to understand reality, scientists build theories that partly determine the very form of the experience they intend to explain. In other words, through their own concepts of the world, scientists model reality, which thus assumes forms that, according to them, allows them to classify and arrange it. Nevertheless, even if the ability to manipulate reality makes it easier for scientists to develop and verify their own theories, very often they run up against anomalous data that compel them to revise their own hypotheses. In the same way, even though individuals model their own environment through their attitudes toward reality and consequent problem-solving procedures, they often run up against "anomalous" experiential data that cannot be explained by the view of self or the world that they have adopted.

As already mentioned, an individual's concept of self and the world is continuously interacting with environmental data and thereupon undergoes incessant remodeling and readaptation in response to the changeability of environmental situations. To take into account simultaneously both the trend toward maintenance and the trend toward remodeling of personal identity, one could say that, within a determined attitude toward reality, the range of possible changes is already defined, so that when they occur they do not produce appreciable modification in the individual's personal identity.

For example, a man who considers himself as a worthless person can define his own attitude toward reality by never revealing his thoughts or emotions, since people would then realize how undeserving he is. Now, let us suppose that a friend provides him with such a guarantee of kindness, understanding, and devotion that our man is persuaded to reveal his own moods. In a sense this event constitutes a notable change in attitude, since the man decided to trust someone and talk about himself for the first time in his life. Nevertheless, this change must be considered as part of that "range" of possible ones (regarding his own attitude toward others) that allows for the unaltered maintenance of his own personal identity. In fact, he will probably attribute his own change to his friend's particular characteristics by elaborating, for example, ad hoc theories of the following type: "He is definitely an outstanding person; I can trust him." In this way the "anomalous" experiential datum (made up of the possibility of confiding in someone without the feared consequence occurring) will be able to produce exclusively a partial modification of his attitude toward reality without implicating the modification of his preexisting self-image.

Individual Deep Change

More than "superficial" changes in the attitude toward reality, "deeper" modification of the structures of personal identity is interesting from a clinical viewpoint. In our opinion the urges capable of determining this deeper change are the product of two distinct pressures, which are exerted upon personal identity within the structured arrangement of knowledge (see Table 3-1, p. 73). On the one hand, there may be anomalous experiential data that come from the attitude toward reality and that cannot be explained by the structured self-image; on the other hand, anomalous data may elicit further implications derived from the individual's self-knowledge, and these, in turn, would require processing and incorporation in personal identity.

From this perspective, a deep change is identified with the change in attitude toward oneself obtained through the explication and reconstruction of new rules that come from self-knowledge. The changed attitude toward oneself will consequently provoke a modification of personal identity; this, in turn, will produce a restructuring of the attitude toward reality through which the world can be seen and dealt with in a different manner. On the other hand, it is appropriate to bear in mind that, given the strong tendency toward maintaining one's own personal identity, any request for whatever degree of deep change must be considered a challenge for the individual. Thus one may expect that the deeper the requested change, the stronger the resistance and the emotional stress. Furthermore, even though the individual is willingly on the way toward a self-transformation, the stronger the emotional stress, the more he or she will presumably try to safeguard the structures of personal identity—at least by slowing down the process.

The patterns of individual deep change differ greatly from one person to the next. However, they share the need for the individual to have an alternative self-image in order to make possible a modification of identity without his or her experiencing any interruption in the sense of subjective continuity. Such an interruption would be equivalent to losing the very sense of reality. In the face of such an impending psychological catastrophe, almost everybody would be unavoidably compelled to reconfirm and maintain his or her habitual self-image, however inconvenient this might have proved.

Although attempts at deep change can be developed with a wide variety of cognitive processes and possible final results, for the sake of conciseness, we describe here only the cases illustrating the more extreme procedures and results, that is, where the attempt to modify attitude toward oneself and to restructure personal identity succeeds and where this attempt fails.

Attempts That Reflect a Progressive Shift. As we have said, the challenging of one's attitude toward reality by anomalous experiential data sets in motion further implications for self-knowledge; these implications exert pressure on the attitude toward oneself, to be made explicit and incorporated in personal identity. This homeostatic and adaptive process yields new possible rules on the basis of which the individual can reelaborate his or her self-images, so that it again becomes able to adapt to the mutable surrounding reality.

The new implications of self-knowledge appear in the subject's mental processing in the analogical code with which tacit self-knowledge is generally expressed. Therefore they essentially take the form of nonverbal and emotionally charged representations (images, fantasies, dreams, sudden recollections, etc.) phenomenally experienced as unexpected and fleeting "intuitions." These knowledge contents may more or less reverbe:..e in the individual's internal representations and initially may not be considered particularly meaningful personal experiences. The prompt attribution of meaning to these reverberating images is made difficult by the fact that they usually assume quite different forms, even in a single day.

For example, at times, images accompanied by specific feelings may suddenly insert themselves in the individual's thought processes, sometimes as a consequence of apparently irrelevant perceptions. At other times, they become present in a more continuous way, as a kind of background to the individual's representational activity. For example, as soon as the individual faces a semiautomatic task, deep-knowledge contents may assume the form of daydreams or semi-intentional fantasies that he or she considers desirable, but impossible, to accomplish (cf. Singer, 1974). Such contents are almost always accompanied by a specific emotional coloring, although generally less intense in this background activity than in unexpected "intrusive" imagery.

Finally, at yet other times—and generally after the initial reverberation phases, when a tacit processing of such contents has begun—some intuitions can appear as true "alternative visions" of self and reality. According to Franks (1974), these intuitions are to be considered as phenomenal indicants of new sets of rules that are being structured in the tacit self-knowledge as a consequence of the information processing that is taking place in it. At the beginning, these intuitions appear in a rather vague and sudden form, and only with later processing may they acquire a more defined form that allows the individual to understand their meaning. The duration of the reverberation period and of subsequent, more organized processing varies widely from case to case. However, even in more favorable situations, the process should always be considered as gradual and accompanied by varying degrees of affective distress. In particular, the latter will be more intense the more deeply one modifies the attitude toward oneself.

The process of deep change approaches a conclusion when the individual succeeds in defining explicitly and stably incorporating the alternative vision of self into his or her personal identity, thus making it a new point of reference and continuous comparison. In parallel, the individual's attitude toward reality is modified, producing a new way of seeing the world and the self in the world, which is translated into more or less extensive modification of the life program. Generally, the phase in which the change process is approaching a conclusion is characterized by the subjects "suddenly," after a relatively long period of instability, beginning to have explicit knowledge of the modification being experienced and of the life objectives toward which he or she is directed.

The mechanisms that regulate the emergence of this explicit knowledge, which sometimes assumes the form of a sudden "discovery," are poorly understood. It is likely that such mechanisms have analogies with the process of "grasp of consciousness" described by Piaget (1974). This process is not identified by a kind of insight that suddenly throws light on aspects of self that up until now had remained obscure. Rather, the grasp of consciousness corresponds to a real reconstruction of something that has been processing and organizing at a tacit level. Although the process of reconstruction is slow and gradual, final understanding comes relatively rapidly and suddenly. This usually takes place when a new set of rules of self-knowledge has been almost completely organized, influencing considerably the individual's attitude toward himself or herself. Thus only the act of grasping consciousness is characterized by a certain suddenness, whereas the preceding tacit construction is gradual.

Grasping consciousness gives rise, in turn, to a new conceptualization, through which the individual reorganizes his or her own personal identity so as to incorporate the ways of thinking and acting that have been gradually structured. Briefly, the change in attitude toward oneself with which the individual arrives at a restructuring of his or her own personal identity presents the following characteristics:

- The new self-image is the outcome of the conceptual reconstruction of new sets of rules that emerge from tacit self-knowledge. Therefore, although it has been elicited from environmental data of experience, the new way of seeing oneself is determined largely by the heuristic power that is intrinsic to the individual's self-knowledge.

- The new self-image does not cancel the previous beliefs that one had about oneself. On the contrary, the old beliefs are organized along with the new emerging beliefs in a different overall structural relationship in which they acquire different meanings as compared to the past—even if, with different meanings and implications, the conservation of the old beliefs permits the maintenance of that sense of subjective continuity of self on which one's personal indentity is founded.

- Only from the reconstruction of personal identity can one consequently proceed toward the reorganization of one's attitude toward reality. That is, the new implications of self-knowledge that have been processed become part of the representational models of reality, providing the individual with new prospects and objectives.

Attempts That Reflect a Regressive Shift. Situations where the change in attitude toward oneself and the consequent restructuring of personal identity do not take place, notwithstanding the presence of environmental urges toward such a change, are frequently encountered in clinical practice. For this reason, we will describe the process only schematically here, referring the reader to the next chapter for clinical examples.

The beginning of the process is analogous to that of the previously described situation. On the basis of anomalous experiential data that question the individual's attitude toward reality, the implications of self-knowledge exert pressure, within the attitude toward oneself, to be made explicit and to be incorporated in personal identity. The new emerging content of self-knowledge, potentially susceptible to processing, begins to propose itself, in the individual's inner representation, through its typical analogical code.

The element that differentiates the "failing" process can be found in the particular attitude toward oneself that the individual has structured (see Note 1). This attitude has induced the construction of a rather rigid, partial, and/or contradictory self-image as compared to the range of possibilities contemplated by self-knowledge. The consequent effect is that the new request for change proposed by tacit self-knowledge is completely foreign to and/or incompatible with the structured self-identity to which the individual adheres. In this situation the processing of new deep rules, with their reverberation in internal representation, does not have many possibilities of reaching a successful conceptual reconstruction. In fact, as stated previously in this chapter, by means of the continuous confrontation with the structured self-image, individuals are able to regulate their own selective attention and therefore to exclude information that comes from themselves and that is incompatible with their own images. If such an exclusion fails, and the information emerges in consciousness, it is distorted or denied, or its meaning is removed.

On the other hand, it should be kept in mind that the continuous proposing of the new data of self-knowledge is constantly accompanied by an important emotional coloring. When it is impossible to make such data explicit, it consequently becomes impossible to explain and thus control the emotional component that accompanies them. Therefore the emotional component is experienced as a more or less continuous emotional distress, which makes the adaptation of reality precarious. The consequences of this emotional distress are reflected in both the attitude toward oneself and the attitude toward reality.

The situation can be schematized in this manner:

- Attitude toward oneself. At this level, a kind of instability is produced in the structures of personal identity, since the individual is not able to recognize the distress that he or she notices more or less continuously as a personal emotional experience. Then we witness the proliferation of ad hoc theories, which have the purpose of explaining the nature of emotional distress while maintaining the structured self-image unchanged. These theories share the common feature of the *external* causal attribution to emotional distress. That is, the cause is identified each time in illness (somatic or psychic, but in any case perceived as not subject to one's control) or in presumed hostilities in the domain of interpersonal and social relationships (refusal, betrayal, conspiracy in the work environment, etc.). In this way striving for the maintenance of the attitude toward oneself can start the development of a full-fledged clinical syndrome.
- Attitude toward reality. The maintenance of personal identity consequently prevents modification of the attitude toward reality. For this reason the individual will be unable to offer

alternative solutions to those problematic situations that have created the urgent request for change. The individual's re-actions to these situations becomes increasingly stereotyped and repetitious, with the end result being a continuous con-firmation of the way he or she faces problems as the only possible one.

Levels of Therapeutic Intervention. The situation briefly outlined here corresponds to a twofold view of therapeutic goals. In accordance with Arnkoff (1980), two levels of therapeutic modification may be identified: a peripheral change and a "central" one. The first level refers to surface structures, and the second to deep structures of knowledge organization.

From this perspective, a peripheral change coincides with the reorganization of the patient's attitude toward reality within the limits allowed by the maintenance of his or her attitude toward self. In other words, with the use, say, of behavior therapy techniques and/or problem-solving procedures, it is sometimes possible to modify the stereotyped and repetitious features of the patient's attitude toward reality without having to modify his or her self-image. Thus it is possible to obtain an improvement in the patient's adaptation to the environment and a reduction of emotional distress. Nevertheless, this type of peripheral intervention is usually of limited value, and its effects are short-lived in complex cases.

By "central change" we mean the modification of the attitude toward oneself that follows the restructuring of personal identity. The patient develops a new attitude toward reality that involves an alternative view of the problems troubling him or her.

These two types of change do not exclude one another; rather, according to our clinical experience, it is often possible to reach a central change only through a preceding peripheral change. A fuller account of this topic is given in Chapter 8.

CONCLUSIONS

In the history of science as well as in a single individual's history, the development of knowledge is characterized by a progressive integration of sparse observations and rudimentary theories into more comprehensive and unified ones. Popper (1972), comparing the biological evolution with the evolution of knowledge, points out how both have, like a tree, a ramified structure. The evolution of knowledge tree, however, is turned upside down: While the biological evolution proceeds toward a progressive differentiation (from the trunk to the branches), the evolution of knowledge proceeds toward a progressive integration (from the branches to the trunk). In other words, from more peripheral and contingent theories, knowledge little by little reaches more central and abstract theories, which include the original theories as particular cases.

This progressive tendency toward integration is also evident in the temporal evolution of an individual's knowledge. The period of development is characterized by the elaboration of rather contingent theories strictly bound to the specific observational context. With the onset of logical–conceptual thought, such theories approach a "paradigmatic" generalization, which allows the individual to extract from them a defined and comprehensive view of himself or herself that is relatively independent of the specific environmental context. During adulthood and maturity, the structures of personal identity progressively regulate the individual's attitude toward reality, giving it an increasingly unitary and individualized course.

Actually, a biography would be completely incomprehensible if the life events included in it were arranged in a more or less casual sequence or if this sequence were determined only by genetic factors or environmental stimuli. A person's history and actions become immediately more understandable if they are seen in terms of the formulation and solution of problems, regulated and coordinated by the knowledge of self and the world that the individual has been progressively elaborating. Furthermore, as age advances and experience is accumulated, every individual's concept of self and the world tends to become better defined and to include in an overall comprehensive vision one's past, present, and future, by now more probable or less uncertain.

As Luckmann (1979) has pointed out, personal identity progressively tends to become a historical form of life. Indeed, various authors have introduced terms such as "plan of life" (Popper & Eccles, 1977) or "life theme" (Csikszentmihalyi & Beattie, 1979) to indicate the progressive unification that a human being's knowledge and actions assume in the course of his or her life. And indeed, observing an individual's biography, one has the impression that he or she has, almost without realizing it, followed a kind of "guiding track" or, to use theatre terminology, a "script."

We would like to emphasize that, even though people do seem to follow a "life theme" during the span of their existence, this is *not* the expression of a predetermined guiding line fixed in their minds and accomplished outside of their control. On the contrary, the life theme is something that is progressively and dynamically constructed day by day and year by year on the basis of the events that have characterized an individual's existence, of how he or she has interpreted and dealt with them, and the consequences that have thus been produced. The consequences of one's choices and actions in turn become further events, which, unified in the memory, allow the individual to construct an even more uniform and comprehensive image of self and of his or her own life. Therefore individuals build their self-images on the progressive merging of the memory of both desired and undesired events that have influenced their lives. This memory's unifying process determines, on the one hand, ever greater consonance between the life-style and the self-conception and, on the other, a growing "rigidity" of the life-style (with a concomitant gradual decrease of possible alternatives). Popper (1972), with his usual clarity, explains this aspect of knowledge development as follows:

> How does an animal path in the jungle arise? Some animal may break through the undergrowth in order to get a drinking-place. Other animals find it easiest to use the same track. Thus it may be widened and improved by use. It is not planned—it is an unintended consequence of the need for easy or swift movement. This is how a path is originally made—perhaps even by men—and how language and any other institutions which are useful may arise, and how they may owe their existence and development to their usefulness. They are not planned or intended, and there was perhaps no need for them before they came into existence. But they may create a new need, or a new set of aims: *the aim structure of animals or men is not "given," but it develops, with the help of some kind of feed-back mechanism, out of earlier aims, and out of results which were or were not aimed at.* (Popper, 1972/1979, p. 117; italics added)

NOTES

1. In our opinion the definition and classification of the individual patterns of the attitude toward oneself may, in the future, provide an altogether new vision of knowledge organization, including the problem of conscious life. For the time being,

systematic investigation of this topic is lacking, and we must content ourselves with sparse studies, whose promising implications surely deserve further clinical and experimental research. For instance, Gur and Sackeim (1979) have proposed the concept of "self-deception" in order to define the situation in which—perhaps because of early conflicts—individuals prevent themselves from being conscious of what they in fact know. Hamlyn (1977) has described other patterns of attitude toward oneself, such as "blindness to oneself," characterized by a "refusal" to commit oneself to a line of action through an overriding attention to other things, and the "standing back to oneself," a kind of self-evaluating attitude by which the individual is always seemingly "a step behind himself," continuously watching and judging his or her own emotions and performances.

2. It could prove useful to mention briefly the postulated difference between first- and second-order problem solving, outlined by Watzlawick, Weakland, and Fisch (1974) after the theoretical model proposed by Bateson (1972; see also 1979). In first-order problem solving, individuals work out a solution that they apply directly to the difficulty they perceive. In this way a limited change (the so-called $CHANGE_1$) can be obtained, consisting of solving a contingent problem, with no modification of the attitude toward reality that made possible the very recognition of the difficulty. If this does not happen, the solution applied may not be eliminated and may become a datum of experience and a further feature of the nature of the perceived difficulty. Thus the solution coincides with the problem, and the impossibility to solve the problem becomes a determining part of the individual's attitude toward reality.

The second-order problem-solving procedure is completely different; most of the time it comes into action once first-order problem solving has proved ineffective. In this case the whole process is applied, consciously or unconsciously, *to the tried solution* (i.e., to what the individual is already doing to solve the problem) *rather than to the difficulty itself*. Therefore, in second-order problem solving, the solution is evidently reached through a "logical gap" involving a change of the individual's attitude toward reality (the so-called $CHANGE_2$).

5

THE ETIOLOGY OF
COGNITIVE DYSFUNCTION

A form of adaptation is thus achieved by narrowing and distorting
the environment until one's conduct appears adequate to it, rather
than by altering one's conduct and enlarging one's knowledge till
one can cope with the larger, real environment.—Craik (1943)

In the preceding chapters we tried to point out how the development
of knowledge is a unitary and systematic process, which unfolds
without interruption during life, even though with variable rhythms
and courses. In this sense the temporal becoming of knowledge is
marked by a continuous process of restructuring and remodeling,
through which the experiential data that emerge from the interaction
with reality are processed and integrated. When a rigid attitude
toward oneself prevents the restructuring of the self-image and of the
attitude toward reality required in order to cope more effectively with
the emergent experiential data, the individual's interaction with reality
becomes stereotyped and repetitious. Consequently, the assimilation
of experiences will be hampered, and the individual will generally
become somewhat maladapted to the environment. It is precisely on
the basis of the emotional distress that accompanies such maladapta-
tion that a cognitive dysfunction[1] usually begins.

It is widely believed that the determinants of a rigid attitude
toward oneself (hampering an eventually needed restructuring of
personal identity and attitude toward reality) are to be found not only
in early experiences per se, but also in the way these experiences have
influenced the subsequent development of knowledge. Although the
"traumatic" experiences and their influences on cognitive growth are
too manifold to permit a classification, at least at the present stage of
research, we believe it is possible to reconstruct the main lines of
development that lead to a potential cognitive dysfunction, taking

advantage of attachment theory (intended as an integrative paradigm of human development; see Chapter 1).

In this chapter we outline a tentative unitary etiology of cognitive dysfunction, based on the quality and course of attachment during the developmental period. We then deal with the way in which specific patterns of pathological attachment may influence knowledge organization, so that the basis is laid for the potential emergence of some common clinical syndromes, which are described more fully in the third part of this book.

PATHOLOGY OF ATTACHMENT

GENERAL REMARKS

Attachment and exploratory behavior are two interrelated classes of behavior, both controlled in the beginning of life mainly through the relationship between environmental contingencies and what Konrad Lorenz calls the species-specific inborn knowledge encoded in the brain and memory mechanisms (Bowlby, 1969, 1973, 1977a). Particularly strong emotions are engaged in the unfolding of attachment and exploratory behavior.

The interrelationship between attachment and exploration is particularly complex. In one sense exploratory behavior depends on the availability of a "positive" attachment figure (remember Blurton-Jones's "smiling" mothers; see Chapter 2). In another sense exploratory behavior is antithetical to attachment behavior, since it implies *detachment* or *active separation* of the child from his or her attachment figure. This complex interrelationship accounts for many possible distortions in the progressive unfolding of attachment and exploration. The following are just the main classes of pathological attachment and hampered exploration:

- Both attachment and exploration can be hampered by the relative absence of reliable attachment figures.
- An anxious attachment, defined by the *expectation* of losing an attachment figure, impedes autonomous exploratory behavior, since the child will refuse to leave the proximity of this attachment figure.

- An attachment figure may actively prohibit autonomous exploration, through threats and punishment.
- The behavior of attachment figures can be so contradictory and misleading that it is impossible for the child to develop a coherent, precise, and unambiguous set of expectations about his or her capabilities of establishing attachment, about exploratory ability, and about the reliability of other people in affectional bonds.

Once one of these abnormal patterns of attachment is established, it influences—usually within the limits of a specific domain of experience—the subsequent cognitive growth.

ATTACHMENT, SELF-KNOWLEDGE, AND FAILED DISTANCING

The three main arguments for explaining the etiology of cognitive dysfunctions according to attachment theory can be summarized as follows:

1. Self-knowledge, which is progressively constructed, is the element that coordinates and integrates cognitive growth and emotional differentiation. During the developmental period, the presence and the behavior of other people are determinants in this process. According to the "looking-glass-self" theory (or the "looking-glass effect"; cf. Chapter 2), children can begin to structure a self-image through interaction with the people who are present in their environment. When parents turn their attention toward their children, they furnish them with an enormous amount of information on both a nonverbal and a verbal level (evaluations, instructions, definitions of their behavior, etc.), and it is through this information that children progressively learn to recognize the attributes that define them as individuals to others—and consequently to themselves. In other words, parents, as a mirror, provide children with a self-image; this does not remain a mere sensorial datum to be stored away as such, but rather orients and coordinates children's self-perception until they are able to perceive themselves in keeping with the image that is supplied to them.

The importance, for satisfactory cognitive–emotional development, of a balanced attachment relationship between the child and his or her caregivers is therefore evident. Every pathological feature of attachment will necessarily be reflected in the developing self-knowledge. In addition, the slow unfolding of human cognitive growth makes the established self-image quite stable and thus not easy to change. The view of oneself implied by the early attachment relationship corresponds, for a rather long period, to the very way the child has of experiencing himself or herself. In other words, because of the effects of the early interaction with the caregivers, a "nucleus" of self-knowledge is formed long before the child is able to remember and reflect upon it. Included in this nucleus are the early rules with which the child comes to perceive and recognize the invariant aspects of self and others. These "tacit" rules will function as a bias for directing the subsequent making and matching processes through which self-knowledge will achieve further development and organization.

2. In the human species, attachment and contact with parents present distinctive features, which are unprecedented on the zoological scale. The process of attachment continues for years, generally way beyond adolescence; during this time, the process is qualitatively enriched, so that from early infancy's simple physical attachment, an emotional and "representational" attachment develops and becomes the basis for identification. While children spend a long period of their lives in their own domestic environment, their parents—whose vision of interpersonal relationships has guided their attachment behavior to the children—probably will not change their own cognitive style very much. Thus, given the persistence of the same relationships that have permitted its first definition, the self-image structured during infancy will probably receive continuous confirmation. This process of confirmation and reinforcement, which continues without interruption until adulthood, can be partially modified by the intervention of the following variables:

- The kind of cultural stimulation provided by the family's social network. (Presumably, a rich and varied cultural stimulation permits further articulation of the original self-image.)
- The availability of alternative identification models in the social network. (Presumably, these models can compensate for the shortcomings derived from a qualitatively and quantitatively insufficient attachment to parents.)

- The life events (illnesses, bereavements, financial changes, geographical moving, etc.) that occur during the course of development. (These can modify the ongoing relationship with the parents or can supply the child with other relational contexts for his or her identification processes.)

3. If the self-knowledge that is being structured is the integrating element of the developmental processes, then it is no wonder that a distorted self-conception may multifariously interfere with such processes. In particular, it is highly probable that, if distorted self-conceptions regarding fundamental aspects of identity (lovableness, personal value, etc.) have been formed, these not only will determine a particular attitude toward reality, but also will notably influence the cognitive and emotional processes in course. In fact, these negative and/or distorted self-images will inevitably elicit a rather rigid and defensive attitude toward oneself, which will make problematic the subsequent interaction between the structures of personal identity and the emerging data of reality. The consequence is a failure in distancing and decentering from many ideas related to these distorted self-conceptions. Consequently, these distorted self-conceptions will remain anchored to the forms of prelogical thinking typical of childhood and will be difficult to make explicit after adolescence in the form of conceptual and critical knowledge.

This failed distancing will influence, in turn, emotional development, so that the emotional component which accompanies these concepts will remain rather undifferentiated, scarcely controllable, and therefore prone to "dramatic" expression. It is precisely the intensity and uncontrollability of these emotions that will indirectly contribute to a rigid and defensive attitude toward oneself (which makes plausible to the individual his or her own idiosyncratic and excessive reactions toward certain events). More explicitly, one could say that the activation of primitive, undifferentiated emotional schemata (according to Duncker's concept of functional fixedness as suggested by Shaw, 1979) conveys a form of dogmatic or mythical thinking (see Chapter 3) that contains elements that were typical of the Piagetian stage of cognitive growth during which those schemata were constructed. In this way the images and inner dialogue flowing in the stream of consciousness will be perceived as being congruent with the feelings experienced and with the attitude assumed. As a result, those emotions and corresponding thoughts will, later on, be equated with reality (inability to distance).

With respect to cognitive growth, these distorted self-conceptions, functioning as a set of tacit rules, will coordinate thinking and deductive reasoning on the basis of the mythical and dogmatic "logic" to which they are still bound. In this way they can set into motion typical patterns of reasoning filled with all those inferential errors and "disorders" in thinking (personalization, polarized thinking, arbitrary inference, selective abstraction, overgeneralization, etc.) that are amply described by Beck (cf. Beck, 1976, pp. 89–101). These aberrations in thinking, inserted in the procedures with which the individual formulates and attempts to solve problems, lead to a whole series of stereotyped and repetitious patterns, which essentially produce the confirmation of the original conceptions. Confirmations so produced will further establish these conceptions and the rigid and defensive attitude toward oneself that accompanies them, further precluding a different articulation of these concepts with experiential data. Thus, in spite of the passing of time, the individual remains anchored to the patterns of organizing reality typical to immature or primitive thinking (cf. Beck, Rush, Shaw, & Emery, 1979, p. 15), characterized by one-dimensionality, globality, invariance, and irreversibility.

ABNORMAL PATTERNS OF ATTACHMENT AND CORRESPONDING COGNITIVE DISTORTIONS

On the basis of the arguments we have presented, we will attempt to outline the main lines of development of the principal cognitive dysfunctions. The purpose of this outline is only that of leading the etiology of these dysfunctions back to a unitary model derived from the attachment theory; for an extensive treatment of the clinical syndromes centering around these aberrations in thinking, see Part Three of this book.

The specific distortions and/or deficiencies that can occur in conjunction with attachment have long been under study as probable etiological factors. Recently, Bowlby (1977a) proposed a comprehensive view of psychiatric etiology and psychopathology in light of the attachment theory. Starting from the model proposed by Bowlby, and integrating it with the concept of development explained in Chapter 2 and with our own clinical experience, we can define four abnormal patterns of attachment that correspond to the same number of clinical syndromes: agoraphobia (and related multiple phobias), depression, eating disorders, and obsessive–compulsive patterns. The other neurotic and psychotic disturbances among the patients we have followed in therapy during the past 10 years have not been representative enough to give us sufficient data for an analogous description.

AGORAPHOBIA

The course of attachment is characterized by a detachment blockage, with more or less conspicuous hampering of exploratory behavior. The detachment blockage is usually created with indirect patterns, as opposed to a direct prohibition of exploration. The more common of these patterns (which can also present themselves in combination) are:

1. Continuous warning from hyperprotective parents on the dangers of the outside world and therefore on the difficulties in dealing with it.
2. Insistence on the child's presumed physical and/or emotional weakness, which makes him or her particularly exposed to the world's dangers.
3. Modeling on the agoraphobic parent who, fearing loneliness, keeps the child with him or her.
4. Threats of desertion or family scenes that make the child insecure outside of the home (cf. Bowlby, 1973, Chapter 19).

The anxious attachment that emerges from this context generally provides the child with a conflicting self-image, which will require considerable effort on his or her part in order to reach a satisfying integration. In fact, the continuous contact and attention that the hyperprotective parents shower on the child provide him or her with a self-image as a lovable and valuable person, whereas, the continuous limitation of exploration furnishes him or her with a weak and/or fragile self-image within a threatening and hostile world.

Given this conflicting self-image, the individual will tend to structure progressively a rigid attitude toward self, centered on extreme control of every minimal "weakness" or emotional frailty. Thus it will be possible to combine the idea of being weak and "different" together with that of being lovable and worthy of much attention: "As long as I can maintain control over every weakness, I can have self-respect."

In structuring the attitude toward reality, the individual also must try to integrate decidedly conflicting aspects. On the one hand, the obstacle to the inborn disposition to explore the environment is perceived as an intolerable constriction, which causes the person to develop an absolutely overwhelming need for freedom and independence: He or she will become selectively attentive to the "constrictive" aspects of reality. Simultaneously, the imagined dangers of the extra-familial world and the individual's presumed weakness create, on the other hand, the need to feel protected by reassuring or familiar figures: He or she will continuously search for the company of "protective" people. Therefore the individual must attempt to settle a dilemma of this type: how to find an equilibrium between the need for freedom and independence, which imply loneliness (and therefore danger), and the need for protection, which implies dependence on others (and therefore a likely repetition of the constricting experience). This difficult equilibrium is reached, in the majority of cases, by structuring an attitude toward reality that centers on the achievement and maintenance of control in interpersonal relationships. In this way the individual can succeed simultaneously in obtaining the protection he or she considers necessary and in maintaining the sense of freedom and independence regarded as indispensable.

The equilibrium that this attitude toward reality permits can have a variable course and duration according to the circumstances, but it is destined to become precarious as soon as the individual finds himself or herself confronting those specific situations that re-present the dilemma, that is,

- Possible loss of protection (e.g., a situation of loneliness threatened by the possible breaking off of a sentimental relationship).
- Possible loss of the sense of freedom and independence (e.g., finding oneself involved in a stable affective relationship with a "controlling" partner or with one who escapes the possibilities of control).

Within these two general situations, the equilibrium previously reached can break down, with the establishment of a specific psycho-pathological pattern (see Chapter 10 for a thorough discussion).

DEPRESSION

In this situation the child is exposed, from the early developmental phases, to patterns of attachment that are, in a sense, the opposite of those connected with agoraphobia.

The course of attachment in this case is characterized by the relative isolation and lack of affective contact in the child's environment. If in agoraphobia we are dealing with a situation where the child's active separation from his or her caregivers is hindered or delayed, in depression we are dealing with a situation where the child experiences a precocious and unwilling separation. Obviously, a wide variety of family situations can lead to isolation and precocious detachment. For the sake of conciseness, we describe here only one of the simpler cases, where isolation is experienced by the child without an accompanying feeling of hostility toward one or both of the parents (because the child attributes his or her "loneliness" not to a willing withdrawal of one or both parents, but to objective necessities, such as the illness or death of one of them or the peculiarities of their work). In situations where children are "critical" toward one or both of the parents, and where feelings of anger and hostility come into the picture, the "depressive" cognitive organization becomes more complex.

The prolongation of such an attachment pattern contributes to giving these children a conflicting self-image. On the one hand, the relative lack of parental contact and attention provides them with a self-image of an unlovable person, and this image causes them to look upon themselves with a sense of unworthiness, impotence, and fatalism; on the other hand, the experience of isolation imposes an image of a person who can count only on himself or herself, orienting them toward attributing to their own personal responsibility the failures that inevitably accompany their moving about in an unknown reality. Thus they will progressively structure an attitude toward themselves characterized by a "compulsive self-reliance" (Bowlby, 1977a), which appears to them not only coherent with their "destiny" of loneliness, but also as the only possibility of overcoming their self-attributed unlovableness and low personal worth.

The attitude toward reality also presents paradoxical aspects. On the one hand, these individuals are oversensitive to refusal and rejection, since they expect (given their own perceived unworthiness) to be "left" alone; on the other hand, they are prone to depend only on their own abilities when faced with difficulties (compulsive self-reliance) and therefore actively exclude the available help and companionship of other people.

Indeed, one might say that, for the depression-prone individual, the positive aspects of reality can be identified precisely in their inaccessibility, whereas the positive aspects of self can be identified in his or her continuous effort to try to adapt, at least in part, to this inaccessibility. As a consequence, when certain goals are "unexpectedly" achieved, often their positivity abruptly changes into negativity, as if they, too, must necessarily turn out to be of little worth since they belong to a person of so little value. The depressed person's dilemma is indeed well expressed by Groucho Marx's famous remark "I wouldn't belong to a club that wanted me as one of its members."

Thus a narrow-margin equilibrium is established, which is based on the continuous personal effort to attempt to reduce exclusion from reality, which, however, is expected as ultimately inevitable. This balance is destined to become precarious if it is exposed to a series of situations (bereavement, losses, detachment, etc.) that make unuseful the personal abilities upon which these individuals have previously founded their striving against expected loneliness and their compensation for the deeply perceived unworthiness, with the consequent onset of clinical symptomatology (see Chapter 9 for a thorough discussion).

EATING DISORDERS

The typical family environment of most individuals who develop eating disorders is characterized by a disguised, contradictory communication. The members of the family, particularly the parents, have a distinct tendency to conceal problems and difficulties, avoiding all clear and definite expressions of individual emotions and points of view.

From this communicative context, a rather ambiguous and indefinite attachment style emerges, which has the main effect of preventing the child from recognizing his or her own feelings as personal features.

In fact, in these communicative contexts, the thoughts and emotions that the child experiences are constantly redefined until he or she is able to conform to the general family pattern, excluding definite expressions of personal emotions and opinions (see Chapter 2 for a discussion of more subtle patterns of disguised communication, such as those proposed by Bowlby, 1979). Within an attachment relationship regulated by a disguised communication, the child is not able to structure an authentic sense of distinguished individuality. Thus the self-image drawn from the relational context is vague and indefinite, that is, that of a person who is scarcely able to express his or her own thoughts and emotions and who is capable of defining them only within a relationship that allows the person to infer what is permissible to feel and think.

Especially after early infancy, the child tends to prefer, as an attachment figure, the family member who is least prone to the formless communicative stereotype that characterizes the family's interaction. Generally this figure is the father, who seems to be the only one able to furnish recognition and confirmation of the child's emotions and opinions. Nevertheless, at least in the circumstances where a clinical case develops, this preferential attachment encounters intense disappointment during childhood or adolescence, when the child, after a wide variety of occasional circumstances, discovers that the father's way of doing things and of communicating is only a camouflage for insecurity or ambiguity, similar to that of other members of the family.

From this attachment style, marked by lack of recognition and/or disappointments, children extract a self-image where their own personal worth and lovableness are vague and indefinite. On the other hand, during the course of childhood, they have been able to attain (through the relationship with the father) a possible trace on how to settle this problem: A stable, loving relationship where possibilities of delusion are excluded make it possible to attain a satisfactory identity.

From this indeterminate and/or vague self-image, these individuals structure a rather rigid attitude toward themselves, centered primarily on a continuous monitoring and evaluation of their own value and lovableness, which always keeps wavering since they do not possess precise standards of reference. The attitude toward reality (which is considered disconfirming by nature) is instead defined by the constitution of behavioral patterns with which they accurately avoid exposing themselves by revealing their own emotions and opinions in interpersonal relationships. The only pattern of self-exposure that they consider feasible is related to rather impersonal contexts, in which disconfirmation and redefinition of one's thoughts are unlikely, such as in school. The scholastic performance of these children, as is well known, is usually rather good.

Finally, if in this way these children succeed in reducing further possible disconfirmations that would represent a kind of "attack" on their own identity, which is already felt as wavering and indefinite, they are, on the other hand, still looking for a relationship endowed with suitable guarantees, through which they can succeed in clearly defining their own value and lovableness. The dilemma is the following: To establish such a "saving" relationship, it is necessary to expose oneself; on the other hand, exposing oneself inevitably entails the risk of disappointment, which would make the self-image become still more vague and wavering.

Thus an equilibrium may be obtained through the development of relational strategies aimed at obtaining the maximum possible guarantees while avoiding, as much as possible, commitment and self-exposure in the relationship. This compromise is usually set out of balance in adolescence or early youth, when it is easy to encounter situations (disappointments in affective relationships, teasing from peers, etc.) where the expected "disconfirming" nature of reality seems to be unquestionably "proved." It is at this point that the onset of clinical manifestations becomes very probable (see Chapter 12 for a thorough discussion).

OBSESSIVE-COMPULSIVE PATTERNS

These situations are marked by a peculiar characteristic: The course of attachment is such that it supplies the child with two distinct and opposite interpretations of both self and reality, which in every moment appear equally as plausible.

The most typical example is the situation where a parent is attentive, thoughtful, and totally dedicated to the child's moral and social education, without expressing his or her love with a caress or other affective display. Two possible realities are presented to the child: On the one hand, the parent effectively dedicates himself or herself to the child, which would favor the hypothesis of an exclusive and total affection, but on the other hand, the lack of verbal and nonverbal manifestations of love makes the parent's affective indifference just as plausible. In simple terms, the interpretations "he loves me" or "he is indifferent toward me" both have evidence in their favor and are equally helpful in explaining the same experience. The *simultaneousness* of two conflicting aspects in the parent's behavior—which correspond to the two reciprocally opposite interpretations on the child's part—seems an important prerequisite for the "obsessive" cognitive organization. As an example of such simultaneousness, imagine a father who, while talking to his child about parental love as being one of the most important realities in the world, has a rigid and amimical face and does not express any emotional connotation in support of what he is saying.

An intrinsically contradictory attachment pattern such as the one described here, if prolonged, determines the constitution of a self-image where two antithetical aspects are present. In other words, the child has evidence in favor of both self-lovableness and unlovableness, high and low personal worth, and so forth, and these opposite aspects can equally explain the same experiences. Furthermore, this conflicting self-image is found in a reality that also frequently presents itself with simultaneous opposite aspects.

In such a situation, the achievement of a unitary, noncontradictory image of self and the surrounding reality may easily become the main goal to be pursued. For this purpose, a rather rigid attitude toward oneself is structured, which centers around the idea of one's conforming to precise moral rules. Indeed, the origin of scrupulousness and perfectionism can be identified in the attempt to reach a defined unity of self through a "spotless" and unconditioned adherence to formal rules: "Intrinsically" valued moral canons become a guide to the elimination (or control) of the "wicked" part of self and the fostering of the "positive" part. The simultaneous presence of reality's opposite aspects makes "systematic doubt" the preferential method of approaching problems; thus an attitude toward reality is structured that is centered on an endless search for certainty and order, through repeated hesitations and doubts.

The paradox is evident: The highly valued "certainty" for which the individual so relentlessly strives leads to doubt about everything. The attempt to settle this dilemma leads to an unstable balance, where, before being able to make a decision, it is necessary to have meticulously excluded every possible error. Therefore it is not surprising how all the emotionally charged situations in which it is difficult to discriminate (according to the individual's standards) between "negative" and "positive" choices may jeopardize such a precarious balance (see Chapter 11 for a thorough discussion).

PRECIPITATING EVENTS LIKELY TO ELICIT
COGNITIVE DYSFUNCTION

As a conclusion to these etiological notes, we would like to emphasize the general conditions—stressful or precipitating events—that, in clinical observation, seem likely to elicit a cognitive dysfunction.

The first stressful event is adolescence, an extremely delicate developmental period, given the complex set of actual and required changes taking place during it. With sexual maturation and the onset of logical–conceptual thinking, there is a drive toward detachment from the family and toward the constitution of an independent relationship with reality. However, the possible distorted and/or negative self-images constituted on the basis of family attachment styles can make problematic the definition of an enduring commitment to oneself (see Chapter 3) and, consequently, the structuring of a satisfactory personal identity. This makes critical the attitude toward reality, exactly in the moment when the need for autonomy and independence is felt more strongly. In this way the "debut in life" can coincide with the onset of more or less important maladaptations to the environment.

Other important stressful events that can occur throughout life independently of the developmental phases are the making and the breaking of affectional bonds (Bowlby, 1977a). One can understand how these situations may come to represent precipitating factors for a variety of psychological disturbances, on the basis of at least two considerations:

1. Even though varying in quality and quantity from infancy to adulthood, attachment toward significant others remains one of the more important elements in regulating the course of an individual's life. As Bowlby (1977a) emphasizes, "While especially evident during early childhood, attachment behavior is held to characterize human beings from the cradle to the grave" (p. 203). Consequently, it is possible that, during the formation and/or breaking off of affective bonds, those misconceptions of self which originated from distorted attachment styles in the family and to which the individual has since found apparently stable and satisfying solutions can be "reactivated."

2. The making and breaking of an affective relationship implies, obviously, some modification of the "environmental niche" in

which the individual was living. The ensuing new experiences may be difficult to assimilate or integrate into the already-structured cognitive organization, especially if the attitude toward oneself has remained rigid and defensive. This makes more precarious the equilibrium maintained up until then.

We do not want in any way to generalize for these situations the factors that set off clinical disturbances in predisposed individuals. The complexity of the human organism and the variability of its environmental interactions do not permit linear schematizations. On the contrary, we only wish to call attention to the precipitating events that are more frequently encountered in the "neurotic" population usually treated with psychotherapy, without excluding the existence of other possible determinants that experience and clinical research can document.

NOTE

1. The concept of cognitive dysfunction does not refer to an "absolute" entity, but rather to something that is relative to the historical and social context; in particular, the codes that the specific cultural matrix provides to the individual for interpreting his or her own emotional distress are obviously important in this respect. The individual's "psychological" dimension can be considered as one of the constituents of Western culture, which has by now become part of the very construction of social reality. The same is not true for other cultures. As Berger and Luckmann (1966) have pointed out, within a culture that describes wide domains of social reality as being based on the mysterious game of extrahuman hidden forces, individuals will be inclined toward reconstructing their own personal crises in terms of "demonic possession" or "evil spirits' revenge." Western culture, however, describes an entire set of conceptual instruments (anxiety, neurosis, etc.) that allow its members to define their own and other people's life crises in terms of psychological disturbances or "illnesses."

It should be kept in mind that all the theories (including those that come from the social–cultural context) determine to a large extent the very forms that experience assumes; that is why both feeling evil spirits and noticing the onset of obscure illnesses will have the characteristics of a "real" experience for the individual. Both phenomena belong contemporaneously and in a corresponding way to the individual's subjective reality and to the "objective" reality of the specific social context. Precisely because of this correspondence such phenomena acquire all those attributes that define them as "real."

PART TWO

GENERAL IMPLICATIONS
FOR PSYCHOTHERAPY

6

THE NATURE OF THE
THERAPEUTIC RELATIONSHIP

From a cognitive point of view, any lasting interpersonal relationship could be seen as a matching process between two theories concerning the self and the world. In cognitive psychotherapy the therapeutic relationship is aimed explicitly at a change of those aspects of the patient's self-knowledge that are creating unnecessary suffering. The clear-cut definition of this aim and the corresponding attribution of roles give the therapeutic relationship its unique nature.

In other interpersonal, nonparental relationships, the main purpose of mutual selection is to cooperate, to cultivate friendly or loving feelings, to attain sexual satisfaction or mutual company as a defense against loneliness, to attain an economic gain, or to acquire new knowledge. The unavoidable comparison between the different theories of the self and the world is a secondary aspect, almost an epiphenomenon, if compared with these primary purposes. Complementary or similar personal visions of the world could have determined the mutual choice. A negative or too painful comparison between these different theories could cause a breakup of the relationship itself; such a comparison could bring some important changes in the self-knowledge of either one or both of the people involved. In any case these choices and changes are quite incidental. In the therapeutic relationship, however, they become the aim of the participants' mutual selection, and, moreover, the change is explicitly requested for only one of them.

This clear therapeutic contract, of course, does not prevent the development within the relationship of phenomena different from the cognitive change (even if related to it). Feelings of competition, attraction, protection, refusal, or love can be aroused quite easily and intensively within the therapeutic relationship. However, the therapeutic contract allows the participants to use these feelings to reach, through their analysis, the desired cognitive change. Presumably, within the patient's cognitive organization, the ability to recognize the personal value and meaning of the feelings emerging in the therapeutic relationship is the most significant achievement of the psychotherapist's job. Both the assessment and the therapeutic interventions will have to take into account these emotional and behavioral aspects of the relationship.

To the psychotherapist trainee facing the emotional aspects of a relationship psychoanalysis can offer its theoretical bases: the well-known "transference" and "countertransference" concepts. What can structural cognitive therapy offer in this respect? To begin, it can offer knowledge of the cognitive organization underlying the most frequently occurring psychiatric syndromes.

KNOWLEDGE OF SYNDROMIC ORGANIZATION AND SHAPING OF THE THERAPEUTIC RELATIONSHIP

If the therapist knows the fundamental elements of the cognitive structure that usually accompanies the pattern of disturbed behavior and emotion presented by a patient as the object of change, he or she can behave, from the beginning, in a manner that will build a relationship that is as effective as possible for that particular patient.

If—as we shall see in the third part of this book—the therapist knows in advance that a female patient, for example, suffers from an eating disorder probably due to the idea that other people are intruding upon her and will probably end up by disappointing her, he will avoid asking too many pressing questions about the patient's feelings and thoughts, prematurely giving her casual explanations (or "interpretations") about her disturbances, showing too much confidence in the therapy, or showing himself to be too self-confident. Then the relationship will neither confirm the patient's expectations of the therapist's intruding upon her personal feelings nor encourage the patient's tendency to expect too much and inevitably be disappointed. In other words, the therapist will be able to build up a relationship *that respects the patient's personal identity for as long as possible and that, at the same time, does not confirm the basic pathogenetic assumptions.*

Similarly, the therapist will at first have to respect the fundamental cognitive structures of personal identity in an agoraphobic patient (by leaving him or her a wide margin of control in the relationship), in an obsessive patient (by acknowledging the abstract importance of the "absolute" and "perfect" results, but emphasizing the bigger importance of *practical*, though limited, results), or in a depressive patient (by admitting the advantages of his or her thinking in terms of effort economy). For a fuller discussion of the way of building with the patient, from the very beginning, a relationship that takes into account his or her syndromic organization, see the sections on therapeutic strategy in Chapters 9–12.[1]

When we started the clinical research whose results are presented in this book, we did not have any knowledge about the cognitive organizations related to the different psychiatric syndromes; such knowledge is in fact the main result of our research. Trying to find the best way to establish a therapeutic relationship, we had to proceed through trial and error. Therefore we decided not to introduce into the relationship with the patient any instrument of assessment that could interfere with the initial evaluation of the efficacy of our attempts to establish a relationship respectful of the patient's personal identity. Often, patients who take psychometric tests or who are rated on scales feel that they are "being treated like objects" or "considered like so many guinea pigs." Patients frequently verbalize these opinions by saying, "Doctor, you are more interested in your research than you are in me as a human being" (see Beck *et al.*, 1979).

The introduction of an additional variable, such as a proposed psychometric test, in the early stage of the psychotherapeutic relationship could therefore have hampered our clinical research in achieving its initial purpose, namely, to gather raw data on the kind of relationship that it was preferable to establish in each case of psychiatric syndrome. For this reason we are not yet able to supply precise correlational data to support some of our clinical observations (see Note 1 to Chapter 7). However, it is obvious that these observations lead to testable hypotheses; such testing is currently in progress in our clinical research program.[2]

Another opinion quite similar to ours has recently been suggested by Bowlby (1977b) in an article very meaningful to all psychotherapists. Instead of our notion of syndromic cognitive organization, Bowlby proposes "that any clinician undertaking this kind of work should have at his disposal an extensive knowledge of deviant patterns of attachment and caregiving behavior and of the pathogenic family experiences believed commonly to contribute to them" (p. 422). Without this knowledge, the therapist can hardly avoid establishing a relationship that either will prove to be unnecessarily painful to the patient (e.g., being prematurely forced to give information that he or she does not yet feel like giving) or will provide misleading and incomplete information. As we shall see in Part Three, Bowlby's "knowledge of deviant patterns of attachment" and our own "knowledge of the cognitive organization underlying psychiatric syndromes" have many elements in common. Here we only need to emphasize that, in Bowlby's perspective as well as in ours, the shaping of an appropriate therapeutic relationship is the first step toward making the assessment reliable and the therapy effective (unless one wants to limit one's objective to the kind of therapeutic changes that Arnkoff, 1980, has described as "shifts in the superficial cognitive structures").

Before fully discussing the relevance of the therapeutic relationship to assessment and the therapeutic process, let us now consider another qualifying aspect of the patient–therapist relationship in cognitive therapy: the deliberately constructed atmosphere of co-operation.

THERAPEUTIC COOPERATION

As soon as possible in the early phase of psychotherapy, the therapist should present a thorough rationale for the use of cognitive modification techniques. The fundamental aspect of such a presentation is the therapist's ability to couch it in terms adequate to the patient's level of sophistication and to his or her idiosyncratic use of language—particularly of psychological and medical terms. Some inklings of the very different meanings that patients attribute to the same illness or to the same medical term (e.g., "heartburn," "palpitation," "stomach," "good appetite," etc.) can be found in sociological studies such as those by Boyle (1975) and Zola (1975).

As long as the therapist succeeds in using as much as possible the patient's own language and formulating a therapeutic contract that respects the patient's deep cognitive structures (personal identity), the contextual ground is safe for a noncontradictory, explicit definition of the therapeutic relationship as one based largely upon cooperation. As Bedrosian and Beck (1980) remark, "By regarding the patient as a collaborator, the therapist conveys respect and gains valuable assistance. . . . The presentation of therapy in a mysterious light induces dependency by implying that the patient lacks the ability to understand completely and participate in the therapy" (p. 135). In other words, use of the patient's language allows the therapist not to assume the role of a teacher with a pupil, improves communication, and permits the therapist to explain, in terms that are not too didactic, the principles on which the therapy is based. Once therapists have explicitly appointed patients as collaborators, patients do not feel diminished in self-esteem and feel they are keeping control of the relationship; thus they are discouraged from seeing themselves as totally weak and in need of protection in front of the "omniscient" therapist.

This policy also prevents many hidden competitive and resentful feelings and many artful tactics of the patient to check the therapist's "omniscience" and "omnipotence." It is probably for this reason that the "resistance" phenomenon is so remarkably uncommon in cognitive therapy as compared to psychodynamic therapies. If a cooperative relationship exists, the patient does not feel the need to "counter-control," and the therapist can plainly accept to consider any disagreement, noncompliance, or irritation on the patient's part not as a form of "resistance," but as a source of information on the patient's way of perceiving or construing the therapist's feelings and behavior.

Finally, the therapeutic cooperation is consistent with the idea that therapists' work is similar to scientific debate or research. It has been repeatedly maintained that therapists' adherence to their theoretical models and their confidence in the models validity are an important factor for a positive outcome of treatment (see Frank, 1974). Consequently, if therapists respect Kelly's analogy of the therapist and the patient as "personal scientists" (Kelly, 1955), they will be inclined to think of themselves and their patients as cooperating in an exploration, a research, and a modification. Furthermore, this theoretical model prevents "scientist methodolatry," a mistake against which Weimer (1980) has so persuasively argued.

If one really sticks to the scientist metaphor in his or her diagnostic and psychotherapeutic work, one cannot help but acknowledge that science is much more an admission of ignorance than a pretense of absolute and certain knowledge. As Goethe said, "Gray, my dear friend, is every theory, and green is the golden tree of life."

THE THERAPEUTIC RELATIONSHIP AND THE ASSESSMENT PROCEDURES

If therapists succeed in proving to their patients their general attitude —that they are recognizing and respecting patients' personal identity —and are willing to work with them to obtain the change that *the patient* would find desirable, then the therapeutic relationship becomes a *secure base for exploration*. The therapist and the patient meet in a favorable atmosphere to explore the patient's behavior, cognitions, feelings, and past and present relationships. Even the actual ongoing relationship between patient and therapist becomes a possible object of exploration.

Therefore various aspects of the assessment depend heavily on the probity of the therapeutic relationship. The most important aspects are as follows:

1. Within a relaxed secure relationship, free from mutual judgments, patients feel free to express their emotions directly through nonverbal behavior. Thus, in addition to the actual declarations of patients, the therapist may become aware of the importance and meaning that they attribute to the subject examined.

2. In a cooperative atmosphere, patients may be directly, or better yet indirectly, encouraged to use their own jargon, or habitual idiosyncratic language. The importance of giving consideration to patients' idiosyncratic expressions both for assessment and for the therapy cannot be overemphasized. It is an important part of the therapist's job to study and go into patients' personal jargon: This will avoid basic misunderstandings of the meaning of a term and will permit the therapist to choose metaphors appropriate to each patient's use of the language whenever the therapist wants to convey new information that may prove difficult to explain without a technical jargon.

3. The amount of personal information that patients might wish to cancel or falsify is obviously reduced in an under-

standing and nonjudging relationship. One has to be careful, however, because patients could avoid giving some information about themselves that they consider strongly negative and apt to cause the special relationship that they have established with the therapist to deteriorate.

4. The way in which patients strive to direct, maintain, or preserve their relationship with the therapist is a most valuable source of data for the assessment of their cognitive structures. The therapist should be keenly alert to the ways in which patients are construing his or her feelings and behaviors, to the predictions patients make about the outcome of the therapeutic relationship, and to the actions they take as a result of these predictions. Particularly relevant is the use of interruptions in the course of treatment (e.g., for vacations) in order to observe how patients construe a separation and respond to it. All these data, which can be gathered only as a direct function of the therapeutic relationship, allow us to ascertain what the representational models of attachment figures are like in patients. Data from the assessment procedures concerning other meaningful past and present relationships can be subsequently matched with this reconstruction of the representational models of attachment and separation; thus the way is open to a therapeutic restructuring of them.

5. Cognitive therapy is a "directive" form of psychological treatment. The therapist's directivity does not mean, however, that he or she is disregarding the cues and feedbacks that patients are giving as a response to the assessment and therapy processes. The therapist's role is an active one, but, in order to be effective,

He must recognize that he cannot go faster than his patient, and that by calling attention to painful topics too insistently he will arouse his patient's fear and earn his anger or deep resentment. Finally, he must never forget that, plausible—even convincing—though his own surmises may seem to him, compared to the patient he is ill-placed to know the facts. (Bowlby, 1977b, p. 426)

Thus the therapist does have a directive role in the therapeutic relationship, but this directivity is based upon patients' proposals of their own meaningful life problems and upon responses to, and appraisal of, the therapeutic work.

THE THERAPEUTIC RELATIONSHIP AND THERAPEUTIC INTERVENTIONS

Much of what has been said about the relevance of the therapeutic relationship to assessing the patient's behavior, emotion, and cognitions also applies to the selection and timing of therapeutic maneuvers aimed at changing them.

Studies on the relevance of the relationship to the outcome of the therapeutic intervention have basically tried to define which aspects of the therapist's behavior and personality—for example, Rogers's empathy, genuineness, and warmth (Truax, Frank, & Imber, 1966)—could be positively related to the therapeutic success (see also Truax & Carkhuff, 1967; Truax & Mitchell, 1971). However, it is still a controversial and debated question.[3] Besides the difficulty of reaching a univocal definition of "empathy" (ten therapists can be "empathic" in ten different ways), the variables that actually determine the good results of psychotherapy could concern the relationship's very quality and development. In itself, the fact that the relationship is meaningful to the patient could influence, more than anything else, the efficacy and incisiveness of the therapeutic process.[4] Surely this does not imply that the role of the therapist's personality and his or her skill and experience are irrelevant, but rather it suggests an alternative, in a way a more dynamic point of view on the basis of which the therapist can determine the most appropriate ways and times to start the intervention.

According to this point of view, in order to introduce an effective intervention within the ongoing relationship, the intervention itself will have to be planned and carried out in consideration of two basic factors:

1. The patient's representational models of change inferred from anamnestic and relational data. It is a commonly observed fact that, whereas some persons see a "change" only as a quick turning point in their lives (and therefore once they have assumed this idea, they are ready to do many things in relatively short times), others see it as something that develops slowly and progressively. Keeping these circumstances in mind may help to preserve the quality of the relationship and to avoid useless struggle between the therapist and the patient.

2. The development of the therapeutic relationship. If a satisfying "therapeutic contract" has not yet been obtained, it is
not convenient to start a process that requires from the
patient effort and confidence in the therapist (see, e.g., in
Chapter 11, the "rituals control" in the obsessive neurosis).

We can perhaps summarize the preceding considerations on the
timing of therapeutic operations according to the development of the
therapeutic relationship by reporting the general rule: Each new
piece of information must be accepted by the old, preexisting cognitive
structures. This point is discussed at length in Chapter 8 (p. 161).
Here we merely report some other reflections on the importance of
the nature of the therapeutic relationship to the possibility of changing
the patient's cognitive structures.

First, was we already mentioned, the therapeutic relationship is,
by explicit agreement, one that allows open discussion of patients'
ways of construing the therapist's feelings and behavior, their own
reactions to separation from the therapist, their verbal and nonverbal
behavior aimed at controlling the therapeutic relationship (seductive-
ness, resentment, request for protection, etc.), and so forth. This
possibility—a unique feature of the therapeutic relationship—allows
the open identification of the representational models of attachment
figures and of themselves that preside over patients' perceptions,
predictions, and actions. This explicitness, in turn, is the first step
toward ascertaining how those models may have developed during
the early phases of the patient's life up to adolescence. Patients may
thus be led to recognize that what is happening is, at least in part, a
repetition of their childhood relationships and, as a consequence, they
may be helped to modify their behavior and cognitions in the light of
more recent experiences and of reason. This is the cognitive therapy
counterpart of the Freudian "analysis of transference." The important
difference is that behavior and cognition, not motivation and (sexual)
drives, are the targets for analysis and change: Conscious and "pre-
conscious" notions are held as more relevant than hypothetical unconscious processes. Using the scientist metaphor again, the *causal
theories* of the patient are identified, brought into the open, and
explicitly verbalized together with their behavioral effects; their
"proofs" (childhood experiences) are recognized; the episodical nature
of these proofs is acknowledged and emphasized; and a *new theory* is
developed according to the results of carefully planned new inter-

personal *experiments*, the most important of which is the therapeutic relationship.[5]

Another important aspect of the therapeutic relationship stems from the therapist's awareness of his or her being a model for the patient's vicarious learning. Sometimes this awareness is explicitly transformed in the planning of a therapeutic technique—consider, for instance, role playing during assertiveness training or the modeling procedure for exposing phobic and obsessive–compulsive patients to fear stimuli (Bandura, 1971; Martin & Pear, 1978; Rachman, 1972).

More frequently, the therapist presents himself or herself as a model, throughout treatment, of a scientist's basic attitude. Thus, both directly and indirectly, the therapist teaches the patient how to recognize one's causal theories and their implications, the way of proving and disproving them, the fallacy of causal circularity and dichotomous thinking, the possibility of creating self-fulfilling prophecies, the utility of planning experiments that could *disprove* one's own theories, and, above all, the possibility and desirability of fully and explicitly accepting life in a world of probabilities instead of pretending to live in a world of absolute certainties.

Within the therapeutic relationship, one could expect that a personal revolution, perhaps similar to Kuhn's scientific revolutions (see Mahoney, 1980), will eventually take place, at least in some patients. Revolutions are likely to be rather painful processes. They require the exploration of novel, exciting, and perhaps frightening areas. Such exploration can usually be performed only by departing from a secure base and knowing that one could easily return to that base. The therapeutic relationship is frequently the only secure base for the patient's exploration, and the patient could very well be willing to explore this base first, in order to test its security.

> A therapist should, so far as he can, meet the patient's desire for a secure base, while recognizing . . . that he should enter into the patient's exploration as a companion ready either to take the lead or to be led; and that he should be willing to discuss a patient's perceptions of him and the degree to which they may or may not be appropriate, which is sometimes not easy to determine; and finally that he should not pretend otherwise should he become anxious about a patient or irritated by him. (Bowlby, 1977b, p. 427)

Again using Bowlby's words:

> Clearly, to do this work requires of the therapist not only a good grasp of principles but also a capacity for empathy and for tolerating intense

and painful emotion. Those with a strongly organized tendency towards compulsive self-reliance are ill-suited to undertake it and are well advised not to. (Bowlby, 1977b, p. 427)

Finally, a therapeutic relationship comes to an end. The patient has to leave the secure base, whatever his or her future explorations may be. Separation is a painful process. "Shall I succeed in coping with my problems without your help, Doctor?"; "I think I have fallen in love with you, Doctor"; "Why do you want to get rid of me, Doctor? I believe that you don't like me." Perhaps every therapist has heard these protests and remarks from frightened patients when the treatment is approaching its end. To discuss them in light of the already-reconstructed cognitive organization is often the final step of the therapy process. When the patient recognizes how his or her doubts, feelings of rejection, and love requests originate from the old attitude toward oneself and toward reality, the time has come to say "farewell."

NOTES

1. By the way, we can see that in this way the therapist uses the knowledge gained during clinical research and psychological and psychiatric experimentation. To underestimate the value of the syndromic approach means, in any psychotherapy, starting all over again and overlooking what the experience of others can teach us. The psychotherapeutic relationship would then be based on intuitions that the therapist had on the spur of the moment during initial meetings with the patient or would be led by general and vague rules (empathy, confidence, and so forth), as if the patients did not show, with the existence of *particular* disturbances, the need of *particular* rules. Moreover, this active attitude on the therapist's part is not to be considered Machiavellian. The therapist is honestly led to assume it by his or her knowledge of the patient's particular syndrome and by the awareness that the aim is to change the deep rules from which the syndrome itself originates.

2. As shall be seen in the chapters on the individual clinical syndromes, we have tried to avoid this limitation by referring to as many data as possible from other authors' correlational and statistical studies that could support our clinical observations. At present, after completing the clinical research whose results—the definition of some cognitive organizations relating to precise psychiatric syndromes—are described in Part Three of this book, our group has undertaken a first series of correlational and statistical studies. In fact, we believe we can now pinpoint the effects of psychometric tests on a patient within the known general scheme of the cognitive organization peculiar to the syndrome from which the patient suffers.

3. For a review of criticism of both Rogers's view of empathy, warmth, and genuineness as necessary and *sufficient* conditions for an effective therapy and of Truax and co-workers' studies related to this topic, see Rachman (1971a, Chapter 7) and Bergin and Suinn (1975).

4. Other considerations somewhat compatible with this hypothesis have been expressed by, among others, Cooper (1963) and Meyer and Gelder (1963). These authors, examining the results of behavior therapy and also considering the measure of success that can be obtained by other forms of treatment, have argued that one of the causes of the therapeutic improvement could be attributed to the patient–therapist relationship that develops during the course of the treatment. The relationship's effects seemed to be particularly significant in the more complex and long-lasting disorders.

5. When this point in the psychotherapeutic process is reached, the patient–therapist relationship usually must change. The patient shows intense and even painful emotions corresponding to the beginning of a change in deep rules, which preside over his or her behavior and ongoing cognitions. The patient could experience a feeling of unreality. We could say that, during this phase of the treatment, the patient's personal identity begins to change. In the same way also, the therapeutic relationship, which at first had been meant to respect the cognitive structures of the patient's personal identity, has to change. It is usually necessary that, during this period, the therapist give the patient, within the relationship, a rational and emotional base (see the concluding paragraph to this chapter).

7

ASSESSMENT OF
COGNITIVE STRUCTURES

Men are not altogether rational: Therefore, real history is less
rational than its reconstruction—I. Lakatos*

The assessment procedure in cognitive psychotherapy is an ongoing
process, which, during the whole period of treatment, merges with
change-producing procedures. In the preceding chapter we emphasized how assessment takes place within the context of a meaningful
interpersonal relationship. In the following chapter we shall go
further into the obvious truth that Meichenbaum expressed in a
lapidary exclamation: "Assessment and change are interdependent!"
(Meichenbaum, 1977, p. 259).

In this chapter we shall begin by considering three points implied
by Lakatos's quotation above: The assessment of cognitive structures
is mainly a reconstruction; it has a strong historical character; it is
probably much more "rational" than the real story. How the assessment can be practically performed during a process of cognitive
psychotherapy is the subject of the last section.

THE ASSESSMENT OF COGNITIVE STRUCTURES AS
A PROCESS OF RECONSTRUCTION

Nisbett and Wilson (1977) have gathered in a brilliant review a host
of experimental, anecdotal, and theoretical information all pointing
in the same direction: "The analysis of situations and the appraisal of

*Retranslated from Italian.

the environment . . . goes on mainly at nonconscious level," as Mandler, quoted by Nisbett and Wilson (p. 232), puts it.

What Nisbett and Wilson succeeded in demonstrating is that people are largely unaware of the ongoing cognitive processes that are taking place in their minds while they are solving problems, reducing cognitive dissonance, drawing inferences, attributing causality to events, ascertaining the effects of stimuli on responses, and so forth. Their results are in accordance with the notion, widely held among cognitive theorists, that "it is the *result* of thinking, not the process of thinking, that appears spontaneously in consciousness" (G. A. Miller, quoted by Nisbett & Wilson, 1977, p. 232).

Still, if required, people do make verbal reports concerning their own cognitive processes. Nisbett and his co-workers succeeded in showing, through proper manipulation of experimental variables, how inaccurate these verbal reports actually are with respect to the real cognitive process that, considering the particular experimental situation, should have taken place (Nisbett & Bellows, 1977; Nisbett & Wilson, 1977). Even the rare accurate reports in Nisbett's studies did not provide any evidence of introspective awareness of the cognitive inner changes or of the effects of stimuli on responses. What, then, is the meaning of people's verbal reports about their own cognitive processes? Well, they are the expression of their theories (appearing as the *content* of their consciousness) about their own cognitive processes. People do not have direct access to the higher order of rules governing their own behavior, emotion, memory, problem solving, and so forth, but they usually do have theories about these "deep" rules.

Let us summarize, then, what therapists can assess when observing, interviewing, and testing a patient.

1. Therapists can assess the patient's behavior and the environmental antecedents and consequences of it. Through direct observation manipulation of environmental stimuli, psychophysiological measures, and appropriate questions, they can evaluate the patient's ability to remember and to observe his or her own reactions. This is, of course, the classic functional analysis of behavior. Direct analysis of interpersonal behavior (see, e.g., Meichenbaum, 1977, pp. 249–250) also falls into this category of assessment procedure.

2. Therapists, appealing to the patient's ability for introspection, can also assess a great amount of data to which only the patient has

direct access, that is, data constituting the patient's private knowledge. Personal emotions, dreams, evaluations and plans, Beck's "automatic thoughts" (whether in the pictorial or verbal mode of inner representation), the focus of attention and the current sensations, and a multitude of personal historical facts are all aspects of the patient's private knowledge.

Many of these data appear in the stream of consciousness as intermediate results of a series of nonconscious mental operations, and the *sequential* assessment is important in reconstructing the kind of information processing that is taking place (e.g., polarized thinking, arbitrary inferences). Meichenbaum (1977, Chapter 9) has proposed the term "functional–cognitive analysis" for this kind of assessment procedure, which is best performed through skilled clinical interviewing, but which can also make use of other tools, including guided imagery (see Singer, 1972, for some hints), TAT-like approaches (Meichenbaum, 1977, p. 255), grid–repertory methods after Kelly (see, e.g., Rowe, 1978), rating scales (see, e.g., Beck, 1967; Beck *et al.*, 1979), and a number of other psychometric tests.[1] In assessing data pertaining to the patient's private knowledge through clinical interviews, we should pay attention to both the verbal and the nonverbal aspects of communication and to both verbal *content* and general *theme* of the conversation. Mahoney (1980) has rightly called attention to the fallacies of a too strict adherence to the idea of a rigorous isomorphism between words and beliefs. Quoting Kelly, Mahoney reminds us that a patient can abruptly change the content of his or her speech, but rarely changes the theme so easily; the observation of a change in content while the theme is still the same may be an important clue to identifying the patient's cognitive structures, since evidently the same structure joins, in the patient's mind, the different "contents."

3. Finally, therapists can assess what Nisbett and Wilson (1977) have described as "a priori, implicit causal theories," that is, judgments about the extent to which a particular stimulus is a plausible cause of a given response. The best way of performing such an assessment is to ask the patient questions such as "Why did you react that way to that situation?" and "What do you believe was the cause of such a behavior?" (or feeling, thinking, etc.). When the patient is led to speak about these kinds of causal theories, he not only "says more than he can know" (as Nisbett and Wilson stated), but also is

describing the most significant aspect of his cognitive organization, the one that usually prevents him from changing in spite of his neurotic suffering. At this point in our analysis, we are at the very core of Freud's "neurotic paradox." If, for instance, patients causally connect an emotional acceleration of heartbeats to a hypothetical somatic illness, they show that they have an incorrect theory of emotions (and of the way in which emotions can affect body functions) and at the same time that they are preventing themselves from acknowledging and solving their interpersonal problems, for example (which are "really" responsible for their emotionality and the consequent heartbeats).

It is the matching between the patient's and the therapist's causal theories that allows for the reconstruction of the patient's tacit deep rules. When actors and observers share the same causal theories, a covariation is perceived between stimuli and responses (Nisbett & Wilson, 1977, p. 256). Therefore the cognitive structure that connects stimuli and responses is not recognized as one among various possible truths, but as "the absolute truth." On the other hand, when actors and observers belong to subcultures that have different causal theories about the effects of a certain stimulus, a difference can be detected between the actors' reports about stimulus effects and the observers' predictions about possible reactions to that stimulus. If the observer belongs to the psychoanalytic subculture, for instance, he or she can detect that patients are reacting to a certain stimulus not according to "reality principles," but according to a complex chain of symbolic transformations, whereas the patients may very well maintain that they do not see those transformations at all and that they are following a very logical reasoning in giving their responses.

This fact clearly creates the deceiving problem of "who is right," the actor or the observer. Actors, having private access to the content of their own thinking, are in a favorable position to ascertain what stimuli they are paying attention to and what their intentions were. On the other hand, they can also be misled by their own meaning domain, so that they can attribute causal value to a stimulus that is relevant for them, but that does not really influence their present behavior. Observers may, then, be more accurate precisely because they disregard such relevant, but nondetermining, stimuli. In any case the question of "who is right" is not the central one in the assessment process. Much more important is the possibility, offered by the psychotherapeutic relationship, to match two different causal theories and to reconstruct, out of this matching, the deep rules of patient's tacit self-knowledge.

As human beings, therapists are not altogether rational, and therefore need some degree of "certainty." We need to know whether our reconstruction of the patient's "deep rules" or "deep cognitive structures" (causal theories, basic assumptions, or irrational beliefs *plus* the tacit rules of transformation that lead to the content of the patient's thinking) is tenable, or if it is just a fancy application of our own causal theories, basic assumptions, or rational beliefs. We can satisfy our human need for certainty in the course of the assessment through two main categories of "proofs." The first is to ascertain to what extent our reconstruction of the patient's tacit self-knowledge and cognitive organization allows us to understand those aspects of the patient's behavior that the patient, with his or her own causal theories, is unable to explain. Intrusive images, compulsions, and even undersirable feelings fall into this class. The criteria of "economic value" and "internal consistency" are related to this first way of probing the validity of our reconstruction. The more of the patient's experiences that are accounted for by a logically consistent reconstruction of his or her cognitive organization, the more confident we may feel about its tenability. The second, more positive, category of proofs for our reconstruction is a careful consideration of the history of the patient's development, which gives the assessment procedure its historical character.

THE ASSESSMENT OF COGNITIVE STRUCTURE AS A HISTORICAL RESEARCH

Developmental analysis has been widely neglected by behavior therapists and, unfortunately, also by many cognitive therapists. The deplorable result is that one is frequently induced to think that the consideration of the developmental aspects of psychiatric syndromes is almost a trademark of the psychodynamic approach. This is a serious misbelief. The way in which people recollect their early experiences and the meaning they attribute to them constitute a gold mine for the cognitive therapist. Of course, the cognitive therapist is mainly interested in "conscious" recollections and in the nonconscious rules of transformation, which explain the fact that people frequently attribute different meanings to the same past event when they recollect it within different contexts.[2]

A cognitive outlook of a person's biography can also give a bird's-eye view of his or her "life theme" (see, e.g., Csikszentmihalyi & Beattie, 1979). Our patients' biographies would be simply impossible to describe, for them as well as for us, if life events followed each other randomly or if they were determined only by the forces of genetics and social environment. Our patients, however, are quite able to describe their main life events in an orderly and consistent way in usually no more than five or six sessions. And we are able to report their biographies briefly and meaningfully in our clinical accounts. This is because our patients (and we as well) have a cognitive representation of a set of problems, usually stemming from a fundamental source of stress during childhood, around which grow the multiform interpretations of reality and the ways of dealing with it. The biography is consistent because it moves from this center. Csikszentmihalyi and Beattie (1979) define the "life theme" as a hierarchical affective–cognitive system, composed of a central existential problem, surrounded by interpretations of its supposed causes and by strategies to be used for solving it.[3] As the reader may notice, this is not too far from our own description of the individual's knowledge organization, based on the metaphorical use of Lakatos's research program (see Chapter 3 and the sections on cognitive organization in Chapters 9–12).

Csikszentmihalyi and Beattie (1979) also suggest some guidelines for conducting the historical research needed to find out the individual's life theme. These, too, are not much different from the assessment procedure of personal historical facts that routinely takes place in the course of our cognitive therapy. Two main periods of personal development must be explored: (1) infancy, preschool years, and childhood and (2) adolescence and early youth.

1. Infancy, preschool years, and childhood. The recognition of major existential stress in the first period of life can be attained through the patient's own private knowledge or by inquiring from family sources. Bowlby's theory of attachment is of great use for the therapist's inquiry (see Chapter 1). It must be remembered that the social–familial idiosyncratic "coding" of events is often biased: "Facts" are valued more than attribution of meaning by parents and patients. The ways in which the patient has first acknowledged and labeled the problem originated by this existential stress are also very important topics of the therapist's questioning. The first causal explanations—couched in the egocentric, magical, dogmatic, or other way of thinking typical of the corresponding developmental phase (Flavell, 1963)—are also a possible source of potentially valuable information.

2. Adolescence and youth. During adolescence, the main personal existential problems—provided that the patient is not developing a schizophrenic psychosis—are usually formulated in a way that allows at least a partial solution. "Internal" or "external" control of the problem area is determined (or left, almost deliberately, vague; see the discussion of eating disorders in Chapter 12). Methods of solution are selected (fighting or ignoring difficulties, applying active resignation, withdrawing from other people, acquiring and using more or less "adaptive" skills, etc.). These data are usually easily recollected after a direct probe of the patient's memory. Of course, we have to be satisfied with hints and cues rather than expecting to obtain full accounts. For instance, agoraphobics will recall daydreams about voyages and freedom and promises that they made to themselves that they would "never submit to anybody" (see Chapter 10); obsessive–compulsive patients will recollect their scrupulosity at school and so forth.

Once we have gathered this historical information, we can match it with our reconstruction of the patient's faulty causal theories, basic assumptions, or irrational beliefs and with his or her ongoing inner representation. If the outcome of the match is correct, our need for partial certainty is satisfied, but—much more important—the patient has understood through what sort of experiences his or her particular view of self and reality has developed. The patient's causal theories are now partly changed, or more probably, partly questioned and therefore ready to be changed.

THE ASSESSMENT OF COGNITIVE STRUCTURES INSIDE THE PSYCHOTHERAPY PROCESS

Perhaps the most interesting aspect of cognitive psychotherapy is the therapist's attempt to constantly maintain a scientific behavior. In this way the therapist teaches the patient, directly or indirectly, to deal with his or her personal problems just like the scientist tries to find invariable rules in the relationships between natural phenomena.

The scientist's main concern is to discriminate, as much as possible, facts from theories. While assessing or attempting to remedy a patient's problems, the therapist also has to distinguish "facts" from "theories" and to start with a clear definition of the former. Therefore assessment (and therapy) starts with an accurate *functional analysis of the patient's problematic behavior.* Maladaptive behavior—in the majority of cases, maladaptive *avoidance* behavior[4]—is then selected as the first target for assessment. Patients learn to think in terms of environmental antecedents and consequences of their maladaptive behavior. Unpleasant emotions are analyzed much in the same way, that is, through a sequential and situational analysis.

At this point, the limitations of behavioral analysis are usually evident and may be pointed out to the patient, together with any verbalization of the time-honored basic principle of cognitive therapy: "It is not the things in themselves that trouble us, but the opinion we have of these things" (Epictetus). "Beauty is in the eye of the beholder" (popular proverb). "The human race is governed by imagination" (Napoleon I). "Men are never so good or so bad as their opinions" (Bentham). "If thy morals make thee dreary, depend upon it they are wrong" (R. L. Stevenson). "We invent for ourselves the major part of experience" (Nietzsche). "Elements are preordained by thoughts" (Buddhists' Dhammapada). Only by taking into account the results of one's thinking is it possible to understand the reasons for one's idiosyncratic behavior and emotional reactions to environmental events.

Thus a first important therapeutic step is taken,[5] and the basis for the subsequent *cognitive–functional analysis* is laid. In this second phase of assessment, we are still dealing with facts—facts to which only patients have direct access, facts pertaining to the realm of private knowledge, but still facts. Patients are taught to listen to their "internal dialogue," to recognize and register their "automatic thoughts," and to take into account daydreams and intrusive images as facts perceived within their own private stream of consciousness. There is a close link between this cognitive assessment and the previous behavioral assessment: We are now taking into consideration mainly the cognitions that precede, accompany, and follow the previously assessed problematic behavior and emotions.

While the therapist listens to the patients' reports of their own inner representations, he or she is usually able *to gather some hints of the patient's causal theories, basic assumptions, or irrational beliefs.*

In other words, it becomes clearer what kind of attitude patients maintain toward themselves and reality and in which ways they define their self-identity and cultivate (or debase) self-esteem. Broadly speaking, we may say that the main cues in this regard come from the therapist's careful attention to the way in which the patient conjugates five main verbs: to be, must, can, to need, and to be worth.[6] The manner in which these verbal forms—or their synonyms—follow the pronoun "I" leads to a reconstruction of the patient's self-identity and self-esteem; the manner in which they follow other pronouns ("you," "he," "they") leads to a reconstruction of the patient's attitude toward reality.[7]

For the first time since the assessment (and therapy) began, the therapist is not looking at facts, but at his or her reconstruction of the patient's cognitive structures. Of course this reconstruction is based on the patient's verbal report of his or her own causal theories (e.g., "I refused to accept my wife's offer *because* I thought that I *am* a despicable human being and do not *deserve* her goodness"), but still it is a reconstruction. As we said in the first section, therapists are well aware that they can recognize the patient's theories as such—and not as absolute truths—only because they have different causal theories. Their job is to make the patient well aware that his or her declarations concern nothing but *theories*, and not absolute truths. This is the whole point of the treatment. Moreover, the patient's causal theories with which we are now dealing are not abstract and impersonal, but, on the contrary, are the very rules that direct, maintain, and prevent from changing his or her disturbed behavior and emotions.

For all the preceding reasons, we cannot afford to make any fantastic, though picturesque, reconstructions. We "need" proof. So at this point, instead of directly confronting the patient with the irrationality of the causal theories—asking for proofs of them, challenging them, pointing out that they come from "primitive and faulty information processing," demonstrating their inconsistency, offering more rational alternative theories, and so forth—we usually move on to a *developmental analysis*.

So we are once more confronting facts. Again, only the patient (or his or her relatives) has direct access to these private facts, and it is well known how memories can be distorted by deceitful personal attitudes. However, the private and possibly distorted knowledge from which recollections of developmental facts come is the same one from which the patient's disturbances come. Therefore we must be

more concerned about the internal consistency among past events—
the way they have influenced the patient's life theme and his or
her present reconstructed causal theories—than about the objective
accuracy of the recollected facts. If this criterion of internal consistency
is satisfied, the patient can really take distance from his or her "causal
theories" and can see, together with the therapist, how the present
irrational beliefs developed.

The assessment of cognitive structures is now at an end. The
therapist is able to reconstruct the main elements of the whole
cognitive organization. Using the metaphor of Lakatos's research
program, he or she can consider what the tacit self-knowledge constituting the "metaphysical hardcore" should be like: emotional schemata
(Chapter 1) corresponding to the main existential stresses experienced
in infancy and childhood. "Stress," in this context, does not mean a
dramatic experience: Any continuous obstacle to the normal unfolding
and interplay of attachment and detachment is an important "existential stress" (see Bowlby, 1969, 1973; Chapters 2 and 5). For instance,
a prolonged hampering of spontaneous detachment and autonomous
exploration by an overprotective mother is surely a serious existential
stress, likely to lead to an agoraphobic development (see Chapter 10).
The impossibility of critically discussing this sort of stress during
childhood and adolescence is another major factor of distress (see
Bowlby, 1979; Chapter 2).

The recollection of historical facts—guided mainly by the attachment theory in our clinical work—is the way to assess the probable
metaphysical hard-core. Historical facts plus present verbalized causal
theories and assumptions concerning one's "being," "worth," and
"duties" allow a reconstruction of the "protective belt," that is, of the
theories and hypotheses concerning identity and self-esteem. In other
words, identity and self-esteem are constructed and maintained as an
articulate cognitive structure, which is initially derived from a consideration of the emotional schemata of the metaphysical nucleus
(supposed causes of the stresses, ways of coping practically with
them, consequent rules and expectations of oneself and of the responding reality, etc.) and later on in life prevents the full recognition
of the episodic value of those schemata. The bases of the indiviudal's
life theme are thus laid. This complex cognitive structure is assessed
through the positive match of the individual's own verbal report
about causal theories and basic assumptions against his recollection of

private historical facts. A negative match implies a failure in the assessment.

Patients' efforts to maintain identity and self-esteem, perpetuating, in a way, the original "looking-glass effect" (see Chapter 1), are the source of their attitude toward reality. Rules for the selection and assimilation of experiences, for the evaluation of life events, and for the solution of problems created by the ever-changing and challenging outside world are immediately evident in patients' verbal reports of their ongoing thoughts. Usually, thoughts appearing in the verbal mode of inner representation and in deliberate daydreaming reflect the solution of problems, the evaluation of meanings, and the attribution of causes, whereas "intrusive" imagery often seems to reflect deeper cognitive structures. The assessment of surface cognitive structures depends directly on patients' reports about their ongoing inner representation of outside reality.

With this final step in the reconstruction of a patient's knowledge organization, we are at the end of our exploration. We have gone back to where we started: The patient's problematic behavior is now acknowledged to be the result of his or her cognitive organization and of the striving to maintain this organization in the face of constant challenge by the environment. And it is perhaps wise to remember once again that very likely "the real history is less rational than its reconstruction."

NOTES

1. We have already stated the reasons why we decided to avoid any use of psychometric tests in our clinical research. This makes us unable to tell more about the practical merits and demerits of the clinical interview versus psychometric testing. At present, our only serious regret for having avoided any kind of rating procedure is that we cannot substantiate the clinical impression that there is a linear relationship between the degree of depression and the negative view of oneself that a depressed patient will give as the *first* reason for his or her passivity and withdrawal. (Less seriously depressed patients give a pessimistic view of the future as the first reason for their apathy; see Chapter 9.)

2. More or less similar remarks may be made regarding the cognitive therapist's consideration of nocturnal dreams. During assessment and therapy, we do not usually insist upon these experiences, but whenever they are spontaneously reported, and when patients show that they prefer to discuss their problems by using their dreams as a starting point, we use a "decoding" procedure widely derived from Hall's

cognitive theory of dreams (Hall, 1953, 1959). Sometimes, although in a very heuristic way, we also use Evans and Newman's analogy with computers in order to understand the dream process (Evans & Newman, 1964).

3. The concept of "life theme" of course reminds us of similar concepts that have been repeatedly proposed since the very beginning of modern psychology and psychotherapy: Adler's concept of "life style," Allport's concept of "proprium," existential philosophers' and psychologists' concept of "project," E. H. Erikson's concept of "identity," and Berne's (1961) concept of "script." For a brief discussion of, and appropriate references for, these concepts, see Csikszentmihalyi and Beattie (1979), who fail to report only the last one quoted.

4. We believe that avoidance of harmless or even pleasant situations is a revealing symptom of the patient's cognitive organization. As the reader can infer from our discussion of behavioral aspects (see Chapters 9–12), we usually start our clinical analysis by considering the patient's problematic behavior as an instance of avoidance behavior. Phobic avoidance is an obvious example, as it is the avoidance behavior of obsessive–compulsive patients. The depressive's inertia also may be seen as an instance of avoidance behavior (avoidance of expected moral pain, failure, or useless effort), and the same may be applied to anorectic or obese patients' "avoidance" of intimacy and of letting their feelings and more personal thoughts known by others.

5. The importance of this therapeutic step is evident if one considers the distancing, or disengagement, from one's own thoughts as the basic move in order to criticize them successfully and change them. When patients understand that their suffering is mediated by their own "opinions" and that "opinions" are not absolute truths, they have "begun to learn," as Epictetus might have said.

6. In Italian, "to be worth" is a one-word verb, "valere," which can be used to convey the meaning that human beings have different intrinsic value, worth, or merit *in themselves*. This basic way of verbally reporting one's self-esteem reveals perhaps one of the most erroneous and suffering-producing notions, as Ellis (1962), among others, has so convincingly argued.

7. To give just a few simple examples: "I am afraid of everything, Doctor—*I am* a phobic"; "*I must* succeed in my examination, because otherwise it means *I am* a failure"; "*I cannot* stand this situation, *I am* not strong enough"; "*I need* to be loved"; "I don't *deserve* my husband's attention—*I am* so wicked—I was unfaithful to him five years ago"; and so forth. And: "*He must* be kind to me because he is my husband"; "*She is* wicked: She slaps the children in the face"; "*He needs* me, so I cannot leave him even though I don't love him anymore"; "He made so many mistakes that *he deserves* to be punished"; "My children *could not* stand to know that I love another woman" (the children are 15 and 21 years old and are fully aware of the difficulties of their parents' marriage); and so forth. Causal theories are quickly derived from such verbalizations: If one is afraid, then he is ill ("I am a phobic"); if one fails in something, this proves her intrinsic unworthiness; punishements are the logical consequence of mistakes; if one knows what is going on around him, he will suffer more than if he stays ignorant and "stupid"; bad behavior is the result of an intrinsic wickedness; and so forth.

8

PSYCHOTHERAPY AS A STRATEGIC PROCESS OF COGNITIVE CHANGE

The man in the street, when asked what he thinks about a certain matter, often replies that he does not think at all: he knows. The suggestion is that thinking is a case of active uncertainty set over against conviction or unquestioning assurance.—Dewey (1916)

Psychotherapy has been given many different definitions: an interpersonal situation in which repressed emotions may be given vent to, so that a catharsis is achieved (cf. early Freudian formulations); a procedure aimed at giving the patient insight into his or her own unconscious processes (cf. the classic psychodynamic formulations); an interpersonal relationship in which the warmth, genuineness, and empathy of one member helps the other in regaining self-understanding, self-confidence, and self-esteem (Rogers, 1951); a learning situation in which the patient is guided by the therapist, through a series of empirical experiences, toward the removal of maladaptive habits and the acquisition of new and more adaptive ones (cf. the original definitions of behavior therapy, e.g., Eysenck, 1960); a teaching relationship, in which the therapist trains the patient to acquire self-control and various coping skills (see, e.g., Goldfried, 1980); a rhetorical process, in which the persuasive abilities of the therapist, matched by the patient's direct or indirect receptivity to persuasion (Frank, 1973; Glaser, 1980), are the main therapeutic factors; a translation process, supplying new verbal categories and concepts to replace old ones (see, among others, Lewis, 1972); a rational correction of irrational beliefs (Ellis, 1962); an active, shared exploration of the patient's patterns of attachment and related cognitions, for which the therapeutic relationship provides a secure base (Bowlby, 1977b); a process of deep structural change, that is, of change in the rules regarding the invariants and transformations among events (Arnkoff, 1980), so that a "personal revolution" (Mahoney, 1980) may take place; and infinitely more.

We do not mean, in this chapter, to add another definition to the group; we quite agree with the last few ones quoted (Lewis, Ellis, Bowlby, and Arnkoff–Mahoney) and believe that, at least in some therapeutic circumstances, all of the quoted definitions are partially valid. Rather, we would like to explicitly extend to the therapeutic process the analogy between the scientist's behavior and that of the patient, as put forward more and more frequently in recent years (Kelly, 1955; Mahoney, 1976, 1980; Mahoney & De Monbreun, 1977; Meichenbaum, 1977, p. 214).[1] Of course the analogy between the therapeutic process and the way of developing scientific knowledge through experiments, proofs, disproofs, and logical challenging and confrontation of theories is quite implicit in Ellis's (1962) and Beck's (1976) descriptions of cognitive therapies. Our aim here is to make it more explicit. In doing so, we can start with Dewey's definition given in the epigraph. Presumably, scientists are well aware of the fact that they do not possess any absolute truth: They think. Our patients, however, frequently sound like Dewey's "man in the street": Regarding certain relevant topics, they do not think—they know. Therefore therapists have to "set over a case of active uncertainty against previous unquestioning assurance"; that is, they have to make the patient do some rethinking about the results of his or her own previous thinking. In other words, in order to profit fully from the analogy with the scientist, the therapist should enable patients to *disengage* themselves from certain engrained beliefs and judgments and to consider them as hypotheses and theories, subject to disproof, confirmation, and logical challenge.[2]

During the early assessment procedure, a certain degree of disengagement is usually obtained simply by asking patients to pay attention to their own "automatic thoughts," inner dialogue, daydreams, and fantasies and to record them and report them to the therapist. This simple indication obviously conveys the belief that patients' thinking is relevant to the understanding of their behavioral and emotional problems—that the causal theories that patients entertained concerning such problems can somehow be changed by the assessement procedures, or alternatively, that patients have to acknowledge them explicitly and at least partially disengage themselves from them.

Assessment and change are interdependent (Meichenbaum, 1977, Chapter 9). Another aspect of this interdependence regards the way in which the therapeutic maneuvers and their results are a continuous source of feedback about patients' cognitive structures. Frequently, if not always, there is no other practical way to assess patients' deeper cognitive structures than by attempting to change their more superficial ones through appropriate therapeutic techniques. We may therefore proceed in describing the psychotherapy process (regarded as a strategy for cognitive change) through an outline of some therapeutic techniques that are usually best applied in the first phase of treatment and that are apt to produce both a change in superficial cognitive structures and an identification of deeper rules.

COGNITIVE–BEHAVIORAL TECHNIQUES FOR MODIFYING SUPERFICIAL STRUCTURES AND IDENTIFYING DEEPER COGNITIVE STRUCTURES

During the early stages of therapy, the therapist establishes with the patient a relationship respectful of the latter's probable deeper rules, by referring to his or her knowledge of psychiatric syndromes (see Chapter 6). At the same time or later on, the therapist goes on to define the therapeutic contract and to ascertain the behavioral sequences thereof (target problematic behaviors, antecedents, and consequences) and the representational models and expectations that go with them. By making the patient concentrate on concrete problems and observable "facts," and by discouraging him or her from engaging in purely theoretical discussions (such as "Doctor, do you think my illness is somatic or psychological?" and "I think problems are a result of having had a strict, authoritarian father"), the therapist teaches the patient, by implication, the first rudiments of the scientific method. The answers to such theoretical questions as those just quoted will come later, when enough data are collected to corroborate the theory. In line with this methodology, the therapist can, at this point, propose for the patient certain "experiments" that can prove as being true or false the patient's assessed expectations concerning the environmental and personal consequences of the problematic behavior or of the alternative behavior patterns that he or she avoids following.[3]

"EXPERIMENTS" IN THE THERAPEUTIC SETTING

One of the possible settings in which these "experiments" could take place is the therapeutic situation itself. Especially in the case of patients suffering from complex neurotic disturbances, the therapeutic relationship, if opportunely handled by the therapist, is the best one in which to disprove certain negative expectations about the outcome of interpersonal relationships, the possibility of being criticized and rejected, and so forth.

One depressed and obese female patient avoided describing to the therapist her feelings and problems. The therapist supposed that she thought herself unworthy of attention and that she expected to be rejected. During the third session, the patient took a deliberately provocative attitude, clearly expressed in this question: "Who do you think you are to be able to help me?" Instead of eluding the question, or reassuring the patient, or counterattacking her, the therapist, in conformity with his theory, asked in turn, "Do you expect me to abandon you if you act like this?" Surprised, the woman hesitated, then answered, "Yes." From then on, it was possible to study the expectations of being rejected and the negative view of herself (a deeper structure on which those expectations were based) that enveloped the patient's stream of consciousness and affected her behavior.

Role playing and *assertiveness training* are other examples of "experiments" that can be started and carried on during the therapeutic sessions to disprove the patient's expectations of not being able to assert himself or herself, endure criticism, and so forth. The same can be said about other *behavior therapy techniques* and many *coping skills training* procedures. For a description of these techniques, and of their cognitive aspects, see Foreyt and Rathjen (1978), Garfield and Bergin (1978), Kanfer and Goldstein (1975), Mahoney (1974), and Meichenbaum (1977). (For an attempted classification of cognitive-behavior therapy techniques, see Mahoney & Arnkoff, 1978.) Here we describe only some examples of how these techniques may be used to disprove the patient's expectations and at the same time gather information about the deeper rules governing these expectations.

Phobic patients usually expect not to be able to tolerate the anxiety caused by exposure to feared situations. They sometimes claim that even imagining such a scene evokes unpleasant and unbearable feelings. The therapist—since the positive therapeutic relationship now established enables him or her to do so—at this point asks the patient to submit to an "experiment," which could prove beneficial for his or her own troubles. With these premises, the therapist explains to the patient the principles of imaginal flooding (Boulougouris, Marks, & Marset, 1971; Marks, 1969). In flooding, patients imagine the frightening situations and the consequences expected from an exposure to them while the therapist pressingly describes them, with dramatic tinges, in the form of repeated themes, each one lasting from 10 to 15 minutes. Usually, in a situation such as this, patients feel, right from the start, much less anxious than they had expected (one of our patients—who probably had a strong tendency to oppose authorities such as a therapist is assumed to be— almost fell asleep during the second flooding session) and, as a rule, can see that, the more the imagined scenes are repeated, the more their anxiety decreases or altogether ceases.

At this stage the patient often objects, "All right, Doctor, I can image all these things without feeling afraid, but I could never face them in real life." Thus the therapist is made aware that the patient is starting to express verbally the belief in an existing difference between imagining dangers and facing them in real life and considers this information as the first chance to ascertain the patient's deeper rules. On the other hand, carrying on the "experiment," the therapist can ask the patient to repeat the flooding experience, but this time to imagine actively the themes introduced in the previous sessions while actually experiencing the dreaded situation. An *in vivo* exposure, so prepared and carried out, can prove to patients that their beliefs about the consequences of exposing themselves to phobic stimuli were exaggerated and wrong and also provide them with an ideal and practical tool to recognize the power of their own imagination and to "master" it (see also Chapter 10).

At this stage patients' superficial cognitive structures are modified together with the related problematic behavior and emotions. They admit that the roots of their phobia were in their imaginal processes and that they are able to master them. And, owing to this superficial change, the therapeutic conversation may clearly bring to the surface the patients' deeper rules (the ones that the therapist intended to respect, but not confirm, in his or her initial handling of the therapeutic relationship). In phobic patients the surfacing of beliefs related to the need to keep control is typical at this stage:

Several among our agoraphobic patients, at this phase of the treatment, reported of having thought, after having successfully faced situations they used to be afraid of: "Well, this time I kept control, but will I be able to do the same in case of a more serious attack of my phobia?"[4]

To confront this kind of theory about self-control (which must be done if we want to obtain more than a superficial change), more and different therapeutic techniques are evidently necessary (see Chapter 10).

It is interesting to notice that valuable information about deeper cognitive structures may be gathered also—and perhaps mostly—when the behavioral interventions applied in the early phase of treatment seem not to cause any clinical change. The following example shows a case and its outcome.

Sophia, age 33, suffered from a serious form of thanatophobia[5] ever since the age of 8. She could not remember any traumatic episode with which the phobia could have originated. She could only recall that at the age of 8 she was afraid of passing by the house where another little girl used to live; she had been acquainted with this girl, who had died a few months earlier.

Sophia's parents still lived in that town, while she had moved to another city to study and remained there after obtaining her degree and getting married. Summoned by the therapist, Sophia's parents said they had noticed their daughter's reaction even to the simple sight of a hearse in the street only when Sophia was already an adolescent. As far as they could recall, Sophia had hardly ever spoken to the little girl who had died— perhaps from leukemia—when their daughter was 8 years old, and she had *not* shown a dramatic reaction to the news of that death. She had been a normal, bright, lively girl, who had easily made many friends among the children her age. The therapist inquired whether she could have learned her phobia through modeling, and the result was negative; to the question "Is there or has there been in the family somebody afraid of things related to death?" both Sophia and her parents answered negatively. Nobody in the family suffered from emotional disturbances or nervous breakdowns; only Sophia's father had a slight hypertension, which the doctors considered of psychosomatic origin. They all agreed that the parents got along very well with each other and with their children (Sophia and two others). The assessment of family communication confirmed this statement. Sophia's marriage also seemed to be very satisfying.

The functional–cognitive analysis revealed only that Sophia superstitiously believed and feared that she herself could die of the shock caused by the sight of a coffin or a corpse. The therapist decided to try to disprove this idea to the patient, using the imaginal systematic desensitization technique.

Sophia was able to imagine vividly the various items in the hierarchy of anxiety-causing stimuli, starting from the fleeting sight of an empty hearse down to watching a corpse being dressed and laid in the coffin; although at first she showed great anxiety, later on she calmed down and was able to remain in a state of deep muscular relaxation.

Unfortunately, the results reached in the therapeutic sessions did not extend to real life. Although she could bear to imagine a corpse in a coffin, Sophia still reacted with fear (prolonged tachycardia and great anxiety lasting 1 or 2 days) to the mere sight of a hearse in the street. The clinical study of the reasons for this unusual outcome of desensitization disclosed that the patient, while dutifully imagining the scenes described by the therapist, silently said to herself, "I shall never be able to do this." That is, she imagined the scene, but not *herself* in the scene. When asked why she was convinced of her incapability, Sophia did not reassert her original superstitious idea—by now she knew she could *think* about death without consequences—but maintained that she felt too *tenderhearted and different from others* to stand the sight of funerals and corpses. A deeper cognitive structure concerning the self-image had thus emerged for the first time and had to be disproved.

Since Sophia's case is a good example for other points that we intend to discuss further on in this chapter, we shall continue it later.

OTHER COGNITIVE THERAPEUTIC TECHNIQUES

Other, more specifically cognitive therapeutic techniques than the ones illustrated up to this point are useful for modifying the superficial cognitive structures and identifying the deeper invariant rules. For example, many cognitive therapy techniques involve giving instructions to patients to make them cognitively rehearse fear-, sadness-, or anger-causing situations (*cognitive modeling, coping imagery, self-instructional training, stress inoculation training,* etc.; see, e.g., Mahoney & Mahoney, 1976; Meichenbaum, 1977; Novaco, 1975, 1977). Whenever patients actively substitute, according to such instructions, appropriate monologues or adaptive self-statements to the previous negative ones, not only are the superficial cognitions somehow changed, but the deeper rules governing them are usually brought a little more into the open.

According to Novaco's suggestions (Novaco, 1975), we instructed one of our patients, who was subject to excessive anger reactions, how to prepare himself for provocation (e.g., "This is going to upset me, but I know how to deal with it"), how to confront provocations ("As long as I keep calm, I can control myself"), and how to cope with rising anger ("Time to take a deep breath"). When the patient learned to substitute his previous statements ("I cannot control my anger" and "I must stop the stupid beast from insulting me") with these new ones, he was in fact able to achieve better control of his aggressive behavior. At the same time, a new aspect of his problem became apparent; he found himself thinking, "I can control myself, but what is going to happen now? Perhaps I am behaving like a chicken in spite of my true self!" So, the theory that he was unable to control his own anger was rectified, but at the same time his deeper theory that not reacting aggressively equals being a coward was brought into full light.

Problem-solving procedures (D'Zurilla & Goldfried, 1971; Goldfried & Goldfried, 1975) may be used in the same fashion. Brainstorms offer alternatives to a patient's unsuccessful attempts to solve his or her personal problems and usually enable both the therapist and the patient to recognize the basic attitude toward reality that was determining the rigid problem-solving rules.

A female patient described her main conjugal problem in this way: whether to submit totally to her loving, but also domineering, husband or to accept quarrels and make her domestic life a hell on earth. Therapist-assisted brainstorming generated many other alternatives (e.g., sabotaging the husband's hobbies by complying at the right time to his previous demands of being informed of the wife's daily programs; discussing openly her inner feelings with her husband; joint counseling; joining a feminist group and requesting the help of other women, etc.), but also made the patient realize that her basic attitude toward marriage justified her previous dichotomized way of considering the problem. She believed that conjugal love meant the *total* devotion of one spouse to the other and could not conceive of cooperation and equal rights in marriage. In her view either the husband or the wife has to *dominate*, and the one who accepts being dominated has a right to expect a great love as a reward. Her problem emerged when she began to feel that, although her husband was very much in love with her, the submissive position was hard to bear for a long time. To solve the problem, however, she clearly had to change her basic attitude toward marriage.

Thought stopping (Taylor, 1963) can be creatively used, and not only with obsessionals, in order to prove to patients how false the common theory is that one does not have *any* control over one's own thoughts. Usually, the deeper cognitive structures determining the "intrusive" thoughts become, thereafter, more easily recognizable.

A hypochondriacal patient asserted that he could not stop in any way the distressing thoughts concerning his own health. The therapist asked him to relax, to dwell deliberately on such thoughts, and then, unexpectedly, shouted a very loud "Stop!" The procedure was repeated, and finally the patient was instructed to shout "stop" himself. As a consequence, the patient admitted that he really *wanted* to think continuously about his health, otherwise he could be in serious danger of missing some minor, but perhaps forewarning, symptom of an impending illness to be treated immediately.

All the examples reported point in the same direction as to therapeutic strategy: The "experiments" created by the therapist to disprove patients' theories on the primary causes of their "symptomatic" behavior bring to light deeper theories (Arnkoff, 1980) that usually need to be confronted with therapeutic techniques of a different logical level than those illustrated here. When patients start to verbally express their deeper causal theories, we generally find that they are much more abstract compared with the more superficial and concrete ones that emerged in the earlier stages of treatment. We can again use the metaphor of the scientist in saying that the deeper rules governing our patients' ongoing cognitions represent more and more formalized and abstract theories about themselves and the nature of their interaction with reality. In turn, the therapist's efforts to disprove such theories also must belong to a more abstract logical level than the previously described cognitive–behavioral tactics. We may collect these higher order tactics under the denomination "therapeutic techniques based upon logical debate and logical challenging." They bear some resemblance to the epistemological debate that occupies the phase of experimental research and theoretical development in the growth process of scientific knowledge.

COGNITIVE TECHNIQUES THAT LOGICALLY CHALLENGE PATIENTS' DEEPER THEORIES

Ellis's and Beck's descriptions (Bedrosian & Beck, 1980; Beck, 1976; Ellis, 1962) of their therapeutic strategy are very good and well-known examples of how to effectively confront, on a purely logical ground, the distorted assumptions (or irrational beliefs) upon which a patient's "philosophy of life" is based. We may mention, for example, the "decatastrophizing" techniques, in which the therapist logically demonstrates to the patient how his or her evaluation of the negative influence of certain events and actions is exaggerated; the "reattribution" techniques, in which unrealistic assumptions of responsibility, causing self-blame and guilty feelings, are subjected to logical criticism rather than simply absolving the patient from all responsibility; and the "rational restructuring" techniques, in which the patient learns to generate logical responses instead of illogical cognitions. These techniques frequently make explicit or implicit reference to "semantic" arguments very similar to the ones originally suggested by Korzybski (1941) and especially by Ellis in his clinical work. As will be discussed later in this chapter, our model of knowledge organization, centered on the concept of personal identity (see Chapter 3), suggests a somewhat renewed use of "semantic" techniques within the strategic process of cognitive therapy.

Before discussing the use of logical debates in the psychotherapy process, we must recall that, prior to challenging the patient's causal theories (already identified after the early phase of treatment), we perform a *developmental analysis* in order to find explicit evidence for the causal theories that the patient has collected during his or her developmental history. To profit as much as possible from the analogy with the formation, growth, and changing of scientific knowledge, the psychotherapy process must fully acknowledge the life experiences on which the patient built his or her irrational beliefs and found a confirmation of their truth. Similarly, before criticizing a scientific theory, we must know on what observations it is based. In Chapter 7 we described how this historical research is carried on. Returning to our thanatophobic patient, Sophia, let us now show how the developmental analysis can be intertwined with the therapy itself.

The correction of the superficial causal theory that Sophia held to justify her thanatophobia ("If I watch something related to death and dying, I shall be so scared that I shall die too") revealed a deeper causal theory: "I am different from other people; I am too sensitive, too weak, too tenderhearted to stand the direct sight of death." Of course the consequences of this belief confirmed it entirely: Her tachycardia at the sight of a hearse "proved" her sensitivity, and the fact that others reacted differently "proved" her uniqueness. But how had Sophia come to build her personal identity?

The developmental analysis, resumed at this stage, indicated that she had felt, as a little girl, closer to her father—who was interested in the arts and was sensitive and shy—than to her mother, a very strong and practical woman. Although this state of affairs *apparently* was not directly related to thanatophobia, its acknowledgment was sufficient for Sophia to start considering her view of herself as an idea made up in identification with her father rather than as an absolute truth (disengagement or distancing). The semantic techniques regarding the use of the verb "to be" and of the pronoun "I," which we shall describe further on, made Sophia accept the idea that she *reacted* in an excessively sensitive way, but "*was not* intrinsically and generally hypersensitive" to certain situations such as death and its symbols.

Having thus achieved a further disengagement from the theories of personal identity, the therapist proceeded to modify "experimentally" Sophia's belief that she was incapable of bearing the actual sight of death-related events, by disproving the negative correlation between "sensitivity" and "indifference to death-related scenes." Since the patient was uncommonly capable of deep muscular relaxation and of vivid and accurate imagining, the therapist decided to turn again to imaginal systematic desensitization (perhaps better called, in this case, "coping imagery procedure") before trying an *in vivo* exposure. But this time the death-related scenes were part of larger scenes, in which Sophia imagined herself busy with her usual daily activities connected with her supposed "sensitivity and uniqueness" (she, like her father, used to paint and preferred delicate subjects such as flowers, rosy sunsets, etc.). One desensitizing scene was, for example:

> You are at the window, and you are painting the flowered windowsill of the house in front. Try to see clearly yourself, the picture, the color. Now you see, down in the street, a passing funeral—keep seeing yourself in the scene, and the funeral, and the flowered windowsill, and your picture. Now imagine the funeral going by and disappearing, while you keep painting without turning away from the window.

The effects of this modified desensitization technique were very good. Now Sophia could stand the actual sight of funerals without feeling too anxious. The therapist started to guide, in his presence (the therapeutic relationship was a very good one), the gradual *in vivo* exposure to feared stimuli, for example, taking Sophia to the cemetery, on a nice spring day, to paint the flowers in the flower beds. Thus the patient learned to distinguish between "artistic sensitivity" and "capability of bearing the sight of death."

And at this point, during one of the follow-up sessions, came a surprising discovery.

Sophia had gone to visit her parents in her hometown. An old, distant relative, who lived in the same town, had died the day before, and the funeral was to take place the following day. Smiling, Sophia said to her mother, "You see, the funeral did not prevent me from coming to visit you for a week; you can go tomorrow (previously, Sophia used to ask her parents and her husband not to go to funerals, because she would have felt "almost contaminated" when they got back), but I prefer to stay home by myself. I am not so afraid to follow a funeral any more, but I prefer to avoid it when I can, and then, I am on vacation." To her great surprise, her mother answered, "But you won't be home by yourself; your father is not coming to the ceremony. He could never stand them." Sophia had always believed that her parents had not attended funerals, when she was younger, because *she* had asked them not to, because of her fear.

Now, at age 34, and *only thanks to a 1-year successful therapy* (54 weekly sessions), she knows that things stand differently. Her sensitive, art-loving father, although he did not attribute his avoidance of funerals to fear, had always refused to attend them. Since he did not avoid passing near graveyards or visiting the relatives of a recently dead person, he did not describe himself as a phobic. But Sophia had acquired, probably very early in her life, the *tacit knowledge* of a negative correlation between artistic sensitivity and the attendance of funerals, and generalization plus the inclusion of this notion to her self-knowledge had done the rest. This completion of the developmental analysis, allowed by the previous therapeutic techniques which were successfully applied, ended the therapy.[6]

SEMANTIC TECHNIQUES

In the psychotherapy process, an examination of the evidence that sustains patients' theories on their personal identity usually precedes the logical challenge of those theories. The next step consists of the semantic correction of the use of the pronoun "I" and of such verbs as "to be," "to be worth," "must," "can," and "to deserve," which, as we said in Chapter 7, are the key to grasping the cognitive structures of personal identity. As Raimy (1975) convincingly argues, misconceptions about the self probably play a major role in enduring maladjustments, and their correction therefore constitutes the main goal of treatment.

Whatever the *content* of misconceptions about the self, their logical form is invariably one of global judgments, invariance, and pervasiveness in attributing causes and meanings. In other words, because of its stability, its duration throughout waking hours (and perhaps also during dreams), and its globality, the self-concept constantly defines the individual to himself or herself, both in everyday behavior and in long-term identity. Verbal forms such as "I *am*," followed by some predicate, obviously express this globality, invariance, and pervasiveness of the self-concept. There are several semantic arguments that can show how the logical form corresponding to these verbal forms is wrong, whatever the predicate may be.

For example, let us consider the attributes of the pronoun "I" in the common use of daily speech. "I dream," "I think," "I sleep," "I breathe," "I walk," "I eat," "I speak," "I see," and so forth. Now let us consider the universality of meaning of the verb "to be." Bearing all this in mind, let us go on to consider the sentence "I am a coward." Obviously, it has no logical value. Indeed, what is the sense of saying "I dream like a coward," "I think like a coward," "I walk like a coward," "I breathe like a coward," and so forth? My "I" is made up of my body, my hair, my eyes, my liver, and so forth. What is the logical sense of saying "My body is cowardly," "My hair is cowardly," "My eyes are cowardly," "My liver is cowardly," and so forth? If we replace "cowardly" with any other predicate—good, bad, smart, stupid, strong, weak, tall, short, attractive, ugly—the result will be the same. Because "I" stands for a myriad of different acts and parts, and "to be" is the verb of universality, only a predicate that can logically apply to *all* these acts and parts can make sense in a sentence with "I am." There is only *one* such predicate—"I am a *human being*"—and this is tautological. Therefore, strictly speaking, the sentence "Einstein is intelligent" is more or less meaningless. It makes full sense only in the following form: "Einstein produced some very intelligent ideas in the field of physics" (and perhaps some silly ideas in daily life). By the way, this is said to be the opinion of Einstein himself; when somebody said to him, "Oh, Professor Einstein, what a genius you are!" he answered, "No, I just happened to have one genial idea in my life."

Moreover, attributes such as "intelligent–stupid," "good–bad," "beautiful–ugly," and so forth, do not pertain to dichotomous aspects of reality, but rather to a continuum of judgment, the elements of which are measurable by means of arbitrary and socially agreed-upon instruments (IQ tests, social instruments of moral evaluation).

Such concepts as "duty" and "worth" are also open to semantic evaluations that may prove interesting, useful, and not too difficult for the average patient. But, since the description of the process would be relatively long, considering clinical situations and patients' different degrees of education, we shall not go into it in depth. To give just a hint of the kind of analysis involved, the general idea of "worth" applied to a human being ("I am worth less than he") is logical only if one believes that there is an instrument to measure this worth. Since, clearly, no such instrument exists, the theory that one human being is worth more than another is groundless. All one can confidently say is that some performances are often—but not always —socially more rewarded than others.[7] As for the idea of moral duty ("must"), we can demonstrate that it is founded on two basic circumstances:

1. A social convention, generally *useful* for the whole group (and therefore also for the patient who belongs to it), the violation of which is followed by some form of punishment (and it is *useful* to avoid the punishment, unless one *wants* to recede from the group and adopt other rules).
2. A sort of natural law, inscribed in the species' genetic heritage. Again, it is *useful* for individuals to respect it, for they would be forcing their nature if they violated it. (For example, the bond of affection between parents and children is a "natural law"; therefore taking care of one's children is not an abstract duty, but a compliance with the "innate knowledge" with which one is endowed.) Thus the idea of moral duty can be reduced to a careful and rational evaluation of what is useful for the *person* as a member of the group and of the species.

Of course there is a psychological, if not a logical, necessity to develop a personal identity marked by universal judgments and based on the ideas of "duty" and "worth." These ideas are generalized and therefore abstract, and they regulate the person's behavior so as to sustain his or her self-esteem. However, this necessity exists particularly during growth and until adolescence and then gradually diminishes in adulthood, when the increased capacity of disengaging oneself from the results of one's thinking is fully developed. With adult patients, semantic correction techniques allow, then, such a disengagement from misconceptions about the self.

LOGICAL CHALLENGE OF CONTENT OF
PERSONAL IDENTITY THEORIES

At this stage of the psychotherapy process, patients are ready to acknowledge that the evidence (developmental stresses, etc.) upon which they founded their theories concerning their personal identity are of an episodic nature and that there is neither a logical nor a psychological reason to consider them as having a general meaning. The logical *form* of global judgments related to one's "being" has been modified. This background allows the therapist to attack and challenge directly, on logical grounds, the specific *content* of the theories on personal identity. Decatastrophizing, reattribution, and cognitive restructuring techniques in the fashion of Beck and Ellis are applied.[8]

In our opinion, more important than the specific cognitive techniques used—which can be chosen by the therapist according to his or her own "temperament," or cognitive organization, and verbal abilities—is the *timing* of the therapeutic maneuver. The acknowledgment of the formal, logical, and meaningful relationships that connect the patient's single beliefs into a structure is essential in determining the proper timing of intervention. The other main factor that guides the therapist in selecting one kind of intervention instead of another at a certain point in the treatment is the consideration of the patient's actual life stresses.

Let us assume, for instance, that a patient is expressing the belief that he sometimes acts as a coward. (He has already recognized that this fact does not allow such generalized statements as "*I am* a coward.") He also believes that he is a very sensitive person, or rather, that he reacts with sensitivity to certain events, and that sensitivity and cowardice are positively correlated; in his cognitive structure, beliefs regarding sensitivity are of a higher logical order than beliefs regarding cowardice, inasmuch as not every coward is sensitive, but every "sensitive" person is also a coward. Let us also assume that he believes that he is in absolute need of being loved in order to preserve his own self-esteem (and perhaps also his self-identity) and that he believes sensitive people are lovable, but cowards are not.

Now, suppose that such a patient's mate threatens to abandon him, without specifying why, and that our patient assumes that she is doing so because he "is" such a coward. (The emotional stress makes him forget to use the alternative statement "because sometimes I behave like a coward.") The therapist is confronted with a decisional problem. From a *logical–structural* point of view, the therapist should proceed to logically disconnect one from another, as far as possible, the judgments of "cowardice" and "sensitivity"; then he or she should prove that acting as a coward is not such a catastrophe and that it does not logically imply the consequence of being abandoned (for instance, the therapist might remark that the idea that "nobody can love a coward" was only the opinion of the patient's father, an opinion that, although not totally unconvincing, was based only on his father's limited experience, and not on the knowledge of some general natural law); and finally, he or she should challenge the idea that an adult human being is in "dire need" of being loved and approved by others (Ellis, 1962). From a *practical* point of view, the therapist could, instead, choose one of the following alternatives, considering the patient's present pressing life situation, permeated by the threat of being abandoned:

1. Make a direct, energetic attack on the patient's beliefs concerning the "dire need" to be loved.
2. Ask the patient to ascertain whether his mate really wants to leave him because of his cowardly behavior or for other reasons.
3. Meet the patient's mate for a joint session (provided that she agrees to it) in order to ascertain her reasons for wanting to leave or otherwise to try to clear up a possible misunderstanding between the two.

Clearly such a decisional problem is not easy to solve. We generally would prefer to use the ongoing life stresses to prove to the patient that his expectations, based on deeper personal identity constructs, could be limited or erroneous and to do so in family or joint couple sessions. Even if the joint sessions should prove that the patient's expectations are correct (e.g., the patient's mate explicitly states that she is going to leave him because he once or twice acted as a coward), it is usually easy to show that such evidence for the patient's causal theories is of a limited episodic value. (For example, the therapist could induce the patient's mate to cite two or three of her friends who do not leave their lovers or husbands just because the latter are easily frightened.) The problem of "assortative mating"—

how one is led to select just the kind of partner who proves the validity of one's theories on oneself and reality—may then be taken into consideration in the subsequent therapy sessions.[9] For instance, a patient who strives to conceal his "cowardice" may play the part of the brave hero and therefore attract just the kind of woman who likes the "I-fear-nothing" kind of man. When the play comes to an end, the woman leaves the scene.

After having accomplished this search for evidence and analysis of assortative mating, we can proceed with the deep modification of self-constructs. Only when an attempt to find evidence for the patient's theories directly in his or her distressing interactions with significant others is not feasible (the patient, or relatives or spouse, do not comply) do we resort to immediately dealing with the emotional stress (support, giving vent to emotions, etc.); then, as soon as possible, we proceed along the lines dictated by the logical–structural consideration of the patient's organization of knowledge.

When the logical challenge of the patient's more deeply set rules is accomplished (or when it is well advanced), we can prescribe new behavioral experiments in real-life situations or new cognitive techniques to aid the patient in developing new and more adaptive theories. In this final stage of the therapeutic process, the patient is on the verge of a "personal revolution": His or her own old "paradigm" (cognitive organization, structural causal theories, attitudes toward oneself and toward reality, or belief system) has been deeply criticized, and a new paradigm is not yet fully established (see Mahoney, 1980, for a fuller account of the analogies between Kuhn's structural analysis of scientific revolutions and the personal revolutions achieved through psychotherapy). A positive therapeutic relationship is essential to minimizing the painfulness and dismay that can be expected while such a deep personal revolution is taking place (see Chapter 6). Behavioral experiments and cognitive techniques are also essential in speeding up the process of constructing a new and more adaptive paradigm. Sometimes therapists may resort to established cognitive–behavioral techniques to achieve the production of the alternative paradigm, but usually they have to "create," together with the patient, the appropriate new "experiments."

For instance, an obsessional patient who was prone to "perfectionist" doubting in his search for an impossible certainty came to recognize, by the end of treatment, that his old paradigm was illogical and maladaptive. But how can one give up the distressing habit of thinking continuously about the *future* in order to calculate and prevent the possible negative outcomes of one's efforts and every possible mistake and risk? How can one acquire the ability to concentrate on the present and live in it more fully? The therapist knew of no established techniques suitable for achieving this result. Thought stopping seemed naive and very apt to produce other doubts (i.e., to be incorporated in the old perfectionist paradigm—e.g., "Have I really succeeded in stopping to think about the future?" or "Have I stopped my thoughts at the appropriate time?"). Rational statements —for example, "Now relax; remember that there is no use in trying to make the future controlled and certain"—were easily forgotten or followed by the old self-judgments and doubts—for example, "How can I be sure of the *limit* between proper planning of actions and excessive dwelling upon the risks of the future?" and "I should have anticipated this problem."

Therefore the therapist "created," together with the patient, a new experiment in cognition: The patient had simply to *imagine*, when waking up in the morning, the main expected events and actions of the day, as vividly as possible, without too many verbal thoughts. At the end of the day, he had to recall again, in the imaginal mode of thought, the main events and actions of the day that actually took place. "Future" and "past" were thus restricted to a daily time span. Judgment evaluations ("I was wrong") were limited through the deliberate use of the imaginal mode. The matching between expectations and actual events, and between anticipation and recollection, was ensured, so that the patient could practice and recognize his "normal" ability to plan actions. He could then correct them when unexpected events required him to do so and could note that an environmental novelty was not to be considered as a disruption of his plans. The personal revolution was not too painful for this patient.

Of course not every patient requires a "deep" change in his or her cognitive organization. "Superficial" or "peripheral" changes in a reasonably adaptive paradigm are sometimes sufficient. However, with complex cases of emotional disorders, a true personal revolution has to be aimed for if one wants to achieve an enduring and satisfactory outcome of the psychotherapy. In this case the treatment lasts longer than it usually does in the cognitive–behavioral treatments. In our experience, in complex cases it lasts, on the average, 2 years, totaling 70 to 100 sessions, 1 hour a week at first and 1 hour every 2 weeks thereafter. Follow-up sessions at 1- or 2-month intervals are usually held for one more year.[10]

THE STRUCTURE OF KNOWLEDGE AND COGNITIVE CHANGE IN PSYCHOTHERAPY

In Chapter 4 we stated that cognitive change is usually a gradual process and that the most difficult structures to change are those defining one's attitude toward oneself. The more rigid and defensive this attitude, the more rigid, stereotyped, and repetitive become the rules for assimilating new experiences and solving problems. In other words, it is the structure of self-knowledge that determines the kinds of relationships and connections between assimilated experience data and that therefore, in the long run, gives meaning to the incoming load of information deriving from the individual's interaction with reality.

It is the full acknowledgment of the central role of self-knowledge that prompts the therapist to ascertain as soon as possible the nodal aspects of each patient's personal identity and to behave towards him or her in such a way as to respect—though not confirm—these aspects. In Chapters 9 through 12, we set forth the notions that allow the therapist to form immediate suppositions as to what cognitive structures intervene in defining the personal identity that the patient attributes to himself or herself, starting with the kind of emotional and behavioral disturbances that are allegedly at the basis of the request for treatment.

There is another reason why this acknowledgment and respect for the patient's personal identity should be the first step in the psychotherapeutic process, while the possible change of personal identity should be the final aim of the treatment strategy. As Popper says, "Knowledge is always a modification of earlier knowledge. . . . Observations are always interpreted in terms of previous knowledge; that is to say, the observations themselves would not even exist if there was no previous knowledge which they could modify" (Popper & Eccles, 1977, p. 425). The tacit and explicit rules making up the patient's self-knowledge are the cognitive structures with which new information—provided by the therapeutic relationship—is continuously confronted. The information provided by the therapist's words and attitude and by prescribed behavioral experiments must be recognized, filtered, and absorbed by these preexisting structures if a modification of previous knowledge is to be obtained.[11]

The role of the structural properties of knowledge in acquiring new information makes the analogy between psychotherapy and rhetoric (Glaser, 1980) or persuasion (Frank, 1973) doubtful. More than persuading patients to give up previous assumptions and forcing new ones into their mind, the therapist's job consists of guiding patients toward a full and explicit acknowledgment of their own previous knowledge and of its internal contradictions, paradoxes, and pitfalls. Emotional and behavioral disorders appear as a manifestation of those contradictions, paradoxes, and pitfalls, revealed by an environment that no longer complies with them.

Perhaps this point of view could be helpful in drawing the sometimes uncertain line of demarcation between normal suffering and emotional disorders. In the face of an environmental aggression against one's freedom and emotional ties, suffering is of course normal. Grief, for instance, is a normal reaction to bereavement. One is also free to recognize his or her own contradictions and to decide to maintain them; any suffering coming out of them should then be considered "normal." But whenever one is not aware of one's own contradictions, and they are revealed by a changing environment so that emotional suffering results, then that suffering could be considered "neurotic." It therefore becomes socially and ethically necessary for therapists to make patients aware of the contradictions and paradoxes in their own constructed personal identity before attempting to "persuade" them to give them up. This ethical consideration coincides with the practical usefulness of providing only that information which may be processed into the already-existing cognitive structures.

Once a certain change (considered desirable at that moment by both the therapist and by the patient) has been agreed upon, the therapist applies specific therapeutic tactics. If the information contained in those tactics is recorded and processed by the preexisting cognitive structures, an approximation of the desired change will ensue. The degree, characteristics, and modes of the approximate change are precious sources of feedback information to decide whether to go further into this therapeutic tactic or to move on to a higher level one. Whenever the information conveyed is not processed by the preexisting cognitive structures, the terms of the therapeutic problem should be laid out again and/or another technique should be tried. At the same time, the absence of any cognitive or behavioral change, or even a worsening of the original problem as a result of a therapeutic technique, provides information on the nature of the patient's cognitive structures.

PSYCHOTHERAPY AS A STRATEGY

Thus the therapeutic process is like a strategic procedure, the final aim of which is a modification of the patient's deep rules, regulated, step by step, by the cognitive changes resulting from the applied therapeutic techniques ("tactics"). Obviously, within the same strategy, therapists may choose, from a range of suitable tactics, the ones that they believe are fitted to themselves and their patients. The problem is, then, to decide with a parametric study whether, for example, flooding is really superior to systematic desensitization in the treatment of all complex phobias. In the hands of a therapist who takes into account the structural organization of knowledge in agoraphobic patients, the choice of a tactic such as systematic desensitization, conveniently adapted so as to respect the patient's theories on self-control, may perhaps give better results than flooding (see Boulougouris *et al.*, 1971, for the alleged superiority of flooding as compared to systematic desensitization; Chiari & Mosticoni, 1979, for an example of "strategic" use of desensitization in agoraphobics; Chapter 10, this book, for a detailed exposition of cognitive organization in agoraphobia).

The idea of psychotherapy as a strategy that takes into consideration the structural properties of the cognitive organization also prevents one from regarding some easily obtained cognitive modifications as solutions of complex clinical cases. The following example can better explain this point:

Leila was a 27-year-old single patient who had orgasmic disturbances. She had been brought up in a family who observed strict Catholic religious rules. Leila had sexual intercourse with a man her own age who wanted to marry her, but could not reach orgasm with him, although she said she loved him and felt a strong physical attraction for him. When the patient told the therapist about her disgust and anger in learning that a friend of hers had started an affair with a married man, it was easy for him to connect this reaction with her old moral beliefs on sex. Throughout a whole session, these beliefs, acquired from her family, were discussed, and at the end Leila admitted that they were too strict: All sexual intercourse was forbidden except that between married people which was aimed at procreation. Leila accepted the therapist's arguments, and her negative reaction toward her friend disappeared. But she was still incapable of orgasm.

The cognitive analysis revealed that, underlying the belief that "sex is forbidden outside marriage," there was another one, much more important, that caused her disturbance: "All men end up by deceiving and betraying their wives after marriage, and this is terrible." This belief proved to be much harder to modify because it was connected to other beliefs regarding her personal identity, such as "I am a weak person—I cannot resist sexual temptation"; "I am unattractive—I am bound to be abandoned"; and "I must never trust anyone—those who seem kind and considerate will ultimately let me down and show their selfishness." It became more evident the longer treatment progressed that Leila's attitude toward reality appeared almost paranoid; she had asked for treatment not really because she wanted to enjoy sex, but rather because she feared that her partner might detect her lack of orgasm, that he would tell her friends about her "abnormality," and that finally—she imagined—they might then think that she was a homosexual. She had not reported these basic motives for asking for treatment during the first therapeutic interviews "because otherwise you would have thought that I was crazy and would have refused to help me." Leila was also afraid that the therapist could say to her, "Do you know that you are a latent homosexual?"

So, what at first seemed an easy matter of changing superficial moral beliefs forbidding sex proved to be a very complex task of deep cognitive restructuring.

Leila's case, which turned out to be a serious one even though it looked simple at first, is happily matched by many opposite situations in which what initially appears as a very serious disorder reveals itself as one that is easy to cure.

Alex, age 41, had been cured for many years with intensive antidepressant medications, because of a diagnosis of "manic–depressive psychosis." For 7 years he continuously went in and out of depressive "phases," with the exception of two (dubious) manic episodes. A psychoanalyst he had seen, to try to discontinue medicines that caused such distressing side effects as constipation, hypotension, and dryness of the mouth, told him that psychoanalysis could not cure manic–depressive psychosis. Alex came to one of us almost hopeless, and considering the kind of treatment (behavioral psychotherapy and cognitive therapy) that he knew to be our specialty as "his last chance."

The early behavioral and cognitive analysis made the therapist doubtful about the manic–depressive psychosis diagnosis: Psychogenic depression seemed to be a much more appropriate one. Having this idea in mind, the therapist started to explain to Alex the different kinds of diagnostic labels that are applied to depression and the fact that nobody has yet proved that depression is a chemical illness like diabetes, for example. The therapist also suggested a gradual reduction in the useless antidepressant medications. At the following session, Alex came back in a very different mood: He was smiling (not elated, of course) and said that he had benefited greatly from the previous session's explanation.

Since that session, the fourth in Alex's treatment, 2 years have elapsed and no "symptom" of depression or of manic excitement has appeared. Alex is still in cognitive therapy—one session every 45 days—to ensure that the former diagnosis was erroneous and to maintain the results of the initial sessions. From the beginning his cognitive structures seemed rather well adapted, with the exception of an excessive inclination to think in terms of "duties" and a tendency to what Bowlby would call "compulsive self-reliance" (see Chapter 5). His problem had begun when he was confronted with a rather serious crisis in his marriage, to which he had reacted with "depression." The notion, given by the psychoanalyst he had consulted and continuously confirmed by his wife, that he was "ill" had done the rest. The side effects of drugs added to his belief that he was desperately ill. The two "manic" episodes were euphoric reactions to the idea that he was finally cured. His wife found his ideas of reconquering her love, his planning trips, and his renewed enthusiasm for work excessive, and the psychoanalyst agreed that they were the first signs of a hypomanic phase, to be treated immediately with lithium carbonate. The reader may well imagine the kind of effects that all this produced.

NOTES

1. It is important to emphasize again, at this point, Weimer's caveat regarding the differences between scientific methodology and "scientistic methodolatry" (Weimer, 1980). We do not want to make our patients believe that science is the answer to human problems, but rather that human beings may, if they choose to, live without certainties and without desperation, exploring themselves and the world much in the same way in which scientists approach their research programs.

2. Beck and his co-workers similarly state the importance of setting patients free from certain engrained judgments ("distancing") and from the belief that they are the focal point of all events ("decentering")—see Beck (1976, p. 242 ff.) and Bedrosian and Beck (1980, p. 143 ff). Disengagement—or distancing—from one's thoughts means that patients learn, for instance, to consider statements on them-

selves such as "I am a complete failure" not as an unquestionable truth, but rather as a result of their own thinking processes, a result that is subject to closer scrutiny and rational criticism.

3. We have already mentioned that it is useful to reinterpret the patient's problematic behavior, whenever it is possible, in terms of avoidance behavior. For example, a patient suffering from social anxiety shows avoidance behavior when he does not make advances to a well-disposed girl he likes or when he does not express his opinion. Of course one should first make sure that the patient has in himself, at least in a primitive form, the potentially useful behavior that he avoids practicing. Once this possibility is considered, one is surprised to see in how many cases the symptomatic behavior can be interpreted as avoidance behavior. For example, a patient presenting excessive displays of aggressiveness can actively avoid keeping calm and answering politely for fear of being abused by his opponents. A depressed patient can avoid action for fear of failure, of other people's judgment, or of the effort that she thinks the action implies. A patient suffering from eating disorders can avoid expressing clearly her problems and feelings for fear of being disappointed or of seeing her confidant take advantage of her as a result of knowing her secrets (see Chapter 12). As these notes indicate, to consider the possibility of an avoidance behavior instead of a behavioral excess or deficit can in itself supply quick information on the patient's cognitive structures.

4. According to what was said in the preceding chapter, the therapist must necessarily have causal theories that are different from the patient's in order to recognize these beliefs concerning self-control as partial, wrong, and potentially pathogenic. In this stage of the treatment, our phobic patients usually consider their phobia as something outside the self and therefore as something that has to be controlled. We therapists consider phobia as an emotion deriving from certain aspects of the tacit self-knowledge and therefore as something that must be corrected through a cognitive restructuring instead of being kept under control.

5. In Italy, especially in little towns, funerals have strong social relevance. In addition to following the hearse and wearing black, the dead person's relatives are visited by friends for many days, send black-lined cards by mail, publish black-lined announcements in special sections of newspapers, and sometimes have black-lined posters affixed on the walls to announce the death. The church where the service takes place often shows black hangings at the door. Consequently, a thanatophobia can become seriously invalidating, just like a phobia for elevators can be invalidating for a New Yorker.

6. Sophia's case proves that, once we remove the obstacle of theories on one's personal identity, a new view of reality dawns on the patient. When Sophia gave up her habit of describing herself, cognitively and behaviorally, as a "phobic" and of blaming her phobia for her and her family's avoidance of funerals, she was able to learn about her father's behavior. The example also shows how difficult it can be for the therapist to assess the existence of family models in some patients' symptomatic behavior: Sophia's father was not lying when, during sessions, he stated that he did not *fear* situations connected to death. After the end of Sophia's treatment, the therapist was able to talk again to the man about this, and he maintained that he refused to attend funerals only because of his theories—that he had never expressed to his daughter—on the uselessness of such ceremonies. But as a child, Sophia had

probably noticed that her father avoided funerals and did not like to talk about them. Her observations very possibly started a mechanism similar to the one described by Bowlby (1979): To know something without talking about it confines the notion in the tacit knowledge and prevents the correction of wrong or partial theories based on the notion or induces one to search for evidence for vague and generic theories. The concept of "confirmatory bias" (see, e.g., Mahoney & De Monbreun, 1977) is particularly applicable in these situations.

7. This idea of a personal profit, as opposed to an abstract moral duty, is neither antiethical nor conservative, as it may at first seem. It is not antiethical because we can prove that even very highly ethical systems (e.g., the one that Spinoza strived to demonstrate with a "geometrical method") are based on logical reasoning starting from the psychological and emotional personal advantage. It is not conservative because it does not at all exclude the possibility that individuals may find an advantage for themselves and for others in struggling for an idea that could modify the social reality in which they live.

8. As argued, for instance, by Beck *et al.* (1979, p. 154 and footnote), Ellis's approach is characterized by a more direct attack on patients' "irrational beliefs," whereas Beck's implies a preference for inducing patients to "collect a solid data base" in favor of or against their conclusions, or to "test reality." The essential objective of this reality testing is to enable patients to correct their distortions through personal "discoveries," while the therapist functions mainly according to the Socratic model.

9. Joint *family* sessions are usually helpful in gathering information about the origins of the patient's causal theories. The patient's family often reacts negatively to the perception of the cognitive and behavioral changes that the patient may achieve with individual psychotherapy. These reactions may be used, especially when the patient still lives with his mother and father, to summon the members of the family. In this unbalanced familiar situation, it is usually easy to find the beliefs that the parents transmitted to their children and that are now undergoing a change. Literature on family therapy gives many examples of this kind of phenomenon.

10. Of course the psychotherapy process does not always follow the regular succession described here. The various stages may overlap and merge with one another in different ways during an individual therapy, and of course many "surprises," both pleasant and unpleasant, occur frequently even in the best planned treatment. Every therapist, for example, has had "lucky cases" in which an apparently deep change was obtained through a therapy that aimed only at a peripheral change or even through a casual remark.

An agoraphobic patient, for example, has suffered from his invalidating illness for the past 10 years. The first manifestation coincided with the birth of his first child, which had endangered his wife's life. Since then, the patient never wanted to be out alone, and his wife had become his habitual escort. Moreover, the patient felt that his marriage was strongly constrictive (see Chapter 10), and he seemed to bear a certain degree of latent resentment to his wife, emerging in an irritated and detached attitude every time they went out together. Wanting to reduce at least one of the reasons for the tension that the patient experienced when he was out, the therapist asked him to try to be a little bit more affectionate toward his wife while walking with her, for example, holding his hand on her arm. The effect of the advice was impressive. The patient at once started to widen the limits of his autonomy of movement and to go out alone more and more often, while the personal and sexual relationship with his wife also improved immensely. Interviews revealed that a deep change had taken place. The patient had suddenly realized that his wife could be pleasant company rather than a necessary escort, he had stopped imagining how he could get rid of his marriage, and he had realized that "he was not so weak as to constantly need someone to accompany him." As we shall see in Chapter 10, these are cognitive changes concerning the deep rules of agoraphobic cognitive organization, and they were obtained "spontaneously" as a result of a therapeutic tactic that the therapist meant to be merely "superficial."

11. The notion that individuals may receive and use instructions from outside themselves—instructions that are totally strange to their own structures—is now questioned even at a biological level. Popper (1975) cites in this regard the example of immune reactions. Early theories of antibody formation assumed that the antigen worked as a negative template for the production of the antibody. The invading antigen thus seemingly operated as an instruction from without. Recent research proves to the contrary that the information enabling the antibody to recognize the antigen is literally inborn. It is conveyed by the genetic code of the specialized cells that produce the antibodies. The invading environmental antigen "selects" the cells that "recognize" it; the antigen–antibody complex is thereupon formed, and it is this complex that stimulates the growth of those same cells, so that the immune reaction takes place. Therefore instructions are from within the structure, and what comes from without is a process of selection of instructions. "Selection" here means recognition, trial, and elimination of unsuccessful trials (cf. Popper, 1975, pp. 80–81).

Much in the same fashion, patients and therapists are able to communicate as long as they are able to exchange information that is already recognizable by their preexisting cognitive structures, so that from this matching process new instructions for behavior can be selected. "Teaching new responses," or "cognitive change," therefore comes to mean that a little-used instruction in the learner is selected, its "growth" is stimulated, and it is finally integrated with other instructions and so transformed into a well-established "new" cognitive structure.

PART THREE

CLINICAL APPLICATIONS

9

DEPRESSION

The nosological status of depression is fairly confused. Many subtypes of depression, referring to different phenomenological features or hypothetically different etiologies, have been described during the last half century. Psychotic, neurotic, endogenous, exogenous, involutional, retarded, agitated, psychogenic, reactive, masked—these are some of the labels applied to various subtypes of depression. Also a problem is the relationship of manic–depressive psychosis to unipolar recurrent depression. The main problem in classifying depressive disorders is perhaps that posed by the supposition of two different classes of etiologic factors: physiological (genetic and biochemical) and psychological.

Our clinical experience and our limited knowledge of the psychiatric literature have so far failed to convince us completely of the validity of the proofs for a biological–genetic etiology of "endogenous" or psychotic depression, and even of manic–depressive psychosis. However, to avoid as much as possible the risk of mixing conditions that are possibly heterogeneous in attempting to find out what kind of common cognitive organization could possibly underlie depression, we have limited ourselves to data that pertain to patients who would have been diagnosed as neurotic, psychogenic, or reactive depressives by most psychiatrists.[1]

In view of the assessment method presented in Chapter 7, we shall discuss our results under three headings: behavioral, cognitive, and developmental aspects of depression. We shall substantiate our hypotheses and conjectures whenever possible with pertinent clinical, statistical, and experimental findings drawn from various sources.

BEHAVIORAL ASPECTS

The most typical feature of the behavior of depressed patients—found in forms of retarded as well as agitated depression, where the patient's facial expression gives the impression either of deep sadness or, superficially, of happiness (the "smiling" depression)—is a marked decrease in the rate of behavior.

The depressed patient withdraws from participation in most of the activities that once made up his or her life. As a rule, the patient gives up *pleasant* activities first and only later on tries giving up routine or "necessary" activities. In the most serious cases, the patient may end up avoiding almost any activity at all, including efforts to escape from situations that are even physically painful, and thus reaching total immobility (depressive stupor, "stupor melancholicus").[2]

Seligman (1974) proposed a model for depression based on his experimental findings of a way to produce in animals (dogs) a state that he called "learned helplessness." Dogs subjected to inescapable electric shocks may subsequently fail to escape from other shocks when escape is possible. During avoidance training, "in dramatic contrast to a naive dog, . . . a typical dog which has experienced uncontrollable shocks . . . soon stops running or howling and sits or lies, quietly whining, until shock terminates. The dog does not cross the barrier and escape from shock. Rather, it seems to give up and passively accept the shock" (Seligman, 1974, p. 85). Seligman argues that "it is not trauma as such that produces interference with later adaptive responding, *but not having control over trauma*" (p. 93; italics in original).

There are obvious formal similarities between a condition of learned helplessness and the inertia of depressed patients. Some depressed patients' statements seem to be compatible with Seligman's idea that the lack of control over painful environmental contingencies is responsible for learned helplessness as well as for many behavioral, affective, and motivational phenomena of naturally occurring human depression (apathy, withdrawal, inability to reach decisions, loss of interest and motivation, sense of inadequacy, etc.). Nevertheless, if one considers the historical antecedents of inertia shown by depressed patients, it is difficult to trace environmental events that are clearly similar to the inescapable shocks producing learned helplessness. To consider an affective loss or a serious difficulty at work[3] on a par with the inescapable shocks that Seligman's dogs were exposed to, cognitive variables must also be considered. In fact, the latest research on learned helplessness (Abramson, Seligman, & Teasdale, 1978) has led to a recasting of the model based on the assumption that depressed patients learn to perceive reinforcement as independent of their behavior and that they *believe* the cause of independence is a *stable, negative,* and *internal attribute.*

In a behavioral–functional analysis of a depressive's inertia, three other hypotheses may be considered:

1. That inertia is an operant behavior maintained by external reinforcement (i.e., other people take care of, and give positive attention to, the depressed patient).
2. That it is an impoverishment of the behavioral repertoire consequent to loss of reinforcement (see Ferster, 1974).
3. That it is an instance of extreme avoidance behavior.

Clinical observations quickly reveal that the first two hypotheses apply, at most, to a very limited number of depressed patients. Frequently, the patient's relatives, after a brief period of compliance, react negatively to the patient's apathy: Being admitted to a psychiatric ward is *not* a reward for one's inertia. During the period of withdrawal and passivity, the patient genuinely suffers (he or she may even commit suicide!), which is hardly to be expected in positively reinforced behavior. The loss of important sources of reinforcement applies only to those instances of depression that are a reaction to bereavement; we must also remember that there is a difference between normal grief and clinical depression.[4]

The hypothesis that the patient's withdrawal, passivity, and behavioral retardation could be considered as forms of avoidance behavior deserves more attention. It is possible that all environmental situations that formerly gratified the patient have acquired a punishing tinge, so that the patient actively tries to escape from or avoid them. This is indeed the impression one gets while examining the way in which he or she has "given up." Beck's description of the stages through which the depressed person arrives at almost total inertia is enlightening:

He no longer feels attracted to the kinds of enterprises he ordinarily would undertake spontaneously. In fact, he finds that he has to *force* himself to engage in his usual activities. He goes through the motions of attending to his ordinary affairs because he believes he *should*, or because *he knows it is "the right thing to do,"* because others urge him to do it—but not because he wants to. . . . He feels a strong drive to *avoid* "constructive" or "normal" activities. . . . He may feel *repelled* by the thought of performing even elementary functions such as getting out of bed, dressing himself, or attending to personal needs. A retarded, depressed woman would rapidly dive under the bedcovers whenever I entered the room. *She would become exceptionally aroused and even energetic in her attempt to escape from an activity that she was pressed to engage in.* . . . People generally try to avoid situations they expect to be painful; because the depressed patient perceives most situations as onerous, boring, or painful, he desires to avoid even the usual amenities of living. (Beck, 1976, pp. 121–123; italics added)

Beck's observation of the depressed woman's energetic attempts to escape makes a point that is difficult to explain either by the learned helplessness hypothesis or by the hypothesis that psychomotor retardation is a consequence of a primary biochemical defect in depression (the "physical depletion" hypothesis). Our observations are in accordance with this: Depressed patients seem to have "energy," but choose not to use it, except when they are pressed to give up their "apathy." In such cases, in contrast with Seligman's dog, the patient does "jump the barrier" and escapes from what he or she seems to consider the more painful "shock," that is, to engage in some "constructive" activity. Even suicidal behavior may be regarded as an extreme escape or avoidance behavior: It is the only way to escape from actual suffering and to avoid the future burden of a hopeless and painful life (see Beck, 1976, pp. 123–124, for some examples of how depressed subjects justify their suicidal wishes).

Naturally, still to be explained is how environmental situations that were once pleasant or neutral acquire such punitive and repulsive attributes for the patient. No environmental antecedents justify such transformation in the clinical analysis of all our patients. (Obviously, were human beings to come up against such environmental transformation as to cause the whole world around them to have objectively repulsive features, we would consider neither their inertia nor any attempted suicide as abnormal behavior.) It seems, rather, that depressed patients have in some way *decided* that passivity and withdrawal are the best—or the least bad—solutions to their problems. To know what the problems are, we must proceed to analyze patients' cognitive contents or processes.

However, before presenting the cognitive–functional analysis of depression, we must further examine a sector of the patient's experience that will make it worthwhile to carry out a sequential analysis in terms of environmental antecedents and consequences, namely, his or her emotional reactions and related interpersonal behavior. The reconstruction of the sequences of environmental antecedents and emotional responses during the first psychotherapy sessions with a depressed patient is useful from the point of view of clinical assessment—furnishing, as it does, the basis for the identification of mediating cognitions—and from the point of view of therapy. In fact, the depressed patient often states in his first interviews that "*everything* makes him suffer"; "he is *always* sad"; "he can't stand *any* novelty"; he is irritated or cries "over a trifle"; he feels "anguished by everything"; he is "always ill"—all of which is "probably to be attributed to some deficiency, fault, or incurable disease" of his. When asked to give clear examples of his negative reactions and to consider to what kinds or mixtures of basic feelings (sadness, fear, or anger) his emotional distress can be compared, the patient discovers with the therapist that, in the apparently uniformly gloomy picture of his existence, some selective responses and exact kinds of situations really do emerge. Usually one can observe that depressed patients overreact to environmental events connoting rejection or loss. Reaction is anguish or sadness, sometimes preceded by anger. It can also be observed that, in situations where there is an environmental influence pressing patients out of their inertia, they react with anxiety (if they consider that action is the "right thing to do"), anger (if they feel unjustly pressed on to action by others), or a mixture of these two basic emotions (the most frequent reaction).

The following examples may illustrate this point:

Example 1

John, a mildly depressed 38-year-old married journalist, noticed that, the day before, he awoke "a bit less depressed" than usual, but soon his depression came back again, worse than ever. John thought that this was proof of the endogenous nature of his depression, because a previous psychiatrist had explained to him that sadness is at its worst, for "endogenous patients," early in the morning. During this assessment, John, trying to identify accurately the events that followed his "seemingly good" awakening the day before, was very sad and not much interested in the procedure. He thought that no "real illness" could be cured by talk. The therapist then asked whether his wife had gotten up before him or after him. Taking on a still gloomier look, John answered that she had gotten up after him. He said angrily that his wife completely disregarded his suffering, and that often, taking advantage of the fact that he arose earlier than usual ever since he got "sick," she would ask him to prepare breakfast! It was not hard to make John see that, as soon as he heard his wife saying "Now that you're up, dear, will you get breakfast ready?," his mood changed. He had become angry, just as he did now; he had started to think that his wife did not understand him and did not love him and *after that* he had become sad. Beck (1967, Chapter 21) reports a similar case, and one may wonder how many instances of "endothymic variations of mood state" could be at least partially explained in this way.

Example 2

Barbara, a severely depressed housewife in her late forties, reacted with crying and yelling whenever her husband tried to force her to go out for a walk, to "get her mind off her worries." She usually succeeded in opposing her husband's efforts. The day before she was admitted to a clinic, he asked her to go out to visit her elderly mother, and Barbara experienced violent anxiety: She reported that she felt the "moral duty" to go, but the idea of dressing up and going out was somehow unbearable. This conflict seemed to activate Barbara's next reaction; she began to scream in agitation that she deserved to die because she couldn't even go out to visit her mother. Then she violently accused her husband of trying to force her to go out at all costs. Wavering between self-accusation and accusation of her husband, her speech became so incoherent that the psychiatrist, when summoned, considered it necessary to hospitalize her.

These examples show the consequences that can follow the expression, in interpersonal behavior, of negative emotions evoked by the perception of rejection, loss, or undue pressure. The partners or relatives of depressed patients would probably respond, in turn, with anger ("This is what I get for trying to help you"), with detachment ("It's pointless to speak with you, you're sick"), or otherwise by showing interest that becomes an "undue pressure" (i.e., forcing patients to come out of their inertia or trying to convince them to enter a hospital, etc.). So, depressed patients tend to create a "niche" of interpersonal relationships around themselves, progressively confirming their perception of refusal or affective loss.[5]

It is hardly necessary to remark, in closing this behavioral analysis, that by their inertia depressive patients *actively* cut themselves off from environmental sources of reinforcement.

COGNITIVE ASPECTS

There is no greater cause of melancholy than idleness; no better cure than business.
—R. Burton, *The Anatomy of Melancholy* (1621)

The notion that "there is no better cure for melancholy than business" is time-honored and makes sense. The depressive's relatives usually try, unsuccessfully, to apply it. Orthodox behavior therapists have also applied it, seemingly without much more success. It seems, then, promising to try to assess how and why any attempt to press the depressed patient into "business" is likely to fail. The best available way of performing this assessment is to question the patient in a straightforward manner and then to listen carefully.[6] Four typical categories of answers are obtained, which can be summarized under the following headings: negative view of the future, negative view of the world, negative view of the self, and desire to "spare effort."[7]

NEGATIVE VIEW OF THE FUTURE

Patients' short- and long-run expectations are negative and pessimistic. On awakening in the morning, depressed patients "see" a day ahead of them full of hardships, oppressing obligations, and suffering. (We suspect that this may be the reason for the daily mood fluctuation often considered a proof of the endogenous nature of depression; obviously in the evening the negative expectations of the day are much diminished.) When they plan to initiate some activity, they foresee failure. When inivited to do something that once amused them, they do not expect to enjoy it or even expect to be bored to death. This kind of negative expectation often appears spontaneously in the imaginal mode of thought representation. If patients feel that they are forced—either from within or without—to act, an internal dialogue (verbal mode of representation) is quickly set up, focusing on these pessimistic expectations.

The following dialogue is an example of a rather typical way in which patients can verbalize their attitude toward the future outcome of their actions:

T: I understand that your wife frequently asks you to go out and meet friends. Why don't you?

P: It would be boring.

T: How do you know? Is it a sort of scene that comes to mind, as in a movie? Is it a picture of a boring meeting? Or do you say to yourself in your mind, "It would be boring?"

P: I don't know. I believe that it is more like a picture in my mind.

T: Do you daydream of topics such as boring meetings, unpleasant situations that you will find at work, and so forth?

P: Yes, I believe that sometimes I do. For instance, yesterday I spent some time thinking of what to do during my vacation. . . . I don't feel like going to the sea anymore . . . and I had a sort of picture of a crowded, noisy beach. . . . Beaches are like that now, and the sea is polluted . . . and mountains are so boring . . . but, again, staying in town, it's so hot . . .

T: You told me you quarreled with your wife because of this problem about your vacation. Did you have this picture of a dirty sea and a crowded beach in your mind while discussing it with her?

P: I don't know, perhaps . . . well, not really, I was thinking instead that she ought to understand me a bit better, I'm not well . . .

T: I'm sure that this feeling of yours—of the need to be better understood—deserves to be spoken of at some length. We'll come back to it shortly. Now, please try to remember whether what you had in mind during your discussion with your wife was a sort of internal monologue or was more like a picture.

P (after a pause): Well, I was surely thinking that it was better for us not to go on vacation so that we could save some money. We're going to need it you know. . . . I'm sure next year I won't be able to earn much money any more . . . I haven't told my wife about this. . . . And it couldn't be a picture . . . I'm sure that I haven't seen a bank, or something like that. . . . Yes, I believe that I was mostly speaking to myself.

T: Did this idea of saving money come before your image of the noisy beach, or did it follow it, in the thoughts that you had about a vacation at that time?

P: The image of the dirty beach surely came first.

(*Note:* This is a verbatim report of an interview with a patient who soon proved to be quite capable of recognizing the different modes of thought representation. Often the therapist has to be content only with a patient's self-reports in which "pictorial" and "verbal" cognitions are indistinguishable.)

If the therapist keeps on asking the patient why he makes no effort to act, he will probably be given answers indicative of a negative view of the far-off future,[8] the world, or himself or of the wish to avoid useless effort, according to the way in which the questions are asked. These simplifed examples follow the patterns of the preceding outline:

T: Don't you think a vacation would do you good? You could relax and next year better approach your work so that maybe you'd earn more.

P: No. Nothing will make me feel better. And there is no sense in all of this . . . vacation, work, marriage . . . my life is a failure, and I don't think it will ever change.

T: How can you be sure that the beach will be so unpleasant or that meeting friends will be so boring?

P: Don't you see what a rotten world we live in? And why should my friends care about me?

T: Do you really think your wife doesn't understand you? Maybe she thinks the sea would do you good, too.

P: Yes, maybe . . . I expect too much from her. . . . Poor thing, she's got an utter failure for a husband . . .

T: What comes to mind if you try to think about going on vacation anyway, if only to please your wife?

P: Fair enough. I know I should . . . but it's so laborious; I don't feel up to it; I'm tired; I'm sick all the time. . . . At least at home I avoid useless efforts . . . by the sea I would be an even greater burden for my wife.

NEGATIVE VIEW OF THE WORLD

Sometimes when the therapist asks questions aimed at determining the reasons for a patient's inertia, the latter's answers immediately reveal a negative view of external reality. As a rule of thumb, we would say that, when that happens, the severity of the depressive state is greater than in the preceding example. The negative view of the world in less severely depressed patients tends to emerge only later on during the conversations, for instance, when the therapist asks questions that more directly recall the attitude of the patient toward reality, as in the second example on page 179. As is apparent from this example, the pessimistic attitude toward reality is manifested mainly in statements of rejection, disparagement, and loss. It is important to emphasize that depressed patients see themselves as somehow deserving their "destiny" of rejection, disparagement, and loss. This distinguishes them very clearly from anxious or phobic patients, who *fear* being rejected, and from paranoids, who think that other people are wicked and that they reveal their evil natures by rejecting them or persecuting them, "the good guys."[9]

The attribution of causality for a perceived loss to some personal deficiency or to an impersonal adverse destiny also distinguishes depressive patients from people suffering from actual bereavement (normal grief and mourning). As Beck cogently states, "*the sense of loss is the central theme of depressive cognitions*" (Beck, 1976, p. 105), but, contrary to what happens in normal grief, in depressed patients the loss is usually imagined, anticipated, hypothetical. Depressed patients ultimately see themselves as *destined to loneliness* and deserving this destiny.[10] Therefore, whenever depressed patients give their negative view of the world as a reason for their inertia, successive clinical inquiry quickly brings out their negative view of self.

NEGATIVE VIEW OF THE SELF

Sometimes depressed patients put forward a negative view of themselves as the *first* answer to the therapist's questions regarding their apathy. As we have said, this fact seems to correlate positively with the severity of the depression. Beck and Stein's (1960) research on the self-concept in depression, showing a strong positive correlation between the Depression Inventory's scores and measures of negative self-concept ($r = .70$), seems to support indirectly our clinical impression. Since the correlation between measures of severity of depression (i.e., the Depression Inventory) and of "pessimism" (or negative view of the future) was somewhat lower ($r = .56$), the idea that a dominant negative view of oneself is correlated with a severe depression receives further (feeble!) statistical support (see also Note 7).

As we have said, a negative concept of oneself tends to emerge in almost any case when, on clinical questioning, the therapist investigates the reasons why the patient feels rejected, not understood, or despised by friends or by those who mean something to him or her. Even when the patient is pressed to say what will happen after a negative evaluation of the kind that Beck called "pseudo-losses" (Beck, 1976, p. 106), a chain of expectations and judgments results that reveals a negative view of self. The following example will illustrate such a chain:

Ann was a wealthy married woman of 39 years when she asked for psychotherapy because of a moderately severe form of depression, which had resisted various antidepressant medications for 2 years. Ann awoke very early in the morning, was almost always sad, and often cried for no reason. In the first interviews, she said that her melancholy was caused by her "empty, boring life," that her usual rich-housewife activities and her friendships had become unbearable, and that she often thought about finding a job or going back to the university to break the monotony of her life. Yet, whenever she decided to enroll at the university or start working, she succumbed to strong anguish and crying fits and could not take action.

Trained to recognize her own inner dialogue and her own images, Ann was invited to observe what could happen in her mind when she was supposed to be interviewed for a possible job shortly thereafter. Ann reported that at the time she could not decide whether to go to the interview or not; she noted two orders of thought, one "on the surface" and the other "somewhat deeper." The superficial thought was that the employer would have refused her, considering her the usual rich woman working for a hobby (an image of the interviewer with a critical rejecting attitude, and an internal dialogue on the theme "rich women looking for a hobby"). In the back of her mind, however, there was also a representation not connected with the decision to be made, namely, the thought of having somehow lost the affection of her husband and two children (pseudo-loss). Ann's husband was showing affection and concern for her and had taken the attitude "Go to

work if you like, but if you don't feel like working, it's not a tragedy, either";
he came home shortly after work, was sexually aroused by Ann, and so forth.
Ann was invited to keep firmly in mind the impression that she had lost her
husband's love. She could not tell whether the idea was presented in a
"quasi-pictorial" form, but was certain at any rate that it was not really an
internal dialogue. She was then asked to imagine what would have happened
after this loss, and Ann drew up an image of herself alone at home, taken up
with this thought: "There you are: I deserve it, I am stupid. I couldn't love
anyone; they were right in going away."

It is important when assessing cognition related to a negative
view of the self, the world, and the future to bear in mind that these
apply to the "personal domain" of the patient, that is, to those aspects
of the self and the world that were meaningful and valued before the
onset of depression. For Ann, love was such an aspect. The patient
whose interview is reported on p. 178ff. highly valued the ability to
earn money and to enjoy himself after working hard. John and
Barbara (p. 175ff.) both held reciprocal understanding, care, and
attention, particularly when one is ill or old, as highly important
aspects of interpersonal relationships, and so forth. We shall soon see
how this observation, to which Beck has repeatedly called attention
(Beck, 1967, 1974, 1976; see also Kovacs & Beck, 1979; Shaw, 1979) is
relevant to the following topic.

DESIRE TO SPARE EFFORT

There are clinical and correlational data that allow us to believe that
the elements of the cognitive triad of depression are interrelated
(Beck, 1967, 1970, 1974), that is, that they constitute a structure.
Nevertheless, they are not always identifiable together in every single
case of depression. Above all, ascertaining the negative view of the
world is sometimes not possible because patients can state that it is
right for the world to refuse them since they have an "intrinsically
evil" nature: "I am cast out of the world and I deserve it. How
beautiful it used to be to go to the countryside. . . . Now the trees that
I see are not as beautiful as they used to be. I have lost forever the
ability to enjoy nature." This example is taken from one of our more
educated patients, who clearly shows that he has lost the capacity to
enjoy the world, though the world is still as good as it ever was.

Perhaps the most consistent reason given by depressed patients for inactivity is the desire to avoid "useless effort." Depressed patients often feel tired and weak (muscle tone and artery pressure are sometimes concomitantly low), think that anything they attempt is bound to fail, and think that they have lost control over getting "positive reinforcements" and avoiding punishing consequences (which reminds us of Seligman's "learned helplessness"). In the face of all of this, they feel that their passivity and inertia are a rather rational solution, for they can thus at least spare themselves the efforts that are seen as useless or overwhelming in view of their weakness.[11] Views of problems as overwhelming (Beck *et al.*, 1979, p. 188) and verbalizations such as "It is pointless to try"; "If I try anything, it won't work out, and I'll only feel worse"; "It's much easier to just sit still, I'm too weak to do anything" (Beck, 1976, p. 274ff.; Beck *et al.*, 1979, p. 198)—all these clinical phenomena can be linked to a wish to spare effort.

It seems to us that the idea of effort or toil must occupy a rather central place in the cognitive organization of persons prone to depression. Certain descriptions of the premorbid personality of depressed patients are in agreement with the assumed central role of beliefs about how tough life is and how even tougher one must be to stand up to it. For example, in Chodoff's (1974) review, one can find descriptions of premorbid personality traits such as these: "vigorous," "competitive," "enterprising," "aggressive," "active," "ambitious," "sociable," "people who make mountains out of molehills," "frequently successful," "hard working," "conscientious," "indeed at times his overconscientiousness and scrupulousness lead to his being called obsessional."[12]

The clinical example that Beck *et al.* (1979) use to demonstrate how depressogenic assumptions lead to "automatic thoughts" (i.e., cognitions of the negative triad occupying the stream of consciousness), and how these in turn lead to sadness and anger, also is in accordance with the idea of the central role of assumptions concerning the need to be strong and well-prepared in order to meet life's difficulties. The reported primary assumption of such a patient is, "If I'm nice (*suffer* for others, *appear* bright and beautiful) bad things (divorce, rambunctious children) won't happen to me" (Beck *et al.*, 1979, Chapter 12, Figure 3; italics added). It seems to us that such a patient must have had the difficulties of life (mostly losses) in mind and then resolved that a strenuous preventive effort was to be made.

Beck's cogent considerations of the strict relationship between the "personal domain" and the specific content of the "cognitive triad" are also pertinent to the topic; the same applies to Beck's explanation of the self-reproaches, as follows:

> In reviewing the histories of depressed patients we often find that the patient has counted on the attribute that he now debases for balancing the usual stresses of life, mastering new problems, and attaining important objectives. When he reaches the conclusion (often erroneously) that he is unable to master a serious problem, attain a goal, or forestall a loss, he downgrades the asset. As this attribute appears to fade, he begins to believe that he cannot get satisfaction out of life and that all he can expect is pain and suffering. The depressed patient proceeds from disappointment to self-blame to pessimism. (Beck, 1976, pp. 114–115)

We would like to avoid a full discussion of the links between the depressive cognitions and their emotional consequences; the writings of Beck (1967, 1976) and Shaw (1979) could be consulted for this purpose. We shall limit ourselves to some brief summarizing notions.

1. The perception of loss produces feelings of sadness. Studies of bereavement and grief (Bowlby, 1961, 1969, 1973; Parkes, 1972) strongly support the notion of an "unconditioned" relationship between loss and sadness. Anger appears as a component in the process of mourning, but is not at all the antecedent of sadness. (According to Freud, the sequence is: unconscious hostility toward the deceased love object → guilt and anger directed toward the self → sadness.) Even taking into account the difference between actual and imagined losses, it is obvious that, if loss and loneliness dominate depressives' representations of themselves and the world, they will feel uniformly sad.

2. It is possible to distinguish feelings other than sadness in the depressive's daily experience: Anger directed toward self and others and fear are perhaps the most important. These specific feelings are elicited, in daily experience, by selective stimulus situations and are mediated by the patient's belief system. Useful information about the patient's idiosyncratic cognitions, particularly about the content of his or her "shoulds" (rigid rules for living), can be obtained by an analysis aimed at these specific feelings. It is important to recognize explicitly that in our cognitive model sadness is the "primary" feeling in

depression; that is, it is not secondary to anger or fear, as it is assumed in much of the psychoanalytic writing.

3. Anger, fear, and sadness are connected to specific beliefs, and their relationships are understandable in terms of the relationships among beliefs that constitute the cognitive structure. A hierarchical organization in which personal identity plays a central role is a better way of conceptualizing this structure than as a chain of causal relationships. The sense of loss and the belief that one has to strive energetically to face it seem to be the central themes of the depression-prone individual's cognitive organization. Whenever this striving fails, the organization goes through a series of changes and readjustments, of which the emerging negative cognitive triad is an expression. The problem at this point is to determine how the sense of loss and the need to face it through intense striving could have developed.

DEVELOPMENTAL ASPECTS

> But oh the heavy change, now thou
> art gone,
> Now thou art gone, and never must return!
> —J. Milton, "Lycidas"

An impressive amount of data indicates that there is a fairly high probability that more depressed individuals have experienced the death of a parent before or during adolescence than nondepressed individuals.

In Chapter 14 of his 1967 book, Beck reviews existing data pointing to the association between premature loss of a parent and subsequent adult depression and presents his own data. Figures on the premature loss of a parent are as follows: 41% (Brown's depressed patients), 12% (general population), and 19.6% (medical patients); 36.4% (Beck's depressed subjects) and 15.2% (psychiatric nondepressed patients). In Beck's study the depth of depression was also significantly correlated to the probability of loss of a parent in childhood; girls seemed more vulnerable than boys to this kind of sorrow. In their recent sociological and statistical study, Brown and Harris (1978, p. 179) found that 47% of women who had lost their mothers before the age of 11 developed a depression during the period of observation, as compared with only 17% of the remaining women. These figures are of statistical significance.[13] In our own sample (see Table B-1, Appendix B), 9 of 24 depressed patients (37.5%) and 22 of 174 nondepressed neurotic patients (12.6%) experienced the death of a parent before age 15. A definitive separation between parents while the patient was a child or a teenager was found in two other depressed subjects and in nine of the nondepressed group.

It is obvious that thinking about a loss influences the way one looks at the world, and consequently, the experience of the death of a parent may take the form of an enduring cognitive influence. However, it is also obvious that not every child who experiences the loss of a parent develops depression later in life, even when faced with serious difficulties or further losses. Besides, many depressed patients have never experienced a loss before adolescence (see Birchnell, 1972, for statistical results in which the association between early death of a parent and depression, though significant, seems to be minuscule). Furthermore, how will the experience of early loss influence the cognitive organization of a future depressive? Is it in the direction that Seligman (1975) suggests—that is, helpless predisposition or learning of uncontrollability—or rather in the direction suggested by Bowlby's concept of compulsive self-reliance (Bowlby, 1977a)?

To give some tentative answers to these problems, we must first consider the family background in which the loss occurs, inquire about the interpersonal situations that could possibly bear some resemblance to separation by death, and finally, listen to the verbalizations of our patients that may be pertinent to these problems.

FAMILY BACKGROUND

The family background of depressive patients has been repeatedly studied, with ambiguous results (for a review, see Beck, 1967, Chapter 10). Generally, one could say that there are some hints that future depressives were brought up in families in which a great deal of importance was attached to success, prestige, and competition. The image of a person striving against difficulties seems to fit such a description.

INTERPERSONAL SITUATIONS

Separation from a beloved parent can come about not only by death
or divorce from the other parent, but also in a variety of other ways.
For example, consider the family in which economic necessity results
in both parents' working and leaving the child alone (which was the
case with 3 of our 24 depressed patients). Or consider the case of one
parent's being forced to work abroad for 2 or more years during the
child's early years (which happened to two of our patients). Or
further, consider the possibility of one parent's often being absent
and the other parent's being weak or sick so that the child is not cared
for by anyone and must not only be deprived of affection, but must
also learn to cope by himself or herself (compulsive self-reliance) in
facing life's difficulties. This was the situation with seven of our
patients, three of whom clearly remembered having felt anger toward
the absent and/or the weak and sick parent. (In two cases the
"illness" seemed to be clearly of a hysterical nature.) The other four
patients expressed understanding for the parent who was too busy to
take care of them ("He had to look after everything") and sympathy
for the sick parent ("Mother suffered so much, poor thing, she
couldn't look after me; Daddy had to take care of her and work as
well"). Four patients who had lost a parent clearly remembered their
childhood decision to look after the other parent, so that the situation
described by Bowlby as an "inverted pattern of attachment" came
about. In these cases the compulsive self-reliance concept (Bowlby,
1977a) seemed especially applicable.

From the extensive and accurate statistical findings of Brown
and Harris (1978), one gets the impression that the ability to establish
intimacy in interpersonal relationships is a powerful protective factor
against depression. In the families of our depressed patients, intimacy
was more often shared with the parent about to die or leave than with
the remaining parent. Sometimes intimacy was achieved at the ex-
pense of reversing the attachment pattern, that is, through strenuous
efforts on the part of the child to take care of the parent (who
reciprocated with feeble expressions of gratitude and approval). In
this context it must be stressed that 11 of our 24 depressed patients
had been present during the prolonged depression of (chronic in
three cases), or the mourning for, one of the parents. This parent's
depression seemed sometimes to be of a hysterical nature and other

times of a reactive nature. This fact is important not only for the possible modeling of the child upon a depressed parent or for the decision to have to rely on himself or herself and take care of the parent, but also for the critical light that it can shed on the problem of the hereditary, genetic nature of depression.

PATIENTS' VERBALIZATIONS

Patients' verbalizations concerning their early sense of loss and loneliness deserve to be quoted extensively. This is John (Example 1, p. 175):

> My father was often away from home; he was a salesman and had to travel a lot to other cities. No, I didn't resent his absence; you have to work to live, and life is so hard. . . . He was too tired to play with me when he was at home, but I understood him: His work was really a continuous stress. . . . The rare occasions in which he played with me are the best memories of my childhood. . . . My mother was rigid; all she wanted was for me to be the best in class. . . . She used to say that life is full of difficulties, and you have to be very well prepared for them. . . . I can't forgive the way she behaved when my father grew old and had to retire; she refused to admit that he was really worn down, she wanted him to go on working, she forced him to work in the house, preparing meals and cleaning the floors . . . it was awful. [The reader may perhaps remember John's reaction to his wife when she asked him to prepare breakfast.]

This is Barbara (Example 2, p. 176):

> When my father was ill, I understood how important it is to take care of an ailing person [Barbara's father died when she was 8, after 2 years of suffering and surgery for cancer.]. . . . My mother collapsed after my father's death. . . . Oh how much I wanted to take care of her. . . . My mother sacrificed herself in order to bring me up. . . . She worked hard and refused to marry again because she feared my reactions toward a stepfather. . . . Do you see how I have reciprocated my mother's sacrifice?

The patient with an astounding ability to recognize clearly, from the beginning, the pictorial and verbal forms of his thoughts (see dialogue beginning on p. 178) used to say with a smile:

One has to rely on himself, isn't that so, Doctor? . . . Nobody will take care of you; if you do not, why should someone else? . . . All I want from my wife is a bit more recognition of my illness, that's all. . . . My parents were both hard-working people. Yes, you're right, Doctor: I learned when I was a child that you have to rely on yourself. They didn't have time for me. Life was so hard, we were really poor. . . . I must have decided then that I wanted a lot of money. . . . I thought I could work even harder than my parents did, but I also wanted more money so that I could relax and enjoy myself after working.

This is another (female) patient's recollection:

I was 5 when my father died. The following year I was at boarding school because my mother had to work. I felt isolated, different from other girls. I remember that, while there, I had an hallucination. . . . It wasn't a dream, I was awake in bed. . . . I "saw" a woman, in black garments, looking at me very sadly. . . . It was nobody I knew. . . . I often thought that that woman had come to point out my destiny. . . . I tried to fight back; I worked, got married, had two children . . . but, do you see, Doctor, despite my efforts here I am: The woman in the vision was right.

Here is yet another female patient:

My mother had that terrible headache all the time—but I'm sure it wasn't true. . . . She made life hell for my father and me. He stayed out of the house as much as possible because of that. I hated her. Shortly after Daddy went out, her headache would disappear. I felt good on those rare occasions that I went out with Daddy, but she used to get angry and say that we left her alone. She wanted me to stay with her so she could torture me with all her talk about my father's indifference. I felt lonely when I was at home with her. I have always tried very hard to be different from my mother, and look how it all ends up—I can't find a man; as a woman I'm a failure.

And this is Ann (see p. 181):

Oh Doctor, only now that my father is ill and is not going to live much longer do I realize how much I missed him when I was a little girl. [Her father had become ill 4 months after Ann started psychotherapy.] He was an insignificant person at home; mother did all the ordering and took care of family business. . . . I loved my mother and thought my father was a good-for-nothing. I had not grasped how important his affection and calm were. . . . My mother used to say that you have to be active and preserve your wealth and your own happiness, and only now do I understand that I was always afraid that I wasn't as strong as my mother and that I didn't know how to be happy. . . . Yes, Doctor, you're right, I considered happiness a duty, an obligation, and when I began to fear that I hadn't attained it, I felt awful. . . . I was rich, I had everything—but I wasn't happy or strong and active like my mother. . . . Ever since I was a child, I thought that love was important, and ever since then, I couldn't recognize it. . . . I didn't know how to love my father.

THE COGNITIVE ORGANIZATION IN DEPRESSION

But first I must/Tell you/That I should really *like* to think there's something wrong with me—/Because, if there isn't, then there's something wrong,/Or at least, very different from what it seemed to be,/With the world itself—and that's much more fright-/ening!/That would be terrible. . . . —T. S. Eliot, *The Cocktail Party*, Act II

The loss of a parent. The perception of isolation by a child who is separated from parents who are too busy. Worry over a sick parent, who cannot spend time with the child, as the only form of affective manifestation. An experience of any of these types constitutes the center of cognizance of oneself and of the world held by the depressed person. We can summarize the meaning of these experiences with the word "solitude." This is the basic theme of the depression-prone individual's early emotional schemata. When faced with the experience of isolation, a child can take on one of two attitudes: consider others bad because they left him or her alone or consider himself or herself as somehow deserving that isolation.

The words that Eliot has Celia say in *The Cocktail Party* make it clear why a negative attitude toward the self is preferable. If "there's something wrong with me," I can avoid the paranoid, frightening nightmare of living in a hostile world in which "there's something . . . very different from what it seemed to be." Moreover, if "there's something wrong with me," perhaps I can find in my environment (which is not totally hostile and deceitful and playing wicked tricks) some knowledge that can lead me to a better adjustment. Maybe I can fight off the fate of isolation and misery. The environment, and frequently the family itself, gives such knowledge. If you try hard, if you are strong, if you have enough willpower, if you are nice and never get angry (a good person does not get angry), if you are long-suffering and sacrifice yourself for others, if you work hard, if you are the best person in your class, and if you love people, then perhaps you will succeed in avoiding loneliness and misery. A generic feeling, "there's something wrong with me," and a remedy, "I have to fight my fate," become the foundations for building personal identity. Self-identity is valued if one succeeds in fighting, but devalued if one fails. Self-esteem fluctuates accordingly. A strong propensity toward value judgments is to be expected. The attitude toward reality now becomes more adapted than that of the paranoid. Rules for assimilating experience are formulated in this way: "Find out whether people like you or not"; "see whether there is somebody stronger (or more clever, etc.) than you are around here"; "test the difficulties of this situation and the way to overcome them"; "carefully observe the suffering in people and how you can alleviate it"; "find out the rules determining acceptance or rejection in this environment"; and so forth. Problem solving is dominated by the idea that strenuous striving is probably needed and by "economic" evaluations of the amount of energy required to reach the goal.

This cognitive organization obviously has its pitfalls and contradictions. One of the easiest to recognize, perhaps, is expressed by the statement made by Groucho Marx that he couldn't accept membership in a club that wanted him to join. You have to be accepted after strenuously striving; if your are accepted without it, then either the "club" has failed to recognize that "there's something wrong with you" (and has thus proved that it is stupid), or else it has recognized it, but does not care (and has thus shown what kind of membership it has).

Both Seligman's idea that premature losses teach helplessness or uncontrollability of traumas and Bowlby's concept of compulsive self-reliance are compatible with the cognitive organization outlined here. They appear, so to speak, as the two sides of the coin of personal identity. The side of self-reliance allows for adaptation; when something happens that reverses the coin, and the side of "learned helplessness" shows up, the whole structure goes through the readjustments and transformations recognizable as clinical depression.

Brown and Harris (1978) carefully evaluated precipitating events and major difficulties seemingly responsible for the onset of depression in persons in their sample (114 psychiatric female patients and 458 women selected at random from the general population and matched by age and residence—Camberwell, Great Britain—with the patients' group). They have listed a huge number of possibly relevant life events and difficulties in their interview schedule (Appendix 5 to their book), but we can briefly summarize their main findings with the following quotation:

> Reading through the description of events leaves us in no doubt that *loss* and *disappointment* are the central features of most events bringing about clinical depressions. . . . The experience of loss . . . is seen to include: (i) separation or threat of it; . . . (ii) unpleasant revelation about someone close that forces a major reassessment of the person and the relationship; . . . (iii) a life-threatening illness to someone close; (iv) a major material loss or disappointment; . . . (v) an enforced change of residence, or the threat of it. . . . (Brown & Harris, 1978, p. 103; italics added)

With the exception of Ann, all our patients recognized at least one event among those outlined here as preceding their depression.[14]

Beck (1967, Chapter 18) has called attention to the specificity of stresses that unleash depression with respect to the areas of vulnerability in the patient's cognitive constellation, that is, his or her personal domain. We may now consider how the various provoking agents bring on a readjustment of the cognitive organization. The experience of loss and disappointment—in the extensive sense outlined in Brown and Harris's quotation—reverses the coin of personal identity from self-reliance to lack of control. The individual's self-knowledge already contains emotional schemata related to isolation, loneliness, and misery. The activation of these schemata is matched by the old decision that "there's something wrong with me." The negative attitude toward oneself permeates the thinking and emerges with "automatic thoughts" (see Beck, 1967, 1976). The attributes of the self that are now debased are those that were originally developed in order to fight the "destiny" of isolation. They are useless; the individual has fought and has been defeated, and so the fate of loneliness and misery is to be expected as inevitable. The images and the inner dialogue flowing in the stream of consciousness convey a negative view of the world and of the future. The representational models of reality become such that they allow the assimilation of only negative experiences. In other words, the rules for assimilating experience can be described according to Beck's "thinking errors" or "faulty information processing": arbitrary inference, selective abstraction, overgeneralization, magnification, etc.

From another point of view, one could say that the activation of primitive emotional schemata (according to Duncker's concept of functional fixedness as suggested by Shaw, 1979) brings with it a form of "primitive" thinking, one that contains elements that were typical of the Piagetian stage of cognitive growth during which those schemata were constructed. Globality of judgments ("I *am* wicked"), invariance ("things *always* go this way"), magical thinking ("my *forebodings* . . ."), and above all, lack of distancing ("I know [instead of "I think"] that I have an awful fate") are features of the "primitive" thinking.

Using the scientist's metaphor, one could also say that the challenge to the metaphysical hard-core is matched by a strengthening of the protective belt. Instead of changing the tacit knowledge that loneliness exists and is terrible, and above all, that uncontrollability exists and is frightening, the individual insists that it is in some way his or her fault that the loss has occurred.[15] Consequently, he or she generates a lot of ad hoc hypotheses and theories in order to substantiate the assumption that "there's something wrong with me" (strengthening of the protective belt). A positive heuristic (e.g., arbitrary inferences "proving" that the individual is a loser) and a negative heuristic (e.g., minimization of favorable events) are used to achieve this thickening of the protective belt. The individual's research program thus becomes "regressive." The rules for solving problems are still permeated by the individual's attitude toward reality, that is, that strenuous striving is needed in order to confront the toughness of life, but now the conclusions are reversed: Since one is "helpless" in the face of one's wicked fate, which one deserves, the most rational thing to do is to remain passive, so that at least one will spare effort. Thus we are back to inertia, from which we started our analysis.

Most cases of depression are relatively short-lived: Depression tends to fade away spontaneously. When the recent experience of disappointment and loss fades away in time, and the person recognizes that relative control can be regained over most of his or her life events, the cognitive organization readjusts itself into its adaptive form. No change in personal identity is obtained in this way, so new stresses can put forward again the idea of uncontrollability and can prevail over self-reliance. Depression is a recurring "illness."[16]

PSYCHOTHERAPEUTIC STRATEGY WITH DEPRESSED PATIENTS

If your morals make you dreary depend upon it, they are wrong.—R. L. Stevenson, *A Christmas Sermon*

The treatment of depression has been a major focus of cognitive therapy. Beck (1967, 1976) and Beck *et al.* (1979) have described in detail a host of *techniques* (both behavioral and strictly cognitive) through which a cognitive change can be obtained in depressive patients. They have also suggested the general lines of the *strategy* within which the therapeutic *tactics* have to be couched, so that the therapy will not follow an erratic course based on trial and error.

During the first phase of assessment, the therapist generally gives the rationale for cognitive therapy and teaches patients to observe and record their own "automatic thoughts." A first step toward "distancing" is thus made. At the same time, the therapist precisely defines the problem areas and selects the first target symptoms to be dealt with. Behavioral targets (inertia, passivity, interpersonal problems), emotional targets (sadness, anger, guilt, anxiety, shame), motivational targets (avoidance wishes, dependency, hopelessness, suicidal wishes), and strictly cognitive targets (indecision, overestimation of problems, self-criticism, polarized thinking) can be selected, for a start, either one by one or in various combinations. With more retarded patients, it is almost compulsory to start with behavioral and motivational targets, so as to give these patients— through behavioral techniques—"mastery" experiences and to elicit the cognitions underlying their inertia and avoidance. While treating the target symptoms, the therapist directly and indirectly (modeling) teaches patients how to take an "experimental" attitude: Where are the proofs for each assertion? In this way further "distancing" is obtained, and at the same time much information is usually gained about patients' "depressogenic assumptions" (i.e., "irrational beliefs," "deeper rules," or "personal contructs"). Besides deeper rules, past experiences are usually given by patients as "proofs" for their statements. Data from patients' past histories are brought into the open, in this way giving a glimpse of their personal development and the fondations of their personal identity. The rational critique of these depressogenic assumptions may start at this stage of treatment.

Up to this point, we have summarized the way in which we ourselves have applied Beck's method of cognitive therapy, trying to verbalize the various steps according to the description given by Beck *et al.* (1979). We must now point out a minor difference in our approach: Before confronting patients with the "depressogenic assumptions," we usually attempt, together with each patient, an initial explicit reconstruction of his or her personal history and cognitive organization. This process has three advantages:

1. It gives the therapist a view of the structural and hierarchical relationships among patients' single assumptions or irrational beliefs, allowing him or her to time future interventions so that patients' personal identity is respected as much as possible. The higher order rules should be changed last, if change is required.
2. It gives the patient an essential basis of partial disengagement from his or her own basic view of self and the world, which is absolutely necessary if a change in personal identity is to be attempted.
3. It allows the therapist to hypothesize about the kind of emotional schemata that the patient formed during childhood and thus to discuss openly with the patient the nature of his or her tacit knowledge, which is somewhat different from the concept of the "unconscious" to which he or she may be accustomed.

In confronting the patient's depressogenic assumptions, note is taken of the way in which he or she conjugates the verb "to be." "I am" is substituted, whenever possible, with other forms: "I do," "I experience," "I feel," "I think," "I believe," "I dream," and so forth. The patient is given the logical and semantic rationale for doing so (see Chapter 8). "Shoulds," "worths," and "musts" are similarly corrected. Thus "*I must* be able to stand life's difficulties, or otherwise I *am* an *unworthy* human being" is translated into "It is better (useful) not to give up easily in the face of certain difficulties, but in no case, even if I *make* a serious mistake, is my *worth* as a human being questioned." Thus, while discussing hierarchically the inconsistencies of the *correlations* between the various basic elements of depressogenic assumptions (e.g., "If I am nice, *then* nothing terrible can happen to me") and the magnification of the emotional sense of their *content* ("Certain things are so *terrible* that I cannot stand them"), the therapist indirectly undermines the idea that one may *be* something other than a human being. When patients acquire the notion that human beings cannot *be* intelligent or stupid, but rather can *have* or not have intellectual capacities, they are ready to take a marked distance from their own personal identity as they had defined it up to that moment. At this point we often chose again, together with the patient, homework assignments (mainly in the fashion of assertiveness training, or rather social skills training) intended to prove that the previous assumptions on which the personal identity was based were nothing but theories.

With this kind of preparation, even the feeling of unreality that sometimes accompanies profound changes in personal identity is not felt by patients as unexplainable or frightening.

Single techniques to fight target "symptoms" are thoroughly described by Beck *et al.* (1979) with many detailed examples; techniques for conducting rational critiques of basic depressogenic assumptions are also presented by Beck *et al.* (1979). Some therapists may prefer to use the arguments with which Ellis (1962) disputes his clients' irrational beliefs. Among such beliefs often presented by depressed patients are the following:

1. One must be competent, adequate, and achieving in order to be considered worthy ("I failed; *therefore* I am worthless").
2. One *needs* love and approval from every significant person ("They reject me, how awful!").
3. If one is "wicked," he or she deserves to be punished ("I deserve my fate because I have no willpower").
4. It is awful and catastrophic when things are not the way one would very much like them to be ("Human beings abhor death; hence the existence of death is a catastrophe").
5. Human unhappiness is caused by external events, and people have little or no ability to control their sorrows ("With my past, why should I hope?").
6. It is better to avoid life's difficulties than to face them ("It is too difficult for me").
7. One should be very upset over other people's problems ("My husband is working so hard, and I don't feel sorry for him as I should").

Ellis's arguments against these beliefs (Ellis, 1962, Chapter 3) can prove very useful if used appropriately. However, we think that the essential point is not the choice of this or that technique (the therapist can make up his or her own technique or adapt an existing one to the specific requirements of the case), but that the therapist be aware of the hierarchical relationships between the various beliefs that constitute the chosen target. The therapist should also ensure that the language in which the arguments are expressed is the kind to which the patient is accustomed. Finally, due consideration should be given to the difference between cognitions appearing in the pictorial mode of representation and those represented in the internal dialogue. Logic can be used for internal dialogue, but it is not much use with daydreams. This is one reason why, in speaking of functional-cognitive analysis, we insisted on the need to ask the patient in what representation mode his or her thoughts appear. The other reason is that in many cases the imaginal representations are a cue for quickly assessing the idiosyncratic structures of personal identity. Rowe's use of guided imagery and grid–repertory techniques to assess the deeper aspects of self-constructs exemplifies this statement (Rowe, 1978).

To give an idea of the importance of considering the structural and hierarchical aspects of cognitive organization in timing the thera-peutic tactics, we shall examine what depressed patients and obses-sional patients think about the possibility of making mistakes and being criticized. If the therapist decides to fight the belief that mistakes and criticism are a proof of one's unworthiness (a belief that will be verbalized in similar ways by the two patients), he or she should be aware of the different hierarchical levels the belief occupies in the two cognitive organizations. For depressed patients it is one of the beliefs making up the protective belt, and correcting it means achieving a deep change. For obsessionals (see Chapter 11), however, it is a relatively peripheral belief, since the personal identity is built around opposite contrasting images and around a desire for absolute certainty and perfection. Therefore criticizing this belief will lead to *no* deep change, but rather to a modification of verbal expressions that could make the therapist think the patient is "resisting" the therapy.

Similarly, both depressed and agoraphobic patients sometimes express exaggerated expectations of loneliness, but whereas the former see loneliness as the proof of their helplessness and unworthi-ness, the latter—having formed a personal identity on the idea of their weakness (they do not consider themselves unlovable)—regard it as a condition of nearly physical danger (see Chapter 10). Similar remarks can be made regarding the ideas of uncontrollability of events frequently expressed by patients suffering from eating disorders. Such ideas are more peripheral in the cognitive organization typical of the eating disorders than the ideas of helplessness are in the depressive's organization of knowledge (see Chapter 12). The notion that the structural and hierarchical aspects of cognitive organization give a different meaning to seemingly similar verbalized beliefs is also applicable to many other possibilities of a cognitive "differential diagnosis" (so to speak) between depression and other neurotic syndromes.

The various stages of the therapeutic strategy to be used with depressed patients can be outlined as follows:

1. During the assessment, respect patients' personal identity; that is, *avoid* reassuring them when they talk of their helplessness and confirm their idea that things do require effort. Give the basic principles of cognitive therapy in brief.
2. Suggest behavioral techniques that can increase the environmental rewards and be ready to closely examine patients' reasons for refusing the homework assignments, especially any "economic" evaluations of energy spending ("I was too tired to do it").
3. Whatever the target symptoms chosen for the treatment, face them, remembering that the basic mechanism of patients' problem solving is based on the idea of effort. Every experience that can give them a sense of "mastery" of events without involving a greater effort than they can afford should be encouraged (including the results of verbal disputes between patient and therapist).
4. If disturbing images appear, use them to show the patient the existence of "tacit knowledge." (It is easier to understand its nature with imaginative experience than with verbal reasoning and ruminations.) Be sure to give a positive idea of the functioning of tacit knowledge (e.g., "what allows you to recognize a friend's face without spelling out its single features") and avoid such negative ideas as "the monsters of the id." Use every possible tool in order to obtain some "distancing," "decentering," or "disengagement" from one's thoughts.

5. Once having assessed what are probably the basic depresso-genic assumptions, go back to the individual's developmental history in order to obtain more distancing ("This is how you have learned to see the world and yourself").

6. Start criticizing, in a hierarchical way, the basic depressogenic assumptions. The last to be treated should be the ideas of the uncontrollability of traumas ("There is always at least the possibility of *some* rational control over one's own thought") and the ideas regarding the need to strive in order to reach one's goals (e.g., "*Sometimes* you can relax, and while you are relaxed, good things could happen all the same, but if they don't, it is not your fault"; "most people can wake up in the morning at a given time simply by proposing to do so before falling asleep—this is how the human brain works; decisions and intentions are at least as important as striving to reach a goal").

7. While conducting Stage 6, try to obtain as many verbalizations as possible not containing global and moralistic judgments and "character diagnoses" ("It would be useful" instead of "I must"; "I have done—or felt, or thought—so and so" instead of "I am," etc.).

8. Discuss the hypothetical and instrumental nature of personal identity. Reassess and discuss again basic experiences (loneliness, losses, etc.), starting with those on which personal identity was constructed, and compare them with actual loneliness, losses, disappointments, and so forth, in order to explain the difference between a child's and an adult's world.

(*Note:* At any step, it is important to make sure that the patient has really understood. Repetition is boring, but it is better to repeat points than to overlook the fact that the patient is only superficially complying with the therapist's statements.)

NOTES

1. The reader is referred to Beck's book (1967) for details on the classification and features of depressive disorders. In more than 20 years of systematic investigation on depression, Beck and his associates have produced an impressive amount of

clinical, correlational, experimental, and therapeutic data. Beck's 1967 treatise on depression is so extensive, accurate, well-documented, and widely known that we shall frequently refer to it for details and documentation. For a review of more recent theoretical and experimental contributions to the cognitive model of depression (which Beck first formulated in 1967), the reader is referred to Shaw's review (1979).

2. In agitated depression patients are uneasy, cannot stay still, and even during the night get up and walk incessantly. They usually complain and cry and are always asking to be reassured or forgiven for imaginary faults. However, they cannot concentrate on a purposeful activity any more than they can stay still. The rate of *goal-directed* behavior decreases.

3. These kinds of antecedents were found in only 5 of the 24 depressed patients examined in this study. Moreover, many people react to bereavement with normal grief, which is only in part similar to clinical depression.

4. Ferster (1974) and Lewinsohn (1974) wrote vast accounts of models of depression based on the principles of operant learning. Whereas Ferster's model is easily subject to the criticisms that we have explained here, and to many others (see the discussion following Ferster's paper in Friedman & Katz, 1974), Lewinsohn's is more articulate, adding to a simplistic Skinnerian approach a host of speculative assumptions and ad hoc hypotheses. Lewinsohn's discussion of the role of precipitating factors of depression (p. 161)—a point that immediately reveals the untenability of his model in the face of the very clinical situations that it should explain—is a noteworthy collection of such ad hoc hypotheses. For example, Lewinsohn (who, by the way, does not seem to distinguish between normal mourning and grief and clinical depression), in order to justify cases of depression closely following a professional *success*, states that "a promotion may *actually* involve a serious reduction in the amount of social reinforcement obtained by the individual" (p. 161; italics added). Not a single line is devoted to clinical or experimental data possibly supporting this statement. Note that Lewinsohn is not speaking of the "successful" depressive's expectations of changes in role or social environment. The absurdities resulting from our first attempts to apply these kind of "orthodox" behavioristic models to our clinical real-life situations led us to give up any consideration of operant "theories," while continuing to use behavior therapy *techniques* whenever their empirical value could be demonstrated. This criticism, of course, does not apply to Seligman's model, in which, for instance, the depression following success is explained in terms of rewards that come independently from any ongoing instrumental activity (Seligman, 1975, pp. 96–99).

5. In the early stages of depression, the relatives or the spouses of depressed patients usually take a considerate attitude. Eventually, however, this attitude changes. When efforts to shake the patient out of his or her inertia fail, they feel frustrated, exasperated, and helpless. We have seen only rare cases where the initial considerate, compassionate, understanding attitude is maintained. When it happens, the effect on the depressed patient is usually an increased sense of unworthiness: "My husband is so considerate, and I reward him with my bad mood and leaving all the house chores to him: How base of me!" a patient used to say. In a familiar milieu of steady understanding and acceptance, it is more likely that the feeling sometimes described as "loss of feeling" appears: The depressed person complains he no longer feels

affection for his spouse and children, but just feels miserable because of this "void" that confirms his sense of being unworthy.

6. Beck *et al.* (1979, p. 198) suggest an alternative method for ascertaining the reason for the patient's inactivity: "The therapist may recommend a particular activity . . . that is obviously within the patient's capacity. When the patient expresses his reluctance or inability to follow the suggestion, the therapist asks the patient to detail the reasons for his reluctance." We recommend this method of assessment only if the behavioral prescription is compatible with the strategic plan of psychotherapy.

7. The first three categories constitute what Beck (1967, 1970) has called the "cognitive triad of depression." We have used Beck's terminology in listing them and have put them in an order that, according to our own clinical experience, roughly parallels the seriousness of the depression. That is, when depressed patients are asked why they have reduced their activity, and their *first* answer shows a negative view of the self, the clinical evaluation of the degree of depression tends to be serious. Our methodological policy of avoiding, at the beginning of therapy, the interference represented by psychometric tests and rating scales does not allow us at this point to support this impression with a statistical–correlation study. Research in this direction is currently in process. An indirect confirmation of this clinical impression is in Beck and Stein's research (1960). Barbara's case of severe depression (Example 2, p. 176), in which the assertion "I am nasty—that is why I refused to go out and see my mother" was the alleged reason for her apathy, is an anecdotal example of our clinical guess. The fourth category of answers, which we call "desire to spare effort," is not explicitly mentioned in Beck's work, although there are some hints of observations compatible with our own (see, e.g., Beck *et al.*, 1979, Chapter 9, under the titles "View of Problems as Overwhelming," p. 188, and "Passivity, Avoidance, and Inertia," p. 197).

8. Depressed patients have, as a rule, a restricted time perspective (see Shaw, 1979, p. 155, for a list of recent research on this topic). They anticipate a far-off future only when trying to imagine the end of their suffering or when someone tries to induce them to hope. The future is seen to be as negative as the present, or worse.

9. A famous historical example is Jean Jacques Rousseau, who was frankly paranoid for more than 10 years according to his own autobiographical reports (*Letters to M. de Malesherbes, The Confessions, Rousseau Judge of Jean Jacques, Reveries*); history also records that he accused his benefactor, David Hume, of conspiring with his enemies. Rousseau repeatedly asserted his conviction that no man on earth *was* as "good" as he was.

10. When actual losses happen to be the triggering events of a real depressive state, mourning is manifested in an abnormal way (Bowlby, 1961, 1963). The depressed patient does not go through the three stages of normal grief that Bowlby has described. This "atypical" grief is common to other psychiatric patients for whom bereavement was the precipitating factor of emotional disorders. Alcoholism, phobias, and anxiety neuroses were the most common diagnoses—after "reactive depression," by far the most frequent—in patients referred for psychiatric help, according to studies reviewed by Parkes (1972, Chapter 8). Parkes notes that atypical grief was more prolonged than normal grief, but his most striking finding was that,

whereas ideas of guilt or of self-reproach were reported by 79% of the bereaved psychiatric patients, they were presented in only 0%–18% of different samples of unselected widows (Parkes, 1972, Appendix, Section 12).

11. One way to elicit remarks on this view of passivity and inertia as a "rational" way to avoid at least the pain of useless effort is to ask the patient why he or she does not try to do something irrelevant (i.e., something for which the concept of failure does not apply), just for the sake of experimenting. The answer is, almost invariably, that the experiment with meaningless activity still implies effort.

12. Intermingled with these trait descriptions are others such as "fearful for competitions," "underestimation of the self," "desperate cry for love" (Rado), "love addict," "narcissistic," and "dependent." Ordinarily, psychoanalytic writers have regarded the personalities of depressives as composed of anal (obsessional, aggressive) and oral (dependent) elements in varying mixtures. The relationship between obessional and depressive states in clinically well-documented (Gittleson, 1966a–1966d). In our opinion depressive and obsessive patients share, in their "premorbid personalities," beliefs concerning the need to exert much effort in their enterprises and negative attitudes toward the self. However, these beliefs and attitudes are couched in different cognitive structures: "Effort" for the depressive is a way to oppose a destiny of loneliness or to stand a situation of loss (imagined) or solitude, whereas the obsessional's "efforts" are intended to seek "perfection" and "certainty." The negative attitude toward oneself of obsessive–compulsive persons is both a consequence of their failure to be "perfect" and a part of a view of the self and the world as being made up of opposite elements (see Chapter 11). Depressives' negative evaluations of themselves are a consequence of their failure to avoid losses and derive from a perceived "fate" of loneliness. Depressives' representation of loss and loneliness could perhaps justify behavior and assertions that were considered as proofs of the "oral component" of this personality, such as the "desperate cry for love" or "dependency."

13. It might be worthwhile to cite two cases of artists whose inclination to depression can be detected in their biographies and their works and who ended their lives with suicide. Cesare Pavese's father died when the writer was 6 years old. Poetess Sylvia Plath's father died when she was 9 years old.

14. Before becoming depressed, Ann (see p. 181) had met another young woman who had free sexual morals. Ann had no serious reason to be disappointed in her marriage, but she started to wonder whether her friend—who had asked for a separation from her husband so as to be freer to meet other people—was happier than she was. This started Ann's brooding over her own happiness. Apparently she blamed herself for not doing enough for her happiness: This was the main proof of her unworthiness. However, she had no idea, based on personal experience, of what happiness is. She did have a clear image of unhappiness, consisting of the lack of love.

15. Of course we should not be surprised. The notion of loneliness and despair is hard to change, and that the uncontrollability of events such as death is even harder. However, many thinkers throughout history (Albert Ellis is among them) had something to say about the possibility of not considering even these extreme events as "unbearable."

16. A concluding note concerning the physical symptoms of depression. For a brief review of the scanty literature on the causal effects of cognition on the

autonomic nervous system, see Shaw (1979, pp. 153–154). Here we would like to mention another aspect of the problem concerning the relationship between cognition, mood state, and physical symptoms in depression. There is wide evidence that bereavement is a serious stress (in Selye's sense) and thus affects the autonomic nervous system and the endocrine–metabolic system. It has been repeatedly demonstrated that the rate of morbidity and mortality among widowed persons in the year following bereavement is significantly higher than the average for unwidowed persons in the corresponding age group. After more than 1 year, the mortality rate is again equal for widowed and unwidowed persons (Maddison & Viola, 1968; Parkes, 1972). On the other hand, there are many proofs in accordance with the hypothesis that what one imagines and what one perceives have similar effects upon the autonomic system. It seems reasonable to assume that an imagined loss and a real loss could have somewhat similar effects upon body functions. Once the depressed patient comes to experience physical distress (insomnia, headache, weakness, anorexia, etc.), three interpretations of these unpleasant feelings are compatible with his or her own cognitive organization: (1) "I am ill, I am desperately ill, I am going to die"; (2) "This is a disease, I have no power to control it, I am weak, I cannot do anything but stay in bed"; or (3) "My imagination is the cause of my state, and this proves that there is something wicked in me, which I can't control even if it does me harm." It is really unfortunate to see that sometimes both "organic" interpretations ("It is a disease") and "psychoanalytic" interpretations ("It is my unconscious") can be confirmed by psychiatrists and psychologists.

10

AGORAPHOBIA AND
RELATED MULTIPLE PHOBIAS

The term "agoraphobia" is generally used to describe the condition of those patients who report a strong fear of leaving their own homes.[1] It is a common clinical observation that, as a rule, these patients have other fears: being alone in the house, being held up in traffic jams, using public transportation, going on long trips (especially by train or plane), being in crowded public places (movie houses, theaters, department stores, etc.), sitting in the barber's or beautician's chair, riding in elevators, and so forth. These patients usually experience acute panic attacks induced by anxiety and accompanied by various somatic complaints. Generally the reasons they offer for avoiding frightening situations include the fear of losing consciousness, of falling, of losing control to the point of going insane, of giving a pitiful display of themselves, or of feeling so sick that they could die.

Considering the frequency of multiform clinical descriptions that have in common the fear of being outside, two nosographic attitudes are possible. The first attitude regards the complex clinical picture as the expression of a unitary syndrome, with only secondary differences from one case to another. Different names have been suggested by the authors who have observed and described this syndrome, reflecting their different nosological orientations: multiple phobias (creating the problem of a differentiation from anxiety neurosis; see Beck, 1976, p. 179), anxiety hysteria (cf. Fenichel, 1945, Chapter XI-3), phobic-anxiety depersonalization syndrome (Roth, 1959), and agoraphobic syndrome (Marks, 1969). The second nosographic attitude considers each specific fear of the clinical description separately and contends that the patient suffers from a varying number of specific phobias: agoraphobia, claustrophobia, traffic phobia, subway phobia, phobia of crowded places, phobia of air travel, barbershop phobia (Stevenson & Hain, 1967), elevator phobia, fear of dying, fear of losing control, and so forth. Up until a few years ago, this second attitude seemed to have prevailed in American psychological and psychiatric literature, especially that of a behavioristic tendency. The first attitude is characteristic of the European literature. For reasons explained in detail elsewhere (Liotti, 1980), we prefer the first attitude. In this chapter all the phobias that are present in patients who *declare their fear of facing certain situations alone* are examined unitarily, under the name "agoraphobic syndrome," even though some fears (in one given case) seem to assume greater intensity or significance than the fear of loneliness.

BEHAVIORAL ASPECTS

> Alone, alone, all alone
> alone in a wide wide sea!
> —S. T. Coleridge, "The Rime of the Ancient Mariner"

An initial analysis of agoraphobic patients' avoidance behavior discloses the existence of two large categories of stimulus situations that are avoided: loneliness and constraint ("constriction" is perhaps a more suitable term, since it conveys the meaning of an "encircling pressure"—*Grolier–Webster Dictionary*, 1971). The majority of agoraphobic patients avoid staying *alone* for long periods in their own homes, on the street, or in other public places where there are no familiar or trusted people. Certain situations are also avoided even when a trusted companion is nearby. This is when a quick escape is difficult or impossible: crowded places (theaters, movie houses, lines in public offices, department stores, etc.); streets with many traffic lights and intense traffice; superhighways; planes or trains; elevators; barbers', beauticians', or dentists' chairs; and so forth. Even though they generally are afraid of traveling, some agoraphobics can travel from one city to another by car, accompanied by a trusted person, if the trip is made on state or country roads where a rapid change of direction is possible. The same trip with the same person on a superhighway is avoided because of the impossibility of turning back *quickly.* Avoidance behavior is much more intense and frequent in some agoraphobics when they have to face situations of loneliness. Usually, however, a careful investigation also reveals that situations of constriction are feared and partially avoided. In other agoraphobic patients the opposite occurs: Fear and avoidance of loneliness are limited, whereas phobic reactions to constrictive situations are so imposing that the term "claustrophobia" seems more appropriate. However, even in the extremes of the agoraphobia–claustrophobia continuum, it is important to note the *simultaneous* existence of those two categories of feared stimuli. If this is taken into consideration during the behavioral analysis of various phobias, we believe that different cases of apparently specific phobias, such as of elevator rides and plane trips, can be traced back to the agoraphobic syndrome.[2]

When agoraphobics do not expect to be able to avoid a feared stimulus, or when they are abruptly exposed to it, they experience a violent emotion of fear. The sensations that correspond to autonomic activation can vary from case to case, with somatic complaints due to anxiety primarily at the gastric, intestinal, respiratory, cardiac, or motor level. At times, a given patient has different reactions, depending on whether he or she has been exposed to situations of loneliness or of constraint: In the first case, sensations of tachycardia, weakness of limbs, trembling, falling, or fainting prevail, whereas in the second case, chest pains, difficult breathing, motor agitation, and muscular tension predominate. Sometimes being exposed to frightening situations determines more complex and distressing subjective reactions, such as the experiences of derealization or depersonalization described by patients in various ways: numbness, blurring of the eyesight, variations in body image consistence, perception of the environment as unreal, and so forth (see also Marks, 1969).

The preceding clinical picture generally develops from one or more initial panic attacks, which usually seize patients when they are in a situation of loneliness or constriction, although at times these attacks can occur in apparently "neutral" situations. As a rule, patients cannot explain the origin of these first acute anxiety attacks. The generalization of fear and avoidance behavior often occurs rapidly with serious disabling consequences, as in the case of agoraphobics who practically become confined at home. In more serious cases, patients' phobic behavior becomes a burden on family members who are their necessary companions every time they go out.

Since agoraphobics usually require the companionship of a family member in order to travel around, and often also to stay at home, a careful consideration of the interactions with the accompanying persons is mandatory: How does the escort react to the demands of the situation? How does the patient succeed in obtaining almost constant company? Is a sort of collusion conceivable between the two? In what ways does agoraphobia in a spouse influence the marital relationship?

There are a good deal of clinical—and some correlational—reports concerning these issues. Using semistructured interviews plus five questionnaires and rating scales, Hafner (1977) obtained data supporting the hypothesis of assortative mating between agoraphobic women and their husbands. The theory of assortative mating asserts that partners choose each other on the basis of perceived attributes, some of which are pathogenic. It also implies that improvement in one partner may be resisted by the other on the grounds that it disturbs the balance of the relationship. Roberts (1964, p. 194) reports on a housewife who became housebound after discovering that her husband was unfaithful. Her symptoms ceased when the husband broke off his relationship with the other woman. She relapsed into agoraphobia 5 years later, when her husband was again unfaithful; then the "symptoms" *ceased and have never recurred again since she separated from him.*

Milton and Hafner (1979), on the other hand, report the development of a severe psychosis in a woman whose husband left her after her agoraphobic condition improved. This shows that, even if the relationship contributes to maintaining agoraphobia disturbances, the breaking of the relationship is not always a cure. Treating agoraphobic women through behavioral techniques, Milton and Hafner (1979) were also able to demonstrate a clear connection between growing dissatisfaction in marriage (as assessed by the Marital Questionnaire given to both patients and spouses) and relapses during follow-up. However, 6 of 18 marriages were reported as improving after a successful behavioral treatment.

Whatever correlation there is between marital interaction and agoraphobic behavior, it is evident that it is not a definite and uniform phenomenon. Clinical reports have something to say about the relationship between marriage, separation from the spouse, and development or maintenance of agoraphobic behavior. Fry (1962) observed that the husbands of phobic women often revealed, on careful questioning, fears that were similar or complementary to those of their wives. These husbands were "protected" from dealing openly with their own problems by their wives' "symptoms." Since the wife was the "ill" one, the husband admittedly avoided loneliness only because he had to, unfortunately, protect her from the fear of being alone.

Liotti and Guidano (1976) reported a typical pattern of interpersonal behavior between some male agoraphobics and their wives. Fifteen male agoraphobics (they amount to 19 in the present patient sample) had married women who exerted a constant and excessive control over their husbands' aggressive behavior. Many of these wives showed a real phobia of violence: For example, they were unable to watch violent scenes on television or films, where the degree of violence was on the order of a boxing match. Marital quarrels were matched, on the wives' part, either with exaggerated anxiety or with an immediate emotional withdrawal, followed by a period of resentful silence. The husbands' aggressiveness first, and assertiveness later on, diminished in the course of the marriage. When agoraphobic symptoms made their appearance, a sort of paradoxical balance also developed. The wife seemed to be the "one-up" in the relationship, because she was protecting and accompanying her "ill" husband, but it was the husband who in fact had control of the couple's decisions (i.e., they could go out for shopping only if he felt "fit," etc.).

Hafner (1979) reports on seven agoraphobic women married to abnormally jealous men. The husbands' jealousy negatively influenced the wives' response to treatment. Improvement in the wife met with a strong resistance on the husband's part—motivated by jealousy —whenever the woman attempted to go out alone. If the wife insisted in her attempt, increased morbidity was noticed in the husband.

Wolpe (1976, p. 161) stated that, in his clinical experience, he had found several classes of agoraphobic antecedents. One of the most common ways of developing fear reactions to physical loneliness originated from the presence of recurring fantasies of liberation from an unsatisfactory marriage, unfulfilled precisely because they evoked a great fear.

As a result of the assessment (through two to five joint interviews with the patients and their spouses) of a marital interaction in the married agoraphobics in our sample, we were able to find instances of every pattern just cited, as well as of other patterns not yet mentioned.[3] However, there were also many instances in which the marriage appeared to be totally unrelated to the development and maintenance of agoraphobia, as in a case where the phobia appeared at a time when the patient had not yet met his future wife, was maintained throughout the marriage, and remained unchanged after separation.

Even though the attempt to find a pattern of marital interaction common to every case of agoraphobia is bound to fail, and even though the statement—frequent among clinicians—that agoraphobics are really suffering from an unhappy marriage has only a very limited value, our assessment of a marital interaction in agoraphobics still seemed to offer some impressions that could perhaps be generally valid. We are referring to the strong impression that, while speaking with their spouses, the agoraphobics were responding more frequently to the formal (i.e., contextual and nonverbal) aspect of the interaction than to the contents aspect. This is especially true for female patients; their attention shifted easily following every possible slight change of the spouse's attitude, and their posture varied accordingly, quite quickly, from, say, seductive to resentful or detached. The husbands were more constant in their global bodily attitude. This discrepancy seemed responsible for the therapist's feeling of a vague, but constant, state of misunderstanding between the two, of their being reciprocally "out of phase." The same quick variations of bodily attitude were not detectable following the verbal contents of the interaction. Although this phenomenon is difficult to describe, a particularly clear example may perhaps illustrate what we mean.

Clare, a 29-year-old agoraphobic, and her husband were discussing with the therapist the situation created by the woman's inability to go out alone. The husband was explaining his willingness to help her and also his feeling of lack of freedom because of her requests of constant company. Clare was swinging from one side to the other of her seat, bending alternatively toward her husband and away from him. The husband, steady on his seat, was looking at the therapist, while Clare watched him. The therapist noticed that Clare bended toward her husband whenever his tone of voice was firm and away from him whenever it became uncertain, tired, or sad, with no relation to the husband's words in that moment. (For example, when he said "I surely wish to help her" with a firm voice, she made a move toward him, but when he uttered almost identical words with a hint of sadness, she reversed her attitude.) Once this correspondence was confirmed, it became quite easy to predict the direction of Clare's oscillations.

Once we had observed the phenomenon in couple sessions, we started noticing it also during individual sessions with married and single patients. Agoraphobic women seemed to be particularly sensitive to the affective mimicry of the male therapist, and agoraphobic men to those contextual aspects of the therapeutic relationship which had to do with manhood and control of ongoing events. Of course these are quite common phenomena in psychotherapy, regardless of the patient's symptoms. However, they seem more accentuated in agoraphobic patients. These seem more inclined than the average person to observe contextual and nonverbal cues in interpersonal relationships and to use these cues to "manipulate" the relationship according to their needs for company, protection, and control. The relationship between agoraphobia and field dependence, demonstrated in female patients by Rock and Goldberger (1978), can perhaps be related to our clinical impressions.[4]

CONTEXTS IN WHICH SYMPTOMS FIRST APPEAR

Since agoraphobic behavior is so clearly aimed at maintaining proximity to familiar or trustworthy people, it would be worthwhile to discuss at this point the interpersonal contexts in which the first "symptoms" occur. In our sample the following possibilities applied, with varying frequency:

1. The first anxiety attacks while being out alone begin during adolescence in patients who have already suffered from school phobia. In this case the appearance of symptoms coincides with a generic increase in environmental requests for autonomy and the desire to form new affective bonds as a result of biological maturation. The transition from school phobia to agoraphobia has been described by Berg, Butler, and Hall (1976) and by Berg, Marks, McGuire, and Lipsedge (1974). In our sample this development occurred in three cases.
2. The onset of the syndrome occurs in a life period characterized by the expectation of becoming independent from parents as

a result of a forthcoming work activity. This happened to four of our patients, who clearly matched Weiss's (1964) observation of emergence of agoraphobic symptomatology in a phase of life when the person must make a move toward independence.

3. The first agoraphobic disturbances begin after the loss of a person who is affectively important to the patient. Generally it is the death of one of the parents or a serious abandonment by the husband, wife, or affectively important partner. In our sample this happened to six patients.

4. The first panic attacks occur immediately before or after marriage or coincide with the formation of intense affective bonds. In these cases the relationship between the onset of agoraphobia and a context of marked variations in the structure of affective bonds appears particularly evident.

5. The disturbances begin during a crisis in the marital relationship that drives the patient toward *desiring* or *imagining* the possibility of a separation from the husband or the wife, even though he or she considers a separation impossible for various reasons.

6. The early anxiety attacks coincide with a significant alteration of equilibrium in the interpersonal relationship with the partner (not regarded as a crisis situation). Examples are the birth of a child and the consequent redistribution of domestic chores between husband and wife or a change in the work activity of either the husband or the wife, which makes him or her more or less independent than before. This case and those described in points 4 and 5 are the most statistically frequent in our experience.

It is usually quite easy to obtain this information about the context by asking direct questions about general life circumstances at the time of the first anxiety attacks. It is almost a rule that patients deny that this contextual condition can explain the origin of their disturbances, that they consider it only a general source of tension, or that they think it somehow important, but attribute their main complaints to a mysterious and independent somatic illness. The arguments patients offer in refusing the hypothesis that there could be a connection between the alternation of their affective bonds and the origin of their disturbances deserve to be illustrated.

Example 1. Many couples don't get along very well, but they don't feel physically sick like I feel.

Example 2. It's true that I had my first attack on the train during my honeymoon when I left my hometown. It's also true that, up until a few months before marriage, I often traveled by train or plane without any trouble. But I can't see what connection this can have with my marriage. I love my wife and we get along very well.

Example 3. Yes, little by little, after my marriage, I gave up all my hobbies and many friendships to help my wife look after the children. I also told you that my wife has always been sexually cold and not very affectionate. But all this went on for a couple of years. Why should it have affected me all of a sudden, right on that Saturday when I was at home with her and the children?

Example 4. Yes, I feel anxious when I think that I'd like to leave my husband but can't. I can't because I'm sick and need someone who will take care of me. It's not that I feel really sick when I think that I'd like to leave him because he doesn't satisfy me. I'm only a bit anxious, while that day on the street alone when I had my first attack, I felt really physically sick, and in that moment I didn't think of my husband, but only that I was far fom home and that I felt so weak.

When precipitating events are as clear-cut as in the case of most agoraphobics, neurotic patients usually are able to admit that there must be some connection. Agoraphobics usually fail to do so. One gets the impression that agoraphobics' own theories of emotion do not allow them to recognize the affective nature of certain inner states, so that they are incapable of relating them to their life's events. We have to bear this in mind while dealing with the cognitive features of agoraphobia.

COGNITIVE ASPECTS

I am never less alone than when I am alone.—Cicero, *De Officiis,* Book 3, Chapter 1

Beck (1976, p. 161ff.) has cogently called attention to the common clinical misbelief that the phobic knows there is no danger in the feared situations. Simple, careful listening to patients' speech reveals that they admit they are exaggerating possible dangers only when they are removed from "phobic stimuli." It is usually easy to ascertain, on direct questioning, that, *during exposure* to frightening situations, patients have fantasies or short fragments of dialogue with themselves about terrifying subjects. "I am alone; if I should feel sick here, I could die before someone came to help me"; "If I should feel sick here, I couldn't escape quickly"; "They'll see that I'm ill and I'll make a fool of myself"; I will not be able to reach home"; "If the elevator stops, I'll go insane"—these are some of the fragments of *internal dialogue* observed in patients and referred to by them during exposure to frightening situations. At times, more or less vivid *fantasies* are reported, which have central themes such as loss of control, criticism, scorn or indifference from unknown onlookers toward the patient's suffering, sexual aggression, heart attack, and death. It is important to recognize in these fantasies the presence and the role of other people, the absence of a trustworthy companion, and the presence of unknown bystanders.

Indeed, in agoraphobics' inner representation of the situations that they label as "loneliness," the role of other people is such that the agoraphobics may very well apply to themselves Cicero's remark "I am never less alone than when I am alone." Phobic patients, in their fantasies, do not see themselves as "alone," but rather as surrounded by people, sometimes by crowds of people, and these people are, in the fantasies, very busy criticizing them, hampering their efforts to fly home (the secure base), creating (willingly or unwillingly) unpleasant, if not dangerous, situations, and so forth. Trustworthy people are also represented in phobics' thoughts when they are "alone," say, in a street: The patient is busy calculating how far away they are, how difficult it would prove for him or her to reach them, and so forth.

It is possible to summarize agoraphobics' *internal representations* in frightening situations in three major categories: loss of control, serious threat to physical well-being, and inability to deal with external danger.

The images and internal dialogues that refer to the possibility of *losing control* vary in intensity and content from case to case. It is important to remember that in agoraphobics "the fear of loss of personal control is interwoven with the fear of social disapproval" (Beck, 1976, p. 169). At times the idea of losing control over physiological functions is involved, and the sequence of internal representation that follows concerns "making a fool of oneself," "being ridiculous," and inviting the judgment and contempt of bystanders. Patients imagine themselves losing control of sphincters, vomiting, having violent sexual excitement climaxing in spontaneous orgasm, not being able to coordinate movements, remaining still, or falling. These fantasies, in which a street full of strangers acts as a stage, imply social humiliation. Other agoraphobics imagine they could lose control over behavior and consciousness to the point of going insane. These patients see themselves screaming senselessly, rolling on the ground, tearing their clothes off, insulting passersby, or making obscene gestures.[5] In this case, too, bystanders' contempt is present in the subsequent sequence of images, with the arrival of the police, forced interning in a psychiatric hospital, and so forth. For agoraphobics faced with the possibility of losing control, the trusted companion is a more steady and controlled person who will know how to bring them back to reality or avoid serious dangers.

Internal representations centered on the idea of a serious *threat to physical health* are less variable from case to case. At times they are limited to an image of an intolerable physical indisposition or fainting, but generally they concern heart attacks or apoplectic strokes. The imagined sequence this time includes the indifference and impotence of the strangers present rather than social humiliation. The companion is regarded as a person capable of assisting the patient as soon as he or she feels bad, of taking him or her to a first aid station, and so forth.

Internal representations dominated by the *idea of an external danger* can have the form of a sexual aggression, a theft, an involvement in a violent mass demonstration, or a gunfight between gangsters and police. Here, again, is the idea that strangers can be hostile and dangerous. The trusted companion is seen as a person strong enough to protect the patient from these dangers, which he or she could not handle alone.

When agoraphobics reach therapy, they usually have already failed in their attempts to solve their problems through doctors' reassurances ("You are not physically ill; your disturbances are due to anxiety") and the use of sedatives. This failure occurs because the adopted solutions are incorporated in the problem itself: Anxiety is considered a threat to physical and mental health ("An attack of anxiety could cause a heart attack"; "If I am seized by anxiety, it will not stop and I'll go insane"), and drugs are looked upon as strange and potentially dangerous substances ("It makes me even weaker"; "When I take that medicine, I feel strange. I'm afraid it reduces my control even more"; "In the long run, sedatives are bad for my heart"; etc.). Time and again, patients are left with their own diagnosis of the problem ("I am ill") and the consequent solution, logical to them—"I need someone trustworthy around all the time."

To gain further information about the patient's deeper rules and cognitive structures (and above all, in many cases, to obtain a steady therapeutic result), we have to break down the barrier created by the patient's diagnosis of his or her problem. And of course, in order to break it down, we have to use the elements that constitute it.

We usually follow the strategy of starting to discuss with patients their views of emotional experiences. Then we make clear to them what kind of basic assumptions are necessarily implied by the inner representations that accompany their "symptoms." Finally, we describe what kinds of experiences in childhood and adolescence could have led to these basic assumptions. Needless to say, while this kind of assessment is performed, therapeutic techniques are applied that can relieve the patients from as much of their limitations and suffering as possible. The integration of assessment procedures, cognitive restructuring, and behavior therapy techniques is discussed in the last section of this chapter.

As we have already seen, agoraphobics are continuously striving to be near familiar (protective) figures, yet they frequently fail to recognize any connection between their distress and the context in which it emerged, even if, in this context, definite actual or expected changes as to proximity to protective figures have taken place (e.g., deaths, new work activities, marriage and consequent separation from former family environment). To expose the personal theory of emotions that allows for the failed recognition, we can start inquiring whether or not the patient is sufficiently aware of the relationship between variations in affective bonds and emotional arousal. The majority of our agoraphobic patients possess the notion that variations in affective bonds can provoke intense emotions per se, but only in a very primitive or inarticulate form. They generally acknowledge that a person can feel sad about being abandoned or wish to return to his or her partner. However, they ignore the gamut of possible emotions, which can, in fact, be of considerable breadth, complexity, and intensity. Rather, their ideas on loneliness focus on the practical consequences—particularly the lack of assistance when in need—and, at the other extreme, on fantasies about romantic love and exciting sexual adventures as a remedy for existential loneliness.

That there can be a form of reciprocal control in an interpersonal relationship that goes beyond the direct or immediate effect of a request, a command, or a "seductive maneuver" is even less known to agoraphobics. Also, in this case the practical and concrete aspects of the control that one person can exert over another are noticed and considered.

Agoraphobics are also generally convinced that it is possible to exert *direct* control over one's own emotions. They are not aware that changing thoughts, fantasies, and actions is the way in which they, like all human beings, achieve control over emotions. As a consequence, every state of autonomic arousal that does not seem subject to self-control through "willpower" is not considered to be of an emotional nature, but rather a symptom of a physical or psychic illness. The following example may elucidate how the agoraphobic's theory of emotions operates.

Paul, a 35-year-old successful engineer, developed agoraphobia 3 years after he had married, shortly after the birth of his second (unplanned) child. His verbal skepticism about a possible relationship between his new status as a married man and father on the one hand and his phobias on the other is reported in Example 3, page 212. Two months before that Saturday on which he experienced, while at home, the frightening "sensation of going mad," he had been trapped in an elevator for 10 minutes, together with three colleagues from work. He did not report feeling frightened or even noticeably distressed during the experience, nor had he become in any way "claustrophobic." However, he was able to recollect—as a reply to the therapist's insistence that he remember his thoughts on that particular Saturday—that he had had the sudden impression that his house was "like a closed elevator" just a few minutes before the frightening sensation of going mad. During this recollection, he grew visibly tense and afraid. He said, "The doors and windows were open, and I could have gone out when I liked, so having had such an idea proves that I'm going mad." The therapist suggested that perhaps that idea could be regarded as a self-offered metaphor for the patient's emotional appraisal of his family context, since he was in fact "trapped" in the house by his wife's requests for help and company and by his obligations to the children. The patient's prompt reply was that this was impossible: "An emotion is something I can control, while that feeling of oppression persisted and grew into a great agitation; my wife's requests are not like closed doors—I can go out even if she asks me to stay. . . . The problem now is that I am afraid to move without her, in case I should feel sick again."

After ascertaining the patient's theory of emotions, we usually concentrate on those beliefs of a higher logical order that are implied by the agoraphobic's internal representations in frightening situations. It is easy to reach the following conclusions.

First, agoraphobics believe that only members of the family or people that they know very well are willing to help them in case of danger or indisposition. Strangers are considered indifferent, more prone to criticism or actually hostile, than to giving assistance. Many circumstances are interpreted as troublesome constrictions, even when patients themselves have chosen these circumstances. They can end up considering the environment a constant source of obligations and constrictions that the patients are sure they *cannot* tolerate. Often, agoraphobics may rapidly change their evaluation of certain situations without even noticing it: They can go from seeing a situation as being based on their own needs to seeing the same situation as being imposed from the outside. The following verbatim report from a female agoraphobic patient who also suffered from a recurring backache exemplifies this phenomenon:

P: You know, Doctor, since the last session my backache has come again. . . . It was almost a year since I've suffered from it the last time. . . . Massages were quite good in giving relief last time, so *I decided* to go again to the same massage parlor. I went there Monday, and it seems to work. . . . Oh, the idea that I *must* go again in that place tomorrow annoys me so . . .

T: Were you annoyed when you *decided*, on Monday, that the best thing to do was to go to the massage parlor?

P: Well, no, not really . . .

T: Why don't you *decide* not to go tomorrow, if it disturbs you?

P: Oh, Doctor, how could I? I *must* go! [The conveyed idea was that of external imposition.]

This phenomenon may remind the reader of theories of agoraphobia that have dealt, in one way or another, with the alleged lack of self–nonself differentiation in these patients (see, e.g., Frances &

Dunn, 1975; Rock & Goldberger, 1978; Note 15 to this chapter). Our direct clinical observations do not allow us to go into such theorizing about agoraphobics' "self-differentiation." However, we can confidently state that agoraphobics' typical view of themselves, matches their view of reality as indifferent, hostile, or coercive (with the exception of family figures). It is almost tautological to say that, in the face of a reality conceived of as unsupportive and coercive, agoraphobics see themselves as somehow weak (i.e., needing support) and rebellious (i.e., needing freedom). The vague feeling of personal weakness is inevitably implied in the agoraphobics' internal representation in frightening situations; it is also quite easy to obtain definite declarations of weakness from patients by asking simple, direct questions.

However, the perception of weakness does not reduce agoraphobics' self-esteem. Thus their beliefs on weakness and inferiority can be easily distinguished from those of depressed patients (in whom the belief of factual inferiority is accompanied by the idea of a reduced personal *value*) and from those of people afflicted by social anxiety (in whom the fear of being poorly judged because of being recognized as "inferior" or weak is accompanied by a lack of interpersonal skills for covering up their assumed defects). In other words, agoraphobics consider themselves weak, but not "unlovable", and physically inferior because of an illness, but not lacking basic interpersonal skills; they blame others more themselves when they think that they can be criticized.[6] Their "weakness" is related to a mysterious lack of energy, which hampers their usual and desired capacity for self-control. Should the mysterious illness fade away, patients are sure that their regained ability to control their own emotions, their behavior, and the environment will cancel any trace of their temporary "inferiority." With the exception of patients with long-lasting phobias, who have learned to see themselves as helpless because of the failure of their repeated attempts to get rid of their limitations, agoraphobics are not usually self-blaming persons. If present, self-blame is limited to the negative evaluations of one's capacity for self-control and does not usually extend to the global personal identity as it typically does in depressive patients. Even in advanced cases of agoraphobia, it is quite usual to hear statements such as "When I recover from this damned illness, I'll be the freest and most enterprising person in the world."[7]

Once we have gained this overall view of the patient's cognitions and basic assumptions, we can ask ourselves what kind of developmental influences were apt to have helped the patient in building them.

DEVELOPMENTAL ASPECTS

Fear of danger is ten thousand times more terrifying than danger itself.—D. Defoe, *Robinson Crusoe*

In our clinical sample, patients invariably did recollect a class of childhood experiences that warranted the development of the cognitions just described. This class of experiences comprises serious obstacles to autonomous exploration and therefore to active separation from protective persons. As readers will notice from the following description, our results are compatible with the four patterns of family interaction tentatively identified by Bowlby (1973, Chapter 19) as characteristic of agoraphobia.

Frequently, patients report having experienced direct obstacles to autonomous exploration of the extradomestic environment, recalling for instance, the following situations: being discouraged by the parents (usually the mother) from leaving home alone even for short outings, being kept at home for longer periods of convalescence than necessary after minor illnesses, and not being allowed to go out to play with friends. Invariably the parents did not present these obstacles to detachment and autonomy as their own wishes; they never explicitly affirmed, for instance, that they preferred to have their children nearby for their own pleasure or for company. Instead, the reasons for prohibiting autonomy always concerned an assumed weakness of the child, whether absolute or relative to hypothetical difficulties of the extradomestic environment. In other words, parents denied or restricted their children's autonomy—often beyond adolescence—by emphasizing their "weakness" ("You are fragile"; "You aren't healthy"; "You are not aware of the dangers of the streets"; "You don't know how to control yourself in front of strangers") and the dangers of the outside environment ("They are bad boys—you must not play with them, it's dangerous"; "If you go out alone on the street, they could attack you"; "You could be hit by a car"; "If you get lost, no one will help you").

When there is not such a direct restriction of autonomous exploration, there inevitably is an indirect restriction. The most common example is the parent who threatens to leave the family, attempts suicide, says he or she wants to die, or complains (usually without any valid reason) of being affected by an illness that will cause death in a short while. Another common example is the parent who suffers from chronic anxiety due to loneliness. Usually this parent is a woman who is afraid whenever her husband is a little late and screams out her fear that he could have had an accident. Sometimes the mother is agoraphobic herself and does not tolerate any separation from her husband.[8]

It should be noted that a *real* separation from one of the parents during childhood is rarely found among our agoraphobic patients. Usually detachment is threatened and therefore imagined along with a sequence of hypothetical consequences. Imagining detachment as an imminent danger, the child avoids leaving home as much as possible and tries to stay near the parent he or she is afraid of losing.

It is understandable how the future agoraphobic can dwell upon the idea of being weak and incapable of facing the external environment's difficulties. Regardless of the imagined dangers and the obstacles created by parents, exploratory behavior is strongly genetically motivated. Therefore we could expect children to strive to overcome their fears and the external hampering. They can try to obtain self-confidence and freedom by showing their parents that they know how to control themselves or by building a strong and confident image of themselves in order to fight the imagined dangers. In any case they have had several experiences that prove that others can be coercive without having had the possibility of discussing these restrictions of freedom with the persons responsible. In fact, parents refuse to admit that they are exerting any constraint: They maintain that what they are really doing is protecting their children from danger.

The only way for the children to solve the riddle between the objectively experienced constraint and the protests of willingness to protect them is to leave the idea that there is something coercive in the world within the realm of tacit knowledge. When there is no direct coercion by parents, as in the case of those who talk about their own death or abandonment, there is still reason for the children to feel lonely, without protection, and therefore weak before the world's difficulties. Consequently, they will try to maintain proximity to protective figures and in this effort will sacrifice their biological drive toward active exploration. We can assume that this sacrifice leaves behind an obscure longing for freedom.

It is important to emphasize that all these early constructions of loneliness, environmental dangers, personal weakness, self-control, and freedom are based on other people's verbal descriptions and on the individual's imagination rather than on concrete experiences. The only concrete experience is the limitation on one's urge to explore the environment, and this experience can never be verbalized. Apparently, the concrete experience of isolation and loneliness during childhood causes different cognitive developments in which fear is not so strongly implied, such as those found in depression.

As we have already noted, the idea of being substantially weak, inferior, or different from others does not reduce future agoraphobics' self-esteem. On the contrary, surrounded as they are by their parents' protective attention, they often have sufficient reason for imagining themselves as particularly lovable persons who deserve attention. Also, when an attachment figure threatens to abandon them, they do not think of themselves as undeserving of love, but, at most, not lovable enough to prevent the parent's detachment. The mother of one patient of ours said rather frequently when he was a child, "Oh, my little beloved son, how sad I am at the idea that perhaps I'm going to die and leave you, whom I love so much."

THE COGNITIVE ORGANIZATION IN AGORAPHOBIA

The freest man is the loneliest man.—H. Ibsen, *An Enemy of the People*

The core or agoraphobics' cognitive organization is the tacit knowledge of an experienced limitation to their personal freedom to explore the world, added to emotional schemata in which the self-image has a hypothetical attribute of weakness. The need for freedom (autonomy) and the need for protection ("dependence")—or, alternatively, the fear of constraint and the fear of loneliness—are the conflicting aspects of this ideational core.

Frances and Dunn (1975), starting from a psychoanalytic viewpoint, reached conclusions similar to ours. From this nucleus of unquestionable knowledge ("metaphysical hard-core"), agoraphobics take an easily identifiable attitude toward themselves and external reality: As long as they are able to maintain *control* over their own "weakness" and over the dangers of the unfamiliar environment, they are safe. "Positive" emotional schemata, related to their ability to obtain love and attention, allow them to construct a personal identity into which the attribute "capable of self-control" is easily admitted. Theories of self-identity originating from this controlling attitude gradually develop: Personal emotions are equated with controllable emotions; self-confidence is based upon confirmation of one's ability to get the positive attention of protective people and to resist the pressures and avoid the criticism of coercive or hostile people; self-esteem is maintained as long as self-control is confirmed.

The controlling attitude toward reality is revealed by agoraphobics' representational models of the outside world. Their attention focuses upon the dichotomies in the characteristics of people and situations, such as sympathetic–rejective, protective–indifferent, friendly–hostile, domineering–submissive, and coercive–uncontrolling. As we have seen, rules for assimilating new experiences are such that they make the individual concentrate more upon the formal than upon the actual aspects of a relationship since the former are more apt to promptly reveal how the relationship can be controlled. Rule for everyday problem solving also depend heavily on this basic controlling attitude; whenever an interpersonal problem arises, the solution falls into one of the following categories: fight (a figure considered aggressive), flight (from coercion, routines, or affectional bonds with controlling partners), or dominate (every other situation, so that mastering can ensure freedom).

Many anecdotal examples might illustrate how this cognitive organization works in regulating everyday behavior. For instance:

1. Most male agoraphobic patients in our sample were quite enterprising and successful in their work, at least before the onset of their disturbances. Also, they were socially quite brilliant, outgoing, and assertive persons. They seemed to strive for mastering every interpersonal situation (see Liotti & Guidano, 1976).

2. A fair proportion of our male and female agoraphobics described themselves before the onset of the clinical syndrome as very reluctant to establish stable and obliging emotional bonds. They were not shy persons, however, and they did have many superficial adventures, charged predominantly with sexual interest. Seductive attitudes were frequently de-

tected in these patients and appeared to be aimed at controlling other people's behavior, getting positive attention, or "manipulating" the relationship.

3. Orgasmic dysfunction is a very frequent complaint in female agoraphobics (60% in our records, 53% in Roberts, 1964, p. 193). There were many hints suggesting that this disturbance was related to an almost deliberate effort to maintain control in the relationship with the sexual partner. Some patients explicitly expressed their idea that having an orgasm meant "losing control" and "being at the other's mercy." Almost every patient with such a complaint found it more comfortable to be in the upper position during sexual intercourse; when the reverse happened, they felt "oppressed" and "dominated."

4. Our patients dwelled a lot, during their life, upon the problem of preventing or controlling interpersonal situations in which other people could become very aggressive. Most of them were not, however, really frightened by the idea of violence, and they were also quite able to react aggressively. Three of our male agoraphobics used to go around with guns in their cars or at their waists; no other patients in our general sample did so. When asked the reason for this habit, one patient replied, "I want to be in the one-up position even in front of a stronger man, should he menace me in any way."

5. Without exception, when it was possible for patients to recollect their fantasies during adolescence, they contained themes such as "I don't want to submit to anybody in my life"; "I will never work under a boss"; "I don't want to marry and be bound"; "I would like to travel a lot and be free from every constraint"; "Freedom is the best thing on earth."

While the preceding cognitive organization is successfully built and maintained through confirming experiences, it ensures a balance between the contrasting needs for protection and for freedom—without, of course, allowing any change in the "metaphysical hardcore" from which it stems. Agoraphobic patients whose disturbances develop as an adolescent transition from a school phobia obviously fail to reach such a balance, but they are a minority in the total agoraphobic population. Other adult agoraphobics did remember having suffered from school or other phobias during their childhood (around 50% in sample of Roberts, 1964, p. 192; about 29% in our own), but they had recovered from them and stayed well up to the onset of the present disorder. During the period of well-being preceding adult agoraphobia, the therapist could frequently detect, on recollection, "traits" such as an inclination to be anxious or a tendency to worry, but they were not so prominent as to negate a global description of most patients' "premorbid personality" as fundamentally lively, outgoing, and enterprising. Going about alone does not create a problem. The individual can usually go on trips without any subjective discomfort and can appreciate the experience very much. Only a careful clinical investigation could perhaps reveal the weaknesses and contradictions of the underlying cognitive organization.

The price to be paid for such a balance is, however, fairly high. Having to concentrate upon formal aspects of human relationships and upon very practical aspects of interpersonal and intrapersonal control (remember Lakatos's positive heuristic), future agoraphobics miss the knowledge of the power and subtleties of human emotional reactions to change in the network of attachment bonds (remember Lakatos's negative heuristic). Being bound by their childhood or adolescent decision to avoid any expression of personal "weakness," these individuals cannot "cultivate" (and therefore recognize) any emotion that could be perceived as a synonym for weakness. Flying away promptly from any binding affectional relationship, they fail to ascertain properly what kind of personal traits would be desirable in a lifetime companion. In selecting a spouse, they frequently misjudge the very personal characteristics that they were looking for in people during their whole lives, as, for instance, noncontrolling or protective attitudes. The following excerpt from an interview with a couple gives a striking example of such misjudgment.

H: I decided to marry my wife, I remember, mostly because she is really free-minded. She doesn't control me continuously. I could not have endured being continuously supervised by a wife, as my mother [who is probably agoraphobic herself] did with my father.

T: How did you recognize your wife's free-mindedness?

W (*superimposing*): I believe that he was really impressed when I told him, before marriage, that I would not have cared if he had superficial sexual relationships with other women while married to me. All I wanted and asked was to be informed of any such relationship, in order to ascertain that it was really superficial, you know.

H: True. This was really impressive. I had never heard anything like that from a woman before. That proved how uncontrolling she was.

The preceding exchange shows clearly how "controlling" the woman actually was: *She wanted to know every detail of her husband's behavior with other women,* in order to be sure that he was not falling in love with them. After 4 years of marriage, during which the husband occasionally had intercourse with other women and every time reported them to his wife, he felt the "funny wish" to have a "secret" extramarital affair. He fulfilled his wish. His wife (revealing again an extreme inclination to supervise her husband) discovered the unfaithful husband's secret. She took her revenge, having, in turn, an extramarital affair (her first) and letting her husband know about it together with her reasons. He became agoraphobic shortly thereafter, presumably because of the inescapable feeling of being controlled and because of the added fear of being deserted by his wife should he again "choose freedom." Several agoraphobic women in our sample selected a husband because he was calm, protective, stable, and "the kind of man that does not desert you," only to discover, shortly thereafter, that he was in fact indifferent, apathetic, passive, and "the leave-me-alone-please" kind of man.

It is now easy to understand how the precipitating events described on page 210 and following can cause decompensation in agoraphobics' cognitive organization. Making new affective bonds, breaking old ones, or perceiving growing isolation or constraint in already existing fundamental relationships can lead to life situations that cannot be dealt with in terms of "self-control." Marriage is a simple example; patients have reasons for ongoing inner representations concerning both the separation from their "protective" parents and the creation of a new bond that restricts their freedom. Rather strong emotional experiences are derived from these representations. Patients do not possess articulate cognitive structures capable of dealing with these emotions. Proper labeling and causal attribution are needed for an emotional experience to be articulate and manageable. Emotions deprived of cognitive labels and casual attribution are recognized as unpleasant and alarming autonomic arousal (Marshall

& Zimbardo, 1979; Maslach, 1979). When the representations of loneliness (because of detachment from protective people) and constriction (because of the new bond) become frequent and vivid enough, the autonomic activation grows so intense that the individual considers it the symptom of an illness. Such an interpretation produces, in turn, new fear, which only worsens the physical discomfort and closes the vicious circle.[9]

Even if a consulted physician explains that the attack was of an emotional nature, and if the patient accepts this explanation as valid, the problem does not change: The *nature* of this assumed emotion remains unknown, the emotion itself is not controllable, and therefore the representations of a threat *external to self* are intact. Such patients begin to think of insanity as an impending threat and hidden cause of their mysterious and painful "emotions." Since the basic cognitions relative to their view of the world as constrictive and of themselves as weak in front of hostile strangers are mostly within the realm of tacit knowledge, these patients usually experience them only in the form of intrusive images evoked by situations of *physical* constraint or loneliness. We could say that the primitive emotional schemata are activated by concrete experiences of loneliness and constraint and that they enhance the appearance, in such circumstances, of distressing images and cognitions of the kind "I must get out of here as soon as possible" (cf. the discussion of the "dual belief system"—with the procession of somatic imaging, visual fantasies, and child-like appraisal of possible dangers following the activation of the primitive immature "system"—in Beck, 1976, pp. 161–165). It is clinically easy to demonstrate in many cases the coherence between the childhood images with which exploratory behavior was hampered by parents and the visual and somatic images now rebounding in the adult agoraphobic's flow of consciousness.[10]

We must remember that, when confronted with this storm of intrusive images and mostly unpleasant emotions, agoraphobic patients are only capable of thinking in terms of *control*. Terrified, they ask themselves how they can control the new threat. They turn to doctors, drugs, personal willpower, distractions, rest, and, above all, the company of reassuring people who can control the danger that they fear they cannot control themselves. As a consequence of these operations, the controlling attitude—which, in our metaphorical use of Lakatos's terminology, constitutes for foundation of the "protective belt"—is strengthened. The protective belt becomes thicker and protects the metaphysical hard-core even more from being recognized and criticized. Subjectively, an idea focused on the fear of losing control appears and develops.

At this point in the syndrome's development, the position of the partner can become very peculiar. If the marriage is unsatisfying, the partner can still be perceived as a negative figure in the patient's life, but he or she is still one of the few people that can ensure protection and control. Frequently, the original situation where the metaphysical hard-core was assumed, is recreated in the patient's present life. A stronger and more self-confident person is nearby; he or she is considered indispensable, even though this person limits the patient's freedom. Such patients once again perceive themselves as weak and in need of protection. These perceptions are considered absolutely true. Avoidance of the situations of loneliness and constriction in which the disturbing intrusive images and emotions were experienced and of similar situations (generalization) confirms patients' belief that they are weak and need protection. The constant request for protective company forces patients into an increasingly dependent position, with a consequent reduction in their assertiveness ("I cannot tell her: I'm afraid that she'll refuse to accompany me anymore") and a growing general feeling of constraint. More and more often, daily events are perceived as coercive, as in the case of the patient who felt that she was "compelled" to go to the massage parlor (see p. 217). The cognitive organization has undergone transformations and re-adjustments, so that it now shows in "agoraphobic" behavior and emotions. In this readjusted form, it is stable and capable of self-maintenance, through a kind of circular causality.

PSYCHOTHERAPEUTIC STRATEGY WITH AGORAPHOBIC PATIENTS

We look forward to a world founded upon four essential freedoms. . . . The fourth is freedom from fear.—F. D. Roosevelt, *Speeches*

Slavery enchains a few; more enchain themselves to slavery.—Seneca, *Epistulae ad Lucilium*, 22, II

The goal of psychotherapy in treating agoraphobics is to make them recognize that the kind of freedom they "need" more of is freedom from their own fear and that they are "enchaining themselves to slavery" through their own fear-motivated "dependence." The initial step that one has to take in order to reach this end is to deal with the problem of self-control. The literature on the effectiveness of behavior therapy techniques shows clearly how important it is to take into account, from the very beginning of psychotherapy, agoraphobics' need of being "in control."

As is well known, imaginal systematic desensitization has been almost entirely abandoned by behavior therapists dealing with agoraphobia, on the basis of many outcome studies emphasizing the superiority of flooding techniques and "*in vivo* exposure" (Boulougouris *et al.,* 1971; Hafner & Marks, 1976; Hand, Lamontagne, & Marks, 1974; Marks, 1969; Mathews, Johnston, Lancashire, Munby, Shaw, & Gelder, 1976). The element that prevents imaginal systematic desensitization from obtaining positive results seems to be agoraphobics' difficulty in achieving good muscular relaxation *when given verbal instructions by the therapist.* In other words, we believe—on the basis of our clinical experience, of sparse clinical reports, and of a confrontation between different outcome studies—that agoraphobics regard relaxation induced by another person as an unbearable lack of control over an interpersonal relationship. However, if biofeedback techniques are used for relaxation, imaginal systematic desensitization seems to work as well with agoraphobics as with simpler monosymptomatic phobics (Chiari & Mosticoni, 1979). The biofeedback techniques leave agoraphobics in complete control over the relaxation situation. They no longer feel they are giving up control in their relationship with the therapist in order to achieve relaxation. The therapist fades away, so to speak, after having given the proper instructions, and the patient is alone with an impersonal apparatus that will help him or her in achieving a new coping skill, that is, the ability to relax. Goldfried's presentation of relaxation as an active coping skill and as a part of training in self-control is very similar (Goldfried, 1971; Goldfried & Trier, 1974). When so presented, relaxation becomes much more acceptable to most agoraphobics, and consequent systematic desensitization becomes possible.

We can confidently say, then, that the initial acknowledgment of, and respect for, the controlling attitude of agoraphobic patients is of critical importance in the beginning phase of treatment. Using Lakatos's research program metaphor, we could say that we had better respect *and recognize* the "protective belt" if we are going to successfully criticize it through the whole research program. Socratic dialogue is a time-honored way to achieve successful criticism of a theory, starting with the initial respect of its basic premises. But how can an analogue of the Socratic dialogue *start* with a patient who is proving that he or she cannot stay alone, through the circular causality of avoiding any situation of loneliness? There are two answers, which can be integrated into one practical answer: The first is derived from behavior therapy outcome studies, and the second from our reconstruction of agoraphobics' knowledge organization. Let us first consider the outcome studies, then the suggestion that arises from the notion of cognitive organization in agoraphobia, and finally the practical integration of the two.

Emmelkamp, Kuipers, and Eggeraat (1978), found that prolonged *in vivo* exposure of agoraphobics to their feared "stimuli" was definitely superior to three main methods of cognitive modification both in bringing about symptomatic relief (which was statistically proved) and in *producing effective cognitive restructuring* (which was tentatively, but also sensitively, argued):

> During treatment with prolonged exposure in vivo clients notice, for example, that their anxiety diminished after a time, and that the events which they fear, such as fainting or having a heart attack, do not take place. This may lead them to transform their unproductive self-statements into more productive ones. . . . *A number of clients reported spontaneously that their thoughts had undergone a much greater change during prolonged exposure in vivo than during cognitive restructuring.* It is possible that a more effective cognitive modification takes place through prolonged exposure in vivo than through a procedure which is focused directly on such a change. (Emmelkamp *et al.*, 1978, p. 40; italics added)

Ellis (1979), in a note on Emmelkamp *et al.*'s study, fully acknowledges the *particular* importance of "*in vivo*" assignments and "exposure" homework in agoraphobics.

Even Freud, as Marks (1969) reports, said that therapists had to work on positive transference in order to bring phobic patients to face their own fears in reality; pure symbolic interpretation, without this reality testing, was not sufficient for overcoming phobic fears. A firm stand can therefore be taken. Therapists, while respecting agoraphobics' need of being in control, should lead patients to expose themselves to real-life situations of loneliness and "constriction." To achieve this goal, therapists can resort *first* to biofeedback-assisted imaginal desensitization (which could perhaps be selected in more severe cases) or to imaginal flooding or can move directly to graded *in vivo* exposure, accompanying patients in the street and then retiring gradually, or to properly adapted forms of self-control training, coping skills training (for a review, see Meichenbaum, 1977), and stress inoculation procedures (Meichenbaum, 1977, Chapter 5). Even direct, simple self-exposure instructions can be useful, although therapist-initiated exposure is required in the more serious cases (for an experimental study on this point, see McDonald, Sartory, Grey, Cobb, Stern, & Marks, 1979).

Is the achievement of self-exposure, though strongly needed, sufficient for obtaining stable benefits for agoraphobic patients? Both on theoretical grounds and in consideration of outcome studies, the answer is obviously no. After self-exposure, patients can see themselves as capable of dealing with situations that they had previously avoided, but this therapeutic change is of the kind that Arnkoff (1980) has described as a "temporary shift in surface structure," which is relatively simple to achieve. In our favored Lakatosian metaphor, neither the metaphysical hard-core ("I am weak in the face of an indifferent–hostile outside environment and a coercive familiar one") nor the protective belt ("I have to control my fundamental weakness and the hostile–coercive environment") is substantially criticized by the self-exposure experiences. Consequently, on theoretical grounds, limited positive outcomes and easy relapses— particularly as long as the environmental (interpersonal) situation remains intact—are to be expected. We have already quoted studies demonstrating how the outcome is poorer and relapses easier when behavior therapy is given to agoraphobics whose marriages are seriously disturbed (Hafner, 1979; Milton & Hafner, 1979).[11] However, with more seriously disturbed agoraphobic patients, one has to expect relapses after the accomplishment of a "temporary shift in surface cognitive structures" *even if the environmental situation has undergone very positive changes* after the successful self-exposure and additive techniques of behavior therapy. The following clinical report is meant to illustrate this point.

Judith developed agoraphobia during her adolescence, after having suffered from a severe school phobia. When she came to one of us (G. L.) for treatment, she was 22 years old and had failed to derive any benefit from either psychotropic medication (antidepressant and tranquilizer) or orthodox psychoanalysis (3 years of treatment). She was very clever and had cultivated her education, although she had no scholastic degree because of her school phobia. She was practically confined to her home, and even if accompanied, suffered from strong feelings of depersonalization while in the street—and sometimes even at home.

Two psychiatrists who had formerly visited her had put forward diagnoses of schizophrenia and "dissociative hysteria." Her family consisted of a quiet, submissive father, very absent-minded, though affectionate; a seriously disturbed, dominating mother, who was herself agoraphobic in her youth and who had "recovered" from her illness when Judith, who was then 9 years old, became housebound; and Judith's youngest brother, a very withdrawn boy who suffered from severe social anxiety, but was eventually able to complete school and get a job. The family was rather poor. Judith greatly benefited from a therapeutic program based upon isolation from the family (she was treated for 6 months as an inpatient in a psychiatric university clinic), graded *in vivo* exposure to feared situations, coping imagery, social skills training, and a brief elucidation of the seriously disturbed family dynamics. While in the hospital, Judith prepared herself for an examination that would give her a junior high school degree, and on discharge she passed this examination, found a job, and had her first sexual encounter (which was satisfactory). One year later, she left her parents and went to live with several female colleagues of hers. A "miracle"? All for the better? No! Two years later she relapsed. Minor difficulties with her job and her roommates caused her to feel "unsupported," "alone," and "in a trap"; thereupon she was again "agoraphobic."

In the face of the insufficiency of the (otherwise necessary) self-exposure program, the unsatisfactory result of marital counseling and family therapy (see Note 11), and the poor results of the cognitive methods used by Emmelkamp *et al.* (1978) in their study on agoraphobia, what could our notion of agoraphobic knowledge organization suggest? The obvious idea is to run through the stages and levels of the cognitive organization in a stepwise fashion, going from the surface structures to the deeper structures, along the following lines:

1. Appropriate relabeling of emotional experiences.
2. Elucidation of the relationship between emotions and ongoing thoughts (Beck's "automatic thoughts," whether in pictorial or verbal modes).

3. "Distancing" from ongoing thoughts (in the sense described by Beck, 1976, pp. 242–244).
4. Identification of the basic assumptions (Beck) or irrational beliefs (Ellis) implied by ongoing thoughts.
5. Descriptions of the developmental aspects of such basic assumptions and of the ways in which they were "confirmed" through daily experiences up to the present moment of the patient's life (i.e., uncovering the metaphysical hard-core and the way the protective belt developed from it).

For each of these steps, appropriate cognitive techniques are required in order to achieve a change, but the crucial point is the correction of the hypotheses that constitute the protective belt (i.e., the personal identity). Only when this result is gained may the "theories" of the metaphysical hard-core be regarded by patients as mere episodes in their lives and no longer function as deep tacit rules governing patients' views of themselves and their world.

Let us now consider how these suggestions that stem from the notion of knowledge organization could be practically applied to the treatment of agoraphobics and integrated with the procedures leading to self-exposure.

Let us imagine the concrete clinical situation from the beginning. We are trying to fulfill the patient's need of being in control, avoiding any aspect of the relationship, any interpretation, and any therapeutic maneuver that might constitute a direct attack on the patient's "controlling" attitudes.[12] We are gradually trying to induce him or her to face feared situations. Which class of situations should we consider first? Which one is presumably more acceptable to the patient and more productive of cues to be followed in order to foster our planned cognitive restructuring?

In most cases it is the "constriction" class of situations. For patients, it is obviously preferable (more compatible with their cognitive organization) to be free than to be alone, so they are well prepared to deal with situations of constraint, not being required to give up the companionship of "protective" persons right from the start. For the sake of cognitive restructuring, the reactions to "coercive" stimuli offer easily understandable hints for a successful cognitive relabeling of emotions. Let us take a verbatim report as a typical example.

P: I have come here today [accompanied by his wife] driving along the road full of traffic lights [which he formerly avoided], as you suggested in the last session [first planned step of an *in vivo* exposure program]. Well, I have tried to notice my reaction, as you asked me to do. Obviously it was fear—fear of having a heart attack just while stopped by that damned red light. At the third light that became red just a second before I could drive through the crossing, my heart started beating. An infarct!, I thought—I must drive away from this trap, and I cannot!

T: This trial was very good of you, and your report could be enlightening. I think we can understand something interesting from it. For instance, could it be that, at the first red light, you have felt just a little bit of irritation?

P: Well, . . . of course. But this is normal, isn't it? I mean, I have reported only abnormal reactions . . .

T: Yes, this is what I asked you to report. But now, let us speculate a little. Could it be that, also, in front of that third traffic light that turned red just before you passed it, you have experienced a little bit of anger before your fear?

P: Well . . . yes . . .

T: I see, most people would have. Don't you think that anger, too, and not only fear, could explain an acceleration of heartbeats?

P: Yes, of course.

T: Very well. Now, it could perhaps be of some use if we deal a little bit longer with a possible relation between thoughts and anger. You were irritated because you felt that the red light was stopping you, obliging you to stop, while you'd rather have preferred to go faster. Wasn't it something like that?

P: Yes.

T: Why didn't you drive through the crossing regardless of the red light?

P (surprised): Why? It's obvious . . . I might have had a serious crash!

T: So you have in some way automatically calculated that it was better for you not to cross, and at the same time you have automatically seen in your mind the red light as a sort of giant that was *obliging* you to stop?

P: Well . . . I have not noticed something like that before . . . but now. . . . Yes, I guess you're right.

T: Anger seems compatible with the idea of the giant forcing you to stop, but not with your chance evaluation and free decision that it was, on the whole, better for you to stop, doesn't it?

P: Yes, it seems logical.[13]

Whether we start from constriction or from loneliness, while patients are making their way through gradual and assisted self-exposure, their experiences are used, through an appropriate Socratic dialogue, as in the preceding example. Knowledge about their dual belief system (Beck, 1976, p. 161 ff.) (e.g., chance evaluation and free decision vs. a view of the world as coercive), acknowledgment of the relationship between automatic thoughts and emotions (e.g., anger related to a view of situations as coercive), and a more accurate labeling of emotions and recognition of their relevance to autonomic activation (e.g., anger *and* fear as determinants of accelerated heartbeats) can be gained by patients without an untimely attack on their controlling attitudes and, moreover, by using their need for self-control in order to foster their curiosity about themselves (which is usually not very strong in agoraphobics, especially males). Also in this vein, distancing from ongoing thoughts is usually obtained and exercised. Alternative coping self-statements (Meichenbaum, 1977) and coping imagery can be given at this point, working as much as possible on already existing cognitive structures. (For example, with a dual belief system such as that identified in the preceding example, one can suggest uttering coping self-statements of the kind "I am choosing to stop at the traffic light" instead of the anger-evoking and frightening self-statement "I am forced to stop while I am feeling so bad.")

The coping procedures by themselves, however, are hardly able to effect stable changes in patients' cognitive organization or marked symptomatic relief. There are two reasons for this. First, there are easily created conflict situations in which both constriction and loneliness are implied, so that coping with constraint means facing loneliness. (And this is too much. Think of a phobic caught in a traffic jam; he can fight his "constraint" thoughts, saying to himself, "Why don't I leave my car here?" Instead of replying "Because I *prefer* to have my car at my disposal tomorrow," he can find himself thinking "Because I *cannot* afford walking alone, so damned weak as I am! Gosh, what a *trap!*") Second, the coping tactic is no good in dealing with emerging problems originating from the underlying controlling attitude. The following example illustrates the second reason:

Jimmy, after 6 months of treatment, managed to go skiing with his girl friend and even took the cable car, which he had been unable to do for the past 7 years. The cable car stopped halfway. He panicked, but was soon able to "cope." He said to himself, "This is only my fear, not an impending tragedy," and "I can manage it." Fear almost disappeared. He was calmer than other people around him. Jimmy experienced a moment of triumph. But soon another thought came to mind: "I was able to control this phobic attack; shall I be able to control a bigger one?" When the cable car began to move again, Jimmy was no longer triumphant.

If the therapist insists on inducing patients to an ever higher degree of control, the menace of an infinite regression appears. Therefore, at this point in the strategic plan of therapy, identification of the basic assumptions concerning self-control is mandatory. Patients are already experienced in distancing from their own thoughts and have learned from the coping tactics that they can "prove" and "disprove" their own beliefs. So they are now ready for a deepening of analysis and therapy. If the therapist summarizes with the patient the main findings of their common research up to the present moment, this is what appears: Two kinds of situations evoke distressing thoughts and frightening images—loneliness and constraint. The contents of inner dialogue and "pictorial" imagery have two main themes: Strangers are seen as potentially criticizing, ridiculing, or hostile (or, at best, indifferent and impotent), whereas familiar people are considered protective.[14] Conjugal bonds are, on the other hand, frequently regarded as coercive and as being needed only because they ensure protection.

With this panorama in mind, one can easily point out to patients that self-control *seems* the only "rational" solution and the one that they have, in fact, adopted up to now in their lives. But what is this "self"? And what, really, is "control"?

The therapist's arguments proceed as follows: Control is not willpower, but has to do with thinking; patients have already experienced this. Control is something upon which patients have based a great part of their life themes, and this is why they are so fearful of losing it. Control is like a two-edged blade, and sometimes an overcontrolling attitude not only does not help the patients in overcoming their fears, but actually fosters the creation of paradoxes that, in turn, may contribute to such odd and unpleasant depersonalization and derealization.[15] For instance, in order to have patients acknowledge the paradoxes of control, we can ask them to reproduce their fears through *deliberate* imagining of the situations they fear most. Usually they fail to reproduce their fears and experience a new possibility of mastering their avoidance behavior through *deliberate* self-presentation of their own previously spontaneous frightening fantasies.[16] However, as soon as they try to use this mastery device in order to increase their freedom of movement, fears come again (at least in a fair proportion of serious agoraphobias). It is easy to demonstrate that the reason for this failure is the fear of losing control over this beautiful mastery (controlling) procedure. To say it better, it is usually patients who state that this is what occurred to their minds.

Control, then, seems a rational solution, but on closer examination it is not the best or the only one. Before criticizing further the controlling attitude (remember, it is the very foundation of the protective belt!), we can now try to answer, together with the patient, the other big question: What is "self"? Using the contents of cognitive analysis, it is easy to answer that, in the patient's own view, "self" is something that is fundamentally weak. And now, at last, we are ready for the final sequence of therapeutic steps.

When and where has the patient learned that strangers could be indifferent, criticizing, or even hostile? That he or she *is* weak and unable to face the difficulties of unfamiliar environments (weak because of intrinsic feebleness, because of lack of control against temptation, or for what other reasons)? That only familiar people are protective, and home is the only safe place? That his or her personal freedom can be very restricted? The answer is now obvious. At this point in therapy, the classical developmental picture that we have described comes into the open. We have only to point out that the main device through which the patient got the *concrete* experience of a limitation in personal freedom was an induced, *imagined* fear.

The stepwise criticism of the main theories of the protective belt is undertaken as the final step. Perhaps, in order to be criticized, these theories could be verbalized using Ellis's (1962, 1979) words: "It is *catastrophic* if I don't get what I need or must have" (where the "need" or "must have" is referred to control of the environment, and the "catastrophic" is referred to the image of loneliness in the face of strangers) and "I can't bear the discomfort of feeling anxious, frightened, and so forth." (where the absolutistic "can't" is at once [1] the expression of the expected "awful" consequences of recognizing oneself as "weak"; [2] the reason why one thinks, circularly, that one "can't," i.e., "I *can't because* I *am* weak"; and [3] of the striving for self-control). However, we find it simpler to let patients use their own words in order to represent, in as many sentences as they like, their basic assumptions regarding hostile strangers in the street, personal weakness, and, above all, the "need" for self-control. At this point it becomes easier to show how these beliefs lead to an improper labeling of emotions, to a mistaken notion of people's characteristics (see p. 224ff.), and, above all, to a perpetuation of one's own basic fears. Patients can also be made aware that the source of their *global* view of the world is nothing but a sequence of episodes (however important) that took place when they were children, and they can be induced to recognize the importance of the emotional accompaniment to attachment and detachment. Perhaps at this point patients can fully understand the meaning of Blurton-Jones's (1972) findings about the freedom of exploration of the smiling mothers' children (see p. 37), that is, that acknowledgment of and freedom from one's own emotional bonds are not two contrasting aspects of reality, but operate reciprocally.

NOTES

1. The term "agoraphobia," introduced by Westphal in 1872 (see Snaith, 1968), means, literally, fear of the marketplace. For many years the word has been used rather imprecisely in the psychiatric literature, but those who have written on the subject have generally implied that they were referring to a collection of situational fears, the main one being the fear of leaving home and being in the open.

2. The dichotomous categorization of "loneliness stimuli" and "constriction stimuli" seemed to us the best way of summarizing the various phobic stimuli that we were able to detect in our 115 patients suffering from agoraphobia (or multiple phobias centered around fear of loneliness). Although we were not able to find among the psychiatric literature a dichotomous categorization similar to ours, an accurate reading of clinical cases in existing correlation studies revealed no data that were discordant or incompatible with it. For example, Snaith (1968) published the scores obtained by 27 agoraphobic patients on the items contained in the Fear Survey Schedule. His results show that patients whose primary fear is of being out of the house also have a "most marked increase" (over 200%) of fears of traffic, crowds,

and narrow streets and an at least moderate increase (between 40% and 200%) of fears of "being closed in." (The schedule does not contemplate specifically fears of elevators, of galleries, of different ways of traveling, etc.)

3. During conversations with Victor Meyer, the well-known behavior therapist from London, we repeatedly heard from him that most agoraphobic women had a basic conflict as a source of their anxiety, namely, between the wish to stay with their protective husbands and the temptations to experience more exciting, but also perilous, adventures with "wolves." The idea of being in the street without their husband could evoke the possibility of being the subject of courting, and hence the conflict. Meyer was obviously very well aware that the idea of the open street unconsciously regarded as opportunity for sexual adventures is an old psychoanalytic explanation for agoraphobia. (K. Abraham, H. Deutsch, and E. P. Ivey, among others, held it; see Snaith, 1968, p. 678.) He wittily explained that psychoanalysts were clever people observing human behavior and that, even if their general theory seemed untenable to him, some of their observations, once translated into learning theory terms, were true and useful even for a behavior therapist. Four of our *married* agoraphobic women (when interviewed without their husbands!) explicitly and spontaneously told us they felt subject to the above-mentioned kind of temptation. Obviously it was not at all unconscious.

4. In the Rock and Goldberger study, female agoraphobics were clearly differentiated from simple phobics by field-dependence measures. Male agoraphobics show the same trend with respect to male simple phobics, but this last difference failed to be of statistical significance.

5. This kind of intrusive imagery has been considered by many clinicians as a proof that agoraphobics are more properly "labeled" as "obsessive–compulsive." In our opinion there is a phenomenological difference between agoraphobics' frightening fantasies of going mad and obsessive–compulsives' "impulses" to scream obscenities, for example. Besides, agoraphobics, in contrast with obsessionals, do not ruminate about going mad when they are not involved in the feared situations, do not test and retest their "mental abilities," and do not ritualize in order to protect themselves from "madness."

6. This is an intentional overstatement. It has been made in order to clarify the difference in cognitive organization between depressives and agoraphobics. Of course, in nature things are not so clear-cut as in our reconstructions. *Some* agoraphobic patients do share many of the depressives' attitudes and "symptoms," and "mixed syndromes" or "mixed cognitive organizations" (e.g., features of agoraphobia and eating disorders in the same patient, or features of obsessional and eating disorders in another patient) are continuously encountered in clinical practice. However, there are also many "pure" cases, in which the described differences can be quite easily detected. In categorizing our patient sample according to diagnosis, our decision was based on the main symptomatic features whenever there was a mixture of elements pertaining to different "syndromes." A typical example of how we made our "diagnostic" decision is given in the following:

A woman in her early 30s asked for treatment because of her inability to travel alone, even for short distances, *outside town*. She was very thin and complained of frequent stomachaches that hampered her in eating. She avoided only one kind of "crowded" situation, namely, restaurants. While walking in distant and unknown parts of the city, she brought with her a packet of biscuits, because she was afraid of fainting as a consequence of her "weakness," which she attributed to her scanty diet. (Agoraphobics usually bring with them tranquilizers, not biscuits, as a safety device when moving away from familiar surroundings.) The patient was assigned to the "eating disorder" (nervous anorexia) group.

7. We could give many examples of agoraphobics' "need for freedom." For the sake of conciseness, we limit ourselves here to the more common ones.

    a. Many agoraphobic patients report frequent nocturnal dreams of pleasant voyages in exotic places.

    b. Almost every agoraphobic energetically states that he or she cannot tolerate being subjected to anybody else's wishes or commands.

    c. "I hate working activities that involve routines" and "I don't want to work under a boss" are other common statements.

    d. One of our patients offers perhaps the most striking illustration of the "need for freedom". While confined almost entirely to his home during 6 years of illness, he learned two foreign languages and studied the geographical features of various foreign countries, holding continuously in his mind his wish to "travel and be free."

8. Strangely enough, we did not have any instance of agoraphobic fathers of agoraphobic children in our clinical sample, whereas five of our female patients and one male patient had mothers who clearly suffered from agoraphobia, which adds the possibility of vicarious learning as a factor in the development of the future agoraphobic. This is not to say that agoraphobic fathers do not exist or that they do not give negative modeling experiences to their children. Two drug-addicted male patients treated by a member of our group had agoraphobic fathers. Three of our male patients who suffered from psychosomatic disturbances and chronic anxiety also recollected memories of housebound fathers.

9. When it is not marriage, but one of the other life events listed on page 210, that constitutes the context in which agoraphobia emerges, it is also very simple to understand how patients might have representations of detachment from protective figures and/or of constrictive new life situations. As stated on page 211 and following, patients are usually able to recollect having had such representations, but deny that they could have any connection with the concomitantly experienced disturbances, and this because they felt they were still "in control." Should those disturbances be "really" of an emotional nature, they would have been able to "control" them: This is their main argument.

10. Some explanatory examples:

    a. A patient whose mother had been very worried about his physical "weakness" when he was a child experienced, while in situations of loneliness, "somatic imaging" (see Beck, 1976, pp. 204–206) relative to pain in his chest. When a child, he had suffered from recurrent respiratory and pulmonary illnesses. His mother used to say, "Cover yourself, take care of your chest!" and "Don't go out, you will cough again, you are feeble, your lungs are always ill!", for example.

b. When one of our female patients was a child, her parents used to speak of the "dangers of the street." She remembered that her mother had always commented on episodes of sexual violence reported in the newspapers. When she was an adolescent, her father had "tyrannically" forbid her to go out alone, because "she would become a bitch." He implied with this statement that she would not be able to resist temptations and sexual proposals if alone in the street. When, shortly before marriage, she became agoraphobic, she feared sexual aggression and had visual fantasies of herself "petrified" and "unable to make a single move" as a consequence of male bystanders' sexual compliments.

c. Another female patient was frequently told by her parents, "You are a tomboy." Her mother continuously tried to restrain, in every possible way, her "too vivacious behavior." She did not allow her to go out to play with the "bad boys" of street. When agoraphobia developed, this patient feared losing control and making obscene and aggressive gestures. She was also afraid of becoming sexually aggressive toward other women in the street and so "discover" that she "really" was a homosexual.

11. The possibility of using family therapy to treat agoraphobics having seriously disturbed marriages was tried in some cases, but our impression is that, at least for agoraphobics, the outcome of family therapy is rather unfavorable. Better results were obtained with joint couple sessions, in which irrational beliefs and expectations of both partners were attacked and corrected, as though they were part of the individual treatment of the agoraphobic spouse.

12. Whenever such an attitude is particularly prominent, as frequently happens with male patients who were especially successful in their work and social life, we start suggesting doubts about the future utility of a cognitive approach. For instance, we say something like the following:

We can start trying some very direct therapeutic techniques, which can give you *more* control over your actual disturbances. Many people are quite satisfied with the results of these techniques. We can then go on trying to understand how your disturbances originated, but this is not absolutely necessary. You can ask for this deeper understanding at a further stage of the treatment or leave treatment when you feel well enough again. There are advantages and disadvantages to each of these choices, so you are really free to decide.

Almost every patient stated quite early that he or she wanted "deeper understanding." By the way, this kind of verbalization has proved useful, in our experience, with agoraphobics, whereas it could be utterly contraindicated with other kinds of cognitive organization. For instance, obsessive–compulsive patients could start having ferocious doubts after it, or depressives could feel that the therapist were already giving up any hope of helping them, though kindly concealing his or her hopelessness under this façade.

13. A funny anecdote was told us by a colleague who applied to a patient this suggestion to use reactions to red lights as a device for making the patient acknowledge his "dual belief system" (Beck, 1976, p. 161 ff.). The patient's major subjective complaint was not agoraphobia, but secondary impotence with his wife and an inability to find other women, because he "needed to have his wife around all the time" and was very reluctant to leave home alone "should anything happen to me— you know, my heart is not strong." After a dialogue on traffic lights much like the one reported here, the patient, at the following session, reported, "You know, doctor, it is funny: I made love to my wife and we have not yet started a therapy for this problem." To the therapist's question of how this could have happened after more than 6 months of "impotence," the patient replied, "I was going to bed, and the thought came to my mind that it wasn't a duty to make love to my wife. I thought that perhaps it was pleasant for me to do so, and I found myself with an erection!" [Of course, we are not suggesting a dialogue about traffic lights with every patient who is impotent with his wife!]

14. One can remark how irrational it is to consider one's spouse as being able to give protection against, say, a heart infarction, while a nearby physician is regarded as potentially indifferent. This is true for many agoraphobics.

15. We are sorry that, for the sake of brevity, we must examine this hypothesis only in a note. Many agoraphobic patients seem to fall easily into a cognitive trap, or paradox: They start describing to themselves their disturbances as something external to the self, that is, as an "illness" and not as a personal emotion, however disturbing. They proceed to base their self-esteem on their ability to control something that, by definition, is uncontrollable, that is, a mysterious illness that even doctors cannot detect properly (or the very common term used to describe uncontrollability: "madness"). Is it surprising that, when this paradox dominates the problem-solving apparatus of the patient, self-esteem and self-identity, are shaken and depersonalization ("I feel as though I am not myself anymore"; "I disappear, I vanish"; "My head is numb, it is like cotton") appears?

During a therapeutic session, we were able to reproduce a feeling of depersonalization in a female patient, inducing exactly this kind of paradox. The patient was asked, in order to "master" her fears, to reproduce them through active, deliberate, intense dwelling upon her frightening images. (This is, by the way, a procedure that we frequently use with agoraphobics because it brings about one of two positive results: The patient, being "in control," does not experience very much fear and so learns to "master" fearful situations, or he or she succeeds in reproducing the fears and "physical distress" and then learns that it is an understandable phenomenon pertaining to personal thoughts and emotions, and not a mysterious illness external to the self.) She did not feel any distress. Then, rather abruptly, while she was noticing the strangeness of this phenomenon, she experienced her usual feeling of depersonalization ("I don't exist, I disappear," was her usual way of describing it). This was the first time that it appeared in the presence of a trustworthy, protective person—as the therapist was surely perceived. When immediately asked about the thoughts that preceded this feeling, the patient said, "It was like a pinwheel in my mind: I can control my fears if I image them voluntarily, but I fail to control them if I want to . . . more or less so . . . this kind of opposing thoughts alternating rapidly in my mind . . . I did not know anymore what was my thinking, what my will." With this patient, the plain description of the controllable–uncontrollable and self–nonself paradox was a decisive step in getting an almost complete cure. To satisfy the reader's possible curiosity, we should add that the patient was Judith (see p. 230 ff.) and that this session was part of the second phase of treatment, that is, the one following her relapse.

16. This technique bears many resemblances to Victor E. Frankl's use of "paradoxical intention," whose utility in the treatment of phobic patients was clinically demonstrated by Gerz (1962, 1966).

11

OBSESSIVE–COMPULSIVE PATTERNS

The term "obsessive–compulsive" is applied to a wide variety of disturbed patterns of thought, emotion, and behavior, having three main features in common:

1. Prolonged periods of rumination and doubting and an inability to reach a conclusion or make a decision: Strong emotions (anxiety, fear, or anger) usually accompany the rumination and doubting.
2. Intense phobias (usually focused upon some category of stimuli regarded as a contaminant) or strong urges to carry out acts unacceptable to the patient (with concomitant guilt and anxiety).
3. Rituals—sometimes elaborate and tinged with superstition and magic—intended to control the consequences of an unavoidable exposure to phobic situations, the emergence of unacceptable urges, or the unbearable insecurity and anxiety of protracted doubting. Very frequently, but not always, patients are aware that these rituals are senseless, time wasting, and distressing. Nevertheless, they maintain that any effort to resist them is painful and useless, and they soon acquire a compulsive character.

This chapter examines the cognitive organization of people suffering from obsessive–compulsive disturbances that emerge on the basis of an *obsessional personality*.

Our definition of "obsessional personality" is somewhat different from the psychoanalytic description of the "anal character." The cognitive and nonmotivational approach tends to consider the obsessional personality traits as manifestations of beliefs or basic assumptions rather than as aspects of a fixation of the libido. Certain beliefs and basic assumptions can rule and coordinate certain domains of cognitive processes, feelings, and behavior, and not others. Thus, in the case of obsessional personality, one particular patient can hold beliefs pertaining to the "*need* to be perfect" that are applicable to only one or two domains of behavior (e.g., work and morals) and not to others (e.g., sports, order in the house, personal cleanliness). Therefore, according to the cognitive view of obsessional personality, the constitutive traits appear only within specific meaning domains and are not necessarily evident in every aspect of the patient's life.[1] Only in this particular sense do we believe that a close connection exists between these traits and the "symptoms" of the obsessive-compulsive "illness."

Moreover, our clinical experience shows that, in some obsessive-compulsive patients, several aspects of the typical anal character—such as orderliness, cleanliness, obstinacy, punctuality, and parsimony—are secondary or altogether absent. On the contrary, we are convinced that other traits are fundamental to the conceptual domains related to each patient's specific symptoms, namely, conscientiousness, scrupulosity in moral matters, overestimation of details, rigidity, perfectionism, and sluggishness and uncertainty in making decisions.[2]

BEHAVIORAL ASPECTS

> With useless endeavour, forever, forever
> Is Sisyphus rolling his stone up the mountain.
> —H. W. Longfellow, "The Masque of Pandora"

Perhaps the most striking common aspect of the different obsessive-compulsive *behavioral* patterns is a generalized and tenacious avoidance behavior, coupled with the repetitive performing of rituals whenever the avoidance tactic fails.

Phobic patients have irrational fears, too, and also frequently emit anticipatory avoidance behavior when confronted with the fear-producing situation. Obsessionals similarly say they fear situations, but in order to avoid them, they spend so much time scanning their environment and monitoring their own actions and thoughts that a particular problem is created by their extreme effort to avoid the feared stimuli. They "create," so to speak, in their internal representation of the world, the very environmental situations that they strive to avoid, even when these situations are factually absent. To quote Mellet's example in the book edited by Beech, *Obsessional States* (Beech, 1974a): "He may claim to fear dirt, and feel compelled to check his clothing for its absence, but he will *go on thinking and looking for dirt* in the cleanest possible situation, when the birdphobic patient will be content in an ordinarily bird-free house" (p. 55; italics in original). Obviously, in such a self-built and frightening environment, avoidance soon becomes almost impossible.

At this point, patients develop specific rituals intended to somehow control the consequences of the imagined exposure to dangerous contingencies. Rituals are repetitive activities, sometimes stereotyped, frequently interwoven with superstitious or magic representations of controlling powers, which result in impairing patients' very happiness and efficiency. They usually, though not always, admit that their hand washing, their testing and retesting of their own performances, their repetitions of prayers, and so forth, are useless, fatiguing, distressing, and, above all, intended to keep under control a danger that is only imagined. Nevertheless, they claim to be compelled by their own fear to do so. A characteristic self-defeating sequence is thus typical of obsessive–compulsive behavior: Fear of certain situations leads to an extreme effort to avoid them; the feared stimuli appear in the inner representations of patients even when they can reasonably doubt their effective presence in the environment; their fear is so intense that they cannot follow their reason; doubting that they avoided what they feared, they appeal to rituals; performing rituals reduces anxiety, but usually induces in patients a negative mood, characterized by depression and hostility; in this depressive state, patients are more apt than ever to muse over the feared situations; and so forth, in an inexorable vicious circle.[3] Since the specific contents of feared situations and rituals vary considerably from one obsessive–compulsive patient to another, it may be useful to describe the most common categories of obsessive avoidance and ritualistic behavior with some examples.

Example 1

Peter, age 34, well-educated, employed, and happily married, was afraid of venereal disease contamination from prostitutes. He was rationally convinced that venereal diseases are contracted during direct sexual contact, but this "abstract" knowledge did not prevent him from fearing contamination even if he just happened to see, while riding in his car, a prostitute waiting for clients on a sidewalk. In such a circumstance, he felt compelled to wash his car and himself. Afterwards, he avoided the street in which he had seen the harlot or performed "compulsive" hand washing if avoidance was prevented by some particularly important necessity. In buses, bars, and stores, Peter watched every woman to find out, by looking at her makeup, clothes, and attitude, whether or not she was a prostitute. When he thought he had spotted one, he avoided that busline, bar, or shop. Again, if avoidance was impossible, Peter would perform hand washing and sometimes an alcohol-disinfecting ritual. Until this ritual was correctly performed, he experienced a sense of impending danger. After completion of the ritual, Peter realized how irrationally he had behaved, indulging in a time-wasting and even physically painful procedure (his hands were red and had rashes after so much washing), and he plunged into a moody or sad state of mind.

Sometimes the avoidance behavior is even more explicitly connected to sexual problems. A relatively common fear is that of being contaminated through the use of public toilets and sometimes through objects that have had only indirect contact with the genitals of persons of the opposite sex. At times the consequence expected from the contact is not an infectious disease, but pregnancy. At other times patients are not afraid of contaminating themselves but others, especially loved ones.

Sexual fears, however, are not always so evident in the avoidance behavior. Often patients are afraid of contamination by infectious diseases or of catching rabies through even indirect contact with animals. Sometimes liquid or air-contained chemicals are considered toxic and feared. In other cases the patients are afraid of contamination from people who have cancer, and they do not feel safer with the knowledge that cancer is not contagious. Finally, contamination from objects even symbolically related to death and corpses is a relatively frequent fear.

In all these cases, washing and disinfecting rituals are common. Sometimes, but not always, these rituals, in order to have an anxiety-reducing effect, must somehow follow a "superstitious" rule—for example, they must be repeated for an even number of times. When washing rituals occur, it is often possible to detect behind their origin, if not in the actual avoidance behavior, some form of sexual anxiety. Frequently they emerge during adolescence, sometimes as a consequence of masturbation experiences or during a sentimental relationship where sexual intercourse assumes special significance.

Example 2

Eva, age 29, married and childless, is a pretty woman with disquieting religious problems. She is constantly observing her own behavior and thoughts in order to check whether they are morally condemnable. Ever since she was a teenager, she has asked for reassurance from several clergymen when she suspects she has done something religiously wrong. The request for reassurance soon acquires a ritualistic aspect, since it has to be repeated twice. Moral errors connected with sexual matters are only a minor concern for Eva. She worries about all sorts of possible errors: disobedience, lack of love for study, overindulgence in eating, and so forth. But Eva's most painful problem is that in church she feels increasigly compelled to swear aloud. Sometimes she thinks she might have changed a word during her prayers, so as to change its meaning into a blasphemy (e.g., "brothel" instead of "brother"). So she starts avoiding going to church and praying, but painfully admits that the avoidance itself is a fault. Thus she takes up rituals. Every time she feels compelled to swear, or thinks she has changed a word in her prayers, she starts reciting to herself with extreme care and attention a special punishment formula. The formula is to be repeated four times. If the repetition contains an error, Eva "erases" it by crossing herself four times and then starts again, so as to obtain four "perfect" repetitions of the formula. Unless she is sure of the perfect completion of the ritual, Eva is afraid something terrible will happen to her or to someone she loves. If anything goes wrong in her daily life—a money loss, a quarrel with her husband, a minor illness—she suspects that it is a possible consequence of some moral fault on her part.

In Eva's case we notice another aspect of avoidance behavior in obsessionals: the avoidance of situations where an internal, unacceptable, and guilty impulse may easily emerge. Such avoidance behavior is accompanied by repeated control rituals, requests for reassurance, recitation of formulas, prayers, and exorcisms.

Example 3

George, age 50, a single and well-to-do lawyer, fears the possibility of losing his memory. One day, when he was in his 30s, he suffered from a depressive syndrome, apparently caused by his overconcern with a minor failure in his work. The depression was successfully treated with seven sessions of electroconvulsive therapy (ECT). After this treatment, he noticed, together with relief, a typical amnesia. At age 47, George again went through some difficulties in his work and again fell into a depressive mood. His psychiatrist this time prescribed antidepressant drugs, but this treatment was slow in showing any efficacy, and George strongly wanted to be in perfect mental shape in order to face his work problem. He was then confronted with a dilemma: ECT was likely to cure his depression rapidly and thus allow him to go back to work before the situation could deteriorate, but it was going to alter his memory, and this conflicted with his need to be in perfect mental shape.

One day, while he was considering this dilemma without being able to reach a solution, George noticed a man working in the front garden. The man disappeared behind a fence. Suddenly George thought of testing his own memory: He tried to remember the color of the man's clothes. When the man came out from behind the fence, George saw that he had remembered correctly and experience sharp relief from the previous anxiety.

After this experience, George started to test and retest his mnemonic abilities, feeling relieved when the test was successful, and anxious and sad when it failed. After a couple of months, this testing habit had greatly swelled and was seriously hampering George's life. He felt compelled to write down almost everything, however irrelevant, that happened outside his personal life's routine: news heard on the radio, titles of newspapers, figures on cars' license plates, and so forth. He wrote everything in a little notebook and then copied the data, as soon and as accurately as possible, into a bigger notebook. He filled up 67 notebooks in 3 years and was terrified of losing even one of them. This was the only way for him to avoid the anxiety of finding that his memory had missed something. George was aware that these rituals were senseless, time consuming and extremely distressing, but he felt "compelled" to perform them. To avoid the compulsions, he had to stay at home as much as possible, blind his eyes whenever he went out (only by taxi) in order not to see cars' license plates, and ask his relatives not to turn on the radio or the television.

In this example we notice two peculiar features of *some* obsessive-compulsive patients: (1) a previous depressive mood is very important for the development of compulsions, and (2) the avoidance behavior originates from compulsive rituals, rather than vice versa. The largest and most systematic study concerning the relationship between depression and obsessions was reported by Gittleson in a series of four papers (1966a–1966d). This study shows how obsessions are relatively common in the course of depressive psychosis and how they are based on the activation of premorbid personality traits. Also relatively common was the observation of patients who had shown clear obsessions before the onset of the depressive syndrome.

The other feature of George's compulsive behavior, his former disturbance that "caused" the avoidance behavior, also deserves comment. Such a connection creates a problem for the simplistic theory, frequently held by behavior therapists, that rituals are merely a displaced form of avoidance behavior.

Example 4

Rita, age 18 and single, was referred for psychotherapy because of a most disturbing syndrome of multiple tics and habit spasms. A psychiatrist had proposed a diagnosis of Gilles de la Tourette's syndrome. However, the clinical examination clearly established that Rita's spasms were *voluntary* and that they were intended to divert her attention from frightening *images* of death, violence, crashes, and disasters involving loved ones or, less frequently, herself. She could not stand to utter or hear such words as "death," "earthquake," or "murder," nor could she listen to news of car accidents, airplane or train disasters, and so forth. She did what she could to avoid these sorts of stimuli, and when her avoidance behavior failed, she resorted to ritualistic spasms and tics in order to cancel the images that such words and news had evoked in her mind. She confirmed that she was afraid that, if these images persisted without an effort on her part to get rid of them, some horrible accident would really happen. She felt literally "compelled" to shake her thoughts out. Since her parents and her boyfriend did not know why she was shaking her body in such an awful way, they tried to force her to stop. This created a state of panic in her, because stopping the spasms would have meant allowing her frightening images to go on, and she expected even more frightening consequences. On the other hand, she could not explain to her parents why she was shaking her body: To make them understand her motives, she would need to utter such words as she would never allow herself to utter. So other people's pressure created a vicious circle, and the spasms grew even more intense, frequent, and ugly to see.

This case exemplifies how interpersonal misunderstandings and pressures may become an inextricable component of an obsessive-compulsive pattern of behavior, a point frequently overlooked in both the psychoanalytic and the behavioristic literature. Furthermore, Rita's case focuses our attention on a peculiar and important phenomenon: the connection between *images* and *words*, and the idea of a sort of "omnipotence" of thought. (In this case the omnipotence was only in the direction of creating evil and suffering, not protection as well, as it was in Eva's case.)

Psychodynamic interpretations of obsessive–compulsive "symptoms" are as many and differentiated as there are numerous and varied aspects and problems relating to the clinical patterns just outlined. Sometimes, sexual guilt and repressed hostile wishes have seemed the most obvious explanations for compulsive behavior. In other cases the need to keep total control over outside reality and one's own behavior —an almost delusional need for omnipotence—has seemed a plausible basis for developing the "symptoms." Still other cases of obsessions have been understood to be a defense against, or a by-product of, depression. The conflicts between obedience and rebellion, between the pursuit of order and moral perfection and the urge to act obscenely or violently, and between behavioral avoidance of certain situations and constant brooding over the same situations have often suggested the idea that ambivalence is the common basis of obsessional neuroses. We think that, from the cognitive–behavioral point of view, priority should be given to the study of *unvarying* cognitive aspects within the variable obsessive–compulsive behavioral patterns rather than to any effort of causal interpretation.

INVARIANT COGNITIVE ASPECTS

If a man will begin with certainties, he shall end in doubts.—F. Bacon, *Advancement of Learning*, Book I

Singer and Antrobus (1972), in a psychometric study of daydreaming patterns as related to personality, succeeded in identifying two main pathological groups. One of these groups clearly seems to represent the obsessional neurotic. They concluded that the person who scores high on the major scales of the factor named "Obsessional–Emotional Daydreaming" might be considerably oriented toward processing imagery and inner experience, but "much of the fantasy would have a *dysphoric quality* and involve *great repetition of a small number of themes* of a somewhat *bizarre nature*, often emerging with an *almost hallucinatory vividness*" (p. 200; italics added). This description brilliantly summarizes what one can observe in clinical inquiry while examining the modes of thought representation accompanying obsessive–compulsive disturbances. Almost invariably, patients, provided they are able to distinguish the imaginal from the lexical (verbal) mode, report the existence of disturbing, vivid, and repetitive images.

Peter (see Example 1 in the preceding section) almost "saw" a sort of very thin dust coming from the prostitute, spreading in the air and sticking to his car. Having touched his car's handles, he almost "felt" this dirty dust on his hands and *then* started to think about hand washing, car washing, and disinfection. He was fully aware of the irrationality and unrealistic quality of these images, and because of this he had some trouble in finding the words to describe them. Words such as "dust" were not proper, he said. It was like a "microscopic" image of millions of germs spreading from the woman. While these images persisted (and the only way to get rid of them was to wash), he *spoke* to himself—that is, he reasoned out his problem. Both the irrationality of the image (resistance to "compulsion") and the "solution" of disinfection were processed in the *verbal* mode of inner representation. When the rational side of the internal dialogue was on the verge of winning the battle (anxiety and self-reproach for his irrationality were obvious concomitants in the conflict), another set of images appeared in his stream of thoughts. He almost "saw" his body covered with pimples and ulcers. This image was so frightening that the contrasting thought that there was no real risk of infection was overthrown. Peter went on to his ritualistic washing.

Peter's case is a clear example of the visual and tactile images that interfere with the rational inner dialogue and rule the avoidance and ritualistic behavior. But every other kind of imaginal mode of thought can be observed in obsessional neurosis.

Eva (Example 2) had auditory images of distorted words in her prayers. After having said aloud, or merely thought, the word "brother," for instance, she, who was constantly monitoring her own thinking, almost "heard" in her memory her own voice uttering the word "brothel." On closer inquiry, even what we previously described as an *impulse* to blaspheme God revealed itself as a vivid auditory image of her own voice uttering horrible obscenities. Eva's guilt-ridden considerations about herself as being responsible for such an awful sin were represented in the verbal mode. Her rituals, although of a verbal nature, were again permeated with an imaginal, almost sensory quality. The mentally recited prayer had to have the same sound quality as the auditory image of the blasphemy in order to be effective.

Rita's images of ravages, destruction, crashes, and death were also very vivid. Both her avoidance and her ritualistic behavior were aimed at preventing and removing such images. The peculiar character of the rituals became understandable on a closer examination of her representations. She was always present in front of the imagined disaster and "felt" herself in this representation as impotent, weak, and helpless. This self-representation had a very distinct kinesthetic quality. By shaking her limbs and contracting her muscles, Rita "canceled" this kinesthetic "image" of weakness, much as Peter did with his images of dirt and Eva with the echoes of her swearing voice. Rita's expectation of misfortunes befalling herself and her loved ones because of her negligence in getting rid of the frightening intrusive images were couched in the verbal mode of thought. "My God, something like this could happen to Daddy!" (or her mother, her boyfriend, or herself) maybe a representative example of the "lexical" comments that she recognized in her own stream of thought.

These three examples describe a very common sequence of thoughts, emotions, and actions detectable in most obsessional patients. Vivid images, accompanied by emotions of fear, disgust, or guilt, emerge in precise environmental contexts (or even later—e.g., while the individuals are reexamining their daily actions in order to judge their conformity with their moral standards). A verbal inner dialogue, full of negative judgments about themselves or the impeding danger, accompanies and follows these images and suggests a remedy: the most careful avoidance in the future and the use of erasing rituals (the so-called undoing) for protection or expiation as soon as possible. During the inner dialogue, patients may consider, before, during, or after accomplishment of the ritual, the irrationality of the images and fears and of the ritual itself. These considerations cause further self-despising, although they do not stop the completion of the ritual. On the contrary, new, more terrifying images may arise from the "rational" conflict of the faulty problem solving contained in the ritual. Finally, there is usually some connection between the sensory nature of the intrusive image and the essential meaning of the ritual (tactile—dirt and washing; auditory—uttered blasphemy and recited prayer; kinesthetic—physical weakness and violent muscular contractions).[4]

Though common, this sequence is not universal in obsessional patients. In George's case (Example 3), for example, it was never possible to find recurring images of a "near hallucinatory vividness." The effort of our cognitive approach is to find constant—or unvarying—aspects; therefore we must go further and find, behind the sequence just described, beliefs, assumptions, or rules enabling us to explain the obsessive–compulsive behavior in cases such as George's.

George was obviously ascribing too much importance to success in his job. The difficulty in his profession that preceded his first depressive reaction was by no means a major one. George did not face on that occasion poverty, the loss of his job, or a serious setback in his career, but only criticism from colleagues in the legal office where he worked. However, George was evidently overconcerned about negative opinions and seemed to identify his worth as a human being with success in his work. Furthermore, he was a perfectionist, so he kept ruminating over every possible mistake made during the day. This description easily fits a cognitive organization leading to depression.

During the second depressive episode, caused by a work problem very similar to the first one, George saw himself as a worthless nonentity. He felt other people's criticism and low opinions to be a fundamental aspect of reality and thought things would get even worse—Beck's classic "triad of depression" (Beck, 1967, 1970). All these notions were processed mainly in the verbal mode of inner representation, and so was the new dilemma that George faced during his second depressive reaction: ECT and efficiency or intact memory and distressing depression? George's doubting and the relief in finding out that he was able to remember the color of the clothes of a man in the garden are to be understood in the context of his "depressogenic" and "perfectionist" view of himself and of the world. Only a memory capable of passing *all* the tests could—George thought —guarantee him quick relief from depression (thanks to ECT) and mental efficiency (regardless of ECT side effects). Nothing less than this *absolute* and *perfect* solution could be accepted by George. On this basis, the first failing in one of the tests on his memory unloosed such a reaction of fear and dejection that George found himself confronted with a new insoluble dilemma: Should he keep testing himself, with the risk of failing again, or should he stop checking his memory, but lose the possible comfort of assessing his toleration of ECT?

Readers familiar with applied learning theory may find George's unsolvable dilemmas similar to the experimental model for the production of fixations described by Maier, Glaser, and Klee (1940) so often used in learning models of obsessive–compulsive disorders (see, e.g., Beech, 1974b, pp. 12–13). In a tempting analogy with the mice that Maier presented with an unsolvable discriminating task, George, too, developed a "fixated behavior" that constantly prevented him from trying to find new solutions to his dilemma. His writing down all information unrelated to daily routines precluded the solving of the problem by giving up the memory tests, but at the same time prevented him from actually testing his memory.

Perfectionism, emotional value attached to his performance in a specific field, and a superimposed dilemma made insoluble by the search for absolutely certain, definite, and perfect solutions are apparently the ingredients of the cognitive antecedents of George's ritualistic behavior. Are the same ingredients detectable behind the sequence of vivid and unacceptable images, faulty problem solving represented in the verbal mode, and ritualistic behavior that we can assess in the cases of Peter, Eva, Rita, and the majority of obsessive–compulsive patients?

The answer is yes. A thorough examination of patients and their solutions to the problems created by their vivid and painful intrusive imagining (or, as in George's case, by any form of insecurity in his own worth) promptly shows how these solutions are *extreme* and rigid. In their research obsessional patients inevitably forget other intermediate concepts, such as the probability of variations in time and relativity of danger with respect to the amount and intensity of infectious agents and toxic substances. The same search for absolute solutions leads to a dichotomizing examination of the environment. Whether or not there is danger is all that counts. For Peter there is almost no difference between a single germ imagined outside his visual field and sexual intercourse with a prostitute. He must avoid *all* possibility of contact with contaminating prostitutes. In the same way Eva does not discriminate between little flaws in her moral behavior and serious faults, and she will not tolerate being distracted. *All* her religious behavior *must* be *perfect* in every detail. Rita cannot afford to be negligent toward her intrusive images *even for an instant*; *she must always* watch out and never leave the slightest room for those images. Therefore, however bizarre the intrusive images may be, the problem-solving mechanism in these patients shows rules based on the belief that perfection and certainty are possible in the relationship between human beings and reality. Ellis's (1962) category of irrational beliefs based on the "need for absolute certainty" seems to be the very core of these patients' approach toward reality. Consequently, whenever a subjective danger seriously involving self-esteem emerges, it rapidly creates the premise for the production of unsolvable dilemmas.

Looking for absolute certainty, and being unable to doubt and postpone as they do when self-esteem is not so directly involved, patients find themselves trying to control the uncontrollable. Rituals in this case seem similar to the stereotyped "fixed" answers obtained by Maier, Glaser, and Klee (1940): They are "false solutions" that do not remove or solve the dilemma, but that are adopted only for their temporary power to reduce the intolerable anxiety of feeling helpless in the face of a "vital" problem. And when the unsolvable dilemma persists, the rituals themselves become repetitive, they show how incapacitating and irrational they are, and patients are confronted with a further unsolvable dilemma: Give up the rituals and undergo anxiety, or keep them and be constantly forced to admit one's own irrationality and helplessness.

Beech and Liddell (1974) have reviewed the experimental evidence for the theory that ritualistic behavior is maintained, notwithstanding its negative effect upon mood states, not simply because of its immediate anxiety-reducing power, but also because of an "overpowering need for certainty in decisions to *terminate* activities" (p. 151; italics added). In looking for evidence that it is absolutely right to terminate the ritual, the patient is "forced" to continue it.

Perfectionism, the need for certainty, and a strong belief in the existence of an absolutely correct solution for human problems are different verbal labels for a cognitive structure that appears to be both unvarying in different obsessive–compulsive patterns and able to explain the construction of unsolvable dilemmas. If this cognitive structure is really fundamental in the organization of knowledge in obsessive–compulsive patients, it should be able to explain the numerous other characteristics of the obsessive style extensively described in clinical and experimental literature.

Doubting, postponing, overconcern for detail, and uncertainty in making decisions are indeed logically reconcilable with this "need for certainty." If there is only one right and certain answer to human problems, scrupulous attention *must* be paid to every detail of the problem before making a decision.[5] Because we live in a probabilistic universe—a fact that obsessionals do not take into consideration—evidence of the correctness of a choice is constantly contradicted by opposing evidence; obsessionals are constantly tormented by doubts and keep evaluating *opposite* options, because their belief in absolutely certain and right solutions prevents them from considering intermediate aspects.

Makhlouf-Norris and her co-workers (Makhlouf-Norris, Gwynne-Jones, & Norris, 1970; Makhlouf-Norris & Norris, 1972), using Kelly's Role Construct Repertory Grid, have experimentally demonstrated how the conceptual structure of obsessive–compulsive neurotics is nonarticulate—that is, clusters of concepts are not linked together by integrative constructs. Makhlouf-Norris argues that nonarticulate conceptual structures permit discrete cataloging of the separate aspects of a person, but cannot bring these together in a single identity. These discrete areas of judgment appear as islands of certainty in a sea of uncertainty. In the uncertainty deriving from his or her inability to give articulate judgments, the obsessional "creates islands of certainty in which he can control events, he tries to create a condition *in which his objective probabilities are invariably 1.00*" (Makhlouf-Norris, 1968, quoted by Fransella, 1974, p. 187; italics added). Doubt and sluggishness in making decisions are the price for maintaining these "islands of certainty": Everything significant has to be examined with extreme care and at length in order to make it fit in this rigid realm of 1.00 probability. Underinclusion (Reed, 1969; see Note 5) is obviously another cost, and so are inability to tolerate ambiguity (Hamilton, 1957), the illusion of living in a symmetric world (Rosenberg, 1953),[6] and the strong, constant fear of criticism (Turner, Steketee, & Foa, 1979).[7] Makhlouf-Norris's conclusion about the self-concepts of her experimental group of obsessive–compulsive patients is also noteworthy: "This conceptual system is predominantly engaged in carrying the meaning that I'm the *opposite* of what I would like to be. . . . The ideal self is described by the *opposite* poles of these (i.e., describing the actual self) constructs" (Makhlouf-Norris & Norris, 1972, p. 283; italics added).

Our analysis seems to support the idea that the need for certainty is indeed a central cognitive structure in the obsessive–compulsive organization of knowledge. The questions that immediately arise then are: How did this cognitive structure come to occupy such a central position? How did it happen that such patients were never able to distance themselves from this way of thinking, so that their theories, now maintained in the face of every possible invalidation, are held as true and continue to regulate their problem solving regardless of the negative consequences and the admittedly irrational "solutions"? To attempt to answer these questions, we shall proceed to an analysis of patients' development.

DEVELOPMENTAL ASPECTS

The way upwards and the way downwards are one and the same way. — Heraclitus

In the clinical literature there are many examples of parents of obsessive–compulsive patients presenting some traits of the obsessional or authoritative personality (see, e.g., Adams, 1973; Laughlin, 1967). A strict, very orderly parent with an inflexible attitude on normal duties may transmit the idea that there are in the world absolute certainties and that it is desirable or necessary to seek them out and behave according to them. In fact, such characteristics were to be found in a majority (but not in all) of the parents of our obsessive–compulsive patients. However, many other neurotic patients' parents had these characteristics, and probably many parents of normal individuals did, too. Moreover, the brothers and sisters of many of our obsessive–compulsive patients never borrowed the parents' attitude. Some other factor than identification must therefore be responsible for the construction of the overwhelming need for certainty by these patients.

As we said in Chapter 5, the pattern of attachment of children that later became obsessive–compulsive patients has one common aspect. The behavior of at least one of the parents is apt to have two opposite interpretations *at the same time*: (1) that he or she takes much care of the child and (2) that he or she is totally unaffectionate or even hostile toward the child. The situation outlined in Chapter 5 is, in this respect, the simplest or perhaps the most common. A morally rigid parent who acts consistently with his or her concept of ethical duties and self-sacrifice is the most prominent figure in the child's familiar milieu. The other parent either approves of this approach or is a minor, relatively dim figure. The rigid parent constantly shows interest in the child, but never expresses affection and is undemonstrative; he or she never plays with nor has fun with the child. Moreover, the parent's interest is manifested chiefly through the teaching of moral rules that the child perceives as bearing renunciation and suffering. "He (she) loves me," "He (she) loves me not" and "I am lovable," "I am not lovable" then become for the child equally possible interpretations of what is going on.

A beautiful literary description of a father similar to the rigid parent described here can be found in the famous autobiographical book by Sir Edmund Gosse, *Father and Son: A Study of Two Temperaments* (1907). In Chapter 2 there is also a poignant description of the childish form of magical thought and the superstitious rituals that the author developed when he was about 6 years old. This description closely follows Gosse's memories of the time he first found out that his father was not infallible or omniscient and the statement that he had then suddenly acquired a sense of his own split individuality: He had discovered that he was himself and at the same time "somebody else living in my own body." Piaget (1926) used E. Gosse's memories in one of his most brilliant definitions of the magic mentality in the child.[8]

Of course, the way to develop a "double-faced" attachment as outlined here is only one of many possible ways. This was transparent in Peter's (Example 1) relationship with his mother, in George's (Example 3) with his father, and in Eva's (Example 2) with both parents. However, Rita's pattern of attachment (Example 4) was somewhat different, as it was for some of our other obsessive-compulsive patients. The following two vignettes exemplify such thematic variations.

Rita's parents were reasonably careful and very affectionate with her and her brother. The mother was also very anxious, worrying about every possible danger. The father soon revealed that he was not able or willing to prevent some of the misfortunes that his wife foresaw. To his wife's reproaches—frequent and often continuing for years—Rita's father reacted by retreating into himself or seeking comfort in his work. He was often out, and when he was home, he would keep saying, very reasonably, that if one is *careful* not to be a prey of fears, he or she will live much better than if always brooding over all the possible dangers. He did not specify what these dangers were or how to avoid thinking about them and "not to be a prey of fear." Sometimes he would just mumble something like "And then, if you keep *thinking* about accidents, you'll end up getting yourself into them." In this context, Rita developed a somewhat stronger attachment to her mother than to her father because she was more often present and was more protective than he was. On the other hand, when she was afraid, she felt closer to her father because her mother was also fear-inducing, whereas her father's attitude toward danger was more reassuring. Rita's construction of her own identity thus centered around this dilemma: Seek protection in the person who induced fears or reassurance in the one who was absent and careless in specifying *how* one could get rid of fears. The double face of her personal identity was evident: She considered herself potentially able, in an unspecified way, to avoid fears and dangers (father's attitude) as well as to be involved in the most terrifying accidents (mother's attitude).[9]

Another female patient, who during adolescence developed an obsession for chemicals (which she considered indiscriminatingly toxic or carcinogenic) and corresponding compulsive hand-washing rituals, had an absent father and a mother who was extremely afraid that her daughter would contract an infectious disease. This mother forced her daughter to wear gloves, even in the summer, while going on the merry-go-round or playing ball. In many other ways, the mother was highly protective and also physically affectionate with the child, but she *almost never listened* when the daughter *asked* to talk to her. The double-faced attachment manifested as gratitude for the protection received and resentment for the absurd demand that she wear gloves and, above all, as a hopeful request for attention versus an angry expectation of a refusal. The patient clearly remembered an episode that contained, in an image, her double attitude toward her mother. The 4-year-old child sat quietly on the beach near her mother, asking her to *talk* to her. The mother, seated on a chaise longue, replied that her back hurt and that she could not talk to her, and she told her to go play somewhere else. The child then went behind the mother's chair and hit her back with her little fists, thinking how she longed to talk to her and at the same time how she wished to hurt her back, since her *good* mother was so *bad* in not wanting to talk to her.[10]

Many authors who have studied the familial roots of obsessional neurosis report observations compatible with our own: H. S. Sullivan, J. Barnett, and J. Ruesch, among others. (For a review of their thought and extensive quotations, see Adams, 1973.) Sullivan described the veneer of convention and sweetness covering unhappiness and cruel attitudes toward the child as a characteristic of at least one of the obsessional parents. Barnett says that, in the obsessional's family, parents camouflaged hostile behavior toward the child with a façade of love and concern. Ruesch stated that "analogic understanding" was undermined in the future obsessive patients because of an excess of verbal communication about abstract or moral topics and a lack of nonverbal manifestations of emotion. Many others reported contrasting attitudes in the parents of the obsessionals, such as overindulgence followed by stringent demands for responsibility, rejection of the child concealed by opposite outward expressions of concern, unrealiability, and unpredictability of rewards and punishments (see, e.g., Laughlin, 1967).

Two great themes of psychiatric literature come to mind when we consider the relationship that obsessionals feel they had with their parents: ambivalence and double bind. Ambivalence has been one of the leitmotivs of psychoanalytic interpretations of the origin of obsessive neurosis. Freud thought that obsessionals' doubts were extensions of their ambivalence and tended to overemphasize the hostile issues as the focal concern in ambivalence. However, as a psychoanalytically oriented psychotherapist remarks, "Ambivalence . . . is also related to the cultural attitudes about loyalty and dedication . . ." (Salzman, 1973, p. 45) and "It is clear that the obsessive person is often incapable of loving another, . . . [but this] is an aspect of his ambivalence and doubting, and not the *result* of it" (p. 40; italics in original). "In one sense, ambivalence is the experience of wanting and not wanting at the same time. After a while it begins to stimulate doubts and uncertainties about one's integrity and honesty" (Salzman, 1973, p. 40).

From our point of view, there are only partial connections between the obsessional's concept of ambivalence and the concept of a relationship that can be interpreted as having simultaneously opposite characteristics. Such an attachment relationship induces in patients a "double" view of themselves and reality, and the unbearability of such a view causes the need for certainty (i.e., the necessity to find out which one of the two sides is the true one) and the need for perfection (the will to act in a way so irreproachable as to conform to the positive side and repudiate the negative one). The doubleness of conflicting emotions is an aspect of the doubleness of cognitive interpretations, rather than vice versa.

The double-bind theme was of major importance in the interpretation of schizophrenia offered by the system model (family therapy). Recently, it has been increasingly considered as a "universal pathogenic mechanism" (Sluzki & Veron, 1976) in the systemic study of abnormal behavior. In fact, there are obvious correspondences between the wider definition of "double bind" (a communicative situation where it is factually impossible not to choose, but where any choice is *logically* wrong) and the unsolvable dilemma experienced by obsessive–compulsive patients in their attachment relationships. Anyway, we are studying the cognitive aspect of the unsolvable dilemma, and only secondarily the interpersonal communication aspects.

These cognitive aspects may be summarized in the image of someone who feels forced, by an unbearable situation of indecision between two opposites, to monitor himself or herself and reality, looking for the *true* nature of things and the right way to behave, without considering the probabilities and variabilities of this world or the innumerable shades and hues between black and white.

THE COGNITIVE ORGANIZATION IN OBSESSIVE–COMPULSIVE PATTERNS

ADAM: How can I help brooding when the future has become uncertainty. . . . Hope is wicked. Happiness is wicked. Certainty is blessed. — G. B. Shaw, *Back to Methuselah*, Part 1

Emotional schemata where the self-image and the image of attachment figures have opposite characteristics are the starting point for understanding the organization of knowledge in obsessive–compulsive patients. In the earlier stages of the organization, when the inner dialogue about primitive images of tacit self-knowledge is structured in an attitude toward oneself, personal identity emerges in a split form. As we already mentioned, it was in this way, somehow split into two, that E. Gosse suddenly acquired the sense of his individuality. This is not the only famous autobiographical description of such an experience.

Nobel Prize for Literature winner Hermann Hesse and Carl Gustav Jung describe similar feelings in their memoirs. Hesse felt his "double" always beside him, suggesting gratuitous and provocative acts. Once the "double" induced the child Hesse to jump into a fountain. Another time Hermann's father, after a harsh reproach for a misdeed, gave him a little calendar as a token of reconciliation; the "double" instantly ordered little Hesse to throw it into the river, and

Hermann, who was very fond of the object, obeyed. Jung remembers being convinced, as a child, that he was made of two different—and in fact opposite—persons, whom he called "Number One" and "Number Two." In his memoirs, collected by Aniela Jaffé (1963), he gives a detailed description of his own and of his mother's two "persons." (He thought that his parents also had a Number One and a Number Two.) Both Hesse and Jung, we may recall, always strained to harmonize the two great opposites: Eastern Wisdom and Western Wisdom, Narziss the theologian and Goldmund the mystic, God and the Devil (in *Demian* Hesse reflects on Abraxas, "the God who was at the same time God and the Devil"), Introversion and Extraversion, the Self and its Shadow together forming the individual, and so forth.

In the face of a split identity, with an attitude toward oneself and an attitude toward reality that simultaneously have opposite valences and that induce one to consider the irreconcilable contrasts of things, there are only two possible approaches. One is to accept the opposing aspects of the Self and the world and to try to compose them in harmonic unity. This is apparently Hesse's and Jung's way. But the persons who are most likely to develop an obsessive–compulsive syndrome choose another way: *Only one* of the two opposites must be "true," or must at least become "true" through a constant effort toward perfection. The opposite negative aspect is then rationalized as a result of an insufficient effort to attain perfection. Mistakes are considered execrable, since they represent the abyss of an evil as absolute as the pursued virtue. The idea of perfection and certainty suggested by parents becomes the key to understanding reality and· regulating one's behavior.

Thus, not yet having attained absolute perfection and certainty, the obsessional keeps focusing his or her attention on the future (a fact often reported by clinicians; cf., e.g., Salzman, 1973, pp. 67–72). In the future, certainty and perfection will be attained if one is able to *foresee* and control all *dangers* that the future brings, without distractions or mistakes. The behavioral and moral rules learned have no practical value and are not considered with regard to their function: They are an abstract "must," which is supposed to lead to an equally abstract perfection (Shapiro, 1965).

The organization of knowledge is thus completed. The original sense of doubleness derived from the tacit self-knowledge data is controlled by an extremely rigid attitude toward oneself. The personal identity is conceived of as a temporarily imperfect personality, straining to become perfect in the future. The actual self, as Makhlouf-Norris and Norris (1972) remark, is construed as the *opposite* of the ideal self. The opposite aspects of the self-image proposed by the tacit self-knowledge are constantly integrated, through a rigid and severe attitude toward oneself, in a steady and unitary personal identity in the present and in another, rigorously defined identity to be reached in the future. The consequent attitude toward reality implies a choice of all the opposite aspects, so as to pursue the positive ones and avoid the negative ones; a careful analysis of other people's behavior; and a constant state of alarm and doubt, so as to avoid danger and mistakes.

In Ellis's words (1962), the following irrational beliefs are specially represented in this theoretical construction:

- "The idea that one should be thoroughly competent, adequate and achieving in all possible respects if one is to consider oneself worthwhile" (p. 63).
- "The idea that if something is or may be dangerous or fearsome one should be terribly concerned about it and should keep dwelling on the possibility of its occurring" (p. 75).
- "The idea that there is invariably a right, precise, and perfect solution to human problems, and that it is catastrophic if this perfect solution is not found" (p. 87).

These kinds of beliefs appear in patients' attitudes toward themselves and reality; they are the basis of the personal identity and work as a sort of protective belt (to use the analogy with Lakatos's model), preventing criticism and admission of the limitedness to particular experiences of the tacit knowledge about the doubleness of self and reality. These beliefs guide obsessionals' representational models of reality toward a rigid dichotomization of the reality data in order to avoid mistakes and danger and to find the "perfect solution." The consequent "polarized thinking" (Beck, 1976) is in keeping with the opposite images of the metaphysical hard-core.

Of course, other irrational beliefs besides the ones mentioned can exist in the cognitive organization of obsessive-compulsive patients, but they are at a secondary level in the conceptual structure. For example, "the idea that certain people are bad, wicked or villainous, and that they should be severely blamed and punished for their villainy" (Ellis's irrational belief n. 3; see Ellis, 1962, p. 65) is logically consistent with the perfectionist attitude of these patients.

Anyway, it is not indispensable for the maintenance of the personal identity and therefore can be easily corrected by psychotherapy or spontaneously. For the sake of perfection, obsessionals may stick to the idea that, for example, one should not judge others, according to the Gospel's teaching ("Judge not, that ye be not judged). Consequently, they can *rigidly* avoid blaming others, but this will not in any way change their notions of perfection and certainty; in fact, it will confirm them. A relevant study by Marks (1966), using the semantic differential, shows how this can happen. The obsessionals used the *central* position of the scales significantly more often than the intermediate, *more discriminatory* positions. It may be argued that the central position on a scale is at least as unambiguous for obsessionals as the scale's extremes and that it also allows them to avoid extremity ratings.

Obsessionals' attitudes toward themselves have a peculiar effect on their own daydreaming and fantasy life. As Singer (1976) puts it,

> The obsessional at his worst is constantly examining and re-examining each sequence of thought and fantasy, splitting each element further into smaller segments, constantly preoccupied with presumed guilts and self-doubts. . . . In an extreme case, . . . an individual may become so obsessed with detail that he allows himself very little free fantasy or inner imagery, and instead prefers to immerse in detailed counting or excessively precise *verbal operations*. (p. 192, italics added)

Imagery is something very close to "analogic" operations, which cannot be easily split into two opposites, whereas verbal operations are "digital" and always imply opposites. Thus again, through the exclusion of free fantasy, the "belt" of perfectionism "protects" the metaphysical hard-core from disproving inner experiences.

In the face of particularly stressful events, recurring intrusive images are likely to appear in the individual's consciousness. These images convey information pertaining to the stressful situations belonging to the tacit self-knowledge, but usually not processed in the verbal mode of inner representation. In obsessive–compulsive patients, these images arouse excessive alarm because of their uncontrollable nature, but mostly because of patients' approaches to everything that appears as dangerous and wrong. (In the face of a stressing event, the unbidden intrusive images inevitably acquire a dangerous or erroneous implication.) Obsessionals intend to control or *totally* annul the danger imagined, with the result of often creating a series of unsolvable dilemmas.

For Peter (Example 1) the stressful event was the game of seduction that an older woman played with him when he was 16 years old. He was then in love with a girl he considered "angel-like." His friends kept trying to persuade him to have together their first sexual experience with a prostitute. He refused and started thinking about his "angel" and about the contrasting "bestiality" of sexual intercourse with prostitutes. He began scrutinizing himself, to see whether he felt even the slightest interest in sex with prostitutes. One day an attractive woman, certainly not a prostitute, whom he had met at an uncle's house, playfully flirted with him. He had the sudden image of this woman dressed like a whore. His first avoidance of contacts—however indirect—with prostitutes was meant to reassure him that he would never be deceived by a harlot who did not look like one. So he found himself thinking of every woman with an easy-going look as a possible prostitute. He had recurring images of prostitutes touching him. A first dilemma was that absolute avoidance of an unpleasant thing implied constant thinking about that thing. The basis for a second dilemma was laid by Peter's belief that he *must* refuse the recurring images of prostitutes; otherwise he had to admit that perhaps he wanted to go with them. To do this, he had to create for himself more and more disgusting thoughts about prostitutes and to wash himself while he had these thoughts. Thus a second dilemma was created: to continue with these reassuring rituals or to stop them because of their irrationality and increasingly distressing "compulsiveness."

In Eva's and Rita's cases, equally "secondary" stressful events led to the creation of unsolvable dilemmas. This is often the case with obsessive–compulsive patients, and the ease with which apparently irrelevant episodes start the process can perhaps explain the inconsistencies among the numerous studies about precipitating factors of obsessional neurosis (for a review of these studies, see Black, 1974). However, in all cases, unsolvable self-made problems give way to further stiffening of the attitude toward oneself and proliferating ad hoc theories, which are repetitive and substantially unfruitful, to explain to oneself the intrusive images and the necessity of rituals. The patient's "research program" (to go back to Lakatos's model) suffers a "regressive shift."

It may be interesting to note that, while the attitude toward oneself becomes more rigid, and fundamental beliefs on which personal identity is based become stronger, the same feeling of doubleness that brought about the organization of knowledge may reemerge (but without integration in personal identity).

Peter said that it was "someone else" who suggested those disgusting images of prostitutes and who prevented the success of his reasoning self, who, in turn, claimed the irrationality of fears and rituals. And he would promptly add, "Doctor, I am well aware that I'm that 'someone,' but I can't help feeling him separated from myself."

Eva said that she was made of two halves, that she would identify with her right side and left side. The right side was good, the left side was bad. The outside world was also divided in two. That is why she had to repeat her rituals four times: The two good halves of herself and the world had to face the two bad halves and cancel them.

Other obsessional patients express their sense of split self by saying "Now it's not me speaking, it's my unconscious" (by a patient who underwent psychoanalytical treatment for many years); "I have two parts, one male, one female, I can't join them together"; "I must touch everything with my right hand, my left hand is clumsy."

PLANNING A THERAPEUTIC STRATEGY

THE SERPENT: . . . I fear certainty as you fear uncertainty. . . . Nothing is certain but uncertainty. If I bind the future I bind my will. If I bind my will I strangle creation. — G. B. Shaw, *Back to Methuselah*, Part 1

Behavior therapy techniques introduced in recent years greatly improved the prognosis of obsessive–compulsive disorders (see Beech & Vaughan, 1978, for an extensive review). Through these techniques it is possible to alter the attitude of patients toward their own rituals, their expectations about what could happen if they do not perform them (Meyer, 1966), and the attitude toward their intrusive images, which, after a modeling and flooding therapy, are no longer considered as something they "cannot stand" (Rachman, 1971b; Rachman, Marks, & Hodgson, 1973). Behavioral techniques by themselves, however, can only lead to a superficial change. In personal communications with us, Isaac Marks and John Boulougouris gave a good example of how such a peripheral change is expressed in the patients' words. They observed a different attitude in phobic and obsessive–compulsive patients who have undergone a treatment based on exposure to the previously avoided situations. The objective estimates of improvement were similar (in terms of ability to face the previously avoided stimuli with a minimum of autonomic arousal), but the *subjective* estimations of phobics and obsessive–compulsive patients were quite different. Whereas phobics asserted that they benefited from the treatment, obsessionals stated that they were as ill as ever.

From our point of view, this is quite understandable, if we consider that the exposure treatment (flooding) does not modify the perfectionist attitude toward oneself. Finding themselves still afraid of certain situations, obsessionals believe that they are not changed in any way. Only a *perfect* total absence of fear would indicate a change; intermediate ratings are excluded.

Thus, the main purpose of a psychotherapeutic strategy with obsessive–compulsive patients should be to alter this perfectionist attitude and the need for certainty. At the same time, the therapist cannot directly and immediately attack the central beliefs of the cognitive organization. Through them the patient sees reality and interprets accordingly whatever the therapist may say. The possibility of misunderstandings and of actual paradoxes deriving from such a frontal attack is fully evident.

The first step of the therapist's strategy, then, should respect, but also exploit, the perfectionist attitude, preparing for subsequent modification and also allowing the start of very concrete and factual work with the patient. The therapist may start by recommending that the patient *not commit himself or herself too much* to the proposed therapy and, above all, to accept from the start the fact that the therapy itself, although requiring a great effort, will give only a *partial result. Only* a majority of one's fears and rituals will disappear. A kernel of the disturbances will have to be kept by the patient.

This method of proposing the purpose of the treatment and of advising patients on their general behavior (not to commit themselves *too much*) may remind readers of the paradoxical prescriptions suggested by the pragmatics of human communication (Watzlawick, Beavin, & Jackson, 1967; for application to the treatment of obsessive thoughts, see Solyom, Garza-Perez, Lewidge, & Solyom, 1972) and the acknowledged efficacy of a "challenging attitude" on the part of the behavior therapist in inducing obsessive–compulsive patients to face the feared situations. We are convinced that this method has other advantages as well:

1. Patients think the therapist is being *honest* in warning them not to expect complete recovery. Since obsessionals attach great importance to ethical behavior, this approach favors a good therapeutic relationship.
2. The idea is *suggested* that something can be done, without implying that it be complete and perfect. This helps to lay the contextual basis for a further explicit and verbalized criticism of the beliefs regarding perfection and certainty.
3. Patients' expectation of being forced to dismiss their rituals— and that this will prove terrible and probably impossible—is disproved. Instead, they are advised not to commit themselves *too much* to this dismissal, suggesting that they might even be tempted to resume them.
4. It is explicitly recognized that a kernel of fears and rituals has a protective value and must be kept. This prepares the way for an exploration of the connection between intrusive images and tacit self-knowledge in order to explain the nature of this protective value.
5. It is then possible to start a behavioral therapy, direct and concrete, and at the same time consistently begin a verbal discussion of the nature and origin of fears and rituals with respect to patients' notions of themselves and the world.

At this point, according to our experience, patients are motivated to follow the prescriptions of a behavior therapy technique even in a normal environment. Only 4 of the 21 obsessive–compulsive patients we have treated in recent years needed a controlled environment, such as a psychiatric ward, and yet they all accepted the guided exposure to the feared situations and the progressive dismissal of ritualistic behavior.

Usually after outlining the treatment just described, we proceed to a modeled "vicarious" exposure to the feared situation. In other words, the therapist asks the patient to *watch* him or her touch some object that the patient considers contaminating or to *listen* to the therapist whispering a text with words the patient does not want to hear. The point here is to make patients feel they control the situation. They are asked, for example, to postpone their rituals till after the end of the session, but at the same time they are asked to guide the therapist's actions, for example, by asking him or her to stop touching the object or reading the book when they feel they can no longer bear the anxiety. Patients afraid of contamination may be asked to open the door themselves at the end of the session, so that the therapist will not touch any other object in the room, not even the door handle; this way patients are sure that, after touching the "contaminating" object, the doctor had no contacts with other objects and that they will be able to go back into the same room for the next session. The therapist may even suggest that patients accompany him or her to the bathroom and turn the water on, so that the next time they can safely use the bathroom. In this example, the therapist will explain that his hand washing after the session is part of the patient-reassuring policy.

To this approach, Peter (who watched the therapist handle a leaf picked from a tree of a street frequented by prostitutes) reacted by saying that "all this was not necessary" (meaning the *therapist's* excessive worries), and he even agreed, at the end of the first modeling session, to shake the therapist's hand, saying that he would wash his only when he got home.

For this initial modeling work and further exposures, the therapist must often show great imagination and must sometimes ask for the cooperation of a psychiatric social worker who will repeat the operations at the patient's house.

In Eva's case, a priest was asked to cooperate by uttering blasphemies while in church with her, specifying that God would not be offended, since the purpose was to reduce Eva's fear of certain *words*, which, after all, are nothing but sounds.

In George's case, the therapist laid on his desk a large number of books with different titles and samples of medicines with the strangest names. Then, after a few minutes, he took everything away from the patient's sight, stating that neither he nor George needed to remember all those names and titles. Afterwards, the therapist crossed out with a pencil a few notes that George had written down in his notebook, again emphasizing the fact that they could go on talking evern without being able to read the notes. Only when George agreed, the therapist crossed out more notes, this time with a pen; after a few sessions, George himself started to tear out a few pages from his notebook.

In Rita's case, the therapist started by reading in a low whisper words such as "death"; later the patient herself was asked to read aloud whole paragraphs of books where such ideas recurred. After 3 months, Rita was able to walk in a graveyard, chatting with the therapist. In this case the contemporaneous help of the family was very important: When the relatives understood the meaning of Rita's muscular spasms, the vicious circle described on page 249 was interrupted. While the modeling and progressive exposure work proceeds, an increasing reduction in rituals is pursued, as suggested by Meyer *et al.* (1974) in the description of their "apotreptic therapy."

During the modeling sessions, therapists also try to obtain from patients a description of their internal representations during exposures like the present one. On the basis of this description, the rigidity and perfectionism of their problem-solving mechanism is pointed out to patients according to a reasoning similar to that described on pages 254–257. The alleged objective for the time being is to obtain a distancing and decentering from, rather than a criticism of, the irrational beliefs listed on page 263 (cf. Beck, 1976, pp. 242–245). Once this distancing is obtained, we can try with patients to reconstruct their attachment and early learning history in order to clarify the recurring aspects of the "couples of opposites" kind. At this stage we usually propose a rational criticism of their irrational beliefs of the kind proposed by Ellis (1962, p. 61 ff.). Here again, rational criticism must start from the most peripheral beliefs (e.g., "certain people are intrinsically bad and should be blamed for that") and then move on to central ones ("There is invariably a right, precise, and perfect solution to human problems, and it is catastrophic if it is not found"). Proceeding this way we can make sure that the background of new notions that patients are acquiring allows them to face possible unbidden images coming from their tacit self-knowledge.

Peter's case again offers a good example of how important it is to keep in mind the hierarchical structure of the patient's organization in timing the different therapeutic interventions. While his perfectionism was being criticized according to Ellis's rational policy, Peter had an intrusive image in which the therapist was a boring teacher showing figures on a classroom blackboard, accompanied by the comment "How presumptuous of him to think he knows everything." Having been prepared in advance, Peter did not accept this image as an objective and adequate description of the therapist, nor did he consider it a further interference from his own "double." On the contrary, he was able to identify it as *one of the ways* with which, making use of his tacit knowledge, he could sort out *one* of the possible aspects of the therapist. Some years earlier Peter had quit psychotherapy because the doctor seemed to him "boring and presumptuous."

At this point of confronting the deep structures of cognitive organization, it is usually possible to suggest to the patient an exercise that has proved especially useful in reducing the disturbing character of residual intrusive recurring images. We ask the patient to dwell on the image instead of eluding it and to try to describe it with words (first with the therapist, then in his or her inner dialogue) down to every detail. According to Klinger's (1980) principle, "focusing attention on an image or on one of its parts often results in a spontaneous transformation of the thing—in the amount of detail, in its form, or in the effect it evokes" (p. 252). The patient, in fact, sees the image fade or reveal significant details of his or her personal history and in any case lose its quality of "impulse" and of disturbing experience.[11] Often at the end of therapy, the patient should be encouraged to trust free fantasy by suggesting the opposite exercise: From time to time, represent with vivid images the contents of inner dialogue.

The therapeutic cycle described here can be accomplished, as a rule, in about 100 sessions over a period of 1 or 2 years. Of course, this length of therapy is necessary for such an ambitious objective as the restructuring of personal identity. A marked symptomatic relief, which may even prove to be long lasting, can be achieved in a much shorter time, in no more than 60 to 70 sessions. Sometimes it is necessary to introduce in the treatment program several interventions in the family (see, e.g., Meyer *et al.*, 1974).

The treatment of obsessive–compulsive patients may be outlined as follows: (items indicated by letters are optional):

1. Paradoxical proposition of the limited aim of treatment, and injunction to avoid excessive efforts.
2. Program of gradual exposure to feared situations (modeling, *in vivo* graded exposures, etc.).
3 a. Prescription of gradual limitation of rituals.
   b. Behavioral intervention in the family, if necessary.

    c. Discussion of the thoughts (pictorial and verbal) emerging during the programmed exposures.

4 a. Starting from the discussion in 3a, pointing out, in general terms, the rigidity in problem solving and of the perfectionism of the patient.

    b. Brief comments on collateral aspects of this perfectionist attitude (e.g., considerations on the asymmetry of life, as outlined in Note 6 to this chapter).

5. Distancing and decentering. (The therapist makes sure that the patient fully understands the difference between one's thoughts and "objective" reality.)

6. Identification and clear verbalization of the central irrational beliefs (or basic assumptions).

7. Recognition and explanation of the basic experiences of early learning and early attachment (the double and opposite aspects of self-knowledge).

8. Rational criticism of the basic irrational beliefs. Related "homework" (e.g., assertiveness training).

9 a. Practice of "translation" from the imaginal to the verbal mode and vice versa.

    b. Discussion of the "contrasting images" that could emerge.

10. Final summary of how self-knowledge and knowledge of the world were organized up to the time of the therapy and of how to maintain the obtained restructuring.

NOTES

1. Makhlouf-Norris *et al.*'s (1970) research on the articulation of the conceptual structure in obsessional neurosis shows that the structure is often "unarticulate" ("monolithic" or "segmented"). In obsessionals more often than in normal persons, there are meaning domains ("primary clusters" of only apparently different concepts) not linked by intermediate meaning concepts (linkage clusters), as opposed to articulate conceptual structures. This makes the obsessional patient more likely than the normal person to appear as "orderly" to someone and "disorderly" to others, depending on the meaning domain to which attention is paid. Perhaps through this kind of reason the paradox voiced by Lewis (1957) can be solved: "In no psychiatric condition is there a more obvious association between illness and preceding personality than here, yet we meet people with severe obsessional symptoms whose previous personality revealed no hint of predisposition."

2. As is well known, there is a discrepancy between clinical and psychometric studies concerning the relationship between obsessive–compulsive neurosis and

obsessional personality. Whereas clinical studies tend to show a close relationship between the two, psychometric studies suggest that the correspondence may be weaker (for an accurate review of these studies, see Slade, 1974). Possibly this discrepancy can be attributed to the fact that psychometric instruments are constructed so as to take into account "global" traits (and not specific meaning domains) and to their consideration of the classical psychoanalytic triad of obstinacy, parsimony, and orderliness as fundamental, whereas in our clinical experience, this triad is of only secondary relevance (see also Shapiro, 1965, Chapter 2).

3. The theory that rituals serve to reduce anxiety and that they are preserved on this account is widely held and seems obvious to most clinicians, both of behavioristic and of psychoanalytic orientation. This theory, however, has found many opponents, who claim that rituals often *increase*, rather than reduce, the amount of anxiety experienced. Beech and Liddell (1974) have extensively reviewed the literature in favor of and opposed to the anxiety reduction theory. We believe that the different findings originated as a result of a different target's being assumed in order to accomplish the research. If the target is emotion (the autonomic arousal) experienced by patients when rituals are forcibly delayed after exposure to feared stimuli, or the *immediate* effect of rituals after such an exposure, then the anxiety reduction theory is valid (Carr, 1970; Hodgson & Rachman, 1972). If the target of the research is the patient's mood over a more extensive period of time—after having performed the ritual or when choosing whether or not to terminate it—then the theory of anxiety reduction will be disproved (Walker, 1967).

4. The so-called motor theories of the mind (Weimer, 1977) offer a good background for the interpretation of this phenomenon. The motor theory asserts that processes underlying perception are identical to those underlying imagination and that determinants of action are encoded in the motor cortex as a field of forces necessary to achieve a functionally specified action. Only "end states" need to be specified, as Pribram (quoted by Weimer, 1977) affirms. The end state for our obsessive–compulsive patients is to get rid of the unpleasant sensory qualities of their images, and they have to achieve this goal through action leading to a perception that is opposite to that "sensory quality."

5. Reed (1969) gave a very accurate description of some aspects that this extreme attention to details, motivated by the need of certainty, acquires. Using a verbal concept task and a nonverbal sorting task, Reed defined a characteristic of the cognitive style of obsessive–compulsive patients that he called "under-inclusion." In defining concepts, the obsessional is overspecific and establishes too rigid and exclusive categories in the effort to avoid mistakes and ambiguity.

6. The attention to symmetry has been frequently observed by clinicians reporting on obsessive thinking. Although this is a somewhat minor aspect of the obsessional's cognition, sometimes in a cognitive therapy it is particularly useful to make the patient realize that we do not live in a symmetric world. The left and right sides of the body are different, the left and right profiles of most people are not exactly overlapping, mostly levorotatory amino acids (and not their symmetric optical twins, dextrorotatory amino acids) are present in living tissues, and so forth. Life is asymmetric. This kind of consideration could enlarge the range of events with which the patient is prepared to deal, without a really direct attack upon central beliefs of certainty and perfection.

7. Rachman (1976) suggested that oversensitivity to criticism could be a characteristic of only a certain group of obsessive–compulsive patients, namely, those who generate testing and retesting rituals (like George, in Example 3). In his words:

> The underlying motive in all of these examples is the attempt to avoid punishment in the form of criticism either from others or self-directed criticism, i.e., guilt. Where the cleaners are mainly trying to avoid coming in contact with danger, discomfort or fear, the checkers are mainly taking steps to avoid criticism or guilt. (p. 270)

Rosen (1975) similarly argues in favor of a distinction between guilt- and fear-motivated obsessionals. This theory is in contrast with our idea that fear of criticism is merely a by-product of the obsessional's "need for certainty." The effort to create conditions in which one's "objective probabilities" are invariably 100% is obviously frustrated if a positively valued person disagrees with the patient's judgments and choices. Therefore criticism is feared, and self-criticism is inflicted if one finds oneself feeling or behaving in contrast with one's rigid moral standards.

The results of these considerations is that, if the need for certainty is an invariant cognitive structure within the different obsessive–compulsive patterns, the consequent oversensitivity to criticism also must be unvarying. Indeed, using the Fear Survey Schedule, Turner et al. (1979) found that "washers" and "checkers" showed more sensitivity to criticism than phobics did, but they did not differ significantly from each other. This was in contrast with their working hypothesis, that is, that phobics and washers (fear-motivated obsessionals) would prove less sensitive to criticism than checkers (guilt-motivated obsessionals).

8. We are convinced that his mother's death was one of the factors that prevented E. Gosse from developing his ritualistic activity in childhood in a full-fledged adult obsessive–compulsive syndrome. His mother shared the father's religious attitude; the stepmother later showed much affection toward and understanding of the child.

9. It may be interesting to note how Rita transferred in her compulsive behavior the vague teaching of her father: "If you keep thinking about accidents, you'll end up getting yourself in one"; Rita amplified this expression to the point of feeling responsible for the actual happening of an imagined accident, unless she shook off the thought immediately. But the father did not specify how to keep thoughts away, so she started resorting to the most common and natural way to do it: She shook her head. Later the shaking extended to the rest of her body.

10. It should be mentioned that this patient was determined, even as a child, not to repeat her mother's absurd fears over infectious diseases. In effect, she was always afraid of toxic chemicals, especially those diffusible in the air, and never feared germs or other infectious agents. This case seems to demonstrate the start of imitative learning and the limited control powers of decisions made on restricted subjects (infectious diseases) when what the model is transmitting is broader (tension and constant alarm when there is even remote danger).

11. We think that the suggested procedure is similar in its effects to the behavior therapy techniques described as imaginal flooding and "satiation" (see Beech & Vaughan, 1978). These techniques, too, imply repeated and detailed *verbal* description of the intrusive images that disturb the patient. The way in which we

propose this kind of therapy to the patient ("translation" from images to words) and, above all, the timing of it (*after* the restructuring of the central core of irrational beliefs) is consistent with our structural and hierarchical view. Intrusive images, according to our theory, come mainly from the tacit self-knowledge. The subject is able to face them properly only after successfully criticizing the protective belt.

12

EATING DISORDERS

In her invaluable book *Eating Disorders* (1973), Hilde Bruch states at the outset that obesity and anorexia nervosa "are closely related through common underlying problems" (p. 3, Routledge & Kegan Paul edition).[1] In succeeding chapters, Bruch actually gives several hints about what "common underlying problems" are. However, although she is accurate in considering the various distinct ways in which eating disorders manifest themselves to clinical observation, she somewhat overlooks the common core of interpersonal behavior, emotional expression, and cognitive organization that can be observed in many cases of eating disorders. Bruch's distinction between reactive obesity, developmental obesity, "thin–fat people's syndrome," psychogenic malnutrition, atypical anorexia nervosa, and primary anorexia nervosa is surely meaningful from theoretical and clinical points of view[2]; on the other hand, the need to describe and distinguish the different clinical syndromes has brought some limits to the examination of "common underlying problems."

In this chapter we treat the topic of eating disorders in a way that is complementary to Bruch's work: We systematically describe the "common underlying problem" of eating disorders and only superficially refer to the many differences between individuals and between the various subcategories. The common aspects of eating disorders, which, according to our clinical experience, are sometimes traceable even when the abnormal eating behavior is part of a schizophrenic syndrome, can be ascribed to three different levels of analysis: behavioral, cognitive, and transactional–familial.

BEHAVIORAL ASPECTS

Watch a man eat. What can that man hide from you? — From an old commentary to I Kings

Three behavioral areas allow us to spotlight common aspects of eating disorders: eating behavior, interpersonal behavior, and sexual behavior. The general activity level deserves consideration as well.

The common aspect of abnormal eating behavior is self-defined: In patients with eating disorders, eating becomes largely independent of hunger and satiety. Abnormal eating patterns can change from case to case, each time involving too strict a diet; constant overeating; sudden periods of abstinence; eating binges or excesses of compulsory overeating (bulimia); spontaneous or self-provoked vomiting; misuse of anorectic medicines, laxatives, and diuretics; and so forth. But if we can identify, within the disordered eating pattern, some episode where the abnormality is more clearly noticeable, and if we analyze this episode (considered as a target behavior) in terms of antecedents and consequences, two aspects common to almost all cases can be observed:

1. The common antecedent of the worsening of already abnormal eating behavior is presumably represented by an unpleasant feeling. It is interesting to note that this feeling is often described by both obese and anorectic patients as "emptiness." Obese patients usually react to their feeling "empty" by overeating, and anorectic patients by reducing their food intake further.
2. The worsening of abnormal eating behavior usually influences the patient's interactions with his or her family. Relatives try to convince the patient to normalize his or her eating habits, and their efforts usually have the opposite effect. The patient feels misunderstood and intruded upon and reacts by persisting in the abnormal eating behavior.

Interpersonal behavior is characterized by an evaluation common to practically all patients suffering from eating disorders: that they are somehow being ignored or "intruded upon" by loved ones. Withdrawal as a reaction to disappointments in an important relationship is also commonly observed in patients with eating disorders. Often, observing the conduct of anorectic or obese patients' families, we also can find some valid reasons explaining the feeling of being misunderstood or intruded upon. However, the patient's way of communicating creates some interpersonal difficulties, even in contexts other than the family. Many descriptions of the behavior of patients with eating disorders during the therapeutic relationship agree on this point (Bruch, 1973; Selvini-Palazzoli, 1963). These patients are said to be reserved, evasive, and not always sincere. Particularly with anorectic patients, the difficulty of communicating within the therapeutic relationship justifies the use of terms generally expressing the schizophrenic's communication deficit, as where Bruch describes the obstacle to spotting some problems peculiar to anorectics, since they "are camouflaged by the *enormous negativism* and *stubborn defiance* with which these patients operate, and which make personal contact so difficult" (Bruch, 1973, p. 254; italics added). With obese patients, these difficulties seem sometimes reduced or completely missing. Careful therapists, however, when examining apparently outgoing obese patients, will notice that they are typically evasive, indecisive, and inaccurate in their answers in at least one of the following conditions: when the therapist tries to examine in detail the characteristics of the patient's abnormal eating behavior; when the patient is asked to describe the physical perceptions and the emotions related to overeating; or when the therapist attempts to define the therapeutic contract.[3]

In this respect, a general rule that should be remembered with almost all patients suffering from eating disorders is that detailed information is not to be expected until considerable therapeutic progress has been made and the patient has learned to trust the therapist. This way of communicating, characterized by evasiveness, indecision, inaccuracy, or even negativism in the most serious cases, obviously leads to simple confirmation of incomprehension and abuse so commonly expected from interpersonal relationships.[4]

Also with regard to interpersonal behavior, it is easy to note how frequently these patients avoid speaking in public. They also avoid relationships requiring a positive commitment. Susceptibility to criticism is remarkable: Schoolmates' teasing comments often precipitate abnormal eating behavior during adolescence. A longitudinal analysis of the most meaningful interpersonal relationships usually reveals great enthusiasm at the beginning, followed by disappointment just as great. As we already said, "withdrawal" is the most common reaction to disappointment.

Disturbed sexual behavior is also common in patients suffering from eating disorders. Bruch (1973) accurately reports the frequency with which these patients show, among their childhood memories, many signs indicating a marked confusion about sex roles. During adolescence, the patients are frequently totally uninterested in sex and have few or no sexual feelings. However, a high percentage of obese female patients later show promiscuous sexual behavior as compared to the average. (This is our clinical impression, applicable to the Italian population.) Orgasmic dysfunction is another common feature of these patients. Many female anorectic patients, as well as some obese patients, even later on in life maintain a complete lack of interest in sex.

Amenorrhea is known to be a characteristic of mental anorexia and is also traceable in many obese female patients. Others have scanty and irregular menstrual periods. The psychosomatic nature of these irregularities is no longer in doubt.

The general activity level deserves some consideration. Hyperactivity is a well-known characteristic of anorexia nervosa. In most obese patients, motor activity is quite reduced. Almost all patients suffering from eating disorders show poorly channeled activity—that is, whether their general level of activity is high or low compared to the average, their undertakings are dispersive and aimless. Although they are often dispersive, the activities of anorectic—but also, in a lesser degree, of obese—patients have a common tendency toward perfectionism.

COGNITIVE ASPECTS

> Where I could put off
> My shame like shoes in the porch,
> My pain like garments,
> And leave my flesh discarded lying
> Like luggage of some departed traveller.
> —D. H. Lawrence, "In Trouble and Shame"

One characteristic of the cognitive organization of patients suffering from eating disorders is the difficulty or inability to recognize biological signs of hunger and satiety. Anorectic patients usually fail to recognize signs of nutritional need and feel satisfied too soon when ingesting small amounts of food. Obese patients, on the other hand, interpret as "hunger" those feelings presumably related to other conditions (boredom, dissatisfaction, etc.), and they often do not recognize satiety.

These observations, however, are less interesting than another one: The abnormal eating behavior is matched, in the ongoing stream of consciousness, by continuous thinking about food and about personal looks. One gets the impression that thoughts and personal feelings are largely replaced by more concrete images of food, of clothes that look either large or small, and of one's own body, as the poem in the epigraph is meant to suggest.

The quasi-verbal aspect of internal representation focuses upon food and eating. The patient plans diets, desires cakes and other "forbidden" fattening food, calculates calories, worries about the possibility of gaining weight after eating too much (or, in rarer cases, about the possibility of malnutrition, leading to weakness and dangerous physical consequences).

The imaginative aspect of internal representation, which more closely reflects the deep structures of self-knowledge, focuses upon an unpleasant or unsatisfactory self-image. As a rule, this unpleasant self-image refers to the body and is described as "being too fat." Whereas for obese patients this self-image corresponds to actual physical aspects, for anorectics it is a "disturbance of delusional proportions of the body image and body concept, . . . the often gruesome emaciation is defended as normal and right, and as the only possible security against the dreaded fate of being fat" (Bruch, 1973, p. 251).

In our opinion, both obese and anorectic patients have in their self-knowledge a self-perception marked by unpleasantness, which shapes itself, in the internal representation, in a body image disfigured by fat. The sole difference is that anorectic patients fight against this image by abstaining from food, whereas obese patients give up, since they feel they are not up to the task. So, from our point of view, the difference between anorectic and obese patients looks rather slight. And it will look even slighter if we consider how often anorectic patients themselves reveal the belief in their fundamental "weakness" toward food. They say, "I do not dare to eat. If I have just a bit more of what I am used to, especially of things that I am fond of, *I am afraid that I will not be able to stop.*" It is well known that anorectic patients sometimes indulge in secret "eating binges" in which they put into practice their belief that they are weak and incapable of controlling the temptation to eat. The simultaneous existence of the fear of gaining weight and an imagination continuously focused on food has made some authors wonder whether the desire for food is primary with respect to the fear of gaining weight, or whether the "weight phobia" (Crisp, 1970) or "morbid fear of being fat" (Russel, 1970) is primary with respect to fasting, and the constant thinking about food consequent to fasting. The direct testimony of a famous anorectic patient, Ellen West (whose case has been described by the Swiss psychiatrist Binswanger under a different diagnostic category) would lead one to consider as primary the continuous thinking about food:

> I do not think that the fear of becoming fat is the real obsession, but the continuous desire for food. The desire, the greed for eating, must be the primary cause. The fear of becoming fat acts like a brake. (quotation from Ellen West's diary, in the English translation reported by Bruch, 1973, p. 220)

In contrast with Ellen West's opinion based on direct experience, most clinicians tend to consider the fear of gaining weight as primary and the continuous thinking about a diet, that is, about food, as secondary (Crisp, 1970; Russel, 1970).

From a cognitive–structural point of view, the problem can be formulated differently. The image of a body disfigured by fat can be considered as the expression of a problem concerning the personal identity cognitive structures, and the continuous thoughts about food as an expression of the patients' attitudes toward themselves and reality. Images and thoughts, together with the feelings that go with them, will therefore become understandable, not so much in terms of mutual causality, but through an analysis of the cognitive structures constituting the personal identity. We have already observed how, beyond the quasi-imaginal representation of a fat body and the quasi-verbal representation of desired food and programmed diets, there is the belief of being somewhat weak and lacking self-control when confronted with the temptation of food. On closer scrutiny, this idea of being weak (for obese patients) or potentially weak (for anorectic patients) with respect to eating seems linked to a belief of general personal ineffectiveness. When facing social duties (school, exams, work trouble) meaningful love affairs, or flirtations, obese patients immediately reveal the same general expectations of failure that accompany their recurring attempts to follow a diet. In anorectic patients this attitude of failure seems at first to be less evident.

However, it is clearly revealed as soon as the patient trusts the therapist enough to give up declarations of self-sufficiency and self-confidence or indifference to the difficulties of his or her life condition. Bruch describes these clinical observations on anorexia nervosa as follows:

> The third outstanding feature is a paralyzing sense of *ineffectiveness*, which pervades all thinking and activities of the patients. . . . While the first two features (distortion of body image and disturbed cognitive interpretations of body stimuli) are readily recognized, the third defect is camouflaged by the enormous negativism and stubborn defiance with which these patients operate. . . . The paramount importance of this third characteristic was recognized in the course of extended psychotherapy. Once defined, it could be readily identified early in treatment. (Bruch, 1973, p. 254)

In further analysis of this "sense of [personal] ineffectiveness," one may note how different it is from the same feeling typical of depressive patients. In fact, it is usually expressed as a general expectation of failure rather than as a definite opinion of little personal worth or of lack of capacities. This fact is clearly described in Ellen West's quoted diary: "I seem to be fighting against sinister powers *that are stronger than I*, but I cannot get hold of them or reach them" (quoted by Bruch, 1973, p. 221; italics added).

It is a peculiarity of anorectic patients that their attribution of causality for the expected failure is undetermined. Neither personal responsibility (as with depressed patients) nor precise external events are used to justify the expectation of a sure failure ("sinister powers that are stronger than I . . ."). In obese female patients, the attribution of causality sometimes seems to be directed more toward personal responsibility. However, if we go over the same topic after some time, we may suddenly come across an attribution of responsibility to the malevolence of others and to external obstacles, as in the following case:

T: So, you are here to try to overcome the obstacles you find in following a diet. During your last attempt to lose weight a dietitian helped you to lose 20 kilograms. Then you suddenly began to eat again. Why did it happen?

P: It is always like that. I really can't do it. Something happens inside me and I begin to eat again. It is my fault.

Two weeks later, talking about her relationship with the dietitian, the patient said:

> He's the one who was wrong. If he had encouraged me instead of criticizing me when I started to eat again. . . . And not one word of praise for all those kilos I had lost. . . . That fellow [the dietitian] is not a good doctor. The only thing he cares about is money.[5]

This shifting of responsibilities from the self to the outside world and back to the self is also typical and has the same meaning as the imprecision of causal attributions evident in Ellen West's diary.

Talking with patients with eating disorders in the way suggested by these examples we get the distinct impression of a sort of confusion or vagueness of the boundaries between the self and the world (if not of an "evanescent" self), which is sometimes explicitly recognized by the patient, as by the anorectic patient described by Eissler (1943), who stated that "her mind was in the mind of other people." When the phenomenon can be explicitly discussed within the psychotherapeutic relationship, other interesting information can sometimes be collected. Seven of our patients with eating disorders (three obese, two belonging to the category of thin–fat people, and two suffering from a mild form of primary anorexia nervosa) remembered that in adolescence they had expected success in just the same general and undetermined way in which they currently expected failure. Thus, even in the times of well-being that had preceded the crisis and the need to start psychotherapy, these patients showed a sort of "emptiness" in personal identity, as though there were nothing definite "inside" them to which they could attribute successes and failures. Similarly, according to the perspective of the "looking-glass effect," there could be nothing definite "outside" to which they could attribute successes and failures.

This peculiar imprecision in the attributional style can easily be referred to other cognitive structures underlying the already-described problematic interpersonal behavior and the fragmented, aimless general activity. In fact, in studying evaluations and expectations that accompany anorectic and obese patients' interpersonal behavior, we distinctly notice, as we have said, that other people are often regarded as inconsiderate or intruding and that the patients expect to be disappointed, or to disappoint, when the relationship is starting well. This kind of representation is obviously consistent with the pervasive sense of ineffectiveness and the general expectations of failure described previously. The imprecise attributional style consequently leads the person to believe that it is useless or dangerous to totally commit oneself to actively searching for a solution to the noticed interpersonal problems. How, indeed, can one make a serious effort to solve a problem when the evaluation of the causes of the difficulty itself is imprecise and inconsistent?

The tendency to avoid interpersonal situations requiring a clear and lasting commitment is, in this respect, perfectly understandable. In the same way, we can see why the general activity of patients with eating disorders seems to be fragmented and relatively aimless, no matter how high the general rate of activity may be. Anorectic patients' hyperactivity and obese patients' apathy are probably due to the arousal or depression of the general drive level, which in turn is related to the inability to satisfy, or the excessive satisfaction of, the hunger drive. In any case, the patients' plans, be they many or few, give an impression of a lack of determination and of aimlessness, seemingly due to inaccuracy in identifying the causes of successes and failures.

Difficulties in communicating with anorectic patients and "counterfeit communication," described by Bruch (1973) as a characteristic of many apparently positive psychotherapeutic relationships with patients suffering from eating disorders, can be considered by-products of the imprecise attributional style. On the other hand, when we succeed in obtaining from patients a description of the beliefs justifying their evasiveness and tendency to lie, we hear statements on the danger and uselessness of telling other people about one's own feelings and opinions. Patients expect their listeners to oppose their points of view and feelings; in other words, they expect others not to satisfy their emotional needs or even to use the information about their inner life for their own purposes.

We have thus revealed a system of beliefs that, on the one hand, justifies the lack of commitment, evasiveness, and even negativism, and, on the other hand, rules a code of communication inducing others to respond in a way that will confirm the belief system.

We are convinced that this distrust in other people's willingness to understand and accept plays a major role in causing indifference to sex in many of these patients and absence of orgasm in many others. Sexual intercourse and orgasm imply an intimacy of communication, meaning the possibility of showing freely one's emotions to the partner, which is totally incompatible with the cognitive structures of anorectic and obese patients.

Another feature deducible from the cognitive analysis of patients suffering from eating disorders is the relatively scarce or contradictory use of abstract concepts (Bruch, 1978, Chapter 3). Possibilities of abstract thinking usually exist, but they are seldom and confusedly applied to the self or to interpersonal relationships. Patients keep on demanding *concrete* and continuous proofs, for example, of their partners' affection; they place much importance on their looks as a means of interpersonal attraction and at the same time say they want to be loved "for what they are" and not because of their looks; and they claim they are not satisfied with themselves, apparently referring to relatively abstract aspects commonly known as "character" or "personality," and then the only definite reason they can give for their dissatisfaction is the physical aspect—"too fat." Bruch (1978), referring to this phenomenon, expresses the opinion that anorectic patients' style of thinking is typical of that phase of childhood cognitive development which Piaget named the "phase of preconceptual or *concrete* operations," or the period of egocentricity. The characteristic adolescent phase involving the capacity to perform formal operations and the ability to think abstractly never completely developed in these subjects.

ANALYSIS OF FAMILY TRANSACTIONS AND OF EARLY DEVELOPMENT

The best brought-up children are those who have seen their parents as they are. Hypocrisy is not the parent's first duty. — G. B. Shaw, *Man and Superman*

There are at least two good reasons to conduct a direct analysis of interactions among the members of anorectic and obese patients' families. The first reason is a practical one: Sometimes, when the patient is totally uninterested in individual psychotherapy, a joint family therapy may be the only way to face the problem. The second reason is of both theoretical and practical interest: A joint analysis of the whole family can give a clear idea of the kind of environment in which the patient grew up and in which the abnormal behaviors are maintained; such observation gives the therapist a fairly good idea of the tacit knowledge acquired by the patient.

Several studies have been carried out on the families of patients suffering from eating disorders, notably on the families of anorectic patients (Bruch, 1973; Minuchin, Rosman, & Baker, 1978; Selvini-

Palazzoli, 1974). Selvini-Palazzoli (1974, p. 202 ff.) describes the contradictions, disguises, and camouflages that characterize the interpersonal relationships in these families. In her opinion, these families are as follows:

> The mother . . . derives no pleasure from nursing the child, control prevails over tenderness and joy. Parental stimulation serves *to stifle any of the child's own initiative.* . . . During the childhood and latency period, an insensitive parent constantly interferes, criticizes, suggests, takes over vital experiences *preventing the child from developing feelings of his own.* (Selvini-Palazzoli, 1974, p. 88; italics added)

Similarly, the reconstruction of the early development of 51 patients suffering from anorexia nervosa performed by Bruch through an analysis of the family frame and transactions pointed out that "encouragement or reinforcement of self-expression had been deficient, and thus reliance on their own inner resources, ideas or autonomous decisions had remained undeveloped" (Bruch, 1973, p. 82). Bruch also recognizes these families' strong tendency to conceal problems and personal difficulties, resulting in a disguised and contradictory communication. She describes similar distortions in obese patients' family transactions and gives some "frightening accounts of the truly contradictory imperatives permeating life in such a family, and *depriving the child of a sense of authentic individuality*" (Bruch, 1973, p. 78; italics added).

Minuchin *et al.* (1978) list four basic characteristics of the family process leading to anorexia nervosa: enmeshment, overprotectiveness, rigidity, and lack of conflict resolution. In our opinion enmeshment is the most important and specific one.

> Enmeshment refers to an extreme form of proximity and intensity in family interactions. . . . On an individual level, *interpersonal differentiation in an enmeshed system is poor.* . . . In enmeshed families the individual gets lost in the system. The boundaries that define individual autonomy are so weak that functioning in individually differentiated ways is radically handicapped. . . . *Family members intrude on each others' thoughts and feelings.* (Minuchin *et al.*, 1978, p. 30; italics added)

These remarks are in perfect agreement with our own, based on joint interviews with the families of 10 anorectic patients, 11 thin–fat patients, and 10 obese patients. In all cases we received the impression that the parents did not acknowledge or confirm the patient's personal thoughts and emotions and that there was a permanent sense of vagueness, contradiction, and imprecision about plans to be carried out together.

The sense of a blurred personal identity, the belief that it is useless and dangerous to get involved in relationships with other people, and the impossibility of defining precisely and concretely the responsibility for action programs and for their failure—the development of this kind of cognitive structure is easy to visualize within such a family context.

In our opinion it is possible to collect from the study of the family frame and transactions other data that are common to nearly all patients suffering from eating disorders and that help in understanding the development of other aspects of the cognitive structures. All these data concern, above all, some dyadic aspects of the interpersonal relationships within the family context, and this is probably why they have not been taken into much detailed consideration in the literature about families of patients with eating disorders. Because they concern dyadic aspects of the family frame, the data we are about to report are remarkably relevant to understanding, for instance, the origin of different neurotic cognitive organizations in two sisters, the one only 2 or 3 years older than the other (they were both under psychotherapy, one for anorexia nervosa and the other for agoraphobia), or of a change in neurotic organization in the same person (a female patient of ours, agoraphobic during her second mariage, who had suffered from anorexia till she divorced her first husband and had been virtually free of symptoms in the time between the two marriages). These data mostly concern the relationship with the father, and its emotional aspect in particular.

In the developmental history of our anorectic patients, we have almost always found experiences of *disappointment in the emotional bond with their fathers* during adolescence or preadolescence (and infrequently during childhood). In the history of obese patients, there often were traces of a disappointment or of an almost complete loss of the relationship with the father at a younger age (childhood). A similar phenomenon—a change for the worse in the image of the father—could be noticed in the few cases of anorectic (two) and obese (five) male patients that came to us for treatment. This experience of emotional disappointment with the father manifested itself in different ways from case to case, but we never succeeded in obtaining descriptions or indirect proofs of disappointment in the relationship with the mother, with either female or male patients. The patients often described their relationship with their mothers as negative, sometimes as positive, and in most cases as something in between. However, it seemed to the patients to have developed uniformly, whereas, on the contrary, the relationship with the fathers was generally marked by a gap, a "disappointment," or a loss.

The importance of this change can be seen more clearly if we consider the significance of a good initial relationship with the father within an "enmeshed" family communication system. In most cases the little girl who later on will acquire the eating disorder establishes a more satisfactory relationship with her father than with any other member of her family. Indeed, among the falsehoods of interpersonal relationships in the family, the father is usually seen as a strong and meaningful figure, and the daughter gets to love him very much. But later something happens (usually, but not always, earlier for obese than for anorectic patients), and the daughter's image of her father changes. Most of the time, she discovers some "weakness" of his, either because he is going through a period of depression or economic difficulty or because the mother more or less covertly manages the relationship with her daughter so as to make her realize her father's "weakness." It can also happen that the different opinion of the father's "worth" depends on "positive" events occurring during the child's development. One of our patients, coming from a poor and uneducated family, was so promising a student that the government decided to give her a scholarship, and she was sent to a boarding school. She went back home after 1 year (she was 11 years old) for summer holidays and suddenly realized how uncultured and obtuse her peasant father was.

There can be other reasons for a daughter's disappointment in her father, originating in their relationship. The daughter may, for instance, come to realize that her father loves the image of himself as the father of such a lovely little girl more than he loves her as a person. Bruch reports the following case (1973, p. 84):

> There were also walks with father on Sunday mornings . . . she was dressed up for this, but always in clothes that she felt were not comfortable, with emphasis on looking nice for father. To him the whole thing was very important: "here I am, a father, taking his daughter for a walk," and he wanted to be proud of her.

In other cases the father must go away because of his work, and this makes the child understand how his job means more to him than his relationship with herself and her mother, although the parents deny this and pretend in front of the child that they are a happy, serene family. In these cases an inquiry regarding the family milieu usually reveals that the necessity to leave the family for work reasons was actually a welcome opportunity to "disguise" a real separation between two people who did not get along.

One obese patient of ours had lived almost solely with her mother ever since she had been born, since her father had an important professional activity that forced him to travel and spend long periods in different towns, while the mother's job "forced" her to stay in the same town. This, at least, was the reason the parents gave for living apart most of the time. The child believed this explanation and had always felt respect and love for her "important" father. Then, one day, when the child was 7 years old, her father was appointed to a high public office in the town where the mother had her job. Although they were neither legally separated nor divorced, the child's parents kept living apart. The father, having to work so much, would sleep in his office and take his meals out. Although the child could neither express her disappointment nor guess her parents' discord—which they denied—she began to form a different image of her father, who now appeared to her as a confused, contradictory man, conceited and caring for the appearance of success, rather than as actually "important."

Although she gives no emphasis to this aspect, Bruch has noticed a peculiarity of anorectic patients' fathers which makes the daughters' disappointment a very likely experience: "The father, despite social and financial successes which were often considerable, felt in some sense 'second best'" (Bruch, 1973, p. 82). Thus the father's image of self-confidence and importance hides a deep sense of insecurity that may suddenly expose him as weak and disappointing to his daughter's eyes. In our experience the number of neurotic reactions (mostly depressive cases) in anorectic patients' fathers when the patients were adolescents is rather high. However, it seldom happens that the father explicitly leaves the family admitting he is not satisfied with his relationship with the mother, or vice versa. Here, too, our observations agree with Bruch's, who has found only two cases of broken homes in her sample of 51 families of anorectic patients, an unusually low incidence considering the divorce rate in the United States (Bruch, 1973, p. 81).

We believe that the relationship with the father during the development of cognitive organization has double importance. First, the patient has emotional schemata regarding an affectional bond representing safety in the middle of confused, contradictory, and deceptive early interpersonal relationships. These emotional schemata will later lead her in search of highly intensive love relationships, conceived of as "safety" or as the sole desirable relationship. This encourages easily aroused enthusiasms and with equal ease leads to disappointments in flirtatious relationships during adolescence and youth. Second, having experienced a very painful disappointment, the patient will be afraid that it may happen again, and therefore from then on she will "test" her partners before getting totally involved in the relationship.[6] She may also form the opinion that all love relationships are inevitably disappointing and consequently choose to have easygoing affairs with persons chosen regardless of affinity and desire.

Moreover, it could happen that only one of the daughters in a family—for instance, the father's favorite—develops with him a relationship liable to disappointment. She is the one who is likely to develop eating disorders later on, while her sister, whose emotional schemata will be marked from the beginning by, say, a sense of loneliness or constriction, could easily be subject to other neurotic disturbances (in this example, depressive or agoraphobic disturbances, respectively). Finally, the experience of a radical change in the emotional relationship with her father gives the patient two possible views of emotional bonds, so that she will tend to build with future partners different, but disturbed, relationships.

A patient of ours, to whom we have alluded previously in this chapter, expected disappointment as much as she hoped for happiness from her first marriage, a typical approach of patients with eating disorders. She began to suffer from a mild anorexia during adolescence (or, more properly, she became a "thin–fat person," according to Bruch's description), which worsened after her marriage, when she felt disappointed by a relationship that was not up to her expectations. After she divorced her husband, she showed no symptoms for 2 years. Loneliness was so unpalatable that she decided to marry a man she did not really like, for the sole purpose of escaping loneliness. She expected nothing from her second husband, because she had come to the conclusion that all men are disappointing. For the same reason, the patient had completely overlooked the second husband's personality, and when, after the marriage, he turned out to be jealous and oppressive, the patient began to wish for and imagine a situation offering greater freedom, but also realized that such freedom was impossible since her husband's jealousy offered her no alternative. To be with him meant to accept his control, and freedom meant to choose loneliness once again. The resulting daydreams about loneliness, aggravated by negative and fearful evaluations, laid the basis for developing agoraphobia.

THE COGNITIVE ORGANIZATION
IN EATING DISORDERS

> And the thought of the lipless voice
> Of the father shakes me
> With dread and
> Fills my heart with the tears of desire,
> And my heart rebels with anguish,
> As night draws nigher.
> —D. H. Lawrence, "Monologue of a Mother"

We can now schematically reconstruct the cognitive organization of patients suffering from eating disorders.

These patients' tacit knowledge includes emotional schemata in which the self-image establishes vague and deceitful relationships with others and in which the expression of autonomous thoughts and emotions is neither recognized nor confirmed. In this desolate picture, where self-expression is denied, the emotional schemata regarding love for the father are exalted by contrast, since they literally represent the only way to self-recognition, as an alternative to the more primitive self-perception through bodily sensations of hunger or movement.

This combination of emotional schemata guides the development of beliefs regarding the importance of love in life; Ellis (1962) would call them "a dire need for love." The idea of love, for these people, joins together the possibilities for communication, recognition, and esteem; it pervades the attitude toward oneself and toward reality. In a way, personal identity is defined through love. All beliefs concerning personal worth, duties to society, and success in school and in life, pivot around the focus represented by this absolute and "saving" idea of love. As Minuchin *et al.* (1978, p. 59; italics added) state:

> The anorexic child's orientation toward life gives prime importance to proximity in interpersonal contact. Loyalty and protection take precedence over autonomy and self-realization. . . . Her expectation from a

goal-directed activity, such as studying or learning a skill is therefore not competence, but approval. *The reward is not knowledge, but love.*[7]

This nucleus of beliefs organized around an absolutistic idea of love is not, by itself, enough to produce the cognitive organization characteristic of persons with eating disorders. As we have seen, our patients have experienced disappointment and delusion in love. For anorectic patients, when the personal identity undergoes full formalization—and perhaps a little sooner for obese patients—the beloved figure loses its charm. Personal identity then becomes uncertain and confused, and the outside reality is deceitful, as though reflecting the self-image in a mirror.

There is no time or way to develop a consistent and precise attributive style or to build a sense of identity independent of outside confirmations and acknowledgments, and yet an accurate attitude toward reality must be developed. Reality provides safety to the self with the possibility of establishing love relationships. But it also bears the possibility of painful, "intolerable" disappointment and of course the risk of negative relationships, full of criticism, rejection, disguises, and misunderstanding, as so often experienced in the family. The rules for assimilating experience connected to these representational models of reality are intuitive: Attention must be focused on figures emerging from the dull screen of incomprehension and vagueness that envelop the familiar relationships, since these figures are the ones capable of giving the ideal love and, consequently, safety. At the same time, care must be taken with regard to the possible defects, no matter how slight, of people who at first seem to possess the ideal requirements. Great virtues and great faults of others are the data of reality filtering through the patient's attitude. At this point, all the patient has to do is to adjust some problem-solving procedures so as to detect magnified virtues and faults *in time* and avoid making wrong choices. For example, one must not feel totally involved in a relationship before one is sure to have made the right choice. Others must be tested before they are shown one's private thoughts and feelings. If they pass the tests, if one can be sure they will not disappoint, they will deserve to be loved and relied upon. Tests will consist of evaluating others' sincerity and their respect for the individual's freedom and independence and, above all, of checking their interpersonal, social, and intellectual potentialities. Of course one must also develop one's own mental and emotional potentialities to the highest levels in order to be adequate to the idealized other. This explains the "perfectionism" that so many authors detect in patients suffering from eating disorders (and that depends on cognitive structures completely different from those of other patients with high standards of aspiration, as obsessionals and some depressives):

> Since the evaluation of what she does is another's domain, the [anorectic] child develops an obsessive concern for perfection. She is both extremely conscious of herself and keenly alert to other people's signals. (Minuchin et al., 1978, p. 59)

> Many parents mention that these starving youngsters spend hours on their homework, and often will not permit themselves to eat a bite until they have completed everything to perfection. Frequently the striving for perfection results in all kinds of additional habits. (Bruch, 1973, p. 273)

Confronted with a negative reality in spite of her careful search for suitable partners and her "perfectionism," the patient has but one solution: to withdraw into herself. This will produce in her, as it would in anyone, a sense of loneliness and frustration. The patient's cognitive structures, however, are not capable of accepting and correctly interpreting this feeling or of suggesting the real nature of the problem and corresponding solutions. Indeed, the personal identity— working as a protective belt that prevents one from recognizing how biased the tacit knowledge is—excludes a clear definition of one's own feeling. What the patient feels as a result of her withdrawal is often vaguely described, sometimes as "a sense of emptiness." In many cases it is confused with the sensation of hunger. This sensation belongs to the primitive level of bodily experiences on which self-perception is based and which become the prevailing aspect of the patient's self-identity when self-recognition within a positive and reliable love relationship is lacking. However, to reduce the unpleasant sense of emptiness by eating implies obvious dangers. To eat means to become fat, and often it was the patient's "plumpness" that caused her adolescent friends' teasing and her consequent withdrawal. To be fat, then, means to be rejected. If a positive relationship with the father in infancy and childhood has gone on for a relatively long time, the patient will probably not immediately lose her self-esteem in meeting the first difficulties and disappointments with other youngsters. She will then fight her tendency to become fat and will go on a diet. The anorectic syndrome has thus officially begun. If disappointment and loss of the relationship with the father occur earlier, however, the patient will probably feel incapable of fighting the disappointment or of excluding reality. Thus, after being abandoned by her first boyfriend, the patient may reduce the unpleasant sense of emptiness by eating. Thus the road to obesity is open.

Overeating or giving up food obviously does not solve the problem, so that a situation of reverberation is created—a sort of regressive shift in the patient's life research program, to use the language of Lakatos's model. The patient insists on affirming the central theories of her "protective belt": Personal identity can be defined only through a love relationship. Consequently, research programs are limited to finding out whether the relationship is impossible because reality is disappointing or because she is unattractive. (Anorectic patients tend to give the first explanation, and obese ones the second, but all patients with eating disorders fluctuate between the two.) Lack of attractiveness is connected to the image of being fat; the solution to the problem, then, is either to become thin and wait for prince charming or to give up hope, stay fat, and find comfort in food.

After adolescence, as the capacity for abstract thinking matures, the patient may recognize that the essence of her problem lies in her relationships with others, notably in the unfulfillment of her need for approval and love. But even this awareness usually cannot change the cognitive organization and eating behavior. On the contrary, the patient can now find out that, if her real problem is that she is not loved and approved, her physical aspect can protect her from, rather than cause, disappointment and exclusion: "What other people refuse is not really me," a patient used to say. "They refuse my fat body." "As long as they do not know me, as long as they only stop to consider how skinny I am," an anorectic patient commented, "they cannot spoil my inner world."

NOTES ON THE ASSESSMENT
OF COGNITIVE ORGANIZATION

In the preceding sections, we have given descriptions and examples of patients' verbalizations, of observations on their interpersonal behavior within the therapeutic relationship, and of studies on the family structure and communication process. All these data allowed us to reconstruct the organization of knowledge just outlined. We think it useful to add another series of verbalizations expressed by patients suffering from eating disorders; they can better explain the possibility of reconstructing the cognitive organization on the basis of what can be heard and recorded during psychotherapeutic sessions.

1. "In my family, to love each other means to have the same opinions." This shows the impossibility of developing an autonomous personal identity because one's own judgments can never be confirmed. It also shows that preservation of love implies, in the patient's experience, a threat to her own independent identity. The love that she has so much longed for becomes menacing, and to preserve it means to give up "being herself."

2. "When I lost weight, as I saw myself in the mirror I thought I was finally an *existing* person." The sense of being "nearly non-existent" is well expressed in this example, and it is correlated with looks, so that it clearly shows the fundamental mistake in the kind of problem solving tried by these patients.

3. "When I am fat, I cannot understand how men can be interested in me and say they accept me as I am." Excessive weight and the sense of not being acceptable to others are so strongly equated in the patient's mind as to resist opposing evidence.

4. "Yesterday I broke the diet. This proves I shall never be able to make it." The patient immediately demonstrates to herself that the image of herself as a failure is correct, even after a small transgression. This mechanism is obviously very important in preventing any progress of obese patients' efforts to lose weight, and it must be taken into account when planning a cognitive–behavioral therapy of obesity (cf. Mahoney & Mahoney, 1976).

5. "Doctor, I feel so grateful to you. I am convinced that, out of 1000 men, 999 are disappointing. Only you will never disappoint me." This is what an anorectic patient wrote in a letter to her therapist after 6 months' treatment. It shows how excessively enthusiastic and thus subject to disappointments these patients are.

In Rowe's book, *The Experience of Depression* (1978), one can find very detailed clinical reports of conversations between the therapist and a patient, Helen, who "came into [the] hospital because there seemed to be no physical reason for her loss of weight other than a refusal on her part to eat" (Rowe, 1978, p. 129). Although Helen's case is included in a book on depression, the progressive uncovering of her problems during the psychotherapeutic process parallels almost step by step what one can expect to find while conversing with an anorectic patient. Rowe's sketch of Helen as a person "who ate so much that she became very thin" reinforces the idea that "anorexia nervosa" could be a better "diagnosis" than "depression," if one wants to put some psychiatric label on people's problems (and Rowe seemingly *does not* want to do so). Since Helen's words are an impressively clear demonstration of the cognitions underlying eating disorders, and since they were obtained in a set that leaves out of consideration our assumptions and hypotheses about eating disorders, we shall extensively quote from and comment on some of them (*Q* stands for therapist's questions, and *A* for Helen's answers).

> *Q:* You say you are frightened when you go out for a meal. What do you think is going to happen? What are you frightened of?
>
> *A: I don't know really.* Perhaps eating in front of other people. I'm very fussy about my food, so *I'm frightened of what others might think of me.* I should turn my nose up to all the different things.
>
> *Q:* What do you think people will think if you do things like that?
>
> *A: I feel that they would notice me.* I don't like being noticed. (Rowe, 1978, p. 131; italics added)

The tendency to give vague or contradictory answers (Helen says "I don't really know" before making a precise statement), sensitivity to criticism, and the certainty that one is better off not getting involved and not being noticed are clearly indicated by this piece of dialogue. After a while, the conversation continues as follows:

> *Q:* Are you saying that within a relationship there is the giving of something, and when you come to give it, *it is all muddled up* and you make a mess of it?
>
> *A:* Mm. Yes. *I suppose so.* I'm also scared of giving to somebody, *I am scared of letting anyone know the real me.*
>
> *Q:* What do you think will happen if you do this?
>
> *A:* I shall be hurt again. (p. 131; italics added)

Here the fear of exposing herself and the tendency to establish confused, undefined relationships begin to show a clear connection. Helen also explains how her fear of letting others see her "real self" can be related to her previous disappointments ("I shall be hurt *again*"). But this effort to avoid being disappointed by others leads to considering oneself as disappointing to others, because of one's very reluctance to get deeply involved:

Helen: It scares me that Chris (a friend she had *recently* met) is getting involved with me. . . . He has this *strong affection* for me, and it's *marvelous* to know he does. I'm scared for his sake.

Q: Why? Why shouldn't he feel like that about you?

A: I'm not really worth it. There must be a lot more people around who can give something back . . .

Q: What is it you haven't got to give?

A: *All* of myself, I suppose. I'm very scared of letting anyone know the real me. They might say, "Well, there you are, take yourself back, I don't want you now." (p. 132; italics added)

The vicious circle created by the fear of disappointment, the avoidance of deep involvement, and the sense of unworthiness because of one's detachment could not be more clearly expressed. But Helen's words also show the tendency to excessive enthusiasm for relationships that are just beginning and that are immediately considered "big romances" ("*strong* affection," "*marvelous*," "*all* of myself," referring to a friend that she has *recently* met). Helen is married to Roger, and her marriage is unsatisfactory. The perception of others as intrusive—of one's identity being threatened by relationships with others—is expressed as follows:

Q: You think that, if you had been the person your parents and Roger wanted you to be, then that would have saved your marriage?

A: Yes.

Q: So if you are the person you want to be the marriage would fail?

A: Yes. (p. 133)

But what kind of person would Helen want to be? When she tries to speak of her own feelings, she is unable to go beyond a very generic description:

Q: What word would you use to describe that feeling?

A: *I suppose* I would say very, very unhappy.

Q: How long have you been very unhappy?

After a long pause, Helen replied: "*I don't know*. It's just every day I get more unhappy. I suppose it's shortly after I got married. (p. 135; italics added)

As we can see, it is difficult for Helen to have a clear idea of her feelings and of their antecedents. Her attribution of causality to feelings is uncertain, and she finds it hard to make developed plans or give her life a purpose ("I think that you should have a purpose in life because then every thing you do will be toward this purpose. . . . All the things I do are for no reason whatsoever." [p. 130]). When she tries to find a reason to justify her existence, *all Helen can talk about is love or other people's interest in her*: "Sometimes I think there must be something worth living for—there must be. *There's Chris and you trying to help*" (p. 136; italics added).

So for Helen others' approval and love are a reason for living. But her behavior toward the therapist seems inconsistent with the preceding statement. The therapist comments:

> You seem to be giving to me two messages at the one time. This is only the second time you have looked at me in over an hour. You give me the impression that you want to be here and yet you don't look at me when you talk. (p. 137)

At this, Helen starts crying, and afterward we can notice a turn in the therapeutic relationship. The patient's idea of her personal identity is analyzed through the use of imaginary characters, Jane and Claire, produced by Helen's guided imagery and is compared with her ideal self and actual self by applying the Repertory Grid Method (Kelly, 1955). To adjust the images of Jane and Claire, the therapist starts from Helen's problem with food:

> *Helen:* The person that I hate is the person who eats too much.
> *Q:* What sort of person is that?
> *A:* A greedy and gluttonous pig. (p. 139)

The guided imagery of this "greedy and gluttonous pig" leads to the identification of Jane, who is about 16 years old, has no friends, and is "big all over," with short legs, greasy hair, and "short, stubby sort of fingers." Jane *has no personality*. Claire is imagined as "the other one, who is trying to keep Jane in order." Claire is "tall, with short hair. Slim, but not skinny . . . would know what is happening . . . would read the newspapers. *She would be able to hold a conversation*" (p. 139; italics added).

After the assessment of personal identity, the therapy continues with a reconsideration of Helen's childhood relationship with her parents, and the patient recognizes how her mother failed to give her approval and how she longed to be loved:

> She is only concerned with how I look. . . . She doesn't want to understand the emotional side of my problem. . . . When I asked her if she had ten minutes to spare to listen to me she made every excuse to *get away*. (pp. 142–143)

I think I am craving love and affection from her. (p. 143)

Previously, Helen had commented on the relationship with her parents as follows:

I'm living with my parents but I feel like a lodger. . . . I don't communicate with them at all. My father is the typical Irishman, but I did think there should be more between my mum and me, but there isn't. I don't know how she can have given birth to me and brought me up and then not feel anything. (p. 133)

Although the therapist never went further into this question, Helen's charges to her mother and exculpation of her father seem to confirm indirectly the existence of an earlier better relationship with her father (who only later disappointed her)—an aspect that we consider typical of anorectic patients' developmental history. At this point, both assessment and therapy were virtually at an end, and Helen was ready to make a series of decisions and changes, including going to live with Chris, despite her fear of failing. Thus, in addition to being a fine example of the assessment of cognitive structures in an anorectic patient, Helen's case, as reported by Rowe, also shows how a therapeutic strategy for patients with eating disorders can be planned.

PLANNING A THERAPEUTIC STRATEGY

May your speech be: "yes," if it is yes, "no," if it is no.—Matthew, 5:37

In treating eating disorders, the therapist will first have to face the difficulties deriving from the patients' own solutions to their problems of contact with reality, that is, avoiding any serious involvement until they are sure that they will be understood and accepted, that they will not be disappointed, and that whatever information they will give about themselves will not be used against their own purposes. Since the patients do not specify what their purposes are (often they are not even able to specify their purposes to themselves, except the desire not to gain weight), the task is, of course a hard one. And no matter how the therapist decides to face this difficulty, the tactic used will have to be in accordance with a larger strategy aimed at a steady correction of the abnormal eating behavior ("superficial goal") or at a deep cognitive restructuring implying a modification of the personal identity.

Empirically, behavioral therapists have found "contract procedure" quite successful in correcting obesity (Abramson, 1973; Harris & Bruner, 1971). It consists of establishing an honest contract with a patient, based on a system of rewards and punishments attached to the loss of weight. The same method is applied in the "Weight Watchers" program. In our opinion this technique meets with relative success because it *implicitly* corrects several key cognitive structures in the knowledge organization of obese patients and at the same time respects their representational models of reality.

For example, if the therapist establishes with patients the contract "For each pound you lose, you will pay one dollar less for the following session; for each pound you gain you will pay one dollar more; the basic fee is $40," the situation thus created is much more interesting than the principles of operant learning may suggest. The patients are confronted with a relationship that is at once honest, defined, and organized and that does not require the disclosure of their feelings and thoughts, which makes it all the more acceptable. Once they accept an honest contract, they learn that they can operate better within a precise system of attribution of responsibility, and this is perhaps the first chance they get in life to establish such an explicit, prolonged, and regular relationship with another person. Receiving no general criticism and judgments of the self, and seeing that a specific behavior is the object of rewards and punishments, patients may reconsider their attitude toward reality, which, up till then, was marked by expectations of general criticism and rejection. The therapist's honesty in respecting the contract gives new strength to the patients' tenuous hope of meeting reliable persons, although this relationship has nothing to do with the great saving romance. In short, there are good chances that the treatment may be at least partially successful in a relatively short time.

The limitation of this therapeutic strategy is clearly its superficial goal. Unless the cognitive structures determining the abnormal eating behavior are *explicitly* recognized, discussed, and corrected, they will be only partly modified by the new learning situation. At the end of the treatment, the patients' interpersonal behavior will probably remain substantially unchanged. In the presence of a disappointment or of a prolonged condition of loneliness, the cognitive organization will again give the same evaluations and false solutions that first caused the "symptoms." In other words, there will be a relapse. Moreover, this "superficial" therapy can hardly be applied to anorectic patients or to patients with more serious cases of obesity.

If we choose as the "deep" strategic purpose the modification of personal identity (so that the patients may add new experiences to their tacit knowledge), two main tactics—an indirect and a direct one—can be selected to fight the difficulty of the patients' will to avoid exposure and involvement. The former is, basically, the one suggested by Bruch:

> For effective treatment it is decisive that a patient experience himself as an active participant in the therapeutic process. If there are things to be uncovered and interpreted, it is important that the patient makes the discovery on his own and has a chance to *say it first*. (Bruch, 1973, p. 338; italics in original)

> For many this close collaborative work with the therapist is a new type of experience; *being listened to*, and not being told by someone else what he really feels or means, is important because his own contributions are being treated as worthwhile. (Bruch, 1973, p. 337; italics in original)

Bruch's approach has resulted in many therapeutic successes, whereas her own previous application of an orthodox psychoanalytic technique had produced mostly failures.[8]

This new approach undoubtedly respects the patients' initial evasiveness and induces them to trust the therapist before exposing themselves. As the therapist confirms their self-discoveries, patients' belief that all they can expect from reality is criticism, rejection, and disappointment will gradually be overturned. In addition to this, the atmosphere of the therapeutic relationship may encourage patients to not only expose themselves, but also admit that their problem originates from their overestimating love and emotional disappointment. However, the therapeutic process cannot be very long, and furthermore, the therapist's passive attitude may possibly make the treatment inapplicable to uncooperative patients. A more direct tactic may therefore be desirable in the early stages of treatment with these patients and in further stages with cooperative patients so as to hasten the therapeutic process.

The direct tactic, in early stages, consists mainly of pressing patients in order to obtain a defined therapeutic contract and in being ready to make them recognize their reluctance to get engaged in a frank contract. We can then propose to devote several sessions to an examination of the nature of this reluctance.

The following is a dramatic example of how the direct initial tactic can be applied:

Elsa was 17 years old when she was urgently taken to a psychiatric hospital because of edema as a consequence of a severe loss of weight. When admitted, she weighed 32 kilograms. Her anorexia had begun 2 years earlier, and since then she had kept losing weight. For 2 days she was fed intravenously, and the edema disappeared, but she refused to eat and kept saying that she could not stay in the clinic. Two days later her parents were summoned for an appraisal of family interpersonal communication, and Elsa started to say (literally), "I cannot stay here; don't ask me to make this sacrifice." Her father answered, "But you know quite well you can't make it outside. We have tried everything else without success." (Elsa had tried many different treatments, including psychotropic drugs and 8 months' intensive psychoanalytic therapy, which resulted in a serious worsening of her conditions, after which the analyst had asked for her hospitalization and withdrew from the treatment.) Elsa repeated, "You can't ask me to make this sacrifice; it's too much for me." Again her father explained that she could not be cured outside the clinic. Elsa once again cried that her father *could not ask her* to make this sacrifice. At this point the reader should have noticed, as the doctor in charge noticed, that the father *was not* explicitly asking Elsa to make the sacrifice of staying in the clinic and that Elsa's way of communicating was, to say the least, a very indirect one. Having made this observation, the doctor (D) decided to try a direct approach to obtaining Elsa's (E) engagement in the treatment. The following dialogue ensued:

D: I ask you to make the sacrifice of accepting hospitalization.
E (*weeping*): No, you cannot ask me that.
D: I am asking you. As you see, I *can* ask you.
E: No, it's too hard on me; you can't ask me.

This went on for about 10 minutes. The patient seemed unable to understand that the doctor *could really* ask her something specific and that she could, just as specifically, answer "yes" or "no." The doctor then clearly stated how he saw the situation:

D: You seem not to understand me. It's clear that I *can* ask you to stay in the clinic, since *I am* asking you. It's also clear that you can answer "yes" or "no." If your answer is "no," we shall say goodbye, and I will not feel insulted by your refusal. If, after answering "no," you will change your mind, I shall be here to help you. Now, I ask you once again to make the sacrifice of staying.

This time Elsa stopped crying: She seemed to think for a while and then answered "no." The doctor said goodbye and led her to the entrance. Her father, who was standing outside, overcoming his surprise, said, "Don't be foolish. Stay." Elsa thought it over, then answered: "All right, I will." The same day Elsa willingly accepted taking her meal with the other patients. She also agreed to discuss with the doctor what had happened and her story, in order to understand the origin of her eating problems. She spoke of the relationship with her father, of how he had disappointed her because he had been irresolute, insecure, and inclined to criticize her. They also discussed her tendency to overemphasize difficulties in emotional relationships.

Inside a month, Elsa was dismissed, with a psychotherapeutic program based on one session every 2 weeks in which she would go on working over the reconstruction of her beliefs about love, relationships with others, and her idea of personal worth. Her menstrual period reappeared 2 months after her dismissal. She kept gaining weight, until she reached about 50 kilograms. Elsa began taking her meals with her family only a year later, but she ate regularly by herself following a diet she had set up with the doctor. After 4 years, Elsa's weight has remained unchanged, even after she broke up with a boy her age.

Each case presents itself for psychotherapy in a special way. Elsa's was particularly dramatic, and the therapist had to take the risk of dismissing a patient in relative life danger, just to show her that she could communicate in a way that was at once clear and respectful of her opinions and decisions. In other cases it is sufficient to emphasize to patients their difficulty in accepting a precise definition of the therapeutic contract and to offer to discuss the origin of this difficulty. This will bring into full light patients' beliefs and expectations about others' incomprehension and probable rejection and hence about the uselessness of exposing oneself and of getting involved. Thus it is easy to collect data concerning proofs gathered by patients during their lives in support of their theories, and the therapist is in an advantageous position to demonstrate that theories are very far from the pure and simple truth.

Always confirming and respecting the recollections brought forward by patients, the therapist can create a favorable condition for them so that they can acquire mental tools that were previously deficient. Patients' inaccurate attributive style can be corrected, and they can verify the usefulness of clearly attributing to themselves or others the responsibility for single successes or failures. This leads to a correction of some cognitive distortions, and the patients learn to rely on their own thinking. For this purpose we can now use the battery of cognitive restructuring interventions set for the correction of faulty inner dialogue, the target being a loss of weight (provided that the patient declares he or she wants it). The battery of cognitive restructuring procedures proposed by Mahoney and Mahoney (1976) is a good example.

At this stage the therapist is very close to the patient's personal identity. Once the attitude toward reality and the abnormal eating behavior have been corrected, coversation moves toward subjects such as the need to be loved and the danger of being disappointed. It is possible to try a direct frontal attack on irrational beliefs concerning "the dire need to be loved" and "the absolute unbearability of disappointment," as suggested by Ellis (1962). However, in most cases we prefer to teach social skills focused mostly on reducing criticism directed toward other people and on increasing approvals and, above all, to reconstruct the development of the patient's theories on love and disappointment, starting from his or her early experiences in the family.[9]

The steps of a deep-goal strategic psychotherapy are summarized in the following outline:

1 a. Definition of a clear therapeutic contract, or
  b. Acknowledgment of the problems met in defining the contract and of the usefulness of inquiring about these problems.
2 a. In case the patient has selected a clear-cut program of weight change, behavioral contracting plus superficial cognitive restructuring.
  b. Spotting of representational models of reality focused upon the expectation of criticism, rejection, disappointment, and so forth. Recognition of the problem-solving procedure based on avoidance of commitment and distinct expression of emotions and beliefs.
  3. Confirming and listening attitude of the therapist (as suggested by Bruch).
  4. Admission of the fact that proofs supporting the attitude toward reality are partial and that the attitude itself is based on a theory rather than on truth (distancing).

5. Behavioral prescriptions aimed at obtaining a more definite attributive style, added to a cognitive clarification of the importance of this point.

6. Behavioral and cognitive prescriptions aimed at weight control, if required or gladly accepted by the patient (e.g., as suggested by Mahoney & Mahoney, 1976).

7. Clear *description* of the beliefs that are fundamental for the definition of personal identity: "the dire need for love" and the "I can't stand disappointment" attitude.

8. Assertiveness training (modified) and/or cognitive restructuring for the preceding items. (This restructuring is best performed after the completion of step 9.)

9. Acknowledgment of the origins of the beliefs concerning "the dire need for love." If needed, joint family sessions can be held in order to give the patient a chance to see what his or her emotional schemata may be.

10. Critical recognition by the patient of her global cognitive organization.

NOTES

1. In this chapter we make free use of quotations from Bruch's work. The original edition by Basic Books, New York (1973), is very difficult to find in Italy, and thus we have referred the reader to quoted material in the Routledge & Kegan Paul edition, London (1974).

2. Clinical observations reported in this chapter refer to three categories of disorders: primary anorexia nervosa, "thin–fat people's syndrome," and developmental obesity. This excludes cases where the abnormal eating behavior in an adult represents a reactive episode to a stressful event (reactive obesity) and cases where psychogenic malnutrition is part of a different psychiatric syndrome (catatonic schizophrenia, epilepsy, mental retardation, severe depression). We also excluded cases presenting marked aspects of hysterical behavior (atypical anorexia nervosa, according to Bruch). The category of "thin–fat people" includes patients of basically normal weight who always feel threatened by obesity and have an attitude toward food similar to that of anorectic patients. These people resort to vomiting when they believe they have had too much to eat or, more often, alternate short periods of irregular overeating and short periods of food abstinence (see Bruch, 1973, Chapter 11).

3. In psychoanalytic therapy the therapeutic contract is often vague with relation to the goal to be reached at the end of the treatment. However, in cognitive–behavioral therapy a distinct purpose is defined from the outset. As we shall see, the

formulation of a precise contract is particularly important in treating eating disorders because it may provide information that is usually difficult to obtain.

4. Several other aspects of these patients' behavior reveal their tendency to act in secret, hidden ways. For example, a tendency to steal has often been noticed. The patients also prefer to wear large, heavy clothes, hiding their figures. From our point of view, this behavior stems from the same attitude: the wish to conceal oneself. Stealing, then, is due to the need to obtain what one likes without letting others know about one's wishes. Concealing the body under sack-like clothes (remember that these patients commonly equate self-image and body image) is another way of hiding oneself.

5. This example shows another very common aspect of anorectic and obese patients' interpersonal behavior: They are inclined to criticize and give continuous negative moral judgments about themselves and others. In a way that can hardly be described, but that can easily be recognized when listening carefully to different patients, criticisms made by patients suffering from eating disorders are different from those made by obsessive neurotics or depressives.

6. We have the impression that this tendency to test possible partners, looking for the slightest shortcoming and even behaving in a provoking way, is more accentuated in persons with eating disorders than in those with other neuroses. Of course, under the spotlight of such careful searching, most suitors will turn out to be disappointing.

7. Experimental data show that these patients are more responsive than the average to emotional stimuli, and particularly to *positive* ones. In Pilner, Meyer, and Blankstein's (1974) study, obese male patients reacted more strongly than normals to the presentation of a slide portraying a "lovable" young girl. Of course, the relevance of this study for our hypothesis of a "dire need for love" as a characteristic of obese patients is only tentative.

8. In our opinion, orthodox psychoanalysis is bound to fail in treating eating disorders because it may easily confirm the main distorted cognitive structures in these patients. For example, the use of interpretation is likely to confirm the sense of unreliability of one's autonomic thoughts; the therapist, being emotionally cold and interpretative, may appear as one more person intruding, criticizing, and interfering with the patient's life instead of helping.

9. At various phases of treatment, we prefer, when possible, to hold joint sessions with the whole family, for two reasons. First, it is sometimes important to offer explanations and emotional support to the whole family (although we do not intend to transform an individual therapy in a family therapy). Second, the study of family interactions may prove very interesting for reconstructing the cognitive organization and the possible pitfalls of development; the results of the study can also be used in the following individual sessions to help the patient reconstruct his or her development and recognize his or her own cognitive organization.

IN CONCLUSION

The report, in the preceding chapters, of our clinical practice and its results is necessarily schematic. Not being skilled enough in written exposition and not wishing to impose on readers longer theoretical descriptions, we decided to omit some collateral clinical observations and additional hypotheses. However, in these last pages we would like to add a few fundamental notes.

The cognitive organizations we have described as typical of each psychiatric syndrome can coexist in a single individual (see Chapter 10, Note 6, and Chapter 12, p. 290). In theory, a person can very well suffer, during childhood, from the early loss of one parent and at the same time be limited in his or her exploratory behavior by the other parent; in this case the bases for a depressive and an agoraphobic development are simultaneously laid. Similar examples could be made in connection with obsessives' cognitive organization and with the organization typical of persons with eating disorders in all the possible combinations. However, in our clinical experience, when such "mixed" organizations exist, one cognitive structure usually prevails over another, and they are either both present at the same time (see the clinical example of Note 6 in Chapter 10) or are evoked, in turn, in consequence of different environmental conditions (see the clinical example on p. 290, Chapter 12).

It is also possible that the disturbance shown by the patient as the main one could be the development of one of the secondary aspects of the described syndromes. Some examples will illustrate this point.

Some patients who presented as their fundamental "symptom" a "phobia of speaking in public" or a "test anxiety," proved to have a cognitive organization very similar to the one pertaining to eating disorders. Others had a cognitive organization similar to the one observed in agoraphobia, depression, or the obsessive–compulsive syndrome, even though they required psychotherapy for problems definable as test anxiety and/or social anxiety. In such cases the test anxiety and the social anxiety show aspects that can be attributed to the patient's basic cognitive structure. For instance, when a test anxiety was based upon a cognitive structure typical of patients with eating disorders, the thoughts that went with it were "I will not be able to express myself"; "The examiner will not understand what I mean"; "They will not grasp the true meaning of my words"; "If my answers are correct, they will expect more and more from me, and I will end up disappointing them"; and so forth. These patients also used to worry too much about their looks. For instance, they cared too much for their clothes or their weight; they sometimes had the tendency to steal in department stores; they suffered from anxiety, usually at a gastric level; they had trouble expressing clearly their feelings and thoughts during the initial assessment; and so forth.

Patients suffering from test anxiety or social anxiety on the basis of an agoraphobic cognitive organization showed their anxiety during examinations or social happenings through thoughts such as "I feel I am forced to sit there and I cannot bear it"; "I feel lonely among all these people"; "It seems that everybody is watching me; I shall make a fool of myself"; and so forth. Their fundamental problems related to loneliness, the need to stay in control, and the sense of constraint were usually clear in other areas as well.

When the test anxiety occurred with an obsessive–compulsive cognitive organization, the internal dialogue focused on the fear of making mistakes, the doubts regarding one's preparation for the examination in spite of previous good results, and an evident perfectionist behavior. Often these patients, before taking the examination, appealed to superstitious or positively "magic" propitiatory rituals.

A patient with a depressive cognitive structure usually expressed test anxiety through such self-definitions as "I am worthless"; "I am not able to study"; "I am a failure, and this exam will prove it"; and so forth.

We believe that there are cases of patients with test anxiety whose cognitive organization is a mixture of the characteristics of those described in the previous chapters and others with a very peculiar and unique cognitive organization. In our clinical experience, we have seen, more than once, patients with social anxiety where the cognitive organization was similar to the one presented by patients suffering from much more serious disturbances of a paranoid nature.

Our experience supplies other examples as variations on this same theme: patients presenting sexual disturbances and difficulties of adaptation to the marital relationship. The inability to have orgasms, for instance, is present in both anorectic and agoraphobic women. Whereas in the former it is accompanied by problems such as a general indifference to sex and tendencies to overemphasize emotional misunderstandings with the partner and to feel easily disappointed, in the latter it is accompanied by the fear of losing control and by an exaggerated sensitivity to the problems of dominance and submission in the couple.

Depressed female patients can become incapable of orgasm because of their idleness and apathy (the general loss of interest and motivations involves the sexual life as well) or because of statements such as "I am not a real woman," "It is not worthwhile to participate in sexual intercourse since he is going to leave me anyway," and "How can a man love a woman like me?"

Obsessive–compulsive female patients often suffer from a moral or religious "perfectionism" concerning sex or, in contrast, from a sort of "technical" perfectionism, in which they try to reach an abstract idea of absolute achievement in sexual intercourse.

Similar considerations can be applied to male patients. In all of these cases the qualifying aspects of the different clinical syndromes (eating disorders, fear of going out alone, compulsive rituals, idleness, gloominess) can be present in varying degrees or completely absent. The cognitive organization that can be deduced and/or the environmental conditions where the patient lives usually explain why the sexual disturbances—or the social anxiety—overwhelm the other aspects, but the syndrome's fundamental features are clear anyway. All of these cases, in which a cognitive organization similar to that of the four syndromes described in this book has been detected a posteriori, have not been included among those presented in Appendix B, Table B-1.

A last and perhaps most important consideration needs the use of a metaphor. We regard the development of cognitive organization as something relatively fluid. It is as though each person, although experiencing loneliness and loss, limitation of freedom to explore the environment, simultaneousness of opposites, and many other fundamental factors of stress, chooses a limited number—or just one—of them as the basic theme on which to articulate his or her life research program. This choice starts and coordinates the whole research program, but does not totally influence it. It provides the fundamental matrix of relationships within which the various life events will find a meaning—and will be "memorized"—but it does not completely determine the quantity and the quality of the information that constitutes the individual knowledge. When this matrix of relationships is sufficiently flexible, that is, when it allows assimilation and transformation of new experiences and is in turn molded by such experiences without losing its identity, then the individual possessing such a cognitive organization will appear to be "mentally healthy." In other words, the "fluidity" of a person's cognitive organization is proportional to his or her capacity to adapt to environmental challenges. Thus the fundamental aim of psychotherapy, from a cognitive-structural perspective, is to augment—through a progressive disengagement from one's own previous "unquestionable assurances"— the flexibility of the person's cognitive organization.

We do not know to what extent we have succeeded in outlining a structural approach to the study of human knowledge and to psychotherapy. But, although we have doubts about the results achieved and presented in this book, we have very little uncertainty about the validity of the basic principles that inspired our approach. These principles are of both a thematic and a methodological nature.

The basic thematic aspect of our approach is the conception of the self as the central and regulating agency of the whole cognitive organization. The idea of the uniqueness of the human species, deriving from biological, evolutionary, and epistemological considerations (self-consciousness, awareness, and the creative power of imagination emerge uniquely in our species), and the sense of the singleness of the individual inside the species (deriving from our immediate experience) confirm this conception. This perspective oriented our idea of the cognitive organizations, often similar because of certain invariant structures, as substantially unique, being expressions of living persons, and not as generic, impersonal patterns of beliefs and emotions.

The main methodological aspect of our approach consists of the effort to adhere to a structuralistic perspective while maintaining a respect for the scientific method. The history of science shows that phenomena frequently can be adequately understood only if we consider the global structure of the situation in which they occur. Besides the many well-known considerations of this matter offered by the study of sociology and anthropology, the history of various other scientific fields easily supplies many proofs of the validity of the structuralistic approach. For instance, a series of phenomena studied by chemistry can be understood only if we consider the spatial structure of molecules, and not merely their composition in terms of constituting atoms.

Similarly, we are convinced that only a consideration of the structure within which the single elements of an individual's knowledge are placed allows us to understand how these elements rule and coordinate that individual's emotions and actions. Of course this opinion is not currently sustained by completely satisfying instruments and methods of psychological inquiry. Therefore we are aware that observations and hypotheses expressed in this book are open to many criticisms from the point of view of scientific accuracy in data collecting, ordering, and comparing. Our hope is that these criticisms may encourage further research, so that more satisfying and complete efforts than our own may come closer to the ideal goal of which we once had a glimpse, reading in the intellectual autobiography by Sir Karl Popper the following enlightening remark:

> I do not deny the existence of subjective experiences, of mental states, of intelligences, and of minds; I even believe these to be of the utmost importance. But I think that our theories about these subjective experiences, or about these minds, should be as objective as other theories. And by an objective theory I mean a theory which is arguable, which can be exposed to rational criticism, preferably a theory which can be tested; not one which merely appeals to our subjective intuitions. (1974, p. 110)

THE STRUCTURE OF PSYCHIATRIC KNOWLEDGE AND THE PROBLEM OF PREMORBID PERSONALITY

The general structure of psychiatric knowledge is based on five main themes.

The first one is the recognizability of syndromes, that is, the regular recurrence of consistent abnormal patterns of behavior, thoughts, attitudes, and emotions in different individuals. Although researchers of different theoretical orientation agree in identifying the major syndromes (depressive, phobic, obsessive–compulsive, paranoid, schizophrenic, etc.), the field of psychiatric diagnosis is still beset with arguments and revisions. The introduction of new nosographic categories (that of eating disorders, proposed by Hilde Bruch, is a recent example), the disappearance of old ones (hysteria is about to be forgotten, just as neurasthenia rightly has been), and the quarrels about the reliability of psychiatric diagnosis are only some examples of the contradictions emerging in this most basic area of psychiatric knowledge.

The second main theme on which psychiatric knowledge is based concerns the ways and the laws through which abnormal patterns of behavior are maintained in the environmental and social context where they appear. Behavior principles, learning theories, interpersonal communication, principles of systems theory, sociological considerations, adverse biochemical influences, and many other factors have been considered in describing the laws of this maintenance, and they have often been extended to the causal explanation of the abnormal behavior's origin. Usually, however, the causes of abnormal behavior are believed to be traceable to the early phases of an individual's development. "In puero homo" is a very old proverb, whose importance for modern clinical psychology is still too frequently overlooked, at least in the clinical practice of many behavior therapists. Undoubtedly, classic psychoanlytic theory is still the most coherent one in accounting for the early causes of abnormal behavior, although new and seemingly more

313

satisfactory theories are now emerging (e.g., Bowlby's attachment theory, which is widely used in the present book; see Bowlby, 1969, 1973, 1980).

The third theme concerns the precise nature of the negative early experiences that make an individual vulnerable to future stressful events, so that he or she reacts to them by developing those patterns of abnormal behavior, emotion, and thought described as clinical psychiatric syndromes. The idea of vulnerability acquired through early negative experiences is rivaled by the concept of a genetic–biochemical predisposition, which, as yet defies any experimental definition (with the exception, perhaps, of the main functional psychoses).

The fourth main theme on which psychiatric knowledge is based is the most confusing and contradictory, but also, in our opinion, the most important. It concerns the mechanisms allowing an individual to maintain a satisfactory adaptation during the period between the early negative influences and the time, in adolescence or adulthood, when precipitating factors produce the clear-cut psychiatric "symptoms." The problem arises regardless of the causal theory in which one believes and of the point of view assumed about the precipitating events. In fact, the following are commonly and clearly experienced in psychiatry:

1. Not all individuals react in the same way to stressful events, even if serious.
2. The antecedents of the same psychiatric syndrome can be quite different from one case to another.
3. Before reaching those particularly serious imbalances that require psychiatric and psychological help, most patients show a certain degree of adaptation to their environment.

Clinical psychiatry used to face these kinds of difficulties with the traditional idea of premorbid personality. According to this concept, whatever the early negative influences have been, individuals have in themselves the mechanisms capable of facing them and of adapting. These mechanisms (e.g., classic defense mechanisms of psychoanalytic thinking; interplay between factors such as introversion, neuroticism, etc.; habits that are adaptive in the original environment but that will show maladaption in a new one) reflect in one's life-style and in one's attitude toward reality—in a word, in the "personality." When an environmental event escapes the coping capacity of these mechanisms, we can observe the development of some premorbid personality traits into full-fledged psychiatric "symptoms."

Everything looks clear up to this point, but here several problems arise. How should we define the exact "traits" of a premorbid personality? How are we to demonstrate the relationship between these "traits" and the psychiatric "symptoms"? How can we connect the mechanisms underlying personality traits and the specific stressful events that precipitate the symptomatology?

It is not only a question of theoretical problems. On the contrary, any attempt to change a psychiatric disturbance permanently should also at least partially alter these basic mechanisms. Since a past event cannot be canceled, nor is it possible, in most cases, to change the environmental conditions that cause the imbalance of the previously reached adaptation, the purpose of psychotherapy should consist mainly of changing the basic attitudes that are revealed by undesirable personality traits. It is precisely this objective, of such great theoretical and practical importance, that the psychological and psychiatric research has failed to achieve, to the extent that the concept of premorbid personality is no longer mentioned in the principal modern studies of psychotherapy and clinical psychology. If readers wish to get an idea of the discord among theories on premorbid personality, clinical research on the relationship between premorbid personality and corresponding psychiatric "illnesses," and psychometric research on the same topic, they should refer to Chodoff's critical review of depressive personality (1974) and Slade's review of obsessive personality (1974). The results of these studies seem constantly ambiguous, vague, contradictory, and of no practical use to the psychotherapist.

Notwithstanding these disappointing results, one fact remains: It would not be possible to recognize, beyond the variety and heterogeneity of the events precipitating the clinical syndromes, a precise class of causes responsible for the subject's vulnerability to those stressful events if some form of premorbid personality were not recognizable as the expression of this latent vulnerability. Thus the fifth main theme on which psychiatric knowledge is based—the therapy process—would in this case be independent from the third theme, concerning early causes. This would mean that psychiatric knowledge suffers from so many gaps that it will, in all probability, collapse under the endless repetition of fragmentary therapeutic interventions, in one case aiming at the direct modification of some aspect of the syndrome, in another hoping to correct hypothetical early causes, and in a third case trying to control the environmental conditions within which the disturbance grows. Although tentative and still to be verified, an attempt to fill these threatening gaps in psychiatric knowledge exists. It is a translation of the premorbid personality concept into the terms suggested by the structural–cognitive approach.

From the standpoint of cognitive–structural psychology, premorbid personality is a concept that can be reduced to that of cognitive organization. Personality "traits" are conceivable as epiphenomena of enduring belief systems or "basic assumptions." Undesirable personality traits should be considered as expressions of specific irrational beliefs (Ellis, 1962, Chapter 5). The bridge between early experiences and actual "symptoms" is no longer the vaguely defined premorbid personality, but the ordered and structured ensemble of beliefs and theories that the individual has developed on the basis of those experiences and that prevent him or her from assimilating the new ones, represented by the precipitating factors of the "illness."

The general pattern of cognitive development that we presented in the first part of this book leads one to consider the formal thinking characteristics, which constitute the so-called cognitive style, as *secondary* if compared with the contents of the structured ensemble of beliefs on which the personal identity is based. Many of the early studies on cognitive style have been made more difficult, as far as the practical importance of their results is concerned, by an inadequate consideration of logical and causal relationships between contents and formal variables. The formal variables (i.e., ways of information processing) were often simply equated to the structural variables (see, e.g., Schroder, Driver, & Streufert, 1967, p. 4ff.). Only rarely was it clearly stated that the "distinction between content and structure is not as neat as it may appear, for what is one and what is other depends on the level of analysis. Though a structure constitutes a relation among elements, it may itself form an element in some superordinate structure" (Scott, 1963, p. 266). Perhaps rarer still were the studies in which content, structural, and developmental variables were taken into account together in considering their causal and logical relationships. A noteworthy exception was Harvey's research on the level of abstractness (a formal property) viewed as a function of the content of the more *central* concepts in an individual "self-system" (Harvey, 1967). Although Harvey's developmental assumptions were rather rough and limited to the individual's experiences with respect to authority, he did take into account their role in the formation of the central concepts in the "self-system" and the *consequent* relationship of some formal characteristics of thinking with these central concepts, but not with concepts of minor centrality and involvement. Referring to the analogy with the concept of "functional fixedness" (Shaw, 1979), we can say that productive thinking becomes unlikely in those areas where the individual's representations are chained to the past. All the *contents* of thinking closely related to the central beliefs of personal identity will then be processed in the "primitive" form of thinking rather than in the "mature" form (see Beck *et al.* 1979, Chapter 1).

From this point of view, we could say that the factors precipitating neurotic reactions act by creating a life condition where the central beliefs of personal identity undergo an unbearable "challenge." "Mature" thinking fades away in the areas of this challenge, and "primitive" thinking takes over. The resulting faulty information processing becomes the foundation of the neurotic "thinking disorder." There is some clinical and experimental evidence supporting the hypothesis that irrational beliefs are primary with respect to formal thinking disturbances in *neurotic syndromes*. (The opposite could perhaps be true in psychotic conditions; that is, primary thinking disorders may cause the appearance of "psychotic" thought contents.) For instance, the good results of therapies based mainly upon the modification of irrational contents of thought (traditional RET; see Ellis, 1962) lead us to suppose that, as a consequence, the faulty information processing is modified too. As opposed to this, there are no equally convincing clinical proofs of quick results obtained by trying to modify the formal thinking mistakes without considering at the same time the content of irrational ideas. Through experimentation, Lloyd and Lishman (1975) found that, when the mood of a group of depressed patients improved, the tendency to selective recollections (a formal thinking disturbance) of unpleasant experiences diminished. Although the authors reach different conclusions from this finding, we think that it is in accordance with the hypothesis that the arousing of depressogenic *contents* of thought implies a growth of the tendency to selective recollection of unpleasant experiences, whereas a subsiding of the depression and a reduced presence of depressogenic contents in the flow of consciousness promote the spontaneous correction of this kind of faulty information processing.

The cognitive–structural view of premorbid personality allows a detailed formulation of a number of testable assumptions and hypotheses.

1. The "traits" of premorbid personality that classic clinical psychiatry attributes to a given syndrome should not be understood to be generally and absolutely true for any individual suffering from that syndrome. On the contrary, they should be sought within each individual's specific meaning domains. Makhlouf-Norris *et al.* (1970) and Makhlouf-Norris and Norris (1972; see also Note 1, Chapter 12) show in their research that the clusters of personal constructs (meaning domains) may be less linked to one another in neurotic patients than in normal individuals. It is one more reason to believe that a certain "symptom" and a certain "trait" of premorbid personality can be correlated only within a certain meaning domain. An obsessive–compulsive patient's "perfectionism," for instance, can show in the way he accomplishes his rituals or in his beliefs on moral behavior, but not in the way he keeps his house (which could be very untidy). If the patient's rituals and morals are correlated within the same meaning domain (e.g., an expiatory ritual of prayer and the desire to follow strictly his religion's requirements), then the perfectionist trait common to both aspects can suggest the existence of a meaningful basic assumption concerning the need to be perfect, even if, in a general psychometric test on "perfectionism," the patient has obtained only an average score. (This may depend on the fact that the test evaluates general aspects of perfectionism, such as order in the house or punctuality, which can be irrelevant for this particular patient.) Although this hypothesis raises questions about the use of instruments such as most of the psychometric scales currently in use, it does not imply the

impossibility of conducting precise studies as does psychoanalytic theory. On the contrary, the definition of the basic irrational beliefs typical of each neurotic syndrome (which should appear in the patient's personality even during periods of well-being) and the use of psychometric instruments (such as Kelly's Repertory Grid Test) allowing the patient to express himself or herself with idiosyncratic verbalizations and the therapist to identify the individual meaning domains could permit both cross-sectional and longitudinal studies on premorbid personality.

2. The range of precipitating events for each neurotic syndrome should become predictable in relation to the identified premorbid personality "traits." It should then be possible to test such hypotheses as those concerning the vulnerability of depressed patients to the loss of a loved person (see Chapter 9), the vulnerability of agoraphobic patients in marriage and to threats of a separation (see Chapter 10), the vulnerability of patients who have eating disorders to criticism about their looks (see Chapter 12), and so forth.

3. The hierarchy of beliefs would explain the different responses of patients to the same stressful events. For instance, agoraphobic and depressed patients are equally vulnerable to threats of abandonment. But, whereas in agoraphobics' cognitive organization abandonment is an unbearable threat, depressed patients expect it as an ineluctable fate they must face and live with. The stressful event will cause the former to panic and to attempt any possible way to annul the threat, whereas the latter will fall into a state of gloominess, thinking that the terrible moment has come and that they cannot do anything to avoid it. Agoraphobics do not consider abandonment as a menace to their self-esteem; rather, it reveals other people's. wickedness or indifference. To depressed patients, abandonment proves their lack of lovableness. The hierarchy of agoraphobics' cognitive organization is dominated by the dilemma between desired freedom and feared loneliness, and the way of reacting to the separation is a consequence of this dilemma. The hierarchy of depressed patients' cognitive organization is ruled by the effort to live with one's fate of loneliness, and separation is regarded as a proof that one's efforts have been in vain.

Once clinical research has shed light upon the main sets of beliefs typical of the premorbid personality of each neurotic syndrome and upon the hierarchical relations within the cognitive organization, a whole series of experimental studies would become conceivable and feasible. We could, for instance, select samples of normal subjects who share the set of beliefs of a certain syndrome (i.e., who have the premorbid personality typical of that syndrome), submit these subjects to the representation of a certain stressful event (e.g., criticism and abandonment by a loved one), and study their cognitive and emotional reactions. Comparison with the reactions to the same imagined stressful events of a group of subjects with a different premorbid personality could confirm or deny that the specific response pattern is a function of the belief system. Experimental studies in this vein have been conducted by Goldfried and Sobocinski (1975) and by Graham, Kabler, and Graham (1962).

4. The question of the intensity of emotional disorders could be seen under a new light. The seriousness of a neurotic reaction, from a cognitive-structural perspective, is in fact a result not only of stressful environmental events or psychophysiological variables, but also, and mostly, of the structural properties of the patient's cognitive organization. By "structural properties" we mean something that involves both formal and content variables and that takes into account the developmental aspects of thinking. Structural properties of cognitive organization are therefore all the *logical relations* (similarity, differentiation, relatedness, integration, generality, deducibility, etc.) and all the *hierarchical-developmental relations* among the *contents* of an individual's conceptual systems. These structural properties emerge in the different forms of "rational" or faulty information processing (inferential errors, selective attention and selective recollection, polarized thinking, rigidity, nondimensional and global thinking, moralistic and absolutistic thinking, overgeneralization, magnification and minimization, magical thinking, etc.). Although a classification of the different forms of faulty information processing with respect to the different structural properties of cognitive organization is yet to be established, it is reasonable to suppose that the more irrational the contents are—and the more they are interconnected within the cognitive structures—the more serious (i.e., resisting changes) the resulting neurotic condition should appear.

APPENDIX B

THE PATIENT SAMPLE

The clinical observations reported in this book derive from a total of 198 psychotherapeutic relationships, the majority of which the authors were personally involved in. The composition of the patient sample is shown in Table B-1.

It is impossible, given the aims of this book, to provide a detailed account of therapeutic outcomes with these patients. Considering as an index of successful treatment complete or major symptomatic relief lasting for at least 2 years of follow-up, we may state that about 70% of our psychotherapeutic relationships ended in success. Around 4% of our patients prematurely interrupted treatment on the basis of a declared dissatisfaction and are therefore to be considered dropouts. The dropouts come from the diagnostic groups of agoraphobics and patients with eating disorders. The remaining 26% are to be considered unsuccessful cases, in which only minor or no symptomatic relief was obtained in spite of a reasonably prolonged treatment.

In successful cases the duration of treatment has been extremely variable, ranging from a minimum of 13 sessions to a maximum of 206 (average: 79 sessions). The frequency of sessions was, in the majority of cases, once a week, and every session lasted about 1 hour.

When the treatment is terminated, we usually ask the patient to return once a month for 1 year and then once every 2 to 3 months for a second year in order to have continuous feedback on the stability of what he or she has achieved from the therapy. In about 30% of the successful cases, we did notice a tendency to relapse, and in these cases we usually resumed treatment with reduced frequency (generally one session every 2 weeks, for an average of 15 more sessions). These booster sessions have proved successful

Table B-1. Patient Sample

	Depression	Agoraphobia and multiple phobias	Eating disorders	Obsessive-compulsive patterns
Number	24	115[a]	38[b]	21
Sex				
Male	10	43	7	12
Female	14	72	31	9
Age				
Extremes	26–57	21–54	14–36	18–50
Average (approximate)	36	30	22	29
Marital status				
Single	7	10	29	13
Married[c]	9	101	8	8
Widowers or widows	4	1	—	—
Divorced (or legally separated)	4	3	1	—

[a]The high number of agoraphobic patients is due to the inclusion in this study of data gathered by the authors and four other therapists during an 8-year clinical study (for the mode of this research, see Liotti, 1980).

[b]Twelve anorectics (2 of whom were men), 15 obese patients (5 of whom were women), and 11 "thin–fat" women.

[c]We have also included in this group the patients who were not legally married, but who had been living with a partner for at least the last 3 years. In our sample, eight patients met this condition.

in regaining the initial benefits in almost all cases in which they were conducted. When the patient is unable or unwilling to come back for the follow-up sessions, we usually obtain the needed data concerning the stability of treatment outcomes through phone calls or letters. However, this indirect procedure has proved necessary in only four cases.

REFERENCES

Abramson, E. E. A review of behavioral approaches to weight control. *Behaviour Research and Therapy*, 1973, *11*, 547–556.

Abramson, L. Y., Seligman, M. E. P., & Teasdale, J. D. Learned helplessness in humans: Critique and reformulation. *Journal of Abnormal Psychology*, 1978, *87*, 49–74.

Adams, P. L. *Obsessive children*. New York: Brunner/Mazel, 1973.

Ainsworth, M. D. S., Blehar, M. C., Waters, E., & Wall, S. *Patterns of attachment*. Hillsdale, N.J.: Erlbaum, 1978.

Arieti, S. *The intrapsychic self*. New York: Basic Books, 1967.

Arnkoff, D. B. Psychotherapy from the perspective of cognitive theory. In M. J. Mahoney (Ed.), *Psychotherapy process*. New York: Plenum, 1980.

Bandura, A. *Principles of behavior modification*. New York: Holt, Rinehart & Winston, 1969.

Bandura, A. Psychotherapy based upon modeling principles. In A. E. Bergin & S. L. Garfield (Eds.), *Handbook of psychotherapy and behavior change*. New York: Wiley, 1971.

Bandura, A. The self system in reciprocal determinism. *American Psychologist*, 1978, *33*, 344–358.

Bandura, A., & Huston, A. C. Identification as a process of incidental learning. *Journal of Abnormal and Social Psychology*, 1961, *63*, 311–318.

Bara, B. G. Changing connections between knowledge representation and problem-solving. In M. Borillo (Ed.), *Représentation des connaissances et raisonnement dans les sciences de l'homme et de la société*. Le Chesnay, France: Editions INRIA-CNRS, 1980. (a)

Bara, B. G. Il tempo del pensiero. In V. F. Guidano & M. Reda (Eds.), *Cognitivismo e psicoterapia*. Milan: F. Angeli, 1980. (b)

Bateson, G. *Steps to an ecology of mind*. New York: Chandler Publishing Company, 1972.

Bateson, G. *Mind and nature*. New York: Bantam Books, 1979.

Beck, A. T. *Depression: Clinical, experimental and theoretical aspects.* New York: Harper & Row, 1967.

Beck, A. T. The core problem in depression: The cognitive triad. In J. Masserman (Ed.), *Depression: Theories and therapies.* New York: Grune & Stratton, 1970.

Beck, A. T. The development of depression: A cognitive model. In R. J. Friedman & M. M. Katz (Eds.), *The psychology of depression.* New York: Wiley, 1974.

Beck, A. T. *Cognitive therapy and the emotional disorders.* New York: International Universities Press, 1976.

Beck, A. T., Rush, A. J., Shaw, B. F., & Emery, G. *Cognitive therapy of depression.* New York: Guilford, 1979.

Beck, A. T., & Stein, D. The self-concept in depression, 1960, unpublished. (Quoted by Beck, A. T. *Depression: Clinical, experimental and theoretical aspects.* New York: Harper & Row, 1967.)

Bedrosian, R. C., & Beck, A. T. Principles of cognitive therapy. In M. J. Mahoney (Ed.), *Psychotherapy process.* New York: Plenum, 1980.

Beech, H. R. (Ed.). *Obsessional states.* London: Methuen, 1974. (a)

Beech, H. R. Approaches to understanding obsessional states. In H. R. Beech (Ed.), *Obsessional states.* London: Methuen, 1974. (b)

Beech, H. R., & Liddell, A. Decision-making, mood states and ritualistic behaviour among obsessional patients. In H. R. Beech (Ed.), *Obsessional states.* London: Methuen, 1974.

Beech. H. R., & Vaughan, M. *Behavioral treatment of obsessional states.* New York: Wiley, 1978.

Berg, I., Butler, A., & Hall, G. The outcome of adolescent school phobia. *British Journal of Psychiatry,* 1976, *128,* 80–85.

Berg, I., Marks, I., McGuire, R., & Lipsedge, M. School phobia and agoraphobia. *Psychological Medicine,* 1974, *4,* 428–434.

Berger, P. L., & Luckmann, T. *The social construction of reality.* Garden City, N.Y.: Doubleday, 1966.

Bergin, A. E., & Suinn, R. M. Individual psychotherapy and behavior therapy. *Annual Review of Psychology,* 1975, *26,* 509–556.

Berne, E. *Transactional analysis: A systematic individual and social psychiatry.* New York: Grove Press, 1961.

Berne, E. *What do you say after you say hello?* New York: Grove Press, 1972.

Biller, H. B. *Paternal deprivation.* Lexington, Mass.: Lexington Books, D.C. Heath, 1974.

Birchnell, J. Early parental death and psychiatric diagnosis. *Social Psychology,* 1972, *7,* 202–210.

Black, A. The natural history of obsessional neurosis. In H. R. Beech (Ed.), *Obsessional states.* London: Methuen, 1974.

Bloom, M. V. *Adolescent–parental separation.* New York: Gardner Press, 1980.

Blurton-Jones, N., & Leach, G. M. Behavior of children and their mothers at separation and greeting. In N. Blurton-Jones (Ed.), *Ethological studies of child behavior.* London: Cambridge University Press, 1972.

Boulougouris, J., Marks, I. M., & Marset, P. Superiority of flooding (implosion) to desensitization for reducing pathological fear. *Behaviour Research and Therapy,* 1971, *9,* 7–16.

Bower, G. H., & Gilligan, S. G. Remembering information related to one's self. *Journal of Research in Personality*, 1979, *13*, 420–432.

Bowlby, J. The nature of a child's tie to his mother. *International Journal of Psycho-analysis*, 1958, *39*, 350–373.

Bowlby, J. Process of mourning. *International Journal of Psychoanalysis*, 1961, *44*, 317–322.

Bowlby, J. Pathological mourning and childhood mourning. *Journal of the American Psychoanalytic Association*, 1963, *11*, 500–518.

Bowlby, J. *Attachment and loss* (Vol. 1): *Attachment*. New York: Basic Books, 1969.

Bowlby, J. *Attachment and loss* (Vol. 2): *Separation: Anxiety and anger*. New York: Basic Books, 1973.

Bowlby, J. The making and breaking of affectional bonds: I. Etiology and psycho-pathology in the light of attachment theory. *British Journal of Psychiatry*, 1977, *130*, 201–210. (a)

Bowlby, J. The making and breaking of affectional bonds: II. Some principles of psychotherapy. *British Journal of Psychiatry*, 1977, *130*, 421–431. (b)

Bowlby, J. On knowing what you are not supposed to know and feeling what you are not supposed to feel. *Canadian Journal of Psychiatry*, 1979, *24*, 403–408.

Bowlby, J. *Attachment and loss* (Vol. 3): *Loss, sadness and depression*. London: Hogarth Press, 1980.

Boyle, C. M. Difference between patients' and doctors' interpretation of some common medical terms. In C. Cox & A. Mead (Eds.), *A sociology of medical practice*. London: Collier-Macmillan, 1975.

Brazelton, T. B., Koslowski, B., & Main, M. The origins of reciprocity: The early mother–infant interaction. In M. Lewis & L. A. Rosenblum (Eds.), *The effect of the infant on its caregiver*. New York: Wiley, 1974.

Bronowski, J., & Bellugi, U. Language, name and concept. *Science*, 1970, *168*, 669–673.

Brown, G. W., & Harris, T. *Social origins of depression*. London: Tavistock, 1978.

Bruch, H. *Eating disorders: Obesity, anorexia nervosa and the person within*. New York: Basic Books, 1973. (Quoted passages are from the Routledge & Kegan Paul edition, London, 1974.)

Bruch, H. *The golden cage: The enigma of anorexia nervosa*. Cambridge, Mass.: Harvard University Press, 1978.

Campbell, D. T. Evolutionary epistemology. In P. A. Schilpp (Ed.), *The philosophy of Karl Popper*. La Salle, Ill.: The Library of Living Philosophers, 1974.

Carr, A. T. *A psychophysiological study of ritual behaviours and decision processes in compulsive neurosis*. Unpublished PhD thesis, University of Birmingham, 1970.

Castaneda, C. *Journal to Ixtlan. The lessons of Don Juan*. Harmondsworth: Penguin Books, 1972.

Chiari, G., & Mosticoni, R. The treatment of agoraphobia with biofeedback and systematic desensitization. *Journal of Behavior Therapy and Experimental Psychiatry*, 1979, *10*, 109–113.

Chodoff, P. The depressive personality: A critical review. In R. J. Friedman & M. M. Katz (Eds.), *The psychology of depression: Contemporary theory and research*. New York: Wiley, 1974.

Cooley, C. H. *Human nature and the social order.* New York: Scribner's, 1902.

Cooper, J. E. A study of behaviour therapy in 30 psychiatric patients. *Lancet*, 1963, *1*, 411–415.

Craik, K. J. W. *The nature of explanation.* Cambridge, England: Cambridge University Press, 1943.

Crisp, A. H. Premorbid factors in adult disorders of weight, with particular reference to primary anorexia nervosa (weight phobia). *Journal of Psychosomatic Research*, 1970, *14*, 1–22.

Csikszentmihalyi, M., & Beattie, O. V. Life themes: A theoretical and empirical exploration of their origins and effects. *Journal of Humanistic Psychology*, 1979, *19*, 45–63.

Curtiss, S., Fromkin, V., Krashen, S., Rigler, D., & Rigler, M. The linguistic development of Genie. *Language*, 1974, *50*, 528–555.

Dawkins, R. *The selfish gene.* New York: Oxford University Press, 1976.

Dewey, J. The natural history of thinking. In J. Dewey (Ed.), *Essays in experimental logic.* Chicago: University of Chicago Press, 1916.

Dickstein, E. B., & Posner, J. M. Self-esteem and relationship with parents. *Journal of Genetic Psychology*, 1978, *133*, 273–276.

D'Zurilla, T. J., & Goldfried, M. R. Problem solving and behavior modification. *Journal of Abnormal Psychology*, 1971, 78, 107–126.

Eibl-Eibesfeldt, I. *Ethology: The biology of behavior.* New York: Holt, Rinehart & Winston, 1970.

Eibl-Eibesfeldt, I. *Love and hate. The natural history of behavior patterns.* New York: Holt, Rinehart & Winston, 1972.

Eissler, K. R. Some psychiatric aspects of anorexia nervosa, demonstrated by a case report. *Psychoanalytic Review*, 1943, *30*, 121–145.

Elkind, D. Cognition in infancy and early childhood. In J. Eliot (Ed.), *Human development and cognitive processes.* New York: Holt, Rinehart & Winston, 1970.

Ellis, A. *Reason and emotion in psychotherapy.* New York: Lyle Stuart, 1962.

Ellis, A. A note on the treatment of agoraphobics with cognitive modification versus prolonged exposure *in vivo. Behaviour Research Therapy*, 1979, *17*, 162–164.

Emmelkamp, P. M., Kuipers, A. G., Eggeraat, J. B. Cognitive modification versus prolonged exposure *in vivo*: A comparison with agoraphobics as subjects. *Behaviour Research Therapy*, 1978, *16*, 33–41.

Erikson, E. H. *Childhood and society.* New York: Norton, 1963.

Evans, C. R., & Newman, E. A. Dreaming: An analogy from computers. *New Scientist*, 1964, *419*, 577–579.

Eysenck, H. J. *Behavior therapy and the neuroses.* Oxford: Pergamon, 1960.

Fenichel, O. *The psychoanalytic theory of the neuroses.* New York: Norton, 1945.

Ferster, C. B. Behavioral approaches to depression. In R. J. Friedman & M. M. Katz (Eds.), *The psychology of depression.* New York: Wiley, 1974.

Feyerabend, P. K. *Against method: Outline of an anarchistic theory of knowledge.* London: New Left Books, 1975.

Flavell, J. H. *The developmental psychology of Jean Piaget.* New York: Van Nostrand, 1963.

Flavell, J. H. *Cognitive development*. Englewood Cliffs, N.J.: Prentice-Hall, 1977.

Flavell, J. H. Metacognitive development. In J. M. Scandura & C. J. Brainerd (Eds.), *Structural/process models of complex human behavior*. The Netherlands: Sijthoff & Noordhoff, 1978.

Foreyt, J. P., & Rathjen, D. P. (Eds.). *Cognitive behavior therapy*. New York: Plenum, 1978.

Frances, A., & Dunn, P. The attachment–autonomy conflict in agoraphobia. *International Journal of Psychoanalysis*, 1975, *56*, 435–439.

Frank, J. D. *Persuasion and healing*. Baltimore: John Hopkins University Press, 1973.

Frank, J. D. Therapeutic components of psychotherapy. *Journal of Nervous and Mental Diseases*, 1974, *159*, 325–342.

Franks, J. J. Toward understanding understanding. In W. B. Weimer & D. S. Palermo (Eds.), *Cognition and the symbolic processes*. Hillsdale, N.J.: Erlbaum, 1974.

Fransella, F. Thinking and the obsessional. In H. R. Beech (Ed.), *Obsessional states*. London: Methuen, 1974.

Fraser, J. T., Haber, F. C., & Mueller, G. H. (Eds.). *The study of time* (Vol. 1). New York: Springer, 1972.

Fraser, J. T., & Lawrence, N. (Eds.). *The study of time* (Vol. 2). New York: Springer, 1975.

Fraser, J. T., Lawrence, N., & Park, D. (Eds.). *The study of time* (Vol. 3). New York: Springer, 1978.

Friedman, R. J., & Katz, M. M. (Eds.). *The psychology of depression: Contemporary theory and research*. New York: Wiley, 1974.

Fry, W. F. The marital context of the anxiety syndrome. *Family Process*, 1962, *1*, 245–252.

Garfield, S. L., & Bergin, A. E. (Eds.). *Handbook of psychotherapy and behavior change*. New York: Wiley, 1978.

Gerz, H. O. The treatment of the phobic and the obsessive–compulsive patient using paradoxical intention sec. V. E. Frankl. *Journal of Neuropsychiatry*, 1962, *3*, 375–387.

Gerz, H. O. Experience with the logotherapeutic technique of paradoxical intention in the treatment of phobic and obsessive–compulsive patients. *American Journal of Psychiatry*, 1966, *123*, 548–553.

Gittleson, N. L. The effect of obsessions in depressive psychosis. *British Journal of Psychiatry*, 1966, *112*, 253–259. (a)

Gittleson, N. L. The phenomenology of obsessions in depressive psychosis. *British Journal of Psychiatry*, 1966, *112*, 261–264. (b)

Gittleson, N. L. The fate of obsessions in depressive psychosis. *British Journal of Psychiatry*, 1966, *112*, 705–708. (c)

Gittleson, N. L. Depressive psychosis in the obsessional neurotic. *British Journal of Psychiatry*, 1966, *112*, 883–887. (d)

Glaser, S. R. Rhetoric and psychotherapy. In M. J. Mahoney (Ed.), *Psychotherapy process*. New York: Plenum, 1980.

Goldfried, M. R. Systematic desensitization as training in self-control. *Journal of Consulting and Clinical Psychology*, 1971, *37*, 228–234.

Goldfried, M. R. Psychotherapy as coping skills training. In M. J. Mahoney (Ed.), *Psychotherapy process*. New York: Plenum, 1980.

Goldfried, M. R., & Goldfried, A. P. Cognitive change methods. In F. H. Kanfer & A. P. Goldstein (Eds.), *Helping people change.* Oxford: Pergamon, 1975.

Goldfried, M. R., & Sobocinski, D. Effect of irrational beliefs on emotional arousal. *Journal of Consulting and Clinical Psychology,* 1975, *43,* 504–510.

Goldfried, M. R., & Trier, C. Effectiveness of relaxation as an active coping skill. *Journal of Abnormal Psychology,* 1974, 84, 51–58.

Gosse, E. *Father and son. A study of two temperaments.* London: 1907. (Italian translation: *Padre e figlio.* Milan: Adelphi, 1965.)

Graham, D., Kabler, J., & Graham, F. Physiological responses to the suggestion of attitudes specific for hives and hypertension. *Psychosomatic Medicine,* 1962, *24,* 159–169.

Grolier–Webster dictionary of the English language. New York: Grolier, 1971.

Gur, R. C., & Sackeim, H. A. Self-deception: A concept in search of a phenomenon. *Journal of Personality and Social Psychology,* 1979, *37,* 147–169.

Hafner, J. R. The husbands of agoraphobic women: Assortative mating or pathogenic interaction? *British Journal of Psychiatry,* 1977, *130,* 233–239.

Hafner, J. R. Agoraphobic women married to abnormally jealous men. *British Journal of Medical Psychology,* 1979, *52,* 99–104.

Hafner, J., & Marks, I. M. Exposure *in vivo* of agoraphobics. *Psychological Medicine,* 1976, *6,* 71–88.

Hall, C. S. A cognitive theory of dreams. *Journal of Genetic Psychology,* 1953, *49,* 273–282.

Hall, C. S. *The meaning of dreams.* New York: Dell, 1959.

Hamilton, V. Perceptual and personality dynamics in reaction to ambiguity. *British Journal of Psychology,* 1957, *48,* 200–215.

Hamlyn, D. W. Self-knowledge. In T. Mischel (Ed.), *The self: Psychological and philosophical issues.* Oxford: Basil Blackwell, 1977.

Hand, I., Lamontagne, Y., & Marks, I. M. Group exposure (flooding) *in vivo* for agoraphobics. *British Journal of Psychiatry,* 1974, *124,* 588–602.

Harlow, H. F. The nature of love. *American Psychologist,* 1958, *13,* 673–685.

Harris, M. B., & Bruner, C. G. A comparison of a self-control and a contract procedure for weight control. *Behaviour Research and Therapy,* 1971, *9,* 347–354.

Harvey, O. J. Conceptual systems and attitude change. In C. W. Sherif & M. Sherif (Eds.), *Attitude, ego-involvement and change.* New York: Wiley, 1967.

Hayes, K. J., & Nissen, C. H. Higher mental functions in a home-raised chimpanzee. In A. M. Schrier & F. Stollnitz (Eds.), *Behavior of non-human primates* (Vol. 3). New York: Academic Press, 1971.

Hesse, H. Kindheit des Zauberers. In *Gesammelte Schriften.* (Italian translation: L'infanzia dell'incantatore. In *Scritti autobiografici.* Milan: Mondadori, 1961.)

Hetherington, E. M. Effects of father-absence on personality development in adolescent daughters. *Developmental Psychology,* 1972, *7,* 313–326.

Hodgson, R. J., & Rachman, S. The effect of contamination and washing in obsessional patients. *Behaviour Research and Therapy,* 1972, *10,* 111–117.

Horowitz, M. J. Image formation: Clinical observations and a cognitive model. In P. W. Sheehan (Ed.), *The function and nature of imagery.* New York: Academic Press, 1972.

Jaffé, A. *Memories, dreams, reflections of C. G. Jung.* New York: Random House, 1963.

James, W. *Psychology.* New York: Holt, 1892.

Kanfer, F. H., & Goldstein, A. P. (Eds.). *Helping people change.* Oxford: Pergamon, 1975.

Kelly, G. A. *The psychology of personal constructs.* New York: Norton, 1955.

Kieras, D. Beyond pictures and words: Alternative information-processing models for imagery effects in verbal memory. *Psychological Bulletin,* 1978, *85,* 532–554.

Klinger, E. Imaginal processes: A glimpse of the Promised Land. In M. J. Mahoney (Ed.), *Psychotherapy process.* New York: Plenum, 1980.

Korzybski, A. *Science and sanity. An introduction to non-Aristotelian systems and general semantics.* New York: Lancaster Press, 1941.

Kovacs, M., & Beck, A. T. Cognitive–affective processes in depression. In C. E. Izard (Ed.), *Emotion in personality and psychopathology.* New York: Plenum, 1979.

Kuhn, T. S. *The structure of scientific revolutions.* Chicago: University of Chicago Press, 1962.

Lamb, M. E. (Ed.). *The role of the father in child development.* New York: Wiley, 1976.

Lakatos, I. Falsification and the methodology of scientific research programmes. In I. Lakatos & A. Musgrave (Eds.), *Criticism and the growth of knowledge.* London: Cambridge University Press, 1974.

Laudan, L. *Progress and its problems: Toward a theory of scientific growth.* The Regents of the University of California, 1977.

Laughlin, H. P. *The neuroses.* London: Butterworths, 1967.

Leventhal, H. A perceptual motor processing model of emotion. In P. Pliner, K. R. Blankstein, & I. M. Spigel (Eds.), *Perception of emotions in self and others.* New York: Plenum, 1979.

Lewinsohn, P. M. A behavioral approach to depression. In R. J. Friedman & M. M. Katz (Eds.), *The psychology of depression.* New York: Wiley, 1974.

Lewis, A. J. Obsessional illness. *Acta Neuropsiquiatrica Argentina,* 1957, *3,* 323–335.

Lewis, M., & Brooks-Gunn, J. *Social cognition and the acquisition of self.* New York: Plenum, 1979.

Lewis, M., & Weinraub, M. The father's role in the child's social network. In M. E. Lamb (Ed.), *The role of the father in child development.* New York: Wiley, 1976.

Lewis, W. *Why people change: The psychology of influence.* New York: Holt, Rinehart & Winston, 1972.

Liotti, G. Un modello cognitivo-comportamentale per l'agorafobia. In V. F. Guidano & M. Reda (Eds.), *Cognitivismo e psicoterapia.* Milan: F. Angeli, 1980.

Liotti, G., & Guidano, V. F. Behavioral analysis of marital interaction in agoraphobic male patients. *Behaviour Research and Therapy,* 1976, *14,* 161–162.

Liotti, G., & Reda, M. Some epistemological remarks on cognitive therapy, behavior therapy, and psychoanalysis. *Cognitive Therapy and Research,* 1980, *5,* 231–236.

Lloyd, G. G., & Lishman, W. A. Effect of depression on the speed of recall of pleasant and unpleasant experiences. *Psychological Medicine,* 1975, *5,* 173–180.

Lorenz, K. *Die Rückseite des spiegels.* Munich: Piper, 1973. (English translation: *Behind the mirror.* New York: Harcourt Brace Jovanovich, 1977.)

Luckmann, T. Personal identity as an evolutionary and historical problem. In M. Von Cranach, K. Foppa, W. Lepenies, & D. Ploog (Eds.), *Human ethology*. Cambridge, England: Cambridge University Press, 1979.

Lynn, D. B. *The father: His role in child development*. Monterey, Calif.: Brooks/Cole, 1974.

Maddison, D. C., & Viola, A. The health of widows in the year following bereavement. *Journal of Psychosomatic Research*, 1968, *12*, 297–303.

Mahoney, M. J. *Cognition and behavior modification*. Cambridge, Mass.: Ballinger, 1974.

Mahoney, M. J. *Scientist as subject: The psychological imperative*. Cambridge, Mass.: Ballinger, 1976.

Mahoney, M. J. Psychotherapy and the structure of personal revolution. In M. J. Mahoney (Ed.), *Psychotherapy process*. New York: Plenum, 1980.

Mahoney, M. J., & Arnkoff, D. Cognitive and self-control therapies. In S. L. Garfield & A. E. Bergin (Eds.), *Handbook of psychotherapy and behavior change*. New York: Wiley, 1978.

Mahoney, M. J., & De Monbreun, B. G. Psychology of the scientist: An analysis of problem-solving bias. *Cognitive Therapy and Research*, 1977, *1*, 229–238.

Mahoney, M. J., & Mahoney, K. *Permanent weight control*. New York: Norton, 1976.

Maier, N. R., Glaser, N. M., & Klee, J. B. Studies of abnormal behavior in the rat: III. The development of behaviour fixations through frustration. *Journal of Experimental Psychology*, 1940, *26*, 521–546.

Makhlouf-Norris, F., Gwynne-Jones, H., & Norris, H. Articulation of the conceptual structure in obsessional neurosis. *British Journal of Social and Clinical Psychology*, 1970, *9*, 264–274.

Makhlouf-Norris, F., & Norris, H. The obsessive–compulsive syndrome as a neurotic device for the reduction of self-uncertainty. *British Journal of Psychiatry*, 1972, *121*, 277–288.

Marks, I. M. Semantic differential uses in psychiatric patients. *British Journal of Psychiatry*, 1966, *112*, 945–951.

Marks, I. M. *Fears and phobias*. London: Academic Press, 1969.

Markus, H. Self-schemata and processing information about the self. *Journal of Personality and Social Psychology*, 1977, *35*, 63–78.

Marshall, G. D., & Zimbardo, P. G. Affective consequences of inadequately explained physiological arousal. *Journal of Personality and Social Psychology*, 1979, *6*, 970–988.

Martin, G., & Pear, J. *Behavior modification*. Englewood Cliffs, N.J.: Prentice-Hall, 1978.

Maslach, C. Negative emotional biasing of unexplained arousal. *Journal of Personality and Social Psychology*, 1979, *6*, 953–969.

Mathews, A. M., Johnston, D. W., Lancashire, M., Munby, M., Shaw, P. M., & Gelder, M. G. Imaginal flooding and exposure to real phobic situations: Treatment outcomes with agoraphobic patients. *British Journal of Psychiatry*, 1976, *129*, 362–371.

McDonald, R., Sartory, G., Grey, S. J., Cobb, J., Stern, R., & Marks, I. M. The effects of self-exposure instructions on agoraphobic outpatients. *Behaviour Research and Therapy*, 1979, *17*, 83–85.

Mead, G. H. *Mind, self and society*. Chicago: University of Chicago Press, 1934.

Meichenbaum, D. *Cognitive-behavior modification*. New York: Plenum, 1977.

Meyer, V. Modification of expectations in cases with obsessional rituals. *Behaviour Research and Therapy*, 1966, *4*, 273–280.

Meyer, V., & Gelder, M. G. Behaviour therapy and complex disorders. *British Journal of Psychiatry*, 1963, *109*, 19–28.

Meyer, V., Levy, R., & Schnurer, A. The behavioral treatment of obsessive-compulsive disorders. In H. R. Beech (Ed.), *Obsessional states*. London: Methuen, 1974.

Milton, F., & Hafner, J. R. The outcome of behavior therapy for agoraphobia in relation to marital adjustment. *Archives of General Psychiatry*, 1979, *36*, 807–811.

Minuchin, S., Rosman, B. L., & Baker, L. *Psychosomatic families: Anorexia nervosa in context*. Cambridge, Mass.: Harvard University Press, 1978.

Mischel, W., Ebbesen, E. B., Zeiss, A. M. Determinants of selective memory about the self. *Journal of Consulting and Clinical Psychology*, 1976, *44*, 92–103.

Mischel, W., & Mischel, H. N. Self-control and the self. In T. Mischel (Ed.), *The self: Psychological and philosophical issues*. Oxford: Basil Blackwell, 1977.

Money, J., & Ehrhardt, A. *Man and woman, boy and girl: The differentiation and dimorphism of gender identity from conception to maturity*. Baltimore: John Hopkins University Press, 1972.

Montemayor, R., & Eisen, M. The development of self-conceptions from childhood to adolescence. *Developmental Psychology*, 1977, *13*, 314–319.

Newel, A., & Simon, H. A. *Human problem solving*. Englewood Cliffs, N.J.: Prentice-Hall, 1972.

Nisbett, R. E., & Bellows, N. Verbal reports: Private access to public theories. *Journal of Personality and Social Psychology*, 1977, *35*, 613–624.

Nisbett, R. E., & Wilson, T. D. Telling more than we can know: Verbal reports on mental processes. *Psychological Reviews*, 1977, *84*, 231–259.

Novaco, R. W. *Anger control: The development and evaluation of an experimental treatment*. Lexington, Mass.: Lexington Books, 1975.

Novaco, R. W. Stress inoculation: A cognitive therapy for anger and its application to a case of depression. *Journal of Consulting and Clinical Psychology*, 1977, *45*, 600–608.

Parkes, C. M. *Bereavement: Studies of grief in adult life*. London: Tavistock, 1972.

Piaget, J. *La représentation du monde chez l'enfant*. Paris: Presses Universitaires de France, 1926.

Piaget, J. *L'épistémologie génétique*. Paris: Presses Universitaires de France, 1970.

Piaget, J. Intellectual evolution from adolescence to adulthood. *Human Development*, 1972, *15*, 1–12.

Piaget, J. *La prise de conscience*. Paris: Presses Universitaires de France, 1974. (English translation: *The grasp of consciousness*. Cambridge, Mass.: Harvard University Press, 1976.)

Pilner, P., Meyer, P., & Blankstein, K. Responsiveness to affective stimuli by obese and normal individuals. *Journal of Abnormal Psychology*, 1974, *83*, 74–80.

Polanyi, M. *The tacit dimension*. Garden City, N.Y.: Doubleday, 1966.

Polanyi, M. Logic and psychology. *American Psychologist*, 1968, *23*, 27–43.

Popper, K. R. *Conjectures and refutations*. London: Routledge & Kegan Paul, 1963.

Popper, K. R. *Objective knowledge: An evolutionary approach.* Oxford: Clarendon Press, 1972 (rev. ed. 1979).

Popper, K. R. Autobiography of Karl Popper. In P. A. Schilpp (Ed.), *The philosophy of Karl Popper.* La Salle, Ill.: The Library of Living Philosophers, 1974.

Popper, K. R. The rationality of scientific revolutions. In R. Harré (Ed.), *Problems of scientific revolutions.* Oxford: Clarendon Press, 1975.

Popper, K. R., & Eccles, J. C. *The self and its brain.* New York: Springer International, 1977.

Pribram, K. H. *Languages of the brain.* Englewood Cliffs, N.J.: Prentice-Hall, 1971.

Pylyshyn, Z. What the mind's eye tells the mind's brain: A critique of mental imagery. *Psychological Bulletin,* 1973, *80,* 1–22.

Rachman, S. *The effects of psychotherapy.* Oxford: Pergamon, 1971. (a)

Rachman, S. Obsessional ruminations. *Behaviour Research and Therapy,* 1971, *9,* 229–235. (b)

Rachman, S. Clinical applications of observational learning, imitation, and modeling. *Behavior Therapy,* 1972, *3,* 379–397.

Rachman, S. Obsessional–compulsive checking. *Behaviour Research and Therapy,* 1976, *14,* 269–277.

Rachman, S., Marks, I. M., & Hodgson, R. J. The treatment of obsessive–compulsive neurotics by modeling and flooding *in vivo. Behaviour Research and Therapy,* 1973, *11,* 463–471.

Raimy, V. *Misunderstandings of the self.* San Francisco: Jossey-Bass, 1975.

Rapaport, D. *The structure of psychoanalytic thought.* New York: International Universities Press, 1960.

Reed, G. F. Under-inclusion: A characteristic of obsessional personality disorder, I–II. *British Journal of Psychiatry,* 1969, *115,* 781–790.

Rheingold, H. L. The effect of a strange environment on the behavior of infants. In B. M. Foss (Ed.), *Determinants of infant behavior* (Vol. 4). London: Methuen, 1969.

Rheingold, H. L., & Eckerman, C. O. The infant separates himself from his mother. *Science,* 1970, *168,* 78–83.

Rheingold, H. L., & Eckerman, C. O. Departures from the mother. In H. R. Schaffer (Ed.), *The origins of human relations.* New York: Academic Press, 1971.

Roberts, A. H. Housebound housewives: A follow-up study of a phobic–anxiety state. *British Journal of Psychiatry,* 1964, *110,* 191–197.

Rock, M. H., & Goldberger, L. Relationship between agoraphobia and field dependence. *Journal of Nervous and Mental Disease,* 1978, *166,* 781–786.

Rogers, C. R. *Client-centered therapy.* Boston: Houghton Mifflin, 1951.

Rogers, T. B., Kuiper, N. A., & Kirker, W. S. Self-reference and the encoding of personal information. *Journal of Personality and Social Psychology,* 1977, *35,* 677–688.

Rogers, T. B., Rogers, P. J., & Kuiper, N. A. Evidence for the self as a cognitive prototype: The "false alarms effect." *Personality and Social Psychology Bulletin,* 1979, *5,* 53–56.

Rosen, M. A dual model of obsessional neurosis. *Journal of Consulting and Clinical Psychology,* 1975, *43,* 453–459.

Rosenberg, B. G. Compulsiveness as a determinant in selected cognitive–perceptual performances. *Journal of Personality*, 1953, *21*, 506–516.

Rosenthal, T. L., & Bandura, A. Psychological modeling: Theory and practice. In S. L. Garfield & A. E. Bergin (Eds.), *Handbook of psychotherapy and behavior change*. New York: Wiley, 1978.

Roth, M. The phobic-anxiety-depersonalization syndrome. *Proceedings of the Royal Society of Medicine*, 1959, *52*, 587–594.

Rowe, D. *The experience of depression*. N.Y.: Wiley, 1978.

Royce, J. E. Does person or self imply dualism? *American Psychologist*, 1973, *28*, 833–866.

Russel, G. F. M. Anorexia nervosa: Its identity as an illness and its treatment. In J. H. Price (Ed.), *Modern trends in psychological medicine*. London: Butterworths, 1970.

Rutter, M. *Maternal deprivation reassessed*. Harmondsworth: Penguin Books, 1972.

Rutter, M. Maternal deprivation 1972–1978: New findings, new concepts, new approaches. *Annals of the Academy of Medicine* (Singapore), 1979, 8, 312–323.

Salzman, L. *The obsessive personality*. New York: Aronson, 1973.

Schachter, S., & Singer, J. E. Cognitive, social and physiological determinants of emotional state. *Psychological Reviews*, 1962, *69*, 379–399.

Schaffer, H. R., & Emerson, P. E. The development of social attachments in infancy. *Monographs of the Society for Research in Child Development*, 1964, *29* (Serial No. 94).

Schroder, H. M., Driver, M. J., & Streufert, S. *Human information processing*. New York: Holt, Rinehart & Winston, 1967.

Scott, W. A. Conceptualizing and measuring structural properties of cognition. In O. J. Harvey (Ed.), *Motivation and social interaction: Cognitive determinants*. New York: Ronald, 1963.

Seligman, M. E. P. Depression and learned helplessness. In R. J. Friedman & M. M. Katz (Eds.), *The psychology of depression: Contemporary theory and research*. New York: Wiley, 1974.

Seligman, M. E. P. *Helplessness: On depression, development and death*. San Francisco: W. H. Freeman, 1975.

Selvini-Palazzoli, M. *Self-starvation: From the intrapsychic to the transpersonal approach to anorexia nervosa*. London: Chancer, 1974.

Shapiro, D. *Neurotic styles*. New York: Basic Books, 1965.

Shaw, B. F. The theoretical and experimental foundations of a cognitive model for depression. In P. Pilner, K. R. Blankstein, & I. M. Spigel (Eds.), *Perception of emotion in self and others*. New York: Plenum, 1979.

Singer, J. L. *Imagery and daydream methods in psychotherapy and behavior modification*. New York: Academic Press, 1974.

Singer, J. L. *Daydreaming and fantasy*. London: George Allen & Unwin, 1976.

Singer, J. L., & Antrobus, J. S. Daydreaming, imaginal processes, and personality: A normative study. In P. W. Sheehan (Ed.), *The function and nature of imagery*. New York: Academic Press, 1972.

Slade, P. D. Psychometric studies of obsessional illness and obsessional personality. In H. R. Beech (Ed.), *Obsessional states*. London: Methuen, 1974.

Sluzki, C. E., & Veron, E. The double bind as a universal pathogenic situation. In C. E. Sluzki & D. C. Ransom (Eds.), *Double bind*. New York: Grune & Stratton, 1976.

Snaith, R. P. A clinical investigation of phobias. *British Journal of Psychiatry*, 1968, *114*, 673–697.

Solyom, L., Garza-Perez, J., Lewidge, B., & Solyom, C. Paradoxical intention in the treatment of obsessive thoughts: A pilot study. *Comprehensive Psychiatry*, 1972, *13*, 291–297.

Sperry, R. W. Lateral specialization in the surgically separated hemispheres. In F. O. Schmitt & F. G. Worden (Eds.), *The neurosciences third study programme*. Cambridge, Mass.: M.I.T. Press, 1974.

Stevenson, I., & Hain, J. D. On the different meanings of apparently similar symptoms, illustrated by varieties of barbershop phobia. *American Journal of Psychiatry*, 1967, *124*, 399–403.

Taylor, J. G. A behavioral interpretation of obsessive–compulsive neurosis. *Behaviour Research and Therapy*, 1963, *1*, 237–244.

Teuber, H. L. Why two brains? In F. O. Schmitt & F. G. Worden (Eds.), *The neurosciences third study programme*. Cambridge, Mass.: M.I.T. Press, 1974.

Truax, C. B., & Carkhuff, R. *Toward effective counseling and psychotherapy*. Chicago: Aldine, 1967.

Truax, C. B., Frank, I., & Imber, S. Therapist empathy, genuineness and warmth and patient outcome. *Journal of Consulting and Clinical Psychology*, 1966, *30*, 395–401.

Truax, C. B., & Mitchell, K. M. Research on certain therapist interpersonal skills in relation to process and outcome. In A. E. Bergin & S. L. Garfield (Eds.), *Handbook of psychotherapy and behavior change*. New York: Wiley, 1971.

Turner, R. M., Steketee, G., & Foa, E. Fear of criticism in washers, checkers and phobics. *Behaviour Research and Therapy*, 1979, *17*, 79–81.

Turvey, M. T. Constructive theory, perceptual systems and tacit knowledge. In W. B. Weimer & D. S. Palermo (Eds.), *Cognition and the symbolic processes*. Hillsdale, N.J.: Erlbaum, 1974.

Tweney, R. D., Doherty, M. E., & Mynatt, C. R. (Eds.). *On scientific thinking*. New York: Columbia University Press, 1981.

Walker, V. J. *An investigation of ritualistic behaviour in obsessional patients*. Unpublished PhD thesis, Institute of Psychiatry, University of London, 1967. (Extensively quoted in H. R. Beech [Ed.], *Obsessional states*, Chapter 6. London: Methuen, 1974.)

Wason, P. C. On the failure to eliminate hypotheses . . . a second look. In P. N. Johnson-Laird & P. C. Wason (Eds.), *Thinking: Readings in cognitive science*. Cambridge, England: Cambridge University Press, 1977.

Watzlawick, P., Beavin, J. H., & Jackson, D. D. *Pragmatics of human communication*. New York: Norton, 1967.

Watzlawick, P., Weakland, J. H., & Fisch, R. *Change*. New York: Norton, 1974.

Weimer, W. B. Psycholinguistics and Plato's paradoxes of the Meno. *American Psychologist*, 1973, *28*, 15–33.

Weimer, W. B. Overview of a cognitive conspiracy: Reflections on the volume.

In W. B. Weimer & D. S. Palermo (Eds.), *Cognition and the symbolic processes.* Hillsdale, N.J.: Erlbaum, 1974.

Weimer, W. B. A conceptual framework for cognitive psychology: Motor theories of the mind. In R. Shaw & J. D. Bransford (Eds.), *Perceiving, acting, and knowing: Toward an echological psychology.* Hillsdale, N.J.: Erlbaum, 1977.

Weimer, W. B. Psychotherapy and philosophy of science: A two-way street in search of traffic. In M. J. Mahoney (Ed.), *Psychotherapy process.* New York: Plenum, 1980.

Weiss, E. *Agoraphobia in the light of ego psychology.* New York: Grune & Stratton, 1964.

Wilson, E. O. *On human nature.* Cambridge, Mass.: Harvard University Press, 1978.

Wolpe, J. *Theme and variations: A behavior therapy casebook.* New York: Pergamon, 1976.

Zola, I. K. Culture and symptoms: An analysis of patient's presenting complaints. In C. Cox & A. Mead (Eds.), *A sociology of medical practice.* London: Collier-Macmillan, 1975.

INDEX